Colored White

AMERICAN CROSSROADS

Edited by Earl Lewis, George Lipsitz, Peggy Pascoe,
George Sánchez, and Dana Takagi

Colored White

TRANSCENDING THE RACIAL PAST

David R. Roediger

UNIVERSITY OF CALIFORNIA PRESS

Berkeley
Los Angeles
London

TO MICHAEL SPRINKER

University of California Press
Berkeley and Los Angeles, California

University of California Press, Ltd.
London, England

First paperback printing 2003

Library of Congress Cataloging-in-Publication Data

Roediger, David R.
    Colored White: transcending the racial past /
David Roediger.
        p. cm. —(American crossroads; 10)
    "The George Gund Foundation imprint in
African American studies."
    Includes bibliographical references and index.
    ISBN 0-520-24070-7 (pbk: alk. paper)
    1. United States—Race relations. 2. Racism—
United States. 3. Whites—United States—Race
identity. 4. White supremacy movements—United
States. 5. United States—Social conditions. 6. Civil
rights movements—United States. 7. Minorities—
United States—Social conditions. 8. Minorities—
United States—Political activity. I. Title. II. Series

E184.A1 R64 2002
305.8´00973—dc21   2001049173

Manufactured in the United States of America
10   09   08   07   06   05   04   03
10   9   8   7   6   5   4   3   2   1

Contents

Acknowledgments

I have benefited greatly from criticism of the ideas expressed in these pages. Invited lectures provided one venue for such criticism. In that connection I wish to thank the Kyoto American Studies Seminar, the Race, Gender, and Class Association, the Labor History Group at the University of Pittsburgh, the Thomas Merton Center, the Havens Center at the University of Wisconsin, the Black Student Union at the University of Binghamton, the Kaplan Distinguished Lecture Series at the University of Pennsylvania, the Atlanta Seminar in the Comparative History of Labor, Industry, and Technology, the Bluegrass Symposium at the University of Kentucky, the University of Iowa Legal History Seminar, the Race Matters Conference at Princeton University, the Ethnic Studies Lecture Series at the University of California at San Diego, the Commonwealth Fund at the University of London, the Newberry Library, the Center for the History of Freedom (Washington University), the Teach-In with the Labor Movement (Columbia University), the Black History Month Lecture Series at Spelman College, the Lefler Lecture Series at Carleton College, the Sidore Lecture Series at the University of New Hampshire, the Committee on Social Theory Lecture Series at University of Kentucky, the Hewlett Lecture Series at Linfield College, the University of California Conference on Whiteness (Berkeley), the "Then What Is White?" Conference at the University of California at Riverside, Dartmouth College's Narrative: An International Conference, the Northern Kentucky University Office of Affirmative Action and Multicultural Affairs, the Theorizing Whiteness Symposium at Williams College, the Bowling Green State University Provost's Lecture Series, the Michael Sprinker Memorial Conference at State University of New York at Stony Brook, the Conference on Inequality at the University of Wyoming, the Zion Baptist Church Summer School (Minneapolis), the *New Left Review* Lecture Series, The Earlham College Convocation Series, the California Humanities Institute Lecture Series, and the Carter Woodson Institute at the University of Virginia, as well as the Departments of History at the University of Toronto, the University of Illinois, Macalester College, Washington University, Saint Louis University, Northern Illinois University, the University of California at Riverside, Southern Illinois University at Edwardsville, the University of Iowa, and Northwestern University, for arranging visits. In addition, the ongoing stimulation of the Race, Ethnicity, and Migration Seminar at the University of Minnesota, the Social Science Research Council Migration Group, and the Southern Education Fund's initiative on the comparative history of race has been important.

Research assistance from Tiya Miles, Josie Fowler, Rebecca Hill, Deirdre Murphy, Rachel Gugler, Jacquetta Amdahl, Felicity Schaeffer, and Steve Garabedian was indispensable. Robert Frame was both a tireless researcher and a very wise critic of the manuscript. Ann Conry, Ana Chavier, Aprel Orwick, Colleen Hennen, and Frame prepared the manuscript for publication with characteristic diligence and skill. The McKnight Research Award and Scholar of the College Award at University of Minnesota and research funds accompanying the Kendrick Babcock Chair at University of Illinois provided crucial practical support. A grant from the Dickerson Fund (University of Illinois) supported the use of full-color illustrations. Connie Day's copy editing enhanced the accuracy, clarity, and style of the book.

In addition to the thank you's in individual essays, I want here to acknowledge the stimulating advice and generous sharing of research given by Randy McBee, Al Young, Jennifer Pierce, Alex Lubin, Martha Hodes, Walter Johnson, Robyn Wiegman, John Wright, George Sanchez, Mia Bay, Joel Olson, Lisa Disch, Jean O'Brien, Henry Yu, Cathy Choy, Erika Lee, John Howe, Mae Ngai, Wolfgang Natter, George Sanchez, David Scobey, Julie Willett, Caroline Waldron, Earl Lewis, Betsy Esch, Tom Guglielmo, Louise Edwards, Susan Hirsch, Micaela di Leonardo, Toby Higbie, Dana Frank, Rudy Vecoli, David Montgomery, Rudolph Vecoli, Neil Gotanda, Kimberlé Crenshaw, Sal Salerno, Jennifer Guglielmo, Alex Lubin, Todd Michney, Tom Sabatini, August Nimtz, Joel Helfrich, and Gaye Johnson.

The book is dedicated to my wonderful longtime editor at Verso, the late Michael Sprinker. Michael's death sadly underscored for me the role of editors in provoking as well as polishing writing. Although sections of this volume that take off from previously published work have been considerably revised, I thank Wahneema Lubiano, Toni Morrison, Rick Halpern, Gay Seidman, Noel Ignatiev, Stanley Engerman, and James Brewer Stewart for specific suggestions and standing invitations that led me to take up new subjects. Bruce Nichols, Will Murphy, and Cecilia Cancellaro energized me in working as editors on related projects. Monica McCormick and George Lipsitz played that role for *Colored White*.

Over the years I have gained clarity and insight over and over again from a group of scholars, friends, and activists who have sometimes read drafts of my work but are always in my mind when I write. They include Angela Davis, Bruce Nelson, Wendy Mink, Donna Gabaccia, Robin D. G. Kelley, Jean Allman, Sundiata Cha-Jua, David Noble, Marcus Rediker, Peter Linebaugh, Susan Porter Benson, Steve Rosswurm, Peter Rachleff, Nell Irvin Painter, Vron Ware, Penelope and Franklin Rosemont, john powell, and Lipsitz. Two such inspirers, Leola Johnson and Jim Barrett, coauthored and emboldened earlier versions of essays in this book. Another, the late Michael Rogin, read the final manuscript with great perception and care.

ONE

Still White

All about Eve, Critical White Studies, and Getting Over Whiteness

Is Race Over?

The cover of a rhapsodic 1993 special issue of *Time* showed us "The New Face of America." Within, the newsmagazine proclaimed the United States to be "the first universal nation," one that supposedly was not "a military superpower but . . . a multicultural superpower." Moving cheerfully between the domestic and the global, an article declared Miami to be the new "Capital of Latin America." Commodity flows were cited as an index of tasty cultural changes: "Americans use 68% more spices today than a decade ago. The consumption of red pepper rose 105%, basil 190%." Chrysler's CEO, Robert J. Eaton, best summed up the issue's expansive mood in a lavish advertising spread:

> At the Chrysler Corporation, our commitment to cultural diversity ranges from programs for minority-owned dealerships to the brand-new Jeep factory we built in ethnically diverse downtown Detroit. And our knowhow is spreading to countries from which the immigrants came. We're building and selling Jeep vehicles in China, minivans in Austria and trucks in Mexico. We're proud to be associated with this probing look [by *Time*] at a multicultural America. We hope you enjoy it.[1]

Remarkably, *Time* sustained such euphoria amid many passages confessing to doubts, troubling facts, and even gloom. In the U.S.-led "global village," readers learned, there were more telephones in Tokyo than in the whole of Africa. The "exemplary" Asian American immigrants had succeeded, but at tremendous cost. The host population that

benefited from the wonders of "our new hybrid forms" told *Time*'s pollsters that it strongly supported curbs on legal immigration (60 percent
to 35 percent). By a smaller majority, those polled also backed the
unconstitutional initiatives being floated in 1993 to prevent the children of noncitizens from acquiring citizenship. One article in this issue
of *Time* held that, "with a relatively static force of only 5600 agents
[patrolling immigration], the U.S. has effectively lost control of its terri-
torial integrity." Richard Brookhiser's "Three Cheers for the WASPs"
fretted that liberty- and wealth-producing White Anglo-Saxon Protestants' values were being elbowed aside as the "repressed" habits of an
"ice person." In one of many bows to an older language of race—
one key article called intermarriage "crossbreeding"—that the issue
claimed to be transcending, Brookhiser lamented that the WASP's "psy-
chic genes" were no longer dominant and revered. The balance sheet
on recent immigration was a close one for *Time*: "Though different and
perhaps more problematic than those who have come before, the latest
immigrants are helping to form a new society."[2]

The ability to keep smiling amid contradictory crosscurrents hinged
on the image that looked out at readers from the magazine's cover.
She was "Eve", the result of sending the computerized photographs of
fourteen models (of "various ethnic and racial backgrounds") through
the Morph 2.0 computer software program. With the aid of a multicultural crew of technicians, the program pictured serially the offspring
likely to eventuate from various couples. The writers had trouble deciding how seriously we ought to take Eve and the morphing process. The
exercise mapped "key facial features" with "pinpoint" accuracy. At the
same time, it was portrayed as merely a playful "way to dramatize the
impact of interethnic marriage which has increased dramatically in
the U.S. during the latest wave of immigration," making for a society
"intermarried with children." State-of-the-art technology made "no
claim to scientific accuracy," but the magazine presented the results
"in the spirit of fun and experiment." The crowning morph ("as in
metamorphosis, a striking change in structure or appearance," a writer
added) was a miracle and a cover story. The managing editor recalled,
"Little did we know what we had wrought. As onlookers watched the
image of our new Eve begin to appear on the computer screen, several
staff members promptly fell in love. Said one: 'It really breaks my heart
that she doesn't exist.' We sympathize with our lovelorn colleagues, but
even technology has its limits. This is a love that must forever remain
unrequited."[3]

But then again, maybe not. After all, *Time*'s cover proclaimed Eve, who was described there as a mixture of "races," (with a caffè latte skin tone) to be the nation's "new face." The beauty of that face helped to explain why the modern Eve had magazine staffers lining up to join Adam in the ranks of apple pickers. But the Eden that she represented mattered at least as much in accounting for her appeal. In connecting her face to the nation's future, *Time* implied that she is what the United States will look like at that twenty-first-century point when, as they put it, "the descendants of white Europeans, the arbiters of our national culture for most of its existence, are likely to slip into minority status." Not only did Eve reassure us that all will be well when that happens, but also she already existed in cyberspace to mock allegedly outmoded emphases on the ugliness and exploitation of race relations in the United States. The collection of morphed photos carried the headline "Rebirth of a Nation." As Michael Rogin's prescient analysis of the cover gently puts it, the title was perhaps chosen "without . . . full consciousness of its meaning." Unlike the racist film classic *The Birth of a Nation*, in which race mixing is cast as Black-on-white rape, the rebirth-in-progress was (con)sensual, even as it was chastely mediated by technology. Although associations with a fall from grace persist, Eve was decidedly presented as good news. Toni Morrison's reminder that race has often been brutally figured on a Black-white axis stuck out like a sore thumb in the special issue. Her telling warnings that immigrants have historically had to "buy into the notion of American blacks as the real aliens" in order to assimilate fully seemed a dour refusal to join the fun of Eve's cyber-wonderland. Morrison was left describing the United States as "Star spangled. Race strangled" at the very moment when the computer could show us the end to all that. An article gratuitously attacking the "politics of separation" on college campuses underlined *Time*'s point that it is time to get over racial (and feminist and gay) politics.[4]

The less slickly marketed recent analysis of demographic trends by the historian and sociologist Orlando Patterson ends with conclusions that precisely mirror those of *Time*. Writing in *The New Republic* under the headline "Race Over," Patterson allows that W. E. B. Du Bois may have been "half-right" in arguing that the "color line" was the problem of the century just past. But, he adds, those who project that problem into the new century are "altogether wrong." Because "migratory, sociological, and biotechnological developments" are undermining race, the outlook for the future is clear to Patterson: "By the middle of the twenty-first century, America will have problems aplenty. But no racial problem whatsoever." Patterson breezily develops four regional patterns. The "California system," destined to prevail on the U.S. and Canadian Pacific Rim, features "cultural and somatic mixing" generating a population that is mostly "Eurasian—but with a growing Latin element." On the West Coast, the "endless stream of unskilled Mexican workers" will drive away "lower-class Caucasians, middle-class racial purists and most African Americans." In the "Caribbean-American system," the Caribbean nations will be integrated into the United States, via economic collapse in the West Indies. Florida will become the "metropolitan center" of this system, which will also produce "transnational and post-national" Afro-Latin communities in northeastern cities. The rest of the Northeast and the urban Midwest will continue to rust, and a declining public sector, the end of affirmative action, and competition from West Indian immigrants will devastate African American and U.S.-born Latino communities. But the Black and Latino poor will be joined in cities and inner suburbs by "European American lower classes." Gated communities will house the middle class. "Social resentment and a common, lumpen-proletarian, hip-hop culture" will produce unity even amid "murderous racial gang fights." The victims of deindustrialization will be "lower-class, alienated and out of control." But they "will be hybrid nonetheless." In discussing the Southeast, Patterson suddenly declines to make a case for metamorphosis. The "Atlanta system" (as Patterson calls it, oddly choosing a southern city whose Third World immigrant population is skyrocketing) will feature continuing segregation. "The old Confederacy," we are told, "will remain a place where everyone knows who is white and who is black and need reckon no in-between." Somehow this prediction still leaves Patterson's "Race Over" prognostications intact, however. Over the next century, "the Southern model will become an increasingly odd and decreasingly relevant anachronism." In any case, science is likely to create new methods of changing hair texture and skin color, enabling African Americans to "enhance their individuality" by "opt[ing] for varying degrees of hybridity" through biotechnology. By 2050, "the social virus of race will have gone the way of smallpox."[5]

Time and Patterson are scarcely alone in arguing that the movement of immigrants, the demographics of intermarriage, and the global consumption of commodities associated with exotic others signal that "race" is over, or at least doomed. The influential website/social movement known as Interracial Voice touts the "intermarried with children" pattern as the key to change. Since, in the view of "Interracial Voice," "political leaders 'of color' and . . . black 'leaders' specifically" prop up the old racial order, the "mixed race contingent" is destined to usher in the "ideal future of racelessness."[6] The journalist Neil Bernstein extols "blond cheerleaders" who claim Cherokee ancestry and the "children of mixed marriages [who] insist that they are whatever race they say they are" as frontline troops "facing the complicated reality of what the 21st century will be."[7] Writing in the *New York Times Magazine*, the critic Stanley Crouch almost precisely anticipates Patterson's basic point, under the title "Race Is Over." Crouch concludes, "One hundred years from today Americans are likely to look back on the ethnic difficulties of our time as quizzically as we look at earlier periods of our history." Although his essay comments on Americans as a "culturally miscegenated people," it is lavishly illustrated with pictures like those in *Time*, serving as "previews" of the future flesh-and-blood individuals who are "Pakistani-African-American," "Russian-Polish Jewish/Puerto Rican," and "Dutch/Jamaican/Irish/African-American/Russian Jewish." The caption of the 20 pictures is "WHAT WILL WE LOOK LIKE?"[8]

The Case against the "Race Is Over" Thesis

It is not possible to assent to the *Time*/Patterson/Crouch vision of an automatic transition to a raceless nation. The many objections to such a view turn on two difficulties. The first of these is an inattention to change over time, and the second is an absence of discussions of power and privilege. In its conviction that everything is new regarding race, the "race is over" school tends to cut off the present and future from any serious relationship to the past. If, as Alexander Saxton argues, "white racism is essentially a theory of history," Eve announces that we are excused from paying serious attention to either racism or history. *Time*'s special issue does offer a short, rosy, and inaccurate history of immigration, but that history is written in such a distorted way as to leave no scars and set no limits. For example, the glories of U.S. multiculturalism arise, according to *Time,* from the nation's "traditional open door policy" toward immigrants. In fact, of course, the historical Open Door Policy of the United States insisted on free movement of American goods in Asia, while Asian migrants were excluded from the United States on openly racial grounds. If everything is new—*Time* writes, "During the past two decades America has produced the greatest variety of hybrid households in the history of the world"—then doing serious history can itself become a symptom of a mordant commitment to raking over old coals instead of stepping into the nonracial and multicultural sunshine. Significant in this regard is the tendency of the "postrace-ists" to keep using the hoary language of biological race as though it carries no meaning, now or in the future, to speak of crossbreeding and refer to the children of intermarriage as hybrids. Indeed, so sure are some advocates of hybridity that mixing and morphing can dissolve race that they put "race" inside wary quotation marks that (rightly) signal its scientifically spurious status but abandon all wariness when "multiracial" is invoked as a category.[9] Inattention to history leaves discussions of the transcendence of race fully saddled with the very preoccupation with biological explanations that it declares to be liquidated.

Taking history seriously also calls into question the proposition that demographic trends can easily be extrapolated into the future to predict racial change. Not only do trends shift, but the very categories that define race can also change dramatically. The idea that "crossbreeding" will disarm racism is at least 140 years old. Demographics simply are not always decisive. Southern states in the nineteenth century with large—sometimes majority—Black populations and very substantial mixing of the races were *slaveholding* states. In the recent past, California celebrated its move toward becoming a white-minority state by passing a raft of anti-Black and anti-immigrant initiatives, becoming, as George Lipsitz puts it, "the Mississippi of the 1990s." That the 1996 anti-affirmative action initiative's triumph occurred in a state in which the population was less than 53 percent white but the registered voters were over 80 percent white reminds us that politics matters at least as much as head counts.[10]

At the start of the twentieth century, as Chapter 9 shows, predictions in which the changed racial character of the United States was plotted and graphed looked very much as they did in the 1990s. Reactions a century ago ranged from a sense of alarm at the threat of "degeneration," of Anglo-Saxon "race suicide," and of "mongrelization," to optimistic rhetoric regarding the creation of a new and invigorated "American race." If immigration continued and mixed marriages spread, the "pure white," "Nordic" domination of the United States was doomed. Immigration from southern and eastern Europe did continue massively for a time, but then it was decimated via political action restricting its flow. Mixed marriages grew dramatically, joining (for example) racially suspect newcomers from Poland, Greece, and Italy with each other and with older groups. But the prediction of racial change never quite became fact. Somewhere along the line, the "new

immigrants" from southern and eastern Europe became fully accepted
as white. It may be that, as *Time* puts it, "Native American-black-
white-Hungarian-French-Catholic-Jewish-American" young people will
lead the United States to an "unhyphenated whole." But the "Polish-
Irish-Italian-Jewish-Greek-Croatian" offspring of the twentieth century
also seemed to hold out that hope. In very many cases they ended unhyphenated, all right, but as whites. We simply do not know what racial
categories will be in 2060. As Ruben Rumbaut's and Mary Waters's
provocative works show, we do not know how the diverse children
imagined in *Time* will be seen or will see themselves in terms of identity.
Although white supremacy can certainly exist without a white majority,
the question of whether such a majority might yet be cobbled together
through the twenty-first century remains. These questions, to which we
shall return at the conclusion of this volume, are political ones, and
even Morph 2.0 cannot answer them.[11]

The important recent work of the population specialists Sharon M.
Lee, Barry Edmonston, and Jeffrey Passel underlines this point. Their
projections for the year 2100 show a U.S. population 34 percent mixed
race, up from about 8 percent today. (Less than a third of the latter percentage actually chose the new "multiracial" category on the 2000 census.) The Asian American/multiple-origin population, in these estimates, will rise to 42 million in the next century, rivaling in size the 56
million U.S. residents whose ancestry is "purely" Asian. Among Latinos, the 184 million persons of Latino/multiple-origin ancestry will
vastly outnumber the 77 million whose ancestry is Latino on both sides.
Among African Americans, lower rates of intermarriage will result in
66 million persons with African American ancestry on both sides
and 39 million persons of African American/multiple-origin descent.
Among "whites," the "pure" population is projected also to outnumber the white/multiple-origin one by 165 million to 90 million. Even
though all of the "purities" are laughable historically, and although the
new century will surely surprise us in many ways, the study's broader
implications are vital. As the authors emphasize, the answer to whether
there might be 77 million, or fewer, or three times that many, Latinos in
2100 will be decided historically and politically, not just demographically. Particularly important will be the actions and consciousness of
those whom Cherrie Moraga calls "21st century mestizos"—those
"born of two parents of color of different races and/or ethnicities." At
issue too is whether the projected relative "purity" of Black-white
racial categories will make that divide more rather than less salient or

leave the 66 million residents with African American ancestry on both sides in a particularly exposed racial position.[12]

Eve leaves studiously vague the possibility that the "new face" of the United States might stay white. She is, the editor tells us, 35 percent southern European and 15 percent Anglo-Saxon but also 17.5 percent Middle Eastern and 7.5 percent Hispanic. Thus, in the curious racelessness that *Time* proposes, Eve remains white even as the text chatters about the nonwhite-majority nation of the future. Chicana students in my classes sometimes see Eve's picture as that of a chicana; Puerto Rican students see her as Puerto Rican; Italian Americans likewise take her as their own. When a new Betty Crocker was introduced as the "mythic spokesperson" for baking products in 1996, the General Mills Corporation's icon morphed into a figure that looks very much like Eve. Her creators announced the marketing value of the figure's ambiguity clearly: "Women of different backgrounds will see someone different: Native American, African-American, Hispanic, Caucasian."[13]

More subtle are the ways in which Eve's seductiveness blurs the line between present and future. Eve appealingly appears—but in cyberspace, not in time. She belongs in some sense to the present, insofar as she is already used to mock antiracist initiatives as anachronistic and wrong. However, Eve exists in 2050, or maybe 2060 or 2100. Those who conjure her up thus ask us to practice (or abandon) the politics of racial justice in the shadow of someone who does not exist. This problem is exacerbated by the fact that white residents of the United States *believe* that whites are a minority in the United States. In a 1996 poll, white respondents estimated whites in the United States population at 49.9 percent. The accurate figure was 74 percent. They thought that the United States was 23.8 percent African American, twice the enumerated Black population. At 10.8 percent, Asian Americans existed in the white psyche in 3½ times their numbers in the census. Hispanics were imagined to constitute 14.7 percent of the population; they represent 9.5 percent. Such misperceptions clearly fueled the anti-immigrant initiatives of the 1990s. Lovable as Eve seemed to the editors, *Time*'s special issue remained equivocal at best on favoring relatively open immigration, and its collapsing of present and future in Eve made nativist folklore credible.[14]

The evasions of questions of power and privilege in the "race is over" literature also obscure the extent to which the fiction of race still structures life chances in the United States. If whiteness continues to confer substantial material advantages, and if large groups of Black and

Latino people exist in grinding poverty, then the wholesale abandonment of older categories of racial categorization and identification seems unlikely. Evidence that such advantages are ending is unimpressive. The *Wall Street Journal*'s dissection of trends from 1992 through 1998 featured a chart with two telling headlines regarding race and wealth. The first was "A Wide Divide in Family Income." Figures under it showed "Nonwhite or Hispanic Income" rising somewhat more rapidly than that of "White non-Hispanics" (10.4 percent to 7.4 percent). These were the good years. From 1970 to 1993, by contrast, the median income of white households rose 3.4 percent; for Black households, the figure was 0.8 percent. Later (1990s) gains still left Black and Latino family incomes at less than 63 percent of white family incomes. More revealing, as Melvin Oliver and Thomas Shapiro have eloquently argued, are patterns of wealth. The *Journal*'s second heading ran "And a Wider Divide in Family Wealth." The boom of the Clinton years left the net worth of "Nonwhite or Hispanic" families at 17.28 percent of the net worth of "White non-Hispanic" families. The rise was infinitesimal, up from 17.23 percent.[15]

Given the prevalence of what the sociologists Douglas Massey and Nancy Denton call "American Apartheid," such gaping disparities in resources are concentrated in communities. As the legal scholar john powell has shown, of the 8 million U.S. residents living in "areas of concentrated poverty" (defined as census tracts where 40 percent of the population have incomes below the official poverty line) in 1990, half were African American and a quarter were Hispanic. Clinton-era "welfare reform" enforces what Alejandra Marchevsky and Jeanne Theoharis call the "racialization of entitlement," using ostensibly *individualistic* criteria to limit eligibility for benefits of racial *groups* isolated from jobs. In future economic downturns, the reforms will further devastate whole communities. In those areas of concentrated misery known as prisons, the growth in numbers of Black and Hispanic inmates has been astronomical. The years 1985 to 1995 saw a 204 percent increase in Black women's incarceration and a 143 percent increase for Black men. About two-thirds of all prisoners are Black or Hispanic. Given a sixfold increase in the prison population between 1972 and 1997, and with the total number of U.S. inmates reaching 2 million, such disparities massively affect communities. Black males born in 1991 are estimated to have a 29 percent chance of being imprisoned at some point in their lives. For Hispanics the figure is 16 percent and for whites just 4 percent. If the imprisoned were counted as unemployed, joblessness in African American and Latino communities would still be at Great Depression levels amid record job creation.[16]

That white poverty is consistently underestimated by the media and by the U.S. residents who are polled makes some sense in terms of such material realities. Poverty among whites appears as situational, not structural, and as unattached to alleged racial traits. Moreover, whereas the poorest 20 percent of the Black population made almost 60 percent of the income of the poorest fifth of the white population in 1967, by 1992 that figure had fallen to 50 percent. The longstanding idea that "whiteness is property," which *ought* to pay off even if it is not doing so at the moment, survives with distressing ease amid such trends, even as income inequalities *within* the Black, white, and Hispanic population have grown tremendously.[17]

The idea that laws, social practices, and the personal opinions of whites in the United States are now "colorblind," and the corollary that antiracism is therefore irrational, counterproductive, or even itself racist, also undergird much of the "race is over" argument. As powell notes, conservatives have increasingly become the leading advocates of "colorblindness." They argue "that since we have learned that race is an illusion, rather than a scientific fact, we should drop racial categories altogether . . . [and that] only those who are either racist or badly misinformed would insist that we continue to utilize these pernicious categories." As Neil Gotanda's riveting work shows, the legal ideology of colorblindness has often also entailed blindness to "white racial domination" where constitutional law is concerned.[18]

The broader notion that whites are generally colorblind animates recent studies arguing for an abandonment of affirmative action and other partly race-based reforms. From the work of Paul Sniderman through that of Stephan and Abigail Thernstrom, to that of Joel Rogers and Ruy Teixeira, advocates of such a position consistently reach sanguine conclusions based on opinion polls in which whites report their own increasing enlightenment on racial matters. We learn, for example, that in 1997 only 1 percent of whites told pollsters that they would or might move if a Black person moved in next door. The changes in polling data are "large and all are in the same direction: *more* tolerance, *less* racism."[19]

These attitudinal shifts, which underpin "race is over" arguments, are suspect for three reasons. One is that racist practices may function despite reported shifts in attitude, and segregation in housing is perhaps the most dramatic example. Second, studies sometimes presume that white respondents are the experts on changing racial attitudes and practices. Polls among people of color may tell a different story. In a recent poll conducted in the Chicago area, for example, 61 percent of white respondents thought that there was "fairly little," "almost none," or no hiring discrimination against Blacks. Only 19 percent of Black respondents agreed; and 43 percent reported believing that there was a "great deal" of discrimination.[20] Finally, although racism may no longer be exhibited openly in political discourse, it is not so decisively defeated in the culture. Huge numbers of whites, for example, tell pollsters that Blacks are relatively lazy. When Charles Murray wrote a proposal for the racist tract he coauthored, *The Bell Curve*, he reportedly promised that it would cause many whites to "feel better about things they already think but do not know how to say." The huge sales of the book combine with polling data to suggest that he was not entirely wrong.[21] In justifying its own interest in *The Bell Curve*, *The New Republic* offered the striking editorial opinion that "the notion that there might be resilient ethnic difference in intelligence is not, we believe, an inherently racist notion."[22]

Specific invocations of the idea that Eve has made race passé often leave unexamined the question of what then is to become of white privilege and instead specifically argue for an end of African American racial identity. The Interracial Voice website, for example, currently features the leading spokesperson of the anti-affirmative action movement, Ward Connerly, predicting that "by 2070, perhaps sooner, 'black,' 'brown,' and 'white' will be historical concepts. Café-au-lait will be reality." The good news is that "in California today, there are more children born to 'interracial' couples than are born to two black parents." The better news for the colorblind right is that the "California trend" will soon sweep the nation. Its fondest hope is that "'African Americans' [will] readily and proudly acknowledge the diversity of their backgrounds [and] then the concept of 'race' will disintegrate." Similarly, mainstream journals of opinion give very respectful attention to the idea that because race is happily over, African Americans should give up their identities. In May 1997, for example, both *Harper's* and *Atlantic Monthly* featured long pleas for an "end of blackness." Meanwhile, the idea that whiteness should disappear is treated as defining the outer limits of academic zaniness.[23] This disparity between the professed goal of nonracialism and the concentration of contemporary fire on the racial politics of activists of color detracts from even so sophisticated a work as Paul Gilroy's recent *Against Race: Imagining*

Political Culture Beyond the Color Line. (Even so, we will miss a great opportunity if debate about Gilroy's book is focused simply on its unfortunate title and not on the possibilities and limits of its insistently antifascist politics.)[24]

A final way in which the "race is over" stance ignores existing inequalities is more subtle. In declaring race to be utterly malleable, proponents of this idea often then turn to gender and sexuality as the "real" differences on which the future is to be founded. *Time*, as Michael Rogin observes, rejected one image produced by Morph 2.0. Because it showed a "distinctly feminine face—sitting atop a muscular neck and hairy chest," the article proclaimed, "Back to the mouse on that one." The insistence on Eve as a love object and on "intermarriage" and "breeding" as the antidotes to racial division defines a future sexual and gender universe as static as the racial frontier is dynamic. Variations on this theme play themselves out more broadly in the abandonment of attempts to build coalitions that address racism and sexism together and in the striking coexistence of usually masculine challenges to the color line with homophobic rants in hip-hop.[25]

The Presence of Race
and the Possibility of Nonwhiteness

Obviously, some of the recent penchant for projecting an assured nonracial future derived from a specific media demand for end-of-decade/century/millennium prognostications. Even so, it seems likely that such predictions will have enduring ideological force growing out of real, though highly complicated, changes in demographics, mass culture, and markets. Sheer exhaustion in the wake of 30 years of grappling with difficult racial questions without effective government commitments to justice and without compelling visions of liberation articulated by a mass movement also make the idea of a raceless new beginning very attractive.

We organize and write, like it or not, in the face of Eve's appeal, and the appeal of Eve's face frankly causes serious problems for antiracists. The charges made against us have decisively shifted. For a long time, such charges were clear: too visionary, too impatient, too little aware of the weight of history and tradition. Now the accusation becomes that we are atavistic—so eager to dwell on the bleak past that we miss the glorious future. With astonishing speed, the idea that race is too fixed a category to allow for the "fixing" of racial injustice has given way to a recipe for inaction that features the fluidity of race: If it ain't fixed, don't bother to fix it. From such an aphorism, it is but a short leap to seeing antiracists as the *cause* of continued race-thinking in an imagined nation whose culture is supposed to be hybrid, whose laws are supposed to be colorblind, whose white citizens are supposed to have gotten over racism, and whose very population is soon supposed to make race irrelevant. If Dr. Martin Luther King, Jr., felt compelled to explain the question "Why we can't wait," we are put in the position of explaining "Why we can't celebrate."[26] In answering, we risk seeming joyless, dated, and parochial. We also run the more serious risk of so defensively insisting on the continuing relevance of race as to miss tremendous changes and the opportunities for resistance that they open. We miss the occasion to decide what we *do* want to celebrate.

At its best, the love of Eve's image expresses a deep desire for the United States to stop being a white nation. We cannot but share that desire. Nor can we ignore the fact that in the last century, the props have been kicked out from under much old-style racism. If white supremacy seemed a century ago to rest on scientific racism, on Jim Crow segregation, on disenfranchisement, and on color bars against the entry and the naturalization of nonwhite immigrants, it survives with none of these barbarisms intact. The arguments being made here thus imply not that struggles for racial justice must continue on the same terrain, but only that they must continue. Indeed, taking advantage of new terrain is one critical task in carrying on such struggles before us.

The title and the structure of this book are intended to convey both the changed situation in which we write and the loads we carry. *Colored White* derives from a line delivered by the great African American comedian Redd Foxx. Playing a junk dealer and crime victim in an episode of his 1970s television series, *Sanford and Son*, Foxx answered an inevitable question regarding his attackers: "Yeh, they was colored— white!" A quarter-century later we are in a much better position to hope that Foxx's barbed point—that whites too carry and act on racial identities—would be broadly intelligible. The much-publicized spate of works in "whiteness studies" (better called critical studies of whiteness) have inched the "white problem" onto mainstream intellectual agendas. These studies have drawn on the works of previously marginalized people of color who had long reflected, and continue to reflect, on why some people think it is important to be white.[27] "Colored white" also carries the connotation that race is, to use Frantz Fanon's term, "epidermal." It is produced in social relations over time and is not biological and fixed. The triumph of such ideas regarding race, although it has been achieved by starts and fits and continues to encounter resistance, is one grand achievement of twentieth-century science and of the century's freedom movements. At the same time, however, that very triumph sets the stage for the conservative and neoliberal arguments rehearsed above, which miss the tragic gravity of Fanon's remarks on the epidermalization of race and indeed seek to forget race by confusing its biological inconsequence and superficiality with the deep inequalities it structures.[28]

Colored White's essays often focus on the history of white identity, and on its presence, as keys to understanding continuities in oppression and the possibilities of new departures. Before I situate this book briefly in the literature on whiteness, two other central underpinnings of the project deserve emphasis. The first is a deliberate effort to move back and forth in time, treating past and present in the same volume, in the same section of the book, and even in the same essay. Thus today's young white kids who profess to "wannabe" black meet Elvis Presley, and Rush Limbaugh is discussed in the company of two of his historical betters, Mark Twain and Eugene O'Neill. Historians often deride such mixing of yesterday and today with the damning adjectives present-minded and (although my spellchecker doesn't like it) *presentist*. Particularly where race is concerned, critics charge that presentminded-ness counterproductively encourages both moralizing judgments on the past from the vantage point of a relatively egalitarian present and exaggerated, romanticized emphasis on the historical success of interracial coalitions as part of an attempt to find a "usable past" of resistance.[29] For example, in placing an article on race and labor history next to a piece on recent labor struggles in solidarity with political prisoner Mumia Abu-Jamal, I deliberately risk such charges. I do so in part because it seems desirable for readers, especially students, to be able to see how historians bring their work to bear on contemporary issues. Indeed, my emphasis is often on identifying not a "usable past" but a "usable present," which enables us to oppose racism today and to pose different and better questions about the past. Thus, paying attention to white working-class conservatism in the 1980s sharpened historical inquiry by forcing us to tackle "presentist" questions regarding when and how some workers had come to identify themselves as white. We then learned that the category "white worker" was articulated by workers from at least the 1830s forward. It was not a "presentminded" import from the politically correct late twentieth century but, rather, had a long and tragic history. Similarly, the question of how immigrants

and "mixed" peoples of the twenty-first century will identify themselves and be identified racially has greatly invigorated scholarship
on the "racial" history of southern and eastern European immigrants
of a century ago. The contemporary politics of immigration has likewise focused attention on the inadequacy of historical approaches that
take race in the United States to mean Black-white relations and has
helped to show how white identity has been formed against multiple
racial others.

The other major concern running through the essays will seem less
familiar. Its prominence has in fact surprised me as the essays have
taken shape. It lies in the need to theorize and historicize the concept of
nonwhiteness in thinking about race in the United States. On one level,
of course, *nonwhiteness* is an offensive term. To refer to people of color
as nonwhites almost perfectly exemplifies the tendency to place whites
at the normative center of everything and to marginalize everyone else.
What I propose here is to think, instead, about how the *nation* can
become something other than white and how those people who are
tempted to identify as white can be, as Franklin Rosemont puts it, "dis-
illusioned" regarding that identity and its alleged ability to produce
happiness. To think in terms of fostering nonwhiteness has several
advantages. One is that it enables us to identify with the sense of possibility and transcendence that attracts people to Eve as the nation's possible new face, even as we resist easy assumptions that the United States
will be automatically transformed. Second, it supplements calls for the
"abolition of whiteness" by providing a phrasing that cannot be mistaken as a threat to the survival of people who think that they are
white. Alice Walker's recent "gift" to white men—to be able to "decide
who you are, *other* than 'white man'"—shows the humanist potential
of setting forth the goal of creating space for nonwhiteness.[30] Third, an
emphasis on expanding the opportunity to live in nonwhite spaces
encourages us to support initiatives attacking institutional racism. If the
state, universities, employers, realtors, loan officers, judges, and police
continue dramatically to privilege white people, we are very likely to
remain a nation in which newcomers struggle to get into the white race
and in which those already so classified opt to retain both whiteness
and privilege. Finally, the theoretical construct of nonwhiteness has the
potential to remind us that coalitions between whites and people of
color need not always and everywhere be the key to social transformation. Coalitions among people of color also represent a critical route to
nonwhite politics.

Demographic changes and the opportunity to challenge the relative payoffs of whiteness at the level of citizenship and of property do more than open the possibility of a future nonwhite United States. They also exemplify the way in which a "usable present" alerts us to the complexities of the past, the way in which critical social movements such as abolitionism were in some senses not white, and the way in which dynamic sectors of the labor movement were not white. They alert us to a history in which immigrants from southern and eastern Europe for a time fell sufficiently short of full whiteness as to encourage W. E. B. Du Bois to propose in the early 1920s that the "Negro, Jew, Irishman, Italian, Hungarian, Asiatic and South Sea-Islander" had sufficient common interests to organize against "Nordic white" attempts to rule the world "through brute force."[31]

Nonwhiteness, History, and the Critical Study of Whiteness

In the individual essays in *Colored White,* a central goal is to convey the richness and promise of studying white identity as a problem whose very existence and re-creation must be explained historically. This introduction is intended to suggest the contours of the critical study of whiteness in order to convey a working knowledge of the scholarship further explored in later essays. What follows, then, is a brief account of the way studying white identity has come into vogue in the recent past and of the far longer and more important tradition of such study by intellectuals of color.

The last decade has seen a dramatic increase in the attention paid to scholarship that casts whiteness as a problem and insists that both the origins and the persistence of white identity demand explanation. Publications that address intellectual and cultural trends have lavished attention on studies of whiteness in the United States. A special issue of *Voice Literary Supplement*, a review essay in *Lingua Franca*, and even an article in the popular music magazine *Spin* all proclaimed the arrival of this putatively new area of inquiry. Special, massive issues of *Transition, Hungry Mind Review,* and *Minnesota Review* quickly appeared. Cleverly titled collections proliferated: *Displacing Whiteness, Off White, White Reign, Whiteness: A Critical Reader, Outside the Whale, Critical White Studies*, and more.[32] Although it has been predominantly a U.S. phenomenon, the study of whiteness has also gathered momentum in Britain and its empire, in Japan, in South Africa, in Australia, and elsewhere, often acknowledging inspiration from, and pointing to problems with, U.S.-centered studies.[33] Most strikingly, the April 1997 "Making and Unmaking of Whiteness" conference at Berkeley drew extensive national and international press coverage.[34]

Such attention has come complete with its share of problems. The new scholarship has been seen as portraying whiteness as just another identity at the table of multiculturalism, thus redirecting scholarly attention to whites in a way that minimizes consideration of power and privilege. As Angie Chabram-Dernersesian's excellent "Whiteness in Chicana/o Discourses" puts it, emphasizing what whites say and feel about their racial identities risks "tak[ing] the jagged edges off the kinds of social practices and material effects" associated with racism. The way in which President William Jefferson Clinton briefly enlisted the uncompromisingly radical work of the historian of whiteness Noel Ignatiev in the service of smoothing out "jagged edges" illustrates both the visibility of the new scholarship and the process that Chabram-Dernersesian describes. In 1998 Clinton gave his jocular, admiring, and fractured version of Ignatiev's *How the Irish Became White*. The president told audiences, "I got . . . this book the other day from a friend of mine who's got a terrific sense of humor who talked about how unfortunate it was that a lot of my [Irish American] forebears turned reactionary, because when we first came here we were treated just like the recently freed slaves."[35]

The clearest barometer of the ease with which the study of whiteness has gotten attention, and of its difficulty in getting a serious hearing, is the insistence of some popularizers that such study is brand new and is a white thing. In 1997, for example, a *New York Times Magazine* reporter interviewed me for her "whiteness studies" story. She led off by remarking that her research was winding down and enumerated those scholars with whom she had spoken. My objection that she had spoken only with white writers was twice waved away. She first held that this was a new field being pioneered by white writers like myself and then shifted to the safer claim that the "news" was that whites were now studying whiteness. Even so, I hoped that our talk had convinced her that such views missed the point of the study of whiteness, that she was overlooking its intellectual leaders, and that she would add interviews and change her emphasis. When the celebrated Minneapolis photographer Keri Pickett later was hired by the *Times* to take my picture for the story, my illusions vanished. Somewhat puzzled, Pickett told me that the magazine wanted oddly adjusted exposures for my picture and those of others who were quoted in the article. When I asked what fooling with the exposure in such a way would do, Pickett replied, "It will make you look whiter." The article itself mocked the study of whiteness as trendy, self-absorbed, and white.[36] Historically and now, however such study has been anything but those things.

If the defining intellectual thrust in the critical study of whiteness is to make white identity into a problem worth historicizing and investigating, it stands to reason that those groups for whom white behavior and attitudes have been most problematic would have inquired most searchingly into the dynamics of whiteness. Indeed, studying whiteness as a problem is perfectly consistent with an African American tradition, extending from Frederick Douglass forward, of insisting that talk of a "Negro problem" missed the point and that the "white problem" instead deserved emphasis. Similarly, the question of white values and the problem of the expansion of the white nationalism of the United States have focused the reflections of Native American thinkers. If slave folklore represents one point of departure for the critical study of whiteness, then the Chicana/o tales collected by Américo Paredes in *Uncle Remus con Chile* define another such point. When W. E. B. Du Bois claimed "singularly clairvoyant" knowledge of the "souls of white folk," his grounding for that claim lay not in any mystique of racial essentialism. Rather, as he, James Baldwin, bell hooks, and others understood, such knowledge was situated in particular "points of vantage."[37] However ignored, intellectuals of color have made searching inquiries into whiteness for a long time. In the writings of Robert Lee, Neil Foley, Cheryl Harris, john powell, Cherrie Moraga, Tomás Almaguer, Gloria Anzaldúa, and bell hooks, such intellectuals have likewise produced the recent texts that have most boldly extended such inquiries.[38] As universities have become less white places, such work has gained influence.

Characterizing the study of whiteness as a project of white scholars thus represents both a continued insistence on placing whites at the center of everything and a continuing refusal to take seriously the insights into whiteness that people of color offer. The enduring and scandalous inability of historians to come to grips with Du Bois as an expert on the past of the *white* South is one index of this failure. More direct evidence comes from the nearly simultaneous denunciation by both *Time* and *Newsweek* of the fiction of the great American Indian expert on race, Leslie Marmon Silko, as somehow "antiwhite," despite her nuanced portrayals of race and her sympathetic development of the view that whites are but a symptom of "witchery" and not the source of evils.[39]

In briefly surveying the content of critical studies of whiteness, it is well to begin with a series of questions posed long ago but still much in need of answers. As World War II ended, the great novelist Chester Himes had a character in *If He Hollers Let Him Go* begin "wondering when white folks started getting white—or rather, when they started losing it." Twenty years ago, in the essay "The Little Man at Chehaw Station," Ralph Ellison puzzled, "What, by the way, is one to make of a white youngster who, with a transistor radio, screaming a Stevie Wonder tune, glued to his ear, shouts racial epithets at black young-sters trying to swim at a public beach?" The oldest of the questions is the most difficult. In a February 1860 contribution to *Anglo-African Magazine*, the Brooklyn schoolteacher William J. Wilson, writing as "Ethiop," framed his subject with a title question: "What Shall We Do with the White People?"[40]

If the critical study of whiteness cannot fully answer the profound questions raised by Ethiop, Himes, and Ellison, at least it offers prom-ising ways to address them. Its first and most critical contribution lies in "marking" whiteness as a particular—even peculiar,—identity, rather than as the presumed norm. This insight crosses disciplinary lines dra-matically. For example, Toni Morrison's work of literary criticism, *Playing in the Dark*, lays bare the tendency to assume that *American*, absent another adjective, means white American. Richard Dyer's essay on cinema, "White," argues that its title describes the normative color of the silver screen. Allan Bérubé joins Baldwin, Siobhan B. Somerville, and others in challenging durable, troubled, and often not consciously noticed connections of whiteness with both "vanilla" heterosexual and queer sexualities. The fact that people of color often regard white iden-tity as crying out for explanation undergirds such important writings as Mia Bay's *The White Image in the Black Mind* and Keith Basso's *Por-traits of "The Whiteman": Linguistic Play and Cultural Symbols among the Western Apache*.[41]

In "marking" whiteness, the historical approach suggested by Himes's question has moved debate forward decisively. Critical studies of whiteness have begun to describe not the origins of generalized white identity but the ways in which specific strata of the population came to think that they are white. In particular, the adoption of white iden-tity by groups themselves subordinated, exploited, and even racialized as "not quite white" has proved fascinating to historians. In his 1935 classic *Black Reconstruction*, for example, W. E. B. Du Bois initiated specific historical discussion of the "white worker" and of why the adjective so often received stronger accent than the noun in the identity of this group. His emphasis on *both* the "income-bearing value" of whiteness and the "public and psychological wages" offered to those categorized as white informs much recent writing on the white worker, including Dana Frank's superb "White Working-Class Women and the Race Question." In Robert Lee's *Orientals*, this body of work is dramatically extended in a deeply gendered account of how the post–Civil War white working class coalesced around the idea of a "family wage" earned by a male breadwinner, in opposition to images of the Chinese immigrant as "a racial Other unfit for white work or white wives." The appearance of scholarship that closely roots white workers in specific locales, labor processes, and political economies marks a further advance.[42]

The painful, uneven ways in which immigrants from European groups were historically seen as racially different and even as less-than-fully-white have long occupied the attention of writers of color. For their deft balancing of "choice" and "coercion" in the process through which immigrants whitened, for their sure sense of racial learning among immigrants as a great drama and tragedy, and for their seminal influence on recent writings on whiteness and immigration, James Baldwin's *The Price of the Ticket* and his "On Being 'White'. . . and Other Lies" deserve specific mention. Outstanding among the recent historical works following the trail Baldwin blazed are those by Robert Orsi, Karen Brodkin, Michael Rogin, and Noel Ignatiev. More impressionistic accounts by the art critic Maurice Berger and the theologian Thandeka perhaps approach Baldwin's boldness even more fully, as does Camille Cosby's article on how her son's murderer, an eastern European immigrant, might have learned to hate Blacks in the United States. Such accounts remind us that whiteness has functioned both as a category, into which immigrants were or were not put, and as a consciousness, which immigrants embraced and rejected in specific circumstances.[43]

The racial identity of white women has engaged the urgent attention of African American thinkers from the slave narratives, through the antilynching agitation of Ida B. Wells, to the recent, provocative, and highly compressed reflections of the philosopher Lewis Gordon. Cheryl Harris's "Finding Sojourner's Truth" offers the closest study of the ways in which gender oppression made the situation of white women like that of African American women (and men), as well as the clearest account of differences that all but ensured that white women would both accept and contest their oppression as women while accepting a white identity. The leading book-length study that takes white womanhood in the United States as a problem for investigation remains Ruth Frankenberg's sensitive ethnography *White Women, Race Matters*, which charts the various ways in which white and female identities interact in daily lives. Vron Ware's *Beyond the Pale* and Louise Newman's *White Women's Rights* cross oceans to put white womanhood and feminism in a context of colonialism as well as of slavery.[44]

Perhaps the central overarching theme in scholarship on whiteness is the argument that white identity is decisively shaped by the exercise of power and the expectation of advantages in acquiring property. This insistence that white identity derived from the experience of dominating, rather than from biology or culture, has long found expression in African American thought. Both Amiri Baraka and Malcolm X, for example, insisted that whiteness is not a color but rather an ideology that developed out of desires to rule and the exigencies of ruling. The leading U.S. historians of whiteness, Theodore Allen and Alexander Saxton, consistently view white identity in terms of class and domination. Equally forceful in connecting whiteness with the exercise of power is Ian Haney Lopez's *White by Law*, the first full treatment of the protracted use of U.S. state power, via naturalization law, to determine who was and who was not white.[45]

The pervasiveness of terror and of the witness of terror—from slave patrols to lynchings to contemporary mass incarceration—in the construction of white identities is another old, and newly rediscovered, theme. When such contemporary writers as Paul Gilroy and bell hooks emphasize that whiteness has been and is still often experienced as terror by people of color, they can easily reach back to the autobiographies of slaves for examples. But those autobiographies also showed how watching and committing acts of racial violence incorporated children, women, and the poor unequally but surely into the white population and kept them there. Gloria Anzaldúa's "We Call Them Greasers" makes poetry out of the impact of such terror. Her poem is narrated by a white man who uses fraud, rustling of livestock, courts, fire, the English language, rape, and murder to gain land from Mexican American victims, some of whom had "black eyes like an Indian." The verses imagine a point at which even "his boys" are so repelled that they refuse to look the father/narrator in the eyes. At that critical juncture, the father requires his sons to lynch the last victim. The story echoes a number of African American works, all written from a "white" viewpoint, on the effects that witnessing terror had on whites. As Ralph Ellison, himself the author of an arresting short story recounting a lynching from the point of view of a white youth, once put it, whiteness worked as "a form of manifest destiny which designated Negroes as its territory and its challenge."[46] In the recent past, Lewis Gordon, Robyn Wiegman, Nell Irvin Painter, and Trudier Harris have likewise described the connections between violence and the development of white collective identities.[47]

The most arresting effort to connect whiteness with power lies in Cheryl Harris's long and remarkable *Harvard Law Review* essay "Whiteness as Property," which is discussed at length in Chapter 8 of this book. Harris moves away from older arguments that simply detail the privileges a white skin confers in obtaining property in the United States to contend that whiteness historically became, and remains, *itself* a form of property. Developing in counterpoint to the dispossession of American Indian property, the owning of slave property, and later, the systematic property advantages channeled toward whites by segregation and other state policies, whiteness itself possesses value and has at times been seen by courts to do so. Harris, like the Chicana writers Linda Lopez McAlister and Linda M. Pierce, features family histories of passing as a member of the white race as openings onto the connections between whiteness and property. George Lipsitz's and Martha Mahoney's accounts of the role of federal housing policies in fostering what Lipsitz calls a "possessive investment in whiteness" merit reading as complements to Harris's article.[48] Ironically, such work is especially important in analyzing the behavior and thought of the millions of whites who acquire no property and the many more who acquire no productive property. Along with valuable emerging scholarship on "propertyless" whiteness, Harris's point that poor whites *do* possess the property of whiteness helps to recast debate on the tragedy of why those who derive so little material benefit from white supremacy often firmly cling to white identity, the only property they hold.[49] Harris's work, like nearly all of the best critical studies of whiteness old and new, implicitly warns us against claims that any significant drama in U.S. history is "really about race" or that any single dynamic is isolated from the social processes within which it unfolds. As we turn, then, to a brief description of the sections of this book, let us first note that the essays seek to place race in dialectical relationship to factors such as class, ethnicity, gender, age, and sexuality in the belief that doing so enhances our understanding of the pervasive presence of race in the United States.

In keeping with the idea of a usable present, the first of *Colored White*'s three parts, "Still White," is the least obviously historical one. After considering Eve and the future, this section makes the case that the United States is "still white" from other angles. The selections on the recent past begin with a description of how whiteness informed the 1999 "smear campaign" of New York City's mayor, Rudolph Giuliani, against the depiction of a Black Virgin Mary by the Afro-British artist Chris Ofili. The next piece critiques the wordless white supremacist sneers delivered by the conservative talk radio host Rush Limbaugh on his mercifully short-lived television show. Like the Giuliani and Limbaugh essays, that on the place of the "white worker" in President Clinton's attempts to distance himself from affirmative action argues that taking a longer historical view is indispensable to understanding the recent past. The section's final essay tackles the racial position of O. J. Simpson—the man and the advertising icon—prior to the murders of Nicole Brown Simpson and Ron Goldman. It disputes the notion that whites in the United States colorblindly embraced Simpson as a man whose achievements counted and not his race. Instead, it argues, Simpson's popularity called on racial images at every turn, not the least when it was used to allow whites to imagine that they had transcended perceptions of color.

The second part of the book, "Toward Nonwhite History," invokes the past to show that the sway of whiteness is not inevitable, unalterable, or simple. It was never the whole story of U.S. history. The section consists of five studies examining whiteness, nonwhiteness, and "inbetween-ness" in the nineteenth and early twentieth centuries. The first two of these selections consider abolitionism as a movement that often drew its membership, its logic, and its inspiration from African Americans—and especially from escaped slaves. The heroism of John Brown and the political maturity of the larger abolitionist movement in responding to the language regarding slavery used by white labor and by members of the women's movement both reflected such influences. "The Pursuit of Happiness," the section's third essay, considers the pre-Civil War United States, avowedly a "white man's country," as a nation in which white identity was shaped not only by slavery but also by relationships with and images of Native Americans and many other "not-white" peoples. The fourth essay considers the racial position of eastern and southern European immigrants in the late nineteenth and early twentieth centuries, finding it to lie "inbetween" full whiteness and the fiercer oppressions inflicted on people of color. The vignette that closes this section introduces the 1929 surrealist map of the world as an early attempt to identify Eurocentrism as a problem and to project a "nonwhite" alternative.

In the final section, three essays probe "The Past/Presence of Non-whiteness," identifying areas in which recent history suggests new possibilities for looking at the past and the future. A selection that considers contemporary "wiggers" (white kids "acting Black") in light of the tensions in racial impersonation embodied by Elvis Presley follows two very differently styled essays on the changing membership base of organized labor and the possible transformation of unions. The concluding pages explicitly confront the question of whether and how nonwhiteness is possible, both for those currently identified as white and for those who may be accepted and coerced into whiteness in the future.

Eve on "The New Face of America." *Time*, Cover. Special issue. September 1993. With permission from Timepix.

Chris Ofili's *The Holy Virgin Mary*. Collage, paint, glitter, map pins, polyester resin, and elephant dung on linen. 1996. With permission of the artist and of the Victoria Miro Gallery.

Smear Campaign

GIULIANI, THE *HOLY VIRGIN MARY,* AND THE CRITICAL STUDY OF WHITENESS

The study of whiteness, both as a category into which some people are placed and as an identity that some people embrace, has gained considerable attention in academia and the popular press in the past decade. Alternately celebratory, dismissive, and bemused, this increased attention reflects the ways in which educational institutions, workplaces, and debates have grudgingly opened up to racial democracy, making the assumption that white privileges, presences, and viewpoints are "natural" more difficult to hold. With biologically based racism in retreat, it has become possible to ask bedrock questions such as "What makes some people think that they are white?" and "When did white people become white?" of a far broader audience. In making whiteness a moral, political, and historical problem, writers like Cheryl Harris, Toni Morrison, Philip Deloria, Cherrie Moraga, Thandeka, and bell hooks have powerfully connected with long-standing critical reflections on whiteness by such towering figures as W. E. B. Du Bois, Americo Paredes, James Baldwin, and Ida B. Wells, all of whom decidedly saw whiteness as a problem long ago.[1] These new and older studies have seldom been brought together, however, and have still less often been deployed in an attempt to illuminate a current political issue. This essay makes such an attempt, sampling an array of critical studies of whiteness with a view toward introducing them to readers and demonstrating their utility in addressing the controversy generated by New York Mayor Rudolph Giuliani's attacks on Chris Ofili's painting Holy Virgin Mary *and on the* Brooklyn Museum *for displaying it. The article's purpose is not to argue*

that the museum controversy "was really about" race and whiteness but
rather to show how powerfully white consciousness operates to shape
debates that are also about religion, politics, and gender.

Seeing Ofili's *Holy Virgin Mary*

The soundbite was consistent if odd. Every time I returned to the hotel
between meetings in New York City in late September 1999, the radio
news echoed Mayor Rudolph Giuliani's charges: An artist had constructed a work by "throwing elephant dung at a picture of the Virgin
Mary," and now the Brooklyn Museum was about to display it, using
public money. Giuliani promised to punish this "hate crime" by with-
drawing museum funds. Sometimes the verbs changed. The dung was
"smeared" or "splattered" on what the Catholic League for Religious
and Civil Rights called a religious painting. But the logic was the same.
As Cardinal O'Connor put it, an "attack on our Blessed Mother" had
occurred and demanded a response." "You don't have a right," Giuliani added, "to government subsidy for desecrating somebody else's
religion."[2]

Because my Catholic upbringing and the time I had spent in West
Africa had given me a clear idea of what both religious paintings of
Mary and elephant dung looked like, it was not hard to generate
images of the offending work. (I did have some doubts about whether
thrown elephant dung would stick to a painting, but I took Giuliani's
word for it.) The controversy held some interest, in terms of the
mayor's senatorial aspirations, censorship, and arts funding, but those
remained far from the research concerns that brought me to New York
City—investigations of race and white identity. Although I leaned
toward the cynical opinion that politics, and not purely religion,
entered into Giuliani's aggressive raising of this issue, I had no reason to
challenge the views of the radio commentators who argued for or
against one or the other of those.

On leaving for the airport, I finally saw a newspaper reproduction of
the offending work, Chris Ofili's *Holy Virgin Mary*. The Virgin gazing
from the newspaper page deflated any conviction that this was a simple
controversy, divorced from the study of race and whiteness. This was
certainly not the "religious painting" of Mary I knew from Missouri and
Illinois churches. Why did no one initially mention that she was Black
and that Ofili was Afro-British? And where was the elephant dung? No
thrown, smeared, or splattered excrement was anywhere in sight.

When I later saw a larger, full-color reproduction in the catalog from Ofili's major exhibition in Great Britain, the mystery of the dung was solved. The Virgin's bare breast was made of the stuff, shaped and processed to a sheen.[3] The painting also sat—unlike what Ofili calls "crucified" paintings hanging from museum walls—on two balls of dung, one labeled "Virgin" and the other "Mary." A catalog described, in a much fuller way than the insidious David Bowie voiceover on the website displaying the Brooklyn Museum's exhibition, why the dung appeared.[4] Ofili had, since a 1992 visit to Zimbabwe, incorporated it into much of his work. Partly a sendup of the British arts establishment's glib, commodified evocations of multiculturalism and "roots" (Ofili took out large ads in trendy arts publications saying simply "Elephant Shit"), the use of dung also reflected an engagement with cosmologies that revere dung as a symbol of regeneration.[5]

The catalog's reproductions and critical works on Ofili also gave form to a vaguer suspicion I had had since I first saw the newspaper reproduction of *Holy Virgin Mary:* the painting somehow seemed admiring, warm toward its subject, and in the end reverent and even Catholic. The draping of Mary, described by one writer as "petal-like," echoed much of Catholic art and doubled the breast's regenerative symbolism. Ofili, himself Catholic, claimed inspiration from the masters of Madonna painting, especially Van Eyck, and alluded to the sensuality of their Virgins. His studio features a sign over the door: "This area is constantly watched and patrolled by the Lord."[6]

The objects surrounding Mary in Ofili's portrayal emerge, on close inspection, as relatively tiny cutouts—one critic calls them butterflies—of buttocks and genitalia from pornographic magazines. The images, largely of Black women, place Ofili's Virgin in a world of racism, misogyny, commodified sex, and dismemberment and they gesture provocatively toward Catholic paintings in which scenes illustrating Mary's "attributes" hover around her. (The artist both critiques and participates in that world.) The sacred and the secular, as Godfrey Worsdale puts it, are thus juxtaposed "in their extremes."[7] A goal of the project, according to Ofili, was to create a hiphop Madonna, reflecting on the sexism of rap but also on the self-assertion—Ofili is specifically fascinated by Lil' Kim—of some women in it.[8] Thus Ofili's *Holy Virgin Mary,* surrounded by the peril of the floating buttocks/balloons/butterflies of pornography and subject to ridicule because of her overdrawn, even minstrelized, African features, is nonetheless neither ethereal nor downcast but self-possessed and sensual.

Having seen, as opposed to merely hearing about, this complex work, I returned to Giuliani's decision to single the painting out for attack much less certain that we could do without a discussion of race in understanding his motivations. The "Sensation" exhibition that brought the *Holy Virgin Mary* to Brooklyn was, after all, designed and endlessly marketed by its entrepreneur/owner Charles Saatchi as "shocking," "offensive," and even vomit-inducing. The works on display included one that brutalized animals and another that seemed to British viewers an homage to a child-murderer.[9] Certainly there was ample room to criticize postmodern art as amoral without singling out Ofili. That the museum was caught in a series of tawdry financial arrangements with Saatchi underlines how effortless it could be to mount such criticisms. To understand why Giuliani zeroed in on Ofili's supposed offenses, why the mayor conjured up the "uncivilized" throwing of elephant dung where none existed, why he regarded the Catholic-inspired painting as an attack by the artist on "somebody else's" religion, why he let dung and not pornography be emphasized, and how he rested assured that even as the painting, with no splattered dung, was reproduced in the press, his know-nothing stance would still work politically, takes us to the heart of whiteness.[10] Although religious faith and gender-inflected political opportunism remain central to explanations of Giuliani's choice of targets, these motivations are themselves so fully tied to white racial consciousness that understanding the *Holy Virgin Mary* affair offers an opportunity to reprise most of the key insights of critical studies of whiteness.

Somebody Else's Madonna

In his certainty that *Holy Virgin Mary* attacked "somebody else's religion," Giuliani turned a phrase significantly. The mayor instantly became the other, the somebody else, the hate crime victim. Ostensibly he did so as a Catholic. The irreligious artist and what Giuliani called the "elite" arts establishment presumably attacked faith in general but Catholicism in particular, as Cardinal O'Connor put it.[11] Indeed, Katha Pollitt's fine *Nation* column on the controversy noted the ease with which it was forgotten that "the Virgin Mary was not Catholic" and nicely quoted the antifeminist Camille Paglia's hints that a "Jewish collector" and a "Jewish museum director" were conspiring to promote "anti-Catholic art."[12] As the stormy debates over Mary in my own Irish Catholic/German Lutheran childhood should have prepared me to know—my parents did not speak for weeks after a Lutheran Sunday School let me color Mary's clothing green rather than the proper blue—religion provides its own sets of significant "others" against which identity forms.[13] But in this case, whiteness overrode internal divisions among Christians.

As Giuliani and his advisers had to know, the stories the mayor orchestrated about Ofili's painting would appear alongside small reproductions of the 6- by 8-foot work. Indeed, *Holy Virgin Mary* was probably the planet's most often reproduced work of art at the millennium's end. The unfamiliar other in those reproductions is not a Protestant Mary but specifically a Black Virgin. Nor, as it turns out, was the artist "somebody else" to the Catholic faith. What then, we ought to ask, was the relationship between the Blackness of Ofili's Mary and Giuliani's ability to assume that she was somebody else's production and to avoid having to defend that assumption even when Ofili's Catholicism was reported in the press?

Critical studies of whiteness help to answer these important questions. In her seminal 1988 article on "white privilege and male privilege," the feminist philosopher Peggy McIntosh set about listing the perks of whiteness that often seem so natural to their owners as to require no second thought. McIntosh described white privilege as "an invisible weightless knapsack of special provisions, assurances, tools, maps, guides, coda books, passports, visas, . . . emergency gear, and blank checks." Its contents, which may or may not be acknowledged consciously, include assumptions that range from the most practical and concrete to the abstract:

· "I can choose blemish cover or bandages in 'flesh' color and have them more or less match my skin."

· "I can expect figurative language and imagery in all of the arts to testify to the experiences of my race."

In convening a recent workshop on race for several hundred Minneapolis social workers, I asked participants to jot down additions to McIntosh's list. The first three volunteers to read their responses were people of color, and they all made the same point: Whites in the United States get to see the central symbols of holiness in the culture almost uniformly portrayed as white. One particularly full response suggested that breaking the commandments against making "graven images" of God had opened the door to white domination. Occasionally, as in the Milwaukee marches against open housing of 1967, when segregationists paraded behind the slogan "God Is White," the assumption of a white deity has been put to explicitly political use. Even in a New York City in which Latino, Asian, and Haitian Catholic populations are significant, and in a world in which Brazil is the nation with the most

Catholics, the image of a white Holy Family survives intact. Listeners at several talks I gave on this subject reported thinking (on the basis of Giuliani's words, poor television and newspaper reproductions of the work, and reigning assumptions) that the painting was a white Virgin made black by smearings of dung on her otherwise white face. Giuliani's "smear campaign" worked because a Black Virgin is somebody else, in a nation in which, as Barbara Reynolds recently pointed out, the government's Postal Service churns out one billion (!) white-Madonna stamps per year. The Harlem-based *Amsterdam News* was almost alone in making this point, headlining a September 30, 1999 editorial "A Black Madonna! Giuliani's Worst Nightmare."[14]

The film scholar and cultural historian Richard Dyer deepens this discussion in his critical 1997 study *White*. Dyer notes that Christianity developed out of a Jewish/Middle Eastern/North African milieu and that its images of holiness did not uniformly privilege whiteness for many centuries. From the Crusades through the Renaissance and European expansion to the Americas, however, Christian symbolism made "national/geographic" others and then racial others into the "enemies of Christ" and/or potential converts.[15] In Renaissance art, Dyer argues, Christ and the Virgin Mary not only are white but also are "increasingly . . . rendered as paler, whiter, than everyone else." They give off light and their hair flows. Their images are both in some ways more physically realistic (Christ's maleness becomes clearer and renderings of his genitals appear) and more preternatural and implausible examples of what Dyer calls "extreme whiteness." Also preternaturally white in some portrayals was the breast milk so frequently associated with Catholic portraits and accounts of Mary—an image in sharp contrast to Ofili's insistence on symbolizing the nurturing and regenerative powers of the Virgin by constructing her bare breast out of a dung both dark and African. Dyer adds that Christianity emerges as a singularly "embodied" religion, obsessed with picturing the holy in human form, and yet "anti-body" in its commitment to the superiority of the spiritual within a cosmology that posits a sharp dichotomy between body and spirit. The wholeness and white body of Mary then powerfully symbolize the ideal and the distance of all women from that ideal. Dyer also observes that in museum-featured religious art, Mary exists at a certain remove from the violence surrounding her life. She is typically not tearstained, wounded, scarred, shadowed, or seen as aging. This image, implausible at once for Mary and for women of the world generally, calls to mind Saidiya Hartman's prescient comments on the impact of seeing the category "woman" as white and privileged: "By assuming that [the term] woman designates a known referent, an *a priori* unity . . . we fail to attend to the contingent and disjunctive production of the category." Hartman adds that in assuming that the violence committed against women of color is attached to slavery or race alone and not also to womanhood, we avoid the "work of feminist criticism . . . the interrogation and deconstruction of this [white] normativity."[16]

A final point concerning the easy pairing of white and Madonna also grows out of the literature critically studying whiteness. At its most healthy, that literature refuses to see itself as the latest hot thing in academia. Instead it roots itself in a long tradition of critical thought about whiteness by people of color. Ofili's work, and Giuliani's reaction to it, may profitably be placed in a long tradition of artistic challenges to the idea of an "extreme white" Holy Family. In very different ways, such resistance appears in the worship of Our Lady of Guadalupe and other saintly images in Asia, Latin America, and Africa; the depictions of Mary as olive-colored by Henry Tanner in *Virgin* a century ago, as brown in William H. Johnson's haunting *Mount Calvary,* and as Black in Romare Bearden's *Come Sunday* (Ofili-like with bare breast and a Christ-child who flies); and the political activism of Albert Cleage's Shrine of the Black Madonna in Detroit. In New York City itself, violence in the bloody white-on-Black race riots of 1834 was sparked in part by the African American preacher Samuel Cox's contention that Christ was dark-skinned. Alain Locke's pathbreaking *The New Negro* (1925) had Winold Reiss's enigmatic "The Brown Madonna" as its frontispiece.[17] Jorge Amado's great Brazilian novel *Tent of Miracles* dramatizes the worship of dark deities and the white-supremacist dread of such worship. Langston Hughes's "Christ in Alabama" (1931) perhaps most closely approximates Ofili's portrayal of Mary as imperiled for her race and her gender:

> Christ is a nigger,
> Beaten and black:
> Oh, bare your back!
> Mary is His mother
> Mammy of the South,
> Silence your mouth.[18]

Italian American Whiteness and Troubles with Madonnas

A second large area in which recent critical studies of whiteness illuminate the position from which Giuliani attacked *Holy Virgin Mary* concerns the mayor's particular experiences as an Italian American New

Yorker. Giuliani's website has him as the grandson of immigrants from Italy, born into a "working-class" family in Brooklyn in 1944. *The Village Voice* contests much of this biography in the noteworthy article "Rudy's White World," which has him growing up in a "blanched Nassau suburb."[19] Wayne Barrett's excellent recent biography of Giuliani clarifies matters. The mayor's father, after serving a term for armed robbery, utilized family connections to get a job tending bar in a Brooklyn restaurant that doubled as a base for loansharking and gambling operations. The family moved from Brooklyn to Garden City, Long Island, which still lacked a single Black family among its residents as late as 1968. In any case a New Yorker, Giuliani grew up in an area in which the racial identity of Italian Americans had been very much at issue in the early twentieth century and beyond. Indeed, in *Do the Right Thing,* Spike Lee's characters roundly questioned Italian whiteness, and in 1999 Lee could cleverly cast the Latino actor John Leguizamo as the leading character in his searching inquiry into working-class Italian American identity, *Summer of Sam.*[20] Giuliani's grandparents came to a nation in which immigrants from Italy were lynched, excluded, and called "guineas" (a slur directly borrowed from earlier usages in reference to African Americans) or "greasers" (a slur directly borrowed from earlier usages in reference to Latinos). They came from a country that had its own sense of racial divisions along a north-south axis. "Africa," lore had it, "begins at Naples." Giuliani was heir to both halves of this division: his father's side came from Tuscany in the north and his mother's from the Naples area in the south.[21]

Recent scholarship on whiteness has looked closely at the process by which immigrant groups regarded as less-than-white upon their arrival in the United States—"inbetween people," as James Barrett and I termed them in a recent article—encountered race and appropriated whiteness. Noel Ignatiev's *How the Irish Became White* and Karen Brodkin's *How Jews Became White Folks* are the best examples of a literature largely inspired by the pioneering essays of James Baldwin. Other accounts make the racialization of Italians central to the racial dramas that unfolded during and after the 1890-to-1920 "new immigration" from eastern and southern Europe. The particular association of "inbetween" status with the poorest immigrant workers and with those doing the dirtiest jobs runs through this literature. So does the frank admission that being victimized as "inbetween" could lead to alliances with people of color (especially, in New York City, among Italian Americans supporting Vito Marcantonio) or, more commonly, to an anxious refusal to avow affinities across racial lines and a desperate desire to achieve a white identity, a desire that was often underwritten by a government-subsidized move to "blanched" suburbs.[22]

The history of Italian and Italian American whiteness was bound up with the images of Madonnas in fascinating ways, some of which could not have been lost on Giuliani. In Italy, and especially in Sicily, depictions of the Madonna and other saints were, and to some extent still are, black. These figures, as Lucia Chiavola Birnbaum's excellent *Black Madonnas* argues, grew out of a social history replete with African, Middle Eastern, and wider Mediterranean contacts. Marina Warner's insightful study of myths and cults that revolve around Mary tellingly explores links of Italian black Madonnas to the sea. Such Madonnas also reflected pre-Christian associations of blackness with strong, mystically powerful women. Leonard Covello, the great student of southern Italian immigration to New York City, wrote 50 years ago of Madonnas as the "chief deity" in the south of Italy, as symbolically more important than Jesus there, and as an index of female power in society. To the extent that they mobilized both pre-Christian and Christian symbolism, black Madonnas represented a particular vulnerability in patriarchal authority. Ofili's *Holy Virgin Mary* captures the spirit of such black Madonnas, and Pollitt not implausibly sees in it "the cheerful mother goddess of an imaginary folk religion." The Church rarely smiled on these images. Attempts to explain away their existence—as, for example, in the contention that fire changed their color—or to hide, marginalize, or repaint them, were rife. Nonetheless, the Black Virgin at Tindari remains one of the most revered Sicilian icons.[23]

In 1952, when Leonard Moss and Stephen Cappannari dispassionately presented their research on scores of images of "dark brown or black madonnas," some of them Italian, to the American Association for the Advancement of Science, "every priest and nun walked out." The next year, when *Scientific Monthly* published Moss and Cappannari's article and ran a picture of a black Madonna on its cover, the chaplain of the Newman Club at Wayne State University denounced them as "campus atheists."[24] This extremely hostile U.S. reaction may reflect what the sociologist Sal Salerno has characterized as a much more thoroughgoing "loss of the symbol" of the Black Madonna among Italian Americans than among Italians. Covello, for example, quotes at length from the reminiscences of an immigrant from Calabria, who made two attempts to enlist the aid of saints to get money for passage to the United States just after the beginning of the twentieth

century. He first asked the black San Filippo to intervene and, that fail-
ing, appealed to the black Madonna of Seminara. Nonetheless, in the
United States, shrines to black Madonnas appear to be absent. Salerno
provocatively links this loss to an "assimilation" into U.S.-style whiteness. It is probably a sign of both the strength and the weakness of such
assimilation that the most popular United States Italian American
entertainer of our time constantly plays across the color line, while
billing herself as Madonna. A decade before the *Holy Virgin Mary* controversy, Pepsi pulled a big-budget Madonna ad campaign and withdrew sponsorship of her concert tour in the context of boycott threats
from a far-right media watchdog group. At issue was Madonna's "Like
a Prayer" video, in which she kissed the feet of a Black saint who then
came to life and romantically embraced her. In reporting Pepsi's decision, and elsewhere, the *New York Times* characteristically made the
embrace raceless," saying that what was at issue was the video's portrayal of "romantic love with a priest or saint."[25]

Whether Giuliani was denied an experience with black Madonnas in
New York's Catholic churches and schools or heard dark rumors of
their existence, he clearly would have known about New York City's
most celebrated Italian American shrine, the Madonna of 115th Street in
East Harlem. The *festa* surrounding the Church of Our Lady of Mount
Carmel there had its roots in devotions begun by immigrants from Pollo,
near Naples, in the 1880s. The celebrations in the Virgin's honor, so brilliantly described in the work of Robert Orsi, became the "central communal event" in Italian Harlem, "drawing immigrants from all over
southern Italy." As Italian Americans (like Giuliani's own family) who
were "finally well-off enough to get out" left the neighborhood (and
often their parents) after World War II, ties of ethnicity and family
became still more bound up with rituals of return to the *festa*.[26] According to Orsi, the Puerto Ricans who transformed the area into Spanish
Harlem had to be imagined as pushing out the Italians who left. Because
of their "proximity" to Italian Americans in color, language, and (for a
time, around Marcantonio) politics, Puerto Ricans represented a particular threat to the security of Italian American whiteness. One strategy in
policing the line between Italian Americans and Puerto Ricans was to
keep the latter unwelcome at the *festa* to the Madonna of 115th Street.
Indeed, Orsi adds, this racial imperative was so strong that the darker,
but less "proximate" and therefore less threatening, Haitians could be
included in the *festa* and could even be considered not so "black" as the
Puerto Ricans. St. Ann's Parish in East Harlem featured, in the image of

San Benedetto (or "Il Moro," as he was known in southern Italy), perhaps the most dramatic statue of a Black Italian saint in the United States. The son of slaves brought to Sicily from Ethiopia in the sixteenth century, Benedetto's feast day was marked early in the century with some African Americans included in the Harlem festivities. Indeed, his transplantation to New York City suggests the possibility of a road not taken, toward an egalitarian pan-Latin challenge to the hyper-whiteness of holiness. Italian Americans more typically took a road to white identity, and in many cases, to the suburbs. Puerto Rican worshippers inherited the statue, although a few Italian Americans persist in the parish. Elsewhere, San Benedetto became known as St. Benedict the Black, the patron saint of African Americans. An Italian American politician in New York City, especially one as successful and well connected as Giuliani, could not help but be aware of the celebrations on 115th Street—Giuliani's father had grown up on 123rd Street in East Harlem—and of the striking racial and neighborhood politics they enacted. Thus, although he was unprepared to see a Black Madonna as holy, Giuliani's ethnicity and location prepared him well to see the need to draw tight the racial boundaries surrounding Mary.[27]

Black Virgin, White Politics

It is in the realm of politics that making the argument that whiteness was a central element in Giuliani's attack on the *Holy Virgin Mary* is most intricate, but also most critical. The politics of religion and gender go so far toward explaining his electoral opportunism that reference to the growing literature on appeals to the "white vote" can seem almost superfluous. As *Time* put it in commenting on the Brooklyn Museum controversy in early October, "To subject this move by Giuliani to crass political analysis is to see brilliance." The votes of "artsy" types were, according to *Time,* lost to the Republicans anyway, but more conservative upstate voters and Catholics statewide would presumably rally to Giuliani's defense of "basic values."[28] *The Village Voice* analysis of "Papal Pandering" similarly found Giuliani to be prospecting for votes outside of the city and appealing to a voting electorate estimated to be 44 percent Catholic statewide. The *Voice* added its opinion that Giuliani was also specifically angling for the support of Michael Long, the Catholic leader of the Conservative Party (CP) of New York. In that state, whose electoral system allows candidates to run on the ballot lines of multiple parties, absence of a CP endorsement has been the kiss of death for statewide Republican candidates for decades. Better relations with Cardinal O'Connor, whose response to the museum controversy eerily echoed Giuliani's, were likely to result from the mayor's stance.[29]

This positioning within Catholic/CP politics came at a time when Giuliani was having serious problems with both groups. Running in New York City, Giuliani had consistently taken a firm prochoice position on abortion and had been a fixture at the gay rights parades that so antagonized the Catholic hierarchy. To the extent that the mayor anticipated his own marriage falling apart and his infidelity being revealed, his Catholic image was further imperiled. (The longer-term political calculations had to be tricky here, however. In early 2001, when Giuliani attacked a work depicting a female and nude Black Christ, as conservative a paper as the *Chicago Tribune* editorialized, ". . . a married man whose mistress receives city police protection is not in the best position to preach against public subsidies to immorality.") Long and the CP, which had not endorsed Giuliani in three previous citywide races, insisted on a reversal in the mayor's position on abortion as a precondition to any possible endorsement. Such a reversal would have carried the large risk of allowing Hillary Clinton to portray Giuliani as without convictions and as beholden to right-wing fringe politics.[30] Moving to the sort of categorical antichoice position that the CP supported both was unpopular with many voters and threatened to galvanize some activist groups, such as he National Abortion Rights Action League, from a neutral position into anti-Giuliani campaigning. The great success of Giuliani's Senate campaign, before it imploded in the context of health problems and scandal, lay in keeping Clinton from opening a "gender gap" among voters. That success was squarely under threat if a sharp shift on the abortion issue were to occur. Even so, appeals to Conservative, Catholic, and Christian-right voters mattered so much that Giuliani's staff apparently sent out test signals regarding a possible move away from a prochoice position six weeks before the museum controversy. He quickly clarified that no change would occur.[31]

With very rare exceptions, commentators did not link the Brooklyn Museum and the abortion issues directly, although the two were repeatedly discussed in proximity to each other. Nonetheless, the ways in which attacking Ofili enabled the mayor to shore up Catholic and Conservative support are striking. By late September, Giuliani had managed to situate himself at the head of a movement in which the Church, the Knights of Columbus, the Catholic League, and the Conservative Party turned out hundreds of demonstrators. For good measure, some orthodox Jewish and Hispanic Christian groups, also courted by Giuliani, likewise mobilized modestly on his side. The "pro-Catholic" quotes coming from city hall and those emanating from the Catholic League were indistinguishable. In defending against a black Madonna and (in somewhat muted tones) decrying the pornographic butterflies surrounding her, Giuliani's words resonated with the attacks on promiscuity and with the endorsements of virginity sometimes made by antiabortion activists. Appearing on "Evans, Novak, Shields and Hunt" on October 10, Giuliani forcefully attacked the museum and *Holy Virgin Mary*. The very next question concerned abortion rights and found Giuliani reaffirming his prochoice stance.[32] Nonetheless, CP leader Long, personally quite estranged from the mayor, had to offer praise: "Of course his actions enhance his plusses with Conservative Party voters. What he did [regarding the Brooklyn Museum] was correct."[33] For a time anyway, the subject was changed, and without shifting his position on abortion, Giuliani shored up support among key constituencies.

And yet these well-tuned and highly gendered appeals *by themselves* take us only so far in understanding either the form or the content of Giuliani's campaign against Ofili's work. With regard to both form and content, recent works in critical race theory and in the critical study of whiteness again provide vital insights. In terms of form, anti-*Holy Virgin Mary* rhetoric consistently strayed toward appeals evoking race as well as religion. This was certainly true at the fringes of the campaign. A minister in Indianapolis, for example, electronically circulated a sermon that eagerly asked, "Should we form a mob and go lynch the 'artist' Chris Ofili?" while a protester at the Brooklyn Museum sported a sign reading "Hitler Was Right When He Got Rid of 'Degenerate Art.'"[34] A vandal desecrated the painting by smearing white paint over much of it.[35]

Giuliani himself put his criticisms of Ofili squarely in the context of culture wars and other defenses of "civilization," which, he added wonderfully, "has been about trying to find the right place for excrement." Such a philosophical gem reminds us that the state-sponsored effort to stigmatize Ofili's work as "shit" and "trash" brought in by outsiders was embedded in Giuliani's larger and long-standing campaigns to "clean up" the city by removing its homeless and its sex workers from sight, by decimating affordable housing, and by massively incarcerating people of color. These campaigns are the centerpieces of the mayor's efforts to build cross-class alliances as he makes the city ever safer for capital and ever more perilous for Black and immigrant victims of police violence. In the context of continuing police brutality, especially killings in custody by the city's police, along with impressive demonstrations against such violence, Giuliani's long-standing strategy of campaigning as anticrime and propolice was compromised. His pro-"civilization" offensives against Ofili and other putative impurities in the city evoke rich connections among excrement, smearing, savagery, blackness, and white (self)images regarding control, anality, and capital accumulation; they could themselves be the subject of a psychoanalytically informed essay. Any such essay would be much in the debt of the groundbreaking psychoanalytical work on race by Joel Kovel, Sandor Ferenczi, Otto Fenichel, and others.[36]

Just as interesting as his remarks on civilization was Giuliani's insistence that "if the painting attacked a 'race,'" it could not have been displayed. This stance, also a staple of talk radio whitelore, ignored the fact that other Ofili works do combine dung with images of his Black heroes, including Muhammad Ali and Miles Davis.[37] The outlandish idea that only the rights of racial minorities, and not those of the white mainstream, are respected today is searchingly analyzed in fine recent work on "racial formation" by Michael Omi and Howard Winant. Omi and Winant argue that in the 1960s, the moral high ground of discourse on race and rights was so successfully captured by the civil rights movement that subsequent racial politics have both marginalized direct appeals to white supremacy and ensured that defenses of the interests of whites were couched in the language of colorblindness, equal treatment, and civil rights.[38] Giuliani's rhetoric regarding "hate speech" against the Virgin Mary and the Catholic League's insistent billing of itself as a civil rights organization further underscore how the (ostensibly post-)racial logic identified by Omi and Winant gave form to Giuliani's campaign.[39]

In terms of the content of Giuliani's vote-catching appeals, race generally and whiteness specifically also greatly matter. In this regard, it is again important not to lose sight of the fact that *Holy Virgin Mary* was massively reproduced even as it was denounced with wild inaccuracy by the mayor. In the absence of the promised splatterings of dung, the work was arresting primarily for the blackness of its subject. Without mentioning race—indeed precisely by not mentioning race when it was patently obvious—Giuliani placed himself in a growing line of politicians who mobilize white votes with ostensibly raceless words. Discussions of this phenomenon place it in a post-civil-rights period in which open appeals to racism are beyond the pale of respectable politics but in which issues such as crime, neighborhood schools, and welfare are powerful in their own right and so saturated with racial assumptions that it is possible to appeal to white voters in what have been called "coded" ways.[40] Many of the most successful and notorious of such appeals have been visual. In perhaps the finest study to date of the political manipulation of racial codes, Doug Hartmann and Darren Wheelock analyze the conservative, talk-radio-fueled effort to stigmatize the meager social spending proposed by the Clinton administration as part of the 1994 crime bill. They show how this campaign used "midnight basketball" as a wedge to call such spending into question as frivolous. Hartmann and Wheelock chart press mentions of midnight basketball, a Jack Kemp brainchild initiated by Republicans. They show how press coverage astronomically increased, became decidedly more negative, and came to identify the program as "liberal." Most important, they show the alarming consistency with which such coverage featured pictures of young African American men, driving home the assumption that midnight basketball was a Black thing.[41]

Such wordless racial appeals stand in a long tradition. Martin Gilens's important study *Why Americans Hate Welfare* quantifies how thoroughly and pictorially the media embraced and fueled right-wing efforts to racialize opposition to the 1960s War on Poverty. At the outset of the War on Poverty in 1964, 27 percent of those pictured in newsmagazine photographs illustrating articles on poverty were Black. By 1967 that figure had reached 72 percent. In Mississippi in 1991, Kirk Fordice's successful gubernatorial campaign featured an advertisement that complained racelessly about welfare liberalism and closed by lingering on a still photograph of a Black mother and her baby. Jesse Helms's ads in the 1990 North Carolina Senate race showed white hands holding a job rejection letter in a largely visual attack on his African American opponent's support of affirmative action. Annenberg School of Communications Dean Kathleen Hall Jamieson has recently conducted focus group research the results of which suggest that the Helms ad carried its racial point by placing a black mark, which interviewees saw as a black hand, in the letter's margin. The celebrated 1988 "Willie Horton" ad from the Bush presidential campaign likewise talked colorblindly about crime as it used Horton's image to racialize the point.[42]

The particular image of *Holy Virgin Mary* opens further fertile ground for such appeals. Although Peter Schjeldahl in the *New Yorker* and Pollitt in the *Nation* both find her "sweet," Ofili's "hiphop" Mary also looks strong, young, and sensual. Breast exposed and surrounded by nudity and danger, she remains unblinking.[43] Reproduction and sexuality coexist in her in a way that they have not been allowed to come together either in plaster representations of Mary or in contemporary popular cultural images of young Black women. Ofili bills her as "simply a hip-hop version of highly sexualized old-master paintings" of the Virgin, but representing Black female sexuality popularly is anything but simple. If, as Hortense Spillers observes, Black women are "the beached whales of the sexual universe, unvoiced, misseen, not doing, awaiting their verb," the problem is even more acute in representations of young Black women. As Tricia Rose's excellent recent work on the hiphop group TLC and on Black female virginity and sexuality shows, young Black women's alternating appearances in the popular culture as hiphop "hotties" and welfare mothers work dialectically to make both their sexuality and their motherhood seem more and more beset with problems.[44]

Rose argues that efforts by TLC and others to embrace sexuality artistically are, however fraught with difficulty, supremely significant. She adds that all such efforts stand in danger of being manipulated.[45] The racial fears on which Giuliani's attack on *Holy Virgin Mary* traded represent just such manipulation. His strategy courted not just a Catholic vote, an upstate vote, a suburban vote, and a conservative endorsement. It also mobilized a white vote. In so doing, it specifically used (just as Fordice's Mississippi ad and Clinton's 1992 diatribes against Sister Souljah had) the image of Black woman to make its "raceless" point.[46]

(How) Does Whiteness Win? A Postscript

In May of 2000, with questions about his health, his infidelities, and his marriage much in the news, Giuliani withdrew from the Senate race. Even before then, it was clear that not even deftly playing to whiteness could solve every personal and political problem. The Conservative Party had denied him an endorsement. Polls showed that his effort to withhold funding from the Brooklyn Museum was unpopular not only in New York City but also in upstate areas. Probably no more than a third of New Yorkers backed Giuliani when the issue was posed on free-speech grounds. The museum easily and predictably prevailed in court, arguing that Giuliani's efforts to withdraw funds amounted to censorship.[47]

On the other hand, Giuliani for a time probably solidified his base among white conservatives. In professing calm over the lack of a Conservative Party endorsement, he emphasized direct appeals to conservative voters rather than to parties. The *Holy Virgin Mary* case was perhaps his most dramatic such appeal.[48] When insider deals accompanying the financing of the exhibition came to light, Giuliani could smile. His actions also forced opponents decidedly onto the defensive. Hillary Clinton's position, summarized by Kira Brunner as "pro-museum, anti-elephant dung," hardly looked decisive. U.S. Senate Democrats meanwhile quickly joined Republicans in supporting a symbolic resolution calling for defunding the museum.[49]

All such outcomes pale, however, before the larger victory for whiteness in this case. What ended up being censored was not the Brooklyn Museum but any serious discussion of religion, gender, race, and power that might have grown out of the art and the controversy. The "colorblind" critical work that emerged did not seriously bring together race and censorship even to the extent that it had, for example, in the recent controversies surrounding Robert Mapplethorpe's photography and 2 Live Crew's lyrics. The views of African American intellectuals were neither featured nor even sought. That African artists and critics had a large stake in the debate was completely ignored by mainstream media. (Indeed, as superb coverage in *Nigeria World News* showed, African critics brought whole new questions to Ofili's work, including searching ones about the ease of his appropriation of elephant dung and bead work). The Clinton camp was eager to see the issues in terms of state policy and censorship, and not of race, just as Giuliani was.[50] With the noteworthy exception of an April 2001 statement of protest against Giuliani's formation of a "decency commission" by the New York local of the Black Radical Congress, the racism of Giuliani's efforts to restrict free expression has gone largely unremarked.[51] Naturalized pictures of white holiness drawn against highly gendered images of "somebody [racially] else," white control of the commanding heights of the media and arts establishments, and the pretense of colorblindness all survived the *Holy Virgin Mary* controversy unscathed and largely undebated. As long as these images and assumptions survive intact, appeals like Giuliani's will have ample time to triumph in the long run if not the short.

P.P.S.

The next burst of Giulianiana in the national media, after his forays into arts criticism, came with his crackdowns on the homeless in New York City in late 1999. At the start of December, homeless-rights supporters mounted a sizeable, integrated demonstration. In it was a large reproduction of Holy Virgin Mary *with the mayor's face standing in for the Madonna's. At this image, protesters threw what looked very much like, but probably wasn't, elephant dung.[52]*

White Looks and Limbaugh's Laugh

The body was burned to ashes; but for many days, the head, that hive of subtlety, fixed on a pole in the Plaza, met, unabashed, the gaze of the whites.

> Herman Melville in *Benito Cereno* (1856), on the execution of Babo, the leader of a slave revolt

The chauvinism and churlishness with which I begin this otherwise modest and even-tempered essay both derive from my having grown up along that part of the Mississippi River that divides Missouri from Illinois. It is easy to be chauvinistic about that stretch of the river, the lone portion of the Mississippi to divide slavery from freedom. Along the river and its banks, from Hannibal to East St. Louis to Cairo and the Missouri Bootheel, great artists and great art have long been made. To an unrivaled extent, that art has challenged the lie of white supremacy both implicitly through its celebration of Black beauty and creativity and explicitly in its probing of the relationship between race and freedom. Geniuses such as Miles Davis, Chuck Berry, Scott Joplin, Katherine Dunham, Redd Foxx, Tina Turner, Quincy Troupe, Josephine Baker, Maya Angelou, Ntozake Shange, and Mark Twain have drawn on experiences along the river to chart, move, explode, and ignore the color line. Along the river in the Missouri Bootheel a half-century ago, adventures with Black and white sharecroppers afforded C. L. R. James seminal insights not only into American life and religion but also, as he remembered, into Hegel's *Phenomenology*.[1] Even T. S. Eliot, the writer ultimately most eager to lose the region's accents, carried much of the racelore and popular culture of the river with him.[2] As a setting for works of genius, the river separating Missouri from Illinois is equally impressive. Huck Finn learns the differences between slavery and freedom drifting down the river and discovers that it is not worth it to be white. Twain sets *Pudd'nhead Wilson,* with its fierce ridiculing of biological racism, in a town between St. Louis and Cairo. Sterling Brown's "Tornado Blues," with its wonderful meditations on race and tragedy, joins others of the finest of Brown's verses in being set in St. Louis.[3] Herman Melville's *The Confidence Man,* on one level a remarkable exploration of whiteness, property, and performance, unfolds on a steamboat bound from St. Louis south.[4]

The churlishness follows from the chauvinism. As I wrote these pages, I seldom made it through a month without hearing or reading— often the source is someone on the left—that "whatever his politics," Rush Limbaugh is a genius. His genius sometimes was said to lie in comedy, sometimes in understanding media, sometimes in knowing how to speak to the American people, and often in all three. I (who can always manage to smile cordially while similar nonsense is trumpeted about William F. Buckley's "seriousness" and "intellect") raged whenever the adulation was heaped upon Limbaugh. The reason lies largely in Limbaugh's hometown being Cape Girardeau, Missouri, and in his roots in the local elite of that southern-Missouri river city. He is my age, and as I grew up in cities north and south of the Cape, his ilk were all too familiar to me. This long-standing distaste for his class and his kind made me bristle when Limbaugh was praised—until I began watching his television show. I then realized how thoroughly his "genius" rests on an utterly unreflective and banal performance of whiteness.

This chapter compares a piece of cultural work on race partly done by Twain with one done by Limbaugh. The juxtaposition underlines not only the difference between genius and banality but also the hard reality that banality sometimes can achieve much more social power than genius where white consciousness is concerned. More broadly, the chapter uses materials from Twain and Limbaugh, as well as from Eugene O'Neill, to take into account what I will call the "white look." The conclusion examines questions of method that emerge from the pairing of Twain's "white look" with Limbaugh's and O'Neill's, suggesting how we might examine historically why certain white looks work and others do not.

"Looking It" at Them

Eugene O'Neill's 1922 play *The Hairy Ape* contains a striking line with great potential to challenge and enrich materialist analysis of race.

The drama of the play hinges on the demise of Yank, a coal handler in the stokehole of an oceangoing ship. In early scenes, Yank personifies all-American manhood, rejecting any and all hints that his work enslaves him, disdaining the hard scrubbing after shifts that other workers viewed as necessary to avoid taking on the complexion of a "piebald nigger," and loudly enjoining others on the gang to ravage the "hungry," dark, and female furnace. Yank's bravado does not survive his obsession over a brief encounter with steel heiress/social worker Mildred Douglas, however. Preternaturally white, paler still in the presence of heat, and "bored by her own anemia," Douglas goes below, convinced that she can find life—or at least diversion—there. She finds Yank—and faints at the combination of his dirt, his ferocity, his power, and his "gorilla face." Yank's mates explain to him that Douglas had come to look at her "slaves," to survey "the bloody animals below," to take in an exhibition of "bleedin' monkeys in a menagerie."[5]

Because Yank was the focus of her gaze and her terror, he was most susceptible to the fear of being seen as "a queerer kind of baboon than ever you'd find in darkest Africy." Lost in anxious reflection, Yank became both nonwhite and inhuman. Declaring himself the enemy of the "white-faced skinny tarts and de boobs that marry 'em," Yank spiraled downward wildly. He came to agree that he was a "hairy ape" and ended his life invading the cage of the gorilla at the New York City Zoo. He wanted to join the "gang" of the gorilla, who savaged him. And yet, the most important line of the play reveals that Douglas probably never called Yank an ape. Responding to Yank's panicked questioning about exactly what she said, the Irish character Paddy tellingly remarks, "She looked it at you if she didn't say the word itself."[6]

The idea that whiteness and nonwhiteness can be "looked at" others sits uneasily in a play saturated with references to the concrete realities of class, work, and power. To see these structural matters as counterposed to the subjectivity of a look is precisely wrong, however. As the best of the substantial recent scholarship on the "imperialist gaze" has demonstrated, looks both frame and capture relations of power. They at once express racism and privilege, reflecting and reinforcing how classes within the imperialist powers see both the colonized and each other. Not merely the symptom of imperial exploitation, the imperialist gaze is a shared social activity that contributes to the domination and to the consciousness that sustains it. In the work of Mary Louise Pratt, for example, the gaze can therefore be a perfect site for the study of the relation of domination.[7]

In many ways, recent writing on the imperialist gaze and imperialist culture illuminates the process by which O'Neill makes plausible the transition from native-born American worker to ape. Douglas displays the desire, so characteristic of imperialist gazers, to categorize and classify—to "investigate everything" (21) in London's slums just as she has in New York. The commanding position of surveying from above, which characterizes imperialist gazes, appears in Douglas's obsession with going below and, negatively, in her collapse when she looks on the workers from their own level. Douglas's search for ersatz interaction with those surveilled also typifies ways in which imperialism "looked." Most important, coal handlers who insisted that Yank (and they) were looked at like zoo animals were precisely right. The zoos, World's Fairs and natural history museums gathered the world's—but especially Africa's and Asia's—animals, *and humans,* classifying and displaying them, creating hierarchies and spectacles. As Donna Haraway has observed, the display of monkeys and apes offered particular opportunities to teach lessons of race and hierarchy. Indeed, Anne McClintock has posited "simian imperialism" as an important link between scientific and popular racism.[8]

The idea that an American-born white worker could be "looked" into nonwhiteness becomes far more plausible in light of the fact that in the early twentieth century, New York City's Bronx Zoo had housed a human with its monkeys and apes in a hugely publicized exhibition. When the African, Ota Benga, was released after protests and his own rebellion, his controllers attempted to transform Benga into a factory worker. Indeed, Cornelia Sears's penetrating recent work on the display of "man-like apes" and "ape-like men" in proximity demonstrates that the animality of humans received emphasis alongside the humanity of the primates. The Bronx Zoo's director, William Temple Hornaday, constructed in his writings a hierarchy of animals from large-brained to small, paralleling imperialist taxonomies. Hornaday supposed that both Ota Benga and other big-brained mammals were "workers" in his zoo. His remarkable "The Wild Animal's Bill of Rights" held that "superior" animals had "no more inherent right to live a life of lazy and luxurious ease . . . than a man or woman has to live without work. . . ." Indeed, real life almost outdistanced O'Neill's art in the case of the Bronx Zoo. In 1924 a blue-eyed young Scottish American proposed that Hornaday confine him in the ape house, to be displayed with the orang-outang and the chimpanzee.[9]

But the imperialist gaze and imperialist culture take us only so far in understanding Mildred Douglas's ability to "look" Yank out of the ranks of white humanity. Rooted in the heritage of U.S. slavery as much as in global realities, Douglas's capacity to do Yank in rested as much on a "white American look" as on an imperialist gaze.[10] Although the ship was at sea, Yank was every inch an American, so much so that at one point he could scarcely recall his own name, having for so long identified totally with his nickname. The play unfolds amid the early 1920s race-baiting of southern and eastern European immigrants, which would culminate in the race-based legislation of 1924 restricting immigration. References to Italian "ginees" (guineas) and "wops" dot the text, alongside slurs against Irish American workers ("paddies" and "micks"), whose whiteness had earlier been questioned. When they expressed discontent, as Herbert Gutman has tellingly shown, these immigrant workers were consistently branded in the press as animals. The references to workers as "slaves," though not peculiar to the United States, carried particular resonances in Yank's nation, the only one to achieve industrial takeoff alongside the presence of a huge slave labor force. Most broadly, the drama in *The Hairy Ape* turns critically on a vicious parody of the blackface tradition of theatrical performance— a tradition that in the United States literally focused on Black-white issues rather than on imperialism.[11] Minstrelsy and vaudeville black- face made comedy out of the ability of white performers and their audi- ences to find fraternity based on the ease with which blackening could be put on and taken off. O'Neill fashioned tragedy, and what James Baldwin called terror, out of a proletarian blackface in which "rivulets of sooty sweat" could hardly be scrubbed out and which ultimately killed Yank.[12] The audience was disinvited to participate in those happy white looks, at the stage and at each other, that made minstrelsy such a powerful force in white consciousness. By contrast, Mildred Douglas's white look was divisive, deadly, and very much open to critique.

Another Look

In 1874, the former confederate soldier Mark Twain sent a pair of sketches to William Dean Howells, editor of the prestigious *Atlantic Monthly*. Twain, trying hard to escape being typed merely as a regional humorist, had high hopes for one of his offerings. The other he titled "A True Story" and touted more modestly. Inviting Howells to pay for it "as lightly as you choose," he explained that it was not his creation. He had merely "set down" the story of an "old colored woman," alter- ing it only by choosing to "begin at the beginning." The ex-abolitionist Howells, cool to the story Twain hyped, bit enthusiastically on "A True

Story."[13] Thus a breakthrough in Twain's career, and the publication of one of his most enduring short stories, took place despite the fact that he professed not to have written the story at all. Instead he presented— as the subtitle avows, "Word for Word As I Heard It"—a marvelous critique of white looking in the form of an "autoethnography" fashioned by an ex-slave.[14]

"A True Story" begins with a paragraph of stage setting from Twain. With other whites, the narrator gazes down from a farmhouse porch onto Aunt Rachel, a "mighty" sixty-year old Black servant who sits on the steps "respectfully below our level." Drawn from Twain's stay in New York state, the tale features at its outset "peal after peal" of laughter from Aunt Rachel, rather than dialogue. Unlike James Fenimore Cooper,[15] who earlier in the century reacted uneasily to Blacks laughing in New York "in a way that seemed to set their very hearts rattling in their ribs," Twain's persona sits utterly at ease. Her work done, Rachel is "under fire" from the white family. The narrator sees her "being chafed without mercy and . . . enjoying it." Her pleasure is natural, it being "no more trouble for her to laugh than it is for a bird to sing." Her performance can be just what the narrator wants it to be. His language echoes fantasies in which men of his race look down on Black women as sexual objects—Rachel would "sit with her face in her hands and shake with throes of enjoyment which she could no longer get breath enough to express"—but his gaze is apparently innocent. "Aunt Rachel," he asks, "how is it that you've lived sixty years and never had any trouble?"[16] Then the story gets true. Rachel "stops quaking," falls silent, and finally sets the narrator straight, saying with deep irony that she ". . . hain't had no trouble. An' no joy." She then recounts her life in a harrowing slave narrative that turns on the sale of all of her children, her resistance to their loss (she had resisted even to the point of using her own chains to strike out at captors), and the spectacularly improbable reunion with one son. White looks saw nothing on this view. [17]

"A True Story" explicitly turns on gazes, but those gazes grow out of the dynamics not of imperialism but rather of races and slavery, U.S.-style. Twain explodes the logic of the white look, not of the imperialist gaze. That he may have had private, careerist reasons for doing so, that what he "heard" is not an untainted truth, and that Twain somehow ended with the byline—and the payment—for a Black woman's story are all of interest. But so is the remarkable set of circumstances that made such a critique of whiteness possible.

That such major literary figures, North and semi-South, as Howells and Twain could validate this critique of the viewpoint of whiteness is remarkable. When Herman Melville made a parallel effort to equate whiteness and blindness two decades before, in his marvelous 1856 novella of a slave revolt, *Benito Cereno,* the reception was largely uncomprehending. At almost the same moment that Melville wrote *Benito Cereno,* a teenaged Twain himself wrote home from the East that "infernal Abolitionists" prevented the return of slaves to bondage and that "in these Eastern States, niggers are [treated] considerably better than white people."[18] But in 1874, a decade after slaves had freed themselves and four years after they achieved full citizenship and suffrage, whites could not look at Black subjects in anything like so fixed a manner. The behavior of many supposedly privileged and loyal former house slaves, who, like Aunt Rachel, came to support the Union Army during the war and to move from the plantation after it, made the possibility that African Americans "are not what they seem" particularly viable.[19] For a time, the leading ex-abolitionist and the leading ex-Rebel cultural figures in the nation could agree that white looks are white lies and could give over the forum of their pages to an ex-slave's self-representation, a view that was simultaneously a searing commentary on whiteness.

Rush to Whiteness

Rush Limbaugh likewise gave over his medium to a Black speaker, but with a look and intent far different from Twain's. He regularly televised videos of excerpts of speeches by prominent African Americans. The replays were chosen for their bombast and grandiloquence, for a point or two that Limbaugh might later challenge, and ideally for their stammers, mispronunciations, or grammatical irregularities. During the clip, Limbaugh appeared in a small box in a lower corner of the screen, as well as live before an overwhelmingly white studio audience. He wordlessly and continually commented on the speech, and on the very idea of Black expertise, with a panoply of rolled eyes, raised brows, nods, snickers, and chortles. At the clip's end, the camera surveyed the studio audience's satisfaction with Rush's performance and Rush's satisfaction with himself. In millions of homes, bars, college "Rush Clubs," and Limbaugh rooms of discount steakhouses, the chain continued. White viewers could look at themselves looking at the studio audience looking at Rush looking at Lani Guinier or at Kweisi—Rush said "Queasy"—Mfume.

Christine Sleeter has written of "white racial bonding" as founded in part on a set of "everyday . . . communication patterns . . . such as inserts into conversations, race-related asides . . . strategic eye-contact, and jokes." Because these interventions are "short and subtle," she continues, we are likely to regard them as harmless and to overlook "their power to demarcate racial lines and communicate solidarity." Because Rush-in-a-Box performed Sleeter's repertoire of white communications wordlessly, he did so all the more effectively. Deep connections between Limbaugh's white looks and the history of imperialist gazes determined that Dr. Jocelyn Elders would be the favorite object of his split-screen attention. Indeed, so treasured were former Surgeon General Elders's appearances that when she was removed from office, Limbaugh and his listeners were nearly inconsolable. That she was an expert African American woman made Elders a prime target for ridicule. Her scientific jargon, her frequent slips, and the play-Army uniform of her office played perfectly into right-wing populist delight in deflating liberal intellectual pretensions, a thread that runs through much of Limbaugh's lampooning of what he calls "the left," Black or white. Through Elders, Limbaugh assembled familiar elements in the long history of imperialist display of nonwhite female bodies. Like the promoters of the nineteenth-century exhibitions of the Hottentot Venus, like P. T. Barnum, and like *National Geographic,* he put the combination of sexual suggestion, images of the bodies of Black females, and scientific expertise before the white male gaze. The wonderful (for Limbaugh) twist in this instance was that the Black woman herself provided the talk about sex and science on which Limbaugh could sit in judgment. Indeed, Elders's final undoing, which resulted from her open discussion of masturbation, put virtually the whole complex of images and actions surrounding *National Geographic* into a house of mirrors.[20]

However, the dynamics of Limbaugh's clowning, leering gambit differ enough from what we know of the workings of the imperialist gaze to suggest again the need to scrutinize the white look as a distinct one. Limbaugh's look clashed dramatically with one much-emphasized attribute of the imperialist gaze: its production of the illusion of an absence of the European male viewer, an absence that Giselda Pollock characterized as the "real meaning of the Orientalist project." Limbaugh not only is present as he looks but is never more active on the show than when he is watching others speak. Moreover, Limbaugh does not occupy the vantage point of the imperial "master of all I survey." He is instead boxed in, dwarfed, low, and *still* in power. His power hinges in critical ways on a sense of reciprocity, as theorists of the imperialist gaze would put it, within the look. But Rush-on-TV seeks none of the reciprocity with nonwhite subjects that Pratt so ably discusses in *Imperial Eyes*. Rather, he cultivates the reciprocity of white entertainer, white studio audience, and white viewers to endow his look with awful power. There is no risk for Limbaugh, as Homi Bhabha argues there is for imperialist gazers, of the "threatened return of the look" by the nonwhite subject.[21]

This white reciprocity rests in large part on Limbaugh's ability to reprise the role of the straight man/interlocutor in countless blackface minstrel entertainments from earlier in U.S. history. He registers the same initial interest and the same growing exasperation with the supposed crudities and excesses of Black speech, appearance, and behavior. This neominstrel ridicule is targeted almost surgically at African Americans rising above "their place," speaking expertly or eloquently, or even attempting to do so. As Nathan Huggins long ago observed, minstrel racism often made a travesty of the very possibility of Black excellence. So too with Limbaugh's venom. To be reminded of this minstrel resonance also evokes the white audience's ritualized watching of blackface comedians and of each other, which had already made the pandering to white looks an important commodity on the U.S. stage by the 1830s. Anne McClintock has recently mounted a critically important argument, centered mainly in the British Empire, that a "commodity racism" that attached imperial conquest to advertised images of domestic products came to replace scientific racism in important ways at imperialism's height. But in the United States, minstrelsy, the massive commodification of Black labor, and more generalized connections of "whiteness" and "property" all linked the commodity form and consciousness of race far earlier and, especially through entertainments, influenced subsequent imperialist gazes. The ubiquitous symbol of commodity racism in the United States, Aunt Jemima, was directly inspired by minstrel performance.[22] The hundreds of millions of white looks at Aunt Jemima's image on boxes helped to allay the anxieties raised by the possibility that the Aunt Rachels were not what they appeared to be. The hundreds of millions of white looks at a chortling Rush in boxes on the screen likewise re-establish control over the meaning and direction of laughter across the color line.

The Workings of Whiteness

Rush Limbaugh's white looks had ratings. His producers could secure figures on just how many viewers decided to tune out and go to sleep as he gaped and guffawed at tapes of "the Reh-vaarh-oond Jock-soon," as he pronounced it. They could determine how many were moved to stay tuned. Sophomoric and repetitive to the point of banality, his gambit was probably more popular than any of the brilliant critiques of whiteness—from the slaves' folktales, to Twain, Melville, James Baldwin and Toni Morrison. This hard fact creates dilemmas in our theoretical and historical approaches to the understanding of white looks.

One temptation is to assume that because a minstrel-derived white look like Limbaugh's still carries so much power, it represents the white look—singular and virtually transhistorical. This misstates the case, as do analyses that posit a singular imperialist gaze. However much one look might work better than others, white looks also come in multiple forms that carry differing class and gender dynamics. The task is to investigate why some looks come to undergird a mass sense of whiteness and others do not. Mildred Douglas's "looking it" at Yank clearly qualifies as a white look and, like all white looks, centers on inclusion and exclusion. But however convincing O'Neill is in showing that it could work to make Yank nonwhite at a particular, early-1920s juncture, its extreme identification of whiteness with great wealth makes race too narrowly and purely a stand-in for class to compete with the populist, "y'all come" whiteness typified by Limbaugh's look. (Indeed, in many shows Limbaugh first delivered his populist performances of whiteness and went on explicitly to defend great differences in wealth as a positive good.)

In understanding why and how white looks work, it is equally crucial to emphasize that such looks are historical. As such, they draw on deep and long patterns of seeing, such as those of the minstrel tradition, but they also change over time. The ability of the white look in "A True Story" to become shared by Twain, Howells, and at least some readers in the era of emancipation was clearly greater than it would have been, for example, in the early twentieth century, a period of reconsolidated white supremacy and diminishing opportunities for Black self-activity. Even Limbaugh's look responds to its historical context in ways that make it far more than just electronic minstrelsy. For all its glee, it remains very much a post-Black Freedom Movement look. Its utter silence—its boxed-in protection from the need to engage in any dialog with the Other—fits snugly into a situation described by Michael Omi and Howard Winant, who argue that recent rightward political motion on race has not easily been able to find an openly racist voice.[23] Even initiatives against racial equality have adopted the rhetoric of equal treatment and have pressed white claims to status as victims, from the anti-affirmative-action campaigns to Limbaugh's own protests that Black folks can get away with saying *nigger* whereas whites cannot.

In this climate, the conviction has grown among the white right that whites have been "silenced." Limbaugh frequently describes his own "rightness" and "excellence" as resting on his saying what listeners already believe. But he equally shares—and for a time embodied—silent white looks. Limbaugh's jowls and blank expression perfectly suited him to come across as a put-upon white everyman at a time when many of his watchers saw their whiteness as a weight, rather than a privilege. But at the same time, silence itself has become far more freighted with meaning. Accordingly, successful 1991 Mississippi gubernatorial candidate Kirk Fordice closed his dramatic antiwelfare campaign advertisement with silence and a still photograph of a black woman and her baby. Fordice trusted that white viewers would connect the dots.[24]

Limbaugh is seldom without words, but he was perhaps never more dangerous than when he was silent. The in-a-box performance enabled Limbaugh to walk the tightrope between the unspoken and the largely unspeakable. He both participated in the refurbishment of openly racist discourse and retained the possibility of defending his performance not only as a joke but also on the grounds that he didn't say a word.

But if this powerful, banal, silent onlooking served new purposes at the end of the twentieth century, it should also remind us of the need to consider the white look in the much longer term. From slave sales and whippings, to highly publicized and massively attended lynchings, to the World's Fair displays of confined nonwhites, to Rush Limbaugh, white consciousness has been formed not only out of terror but also out of the mutual, self-recognizing, and changing witness of terror—out of white looks at the oppression of others and at the privileges of each other. As Rachel DuPlessis has recently observed, the "free white gaze upon blacks is part of the power of whiteness."[25] But it has been neither a simple nor a single gaze.

White Workers, New Democrats, and Affirmative Action

Written originally in 1994, as President William Jefferson Clinton abstained from defending affirmative action in the campaign over Proposition 209 in California, this chapter will strike many readers as counterintuitive, if not flatly wrong. During his second term, President Clinton so attracted loyal African American support, most critically in the crisis surrounding his impeachment, that an account of his failures on a central question of racial justice seems carping. If Clinton has claimed credit for "ending welfare as we knew it," his role in the constriction of affirmative action has been far less clear. Indeed, his advocacy of a "Mend it, don't end it" policy with regard to affirmative action transformed his image into that of a relative defender of the practice in the mid-1990s. The chapter on the politics of race in Christopher Hitchens's searing No One Left to Lie To: The Triangulations of William Jefferson Clinton, *though the book's best, is therefore also its least resonating. Similarly, Adolph Reed, Jr.'s excellent collection* Without Justice for All: The New Liberalism and Our Retreat from Racial Equality, *which powerfully demonstrates the timidity of Clinton's policies on race and reform and shows that the terrain the president defended with regard to affirmative action was precisely ground he had ceded in his 1992 campaign and his first term, struggles to find an audience.[1] All of this invites me to revise both the title and the argument of this chapter radically. However, although I have added new material, I have not undertaken such wholesale revision. Rather, I hope to make a modest contribution to efforts to look at the neoliberal views of race and of class historically.*

"Without a constitutionally structured programme of deep and extensive affirmative action," African National Congress legal theorist Albie Sachs wrote in 1991, "a Bill of Rights in South Africa is meaningless." Sachs added that affirmative action "is redistributory rather than conservative in character. . . . In the historical conditions of South Africa, affirmative action is not merely the correction of certain perceived structural injustices. It becomes the major instrument in the transitional period after a democratic government has been installed, for converting a racist oppressive society into a democratic and just one." Incorporating such logic into its policy documents, the ANC at times drew optimistically on a tradition and a language of affirmative action developed largely in the United States. Thus the draft constitution promised to use race-specific initiatives to eliminate discrimination in "form and substance."[2]

Meanwhile, in the United States, much of liberalism and part of the left has come to see affirmative policies designed specifically to remedy the effects of racism as electoral liabilities, suitable perhaps in moral discourses but not in political ones. That the Republican calls for an end to affirmative action provoked so much "review" and such belated defense of the policy by the Clinton administration is therefore not surprising. Not only was a vigorous political defense of the principles and politics of affirmative action never undertaken by Democratic leaders, but the "new Democrats" of the Clinton administration developed their electoral strategies largely around claims to be uniquely well attuned to voters "fed up" with race- and gender-specific policies. Irony abounds in the United States/South Africa comparison. In a United States in which, theoretically and demographically at least, thoroughgoing affirmative action could substantially improve employment opportunities for a large percentage of the nonwhite population, the demand is seen as utopian and unworkable. In South Africa, where the white population is so small that opening "white" jobs to affirmative action hiring could at best benefit an important but small segment of the nonwhite population, the demand is seen as promising and central.[3]

The relative justice of moral claims to redress by the oppressed cannot account for current differences between the United States and South Africa in attitude toward affirmative action and other race-specific initiatives. It is true that the Nationalist governments in South Africa have implemented what amounts to a huge and more-or-less explicit pro-Afrikaner affirmative action program for decades. But it is likewise true that, as Cheryl Harris has brilliantly shown, the U.S. government

and private industry have recognized and promoted a "property interest in whiteness." Federal relief for victims of the 1993 floods in the
Midwest, Garry Wills quipped at the time, might well have been called
an "affirmative action program" for flood plain dwellers. But, he continued, such relief differed in one important particular from affirmative action designed to remedy inequalities: the government did not
cause the flooding, whereas it did, in large part, the racial and gender
oppression.[4]

The dynamics of electoral politics go a long way toward accounting
for the different places of affirmative action in the South African and
U.S. contexts. In the former case, demanding affirmative action for nonwhites before a largely nonwhite electorate has considerable potential
benefits. In the latter case, demanding affirmative action for nonwhites
before an overwhelmingly white electorate is seen as having considerable potential costs. In such a situation, new Democrats and social
democrats have seemed to have hard-headed, vote-counting logic very
much on their sides as they argue that downplaying race-specific initiatives is not only the approach most likely to yield general social
progress but also the strategy most apt to win reforms that benefit the
Black and Latino poor.

This chapter challenges such a view—a view that, with the success of
the Clinton strategy of abjuring antiracist appeals in the 1992 elections,
and the Republican success at "using" race in 1994, threatened to make
the abandonment of egalitarian race-specific initiatives a hallmark of
liberal political common sense. I will maintain that an emphasis on
short-term vote counting has caused us to leave unexamined the historical precedents, as well as the present vagaries and future implications,
of what is being argued by those who oppose race-specific initiatives. I
will focus especially on the slippery place the white working class occu-
pies in neoliberal discussions of race.

Race, Class, and Commentators Thereon

Leading Clinton strategists assumed that the worker is white and portrayed white workers as so obsessed with race as to be unable to enter
into coalition politics unless issues of racial justice were removed from
the agenda. They offered a confused and confusing analysis of the race-
thinking of such workers, sometimes hinting that the workers were
unfortunately backward and at other times suggesting that they were
uncommonly perceptive. But however confused, this analysis allowed
the Clinton administration to move away from both race and class

politics. Indeed, Clinton himself provided a glowing blurb for one of the most outspoken analyses arguing that Democrats would have to jettison the onus of being the party of special racial interests in order to win back whites, Peter Brown's punningly titled *Minority Party* (1986).[5] Rather than appealing to civil rights constituencies and to labor, even in the highly diluted forms that the old liberalism favored, new Democrats professed the necessity of appealing to white workers, who were, in their view, defined much more by the adjective than by the noun. In so doing, the historical reflections that close the article argue, neoliberals led us to a disastrous misapprehension of the relationship between whiteness and class.

When neoliberalism explained why we in the United States cannot have initiatives such as those proposed by the ANC, the usual suspects got rounded up. It was the fault of white workers or, no, check that, I mean black workers, or, no, the "Black underclass." Although there was considerable talk about the "declining significance of race" inside neoliberalism, such talk was related to economics, not politics, and certainly not to any supposed decline in the depth of racism among white workers. Properly speaking, the arguments of William J. Wilson and others for race's declining significance have centered on the relative weight of race and class in structuring Black poverty. Wilson's mid-1990s work on the "new poverty" expressed especially equivocal positions where causation was concerned. There was, he argued, widespread "employer discrimination" against Black men and the discrimination was sharply rising. Such bias resulted not only from bad "underclass" habits regarding work discipline but also from management's preference for female and immigrant workers, according to Wilson. Cultural/racial conflicts mattered enormously. White flight, in Wilson's view, could be caused by "socially isolated inner city residents . . . enjoy[ing] a movie in a communal spirit." Race had anything but a declining significance *politically* for commentators such as Stanley Greenberg, Thomas and Mary Bryne Edsall, Paul Starr, and Wilson himself. It was, they argued, the potency of race-thinking among white voters, and especially among white working-class and ethnic voters, that necessitated the downplaying of race-specific initiatives.[6] Jesse Helms's use of an ad that encouraged every white voter who ever got turned down for anything to blame affirmative action to help win a 1990 North Carolina Senate election was seen as evidence of both the "virulence of race" and the necessity to shift debate to other issues.[7] An admiring *New York Times* reviewer rightly perceived that the Edsalls argued that "race—not class—

dominates the domestic political agenda." In this important sense, Felicia Kornbluh was directly on target in tracing neoliberal calculation where race was concerned straight back to Kevin Phillips's 1969 tract *The Emerging Republican Majority,* "a book dedicated to President Richard Nixon and Attorney General John Mitchell." Greenberg, a Yale political scientist turned Clinton pollster/advisor, was precise in identifying the race-thinking of white *working-class* "Reagan Democrats" as a key to modern politics. He argued that among these vital voters, African Americans "constitute the explanation for nearly everything that has gone wrong" so that "virtually all progressive symbols and themes have been redefined in racial and pejorative terms."[8]

But as soon as the Edsalls approvingly quoted Greenberg on working-class white Reagan Democrats, they shifted focus to explain that the "significant worsening of social dysfunction of the bottom third of the black community" since 1966 *conditioned* changes in white working-class attitudes.[9] The shift was a significant one. Pegging of white working-class discontent to perceptions of Black social degradation enabled neoliberal opponents of affirmative action to avoid the question of whether working whites really were victimized massively by "reverse discrimination," a troublesome issue on which opponents of "strong" affirmative action have taken a welter of conflicting positions. On the one hand, many commentators strove to see affirmative action as an upper-middle-class, suburban, liberal assault on white, often ethnic, urban workers who were alleged to have paid for the new policies through lost opportunities. On the other hand, critics wanted to emphasize, evidence to the contrary notwithstanding, that only upper-class and middle-class Blacks significantly benefited from affirmative action, which could supposedly offer little help to the ghetto "underclass" and working poor. Moreover, from Barry Gross's 1978 attack on affirmative action to Theda Skocpol's lukewarm 1994 defense, the policy was portrayed as much more successful in reaching university admissions staffs than employers hiring people to fill good working-class jobs. However much these inconsistencies were rooted in an objectively complex and changing context, they have embarrassed neoconservative and neoliberal indictments of affirmative action, not the least by implying that when the bottom of white society loses, the top of Black society gains—a situation that hardly supported the argument that race-specific initiatives were outmoded.[10]

The Edsalls deftly sidestepped this issue. Black underclass dysfunction, they maintained, not only caused Black economic misery but also "assault[ed] efforts to eliminate prejudice" among whites and "crush[ed] recognition of the achievements of liberalism." Moreover, in effusing over Paul Sniderman and Thomas Piazza's *The Scar of Race,* Thomas Bryne Edsall came around to the view that the history of affirmative action was one of rank injustice to white workers and students. His earlier, coauthored work had recognized tragically conflicting claims at play in affirmative action, but his review portrayed employed Black workers as well as the so-called underclass as shouldering a large share of race-specific blame for liberalism's plight.[11] A studied lack of clarity left open the question of whether white workers, as they moved to the right, were reacting as racists or acting as apt observers of Black social pathology and preferential treatment.

The Edsalls discredited race-specific initiatives largely by discussing policies that were and are in fact *not* race-specific but are seen that way by white voters. In fact, almost no positive race-specific policies exist in the United States. Affirmative action procedures cover white women, veterans, the disabled, and many others. Such procedures potentially benefit a large majority of the population and of the working class, and they should be defended in such terms. If we avoid neoliberal formulations that implicitly identify the "worker" as both white and male, affirmative action is far less race-specific than such negative neoliberal-supported policies as expanded capital punishment, the demonization of crack cocaine in sentencing guidelines, and the suspension of constitutional guarantees in federal housing projects. Welfare, including Aid to Families with Dependent Children (AFDC), is both race-neutral and much utilized by whites. In his recent and smart *Race, Money and the American Welfare State,* the political scientist Michael K. Brown charts how AFDC came to be "racially stigmatized" as a program allegedly for African Americans and how welfare programs more generally "have a way of being particularized along racial lines."[12]

As Greenberg's work suggested, a far more consequential issue than that of whether policies are "race-specific" or "universal" is how those policies *come to be seen* in "racial and pejorative" terms. Thus welfare and job-training programs become "nonwhite." Meanwhile, as George Lipsitz has recently demonstrated, the tremendous benefits of Federal Housing Administration loans, home mortgage tax deductions, and federal subsidy of highway construction serving new suburbs are seen as "race-neutral," despite the fact that their benefits accrue overwhelmingly to the white middle class. Indeed, those policies are often not seen as welfare at all. Although the Edsalls offered some perceptive commentary on racial "coding" in U.S. politics, they remained mute on how to prevent racial typing from recurring and stigmatizing new rounds of "universal" reforms that the new Democrats sometimes advocate. Ruy Teixeira and Joel Rogers's recent *America's Forgotten Majority: Why the White Working Class Still Matters* is particularly given to waffling and wishful thinking on this score. Its slight treatment of racism holds that white assent to such statements as "It's really a matter of some people not trying hard enough; if blacks would only try harder they could be just as well off as whites" reflects no "new racism." Instead, Teixeira and Rogers first maintain that such statements "tap into attitudes towards government at least as much as they tap into racial attitudes." Three lines later, racism seems still less of a problem, because "endorsement of such statements has much less to do with white hostility towards blacks than with hostility towards a specifically liberal view of the role of government in racial matters." Nor, in my view, does Martin Gilens's suggestion, in an otherwise very useful study of media, race, and welfare, that we might disaggregate white racist stereotypes in order to disarm them, move us forward. In particular, Gilens holds that the "blacks as lazy" stereotype drives antiwelfare sentiments among whites and is not any longer sustained by a more general racial prejudice. The real problems, for Gilens, come from media distortions regarding race and poverty and from a white belief that the economic system is fair and open.[13] But it never becomes clear how these problems are separable from racism and more easily opposed.

Because of existing inequalities of race, some new benefits will clearly be utilized at different levels across racial lines. Race-neutrality, in other words, does not work in the long run, even on its own terms. The sociologist Douglas Massey has made just this point in a direct challenge to Wilson and to other advocates of "race-neutral" initiatives. Massey argues, "It will not be possible to deal with class-based divisions without addressing race-based issues with equal verve." To put race on "the back burner," he continues, "would leave the field open to those who would undermine the class-based strategies . . . by manipulating racial attitudes that are still there."[14] Both white racism and Black poverty need to be confronted as problems or the cycle that Greenberg identifies repeats itself.

Whatever its serious weaknesses, the strategy of shaping labor/civil rights unity around a program of economic reforms articulated by Bayard Rustin in the mid-1960s was begun as a serious effort to mobilize a constituency based on class interest. Neoliberal racial discourse disguises the fact that neoliberalism utterly lacks even such a limited agenda. It has undertaken no significant initiatives to create a legal and political climate in which the labor movement can be rebuilt, for example. And although it has sometimes identified the white working class as a key voting bloc, it has offered very little to workers and working-class organizations. Compare, for example, the expenditure of political energy and pork on the passage, over fierce labor opposition, of the corporate-sponsored North American Free Trade Agreement (NAFTA) with the Clinton administration's meager mobilization of legislative support for the striker replacement bill. Leading liberal writers on race and politics in recent U.S. history mirror this tendency to treat labor organizations as irrelevant. The AFL-CIO receives three glancing mentions in the Edsalls' detailed and deeply historical treatment of the Democratic party in *Chain Reaction*. Andrew Hacker's *Two Nations* manages to do without any discussion of trade unions, even in a long chapter on "equity in employment."[15]

This absence of attention to class and to class politics is tied intimately to the racial politics of neoliberalism or, perhaps more precisely, to its pretended transcendence of racial politics. We are too ready to assume that the removal of "racial" demands clears political space for class mobilizations. But much of the logic of neoliberalism runs just the other way. Because white workers serve alternately (and often simultaneously) as the backward masses and the honest observers of Black social pathology, the new Democrats have every political reason to take seriously those workers' views as whites and very little reason to consider their demands as workers.

Greenberg's strategy in developing polling data to guide the right and center of the Democratic party in developing a strategy to build coalitions "no longer bedeviled by race" perfectly illustrated the tendency to remove the *workers* from considerations of *white workers*. As his recent book shows, Greenberg chose to concentrate his 1985 and 1989 efforts on understanding why the all-white, largely working-class constituencies of Macomb County, Michigan, had turned to supporting Ronald Reagan's presidential candidacies, why they had not returned to the Democrats in the 1988 Bush-Dukakis race, and how they might be won back by Clinton in 1992. Greenberg's data came largely from "focus groups," which he insisted had to be "homogeneous" so that they would tell the hard truth about their alienation. The homogeneity was designedly racial, and so were the truths in which Greenberg was interested. In 1985, 40 percent of households in Macomb County were union households, the highly integrated United Auto Workers being the leading labor organization in the county. But homogeneous focus groups did not convene on the basis of union affiliations and class position. Macomb County voters were brought together as white residents, not as auto workers. Greenberg gloried that Clinton showed, in a celebrated Cleveland speech, that he understood the concerns reported by these white-identity-politics-based focus groups. That speech, given before the Democratic Leadership Council (DLC), was picketed by Jesse Jackson and others who protested the DLC's support for NAFTA, a treaty bitterly opposed by the UAW.[16]

Neoliberalism's appeals to the white working class under Clinton largely focused on issues that were ostensibly race-neutral but are in fact highly charged in racial terms: being "tough" enough to criticize hiphop and Black parenting, "ending welfare as we know it," implementing and expanding the death penalty, "three-strikes-and-you're-out" incarceration, justification of NAFTA as an insurance policy against Mexican immigration, and so on. If white workers could be won on these issues, no class agenda was required. Still less was a mobilization around the specific interests of white women workers necessary. The difficult issue of building alliances between white feminists and people of color, so fatal to the campaign against Proposition 209's attack on affirmative action in California, went unaddressed. Moreover, despite the apologies of Deirdre English and others who praised the Clinton administration for being "as liberal as it's going to get" in the rightist popular climate in the United States, it was clear that Clinton's search for positions which were impenetrable to Republican appeals to whiteness sometimes took him to the right of the general population on racialized policy issues. For example, a *Time*/CNN poll had only 42 percent of Americans favoring capping welfare when recipients continue to have children. But in the same 1994 issue of *Time* that featured the poll, Clinton supported both a state's right to engage in such capping and the logic of the "reform" itself.[17]

Racial appeals to white workers also resonated with white upper- and middle-class suburban voters, who probably were the real prize being pursued in many invocations of the need to attend to the racial views of white workers. In a fascinating closing section of *Chain Reaction*, the Edsalls suddenly departed from an analysis predicated on the centrality of "Reagan Democrats" and argued for the increasing weight of the "white suburbs," analyzed overwhelmingly in race terms, rather than class terms, for the future of U.S. politics. In their conclusion, the white working class moved from the center to the margins of neo-liberal political analysis with such astonishing ease as to suggest that white-working class Reagan Democrats (and southern "bubbas") were courted by new Democrats not so much as constituencies in their own right but as groups whose putative demands and foibles could reposi-tion the party to appeal to middle-class suburban white voters nation-ally. Indeed, the 1985 Democratic National Committee study on key constituencies that informed much of the Edsalls' analysis was quite suggestive in laying the basis for an effortless transition from white working-class to middle-class concerns. It characterized the grievances of white ethnics and southern moderates as centering on the belief that the Democratic party "has not stood with them as they moved from the working to the middle class."[18]

Three Generalizations

Even if the short-term question of whether we should buy an Edsall is rather easily answered in the negative, the larger one of how we should conceptualize race and class in current U.S. politics remains vital. I do not propose to answer that question in the brief balance of this chapter, beyond offering the opinion that radical South Africans who argue that the way to nonracialism is through race have much to teach us. What I would like to do is to propose, arguing largely from history, three broad generalizations. Bearing them in mind might help us progress toward such a reconceptualization, especially where white workers are con-cerned. These generalizations suggest that even in its Rustin-inspired, social democratic variant—and certainly in its current, neoliberal one—race-neutrality is itself a problematic strategy and also leads away from meaningful mobilizations against class inequality.

The first generalization is that the choice between race and class approaches to U.S. working-class history and to current politics is a false one. Fixation on such a choice obscures the fact that people of color have always formed a large and dynamic sector of the U.S. work-ing class. The class consciousness of white workers has long been, and is today, fully understandable only in the context of race. As I argued in *The Wages of Whiteness* and *Towards the Abolition of Whiteness,* white workers have created racialized class identities by reflecting not only on their roles as the producers and the exploited, but also to their positions as nonslaves and as refusers of "nigger work."[19] As Green-berg remarked in one of his few comments on the United States that attain the standard of his fine earlier work on South Africa, for many working whites "not being black is what constitutes being middle class; not living with blacks is what makes a neighborhood a decent place to live." David Halle's careful 1984 ethnographic study of New Jersey chemical workers underlined Greenberg's point. Halle's white subjects sometimes described nonunion, non-working-class white neighbors as "workingmen" or middle-class like themselves. Their Black union brothers by contrast, were construed as aliens, outsiders, and intruders.[20] One might fairly ask, in such a situation, how class issues could conceivably be raised without a discussion of race.

Halle's observation leads to a second, related generalization. Although, as Barbara Fields carefully notes, common class and union experience can at times act as a "solvent" of some of "the grosser illusions of racialism," race can also dilute, dissolve, and even outlast the impact of class experiences. Historically, radical class organizations in the United States have often unlearned the lessons of interracial unity forged in class struggle. The examples in U.S. history of dramatic turns away from nonracialism even after experience in shared struggle are many, dramatic, and tragic: the National Labor Union and the Knights of Labor (both of which, in their later stages, flirted with supporting mass deportation of Black workers), the early AFL, and, most notably, Tom Watson and much of the populist movement.[21] Nor does shared grief necessarily forge unity across racial lines. Katherine Newman's fine 1988 study of industrial decline provides another revealing New Jersey example of the disfiguring impact of racial ideology on class experience. Newman found that one response of white workers in Elizabeth who suffered through capital flight, runaway shops, and loss of jobs was to blame laws that force employers to hire Black and Latino workers, thus, they supposed, making profitable American industry impossible.[22]

The third generalization is the most unfamiliar and difficult. It holds that the whiteness of white workers is so complex and conflicted as to complicate profoundly both simplistic variants of the neoliberal perception of white workers—that is, seeing white workers as simply racists, on the one hand, or, on the other, as simply observers of alleged social pathologies of the inner cities. As Michael Omi and Howard Winant have observed, white views on race are quite heterogeneous: "There are all sorts of [white] people out there, many who have committed themselves to integrated neighborhoods, churches and schools, recognized the overlaps between racism, sexism, homophobia, and anti-Semitism, and generally struggled to resist the temptations of racial privilege.

White identities remain uneven and contested: white workers, even white ethnics, are not uniformly 'Reagan Democrats.'" Moreover, beyond differences of opinion among whites, important strains and contradictions within the racial consciousness of individual whites lend weight to Omi and Winant's conclusion that the "volatility of contemporary white identities, not their consolidation, is what must be emphasized."[23] White identity, as Eric Lott, Stuart Hall, and others have astutely shown, is compounded of hatred *and* attraction toward nonwhite cultures, of repulsion *and* desire, of "love" *and* theft. African Americanity in particular has historically symbolized the terrifying limit of possible working-class degradation, especially among poor whites in the South and among darker and poorer European immigrant groups. At the same time, it has symbolized an alternative to regimented labor, a refusal to delay gratification endlessly, and a preservation of ties with land and tradition.[24]

This doubleness makes whites notoriously unreliable observers of so-called social pathology among African Americans and of supposed preferential treatment toward nonwhites. During slavery, a good deal of white labor literature maintained that slaves led more leisurely and secure lives than white workers.[25] During the Jim Crow era, polling data showed a large majority of white southerners, and a majority of whites nationally, believing that Blacks had as easy a time as whites in making a living. As David Alan Horowitz's sympathetic account of white southerners' reactions to the pre-affirmative-action phase of the civil rights movement puts it, integration was seen even then by many whites in the South "as providing license for blacks to eat in gourmet restaurants, to sleep in elaborate hotels."[26]

A concrete example renders these often quite tortured perceptions on a human scale. In the 1930s, a Federal Writers Project interviewer in Bridgeport, Connecticut, heard this from a Slovak American woman:

> I always tell my children not [to] play with the nigger-people's children, but they always play with them just the same. I tell them that the nigger children are dirty and that they will get sick if they play. I tell them they could find some other friends that are Slovaks just the same. This place now is all spoiled, and all the people live like pigs because the niggers they come and live here with the decent white people and they want to raise up their children with our children. If we had some place for the children to play I'm sure that the white children they would not play with the nigger children. . . . All people are alike—that's what God says—but just the same it's no good to make our children play with the nigger children because they are too dirty.

The informant added that: "the nigger people can stay up to 3 o'clock in the morning playing and dancing and they don't have to worry about going to work. . . . We [white] poor people can't even have a good time one time a week. . . . The nigger people have a holiday every day in the week." Here, proximity to the oppression of African Americans—Slovaks suffered consistently under the stereotype of being a dirty people—produces not solidarity but a poignant mixture of attraction, guilt, disdain, and despising.[27] Without a politics that challenges white supremacy and indeed critiques whiteness as well—which is to say, given a continued neoliberal recognition of the property right of whiteness—it is the disdain and despising in such a mixture that will predominate politically, if not culturally.

Two decades ago, the London-based theorist Sivanandan wrote that "the white working-class must, in recovering its class instinct, its sense of oppression, both from technological alienation and [from] a white-oriented culture, arrive at a consciousness of racial oppression."[28] In this view, a critique of whiteness is *both* the precondition and the result of *both* class and antiracist struggles. To peg political strategies on such a challenging dialectical formulation is difficult but, I think, necessary. One element of such strategies should include an attempt to take advantage of what Cheryl Harris has called the "destabilizing" character of affirmative action—its tendency to call into sharp question "the illusion that the original or current distribution of power, property and resources is the result of 'right' or 'merit'" and to demand "a new and different sense of social responsibility in a society that defines individualism as the highest good and the 'market value' of the individual as the just and true assessment." Fully aware, with Harris, that affirmative action lacks "any magical capacity to create cross-racial solidarity with the white working class against class exploitation," we should nonetheless champion it both out of a sense of justice and as part of a long process in which whites may lose the privileges, burdens, and illusions associated with their racial identity. To capitulate to race-neutrality, and thus to white supremacy, is to abandon white workers to their own worst impulses and to their society's. It is to close, rather than to open, space for class politics.

"Hertz, Don't It?"

WHITE "COLORBLINDNESS" AND THE MARK(ET)INGS OF O. J. SIMPSON

WITH LEOLA JOHNSON

Remove the appearance of sharp racial differences from *Othello* and the difference in the play is so striking that it makes you wonder how many other stories have been distorted in our imaginations by our historical obsession with race. . . . [A]fter three hours one still leaves this performance thinking mostly about how clear the plot is and how swift its development if all the baggage of race we tend to bring to it is left at the door.

> *New York Times* reviewer D. J. Bruckner, mis-
> understanding and praising a 2000 performance
> of what he calls a "colorblind" *Othello* by the
> National Asian American Theatre Company

A quarter-century ago, O. J. Simpson told of his strategy for responding to racial taunts. It consisted of a sharp jab to the offender's chest, accompanied by a literal punch line: "Hertz, don't it?" The humor rested on the bitter contrast of Simpson's tremendous success as an athlete who crossed over to become a beloved corporate icon, advertising rental cars among much else, with his continued facing of racial hurts and desiring to strike back against them. (The same *Hertz/hurts* punning was repeated endlessly on "O. J. jokes" websites during Simpson's later trials.) Simpson surely knew that he briefly stepped out of character in telling the joke. He followed the remark with laughing reassurances that such jabbing was of course unnecessary. Referring to himself in the disturbing third-person manner common to toddlers and Republican presidential hopefuls, he pointed out that "The Juice" so transcended white racism that he scarcely faced bigotry. He then shifted the discussion to the troublesome African American women who criticized his acting out interracial romances in films and to the insecure African American militants who had tried to draw him into their own wrestling with racial identity. In general, apart from his delivering the occasional line about country clubs flying their flags at half-staff on the days when he was their guest, Simpson's pre-1994 self-presentation was as someone for whom racism was not a problem. As early as 1969, he triumphantly reported that O. J. was thought of as a man, not as an African American. He told reporters that the American public happily saw him as "colorless." In making the latter claim, Simpson also invoked Hertz. The marketing division of the firm, he observed, had generated data that proved his transcendence of race.[1]

As this chapter was being written, lawyers and trademark bureaucrats were deciding a bizarre conflict regarding who owned the initials "O. J." Amid much bad financial news, Simpson prevailed on the orange juice lobby to give up its disputing of his claim to be O. J. Perhaps reflecting a desire not to be much associated with Simpson, the juice industry gave ground on its claims to the initials, except in direct reference to orange juice products. Simpson hoped the decision would enable him to bounce back from his trials and market a range of products—from apparel to toys—under that trademark. Such connections of Simpson to the sale of things were long-standing and wide-ranging: razors, boots, books, videos, juice, clothing, soda, combination juice and soda, sunglasses, televisions, films, dolls, cars, sneakers, sporting goods, chicken, cameras, aftershave, rental cars, and (as both he and others have long observed) his own "image" and "personality." The length of the list suggests why Simpson could still imagine that the white public might see him as without race.[2]

This chapter examines the role of race and the claim of "colorlessness" in O. J. Simpson's life largely prior to the 1994 murders of Nicole Brown Simpson and Ronald Goldman. It seeks to understand why Simpson became the first black sports star to cross over massively from athletic hero to corporate spokesman and media personality. It argues that however passionately Simpson believed that such a crossover also involved a movement beyond color, his success rested on appeals rooted strongly in his race, in the presence of movements for racial justice, and in the history of race and gender in the United States. Although there can be no doubt that Simpson's image became a valuable commodity, commodity and color were inextricably linked in his appeal. This chapter addresses these pre-1994 realities as critical in their own right, murders and trials aside. However, it also acknowledges that all thinking about Simpson now is read as reflecting on "the case"—that books on him are now not shelved in sports or business aisles but in the "True Crime" sections of bookstores. The argument here obviously intersects with one of the aspects of the case that endlessly fascinates: the terrifying juxtaposition of the slashed, maimed, and lifeless bodies of the victims with the feverish rush of media and markets to sell, and of the public to buy, any and every commodity related to the tragedy. The awful fact that the sales of white Broncos skyrocketed, along with sales of the type of stiletto once thought to be the murder weapon, the obscene sensationalizing by the tabloid and mainstream media, the paid-for interviews with witnesses, the seven-figure book contracts, Kato Kaelin's auditioning for further parts from the witness stand, and the nude photo spread of a Simpson "juror with a difference" in *Playboy*—all these provoked horror precisely because they showed how quickly the pursuit of profit displaces and desecrates the memory of the dead. O. J. Simpson, selling his own image from jail (signed, on football cards) and hawking books, videos, medallions, interviews, and even photographs of his children, epitomized this outrageous behavior. Indeed, the prosecution's appeals, from Christopher Darden's warnings against being taken in by high-priced Dream Teamers to Marcia Clark's closing slide show of the victims, offered jurors an opportunity to rescue the dead from the lively rush to profit.[3]

The deeply gendered connections of house, home, and community in Simpson's commercial success, which also receive attention here, underpin another major narrative regarding the case, one especially found in Black reflections on it, from the neighborhood where Simpson grew up to the speeches of Louis Farrakhan. According to this narrative, which has some force, Simpson progressively concerned himself less and less with African American life but was nonetheless unable, when accused, to transcend racism and ironically found significant support within a community he had left behind. Simpson's own writing on the case detailed a growing horror at having to "see race" after a life he characterized as lived entirely on merit. Understanding O. J. as a seemingly "colorless" but in fact fully racialized commodity, brilliantly positioned to be marketed to middle-class white men, is thus vital to comprehending his and the public's reaction to the trial. Simpson emerges then as a key figure in the history of modern white attempts to claim to be "colorblind," a stance wholly unlike the whites in an earlier era, whose racism was clear and open, and equally unlike that of the allegedly atavistic

African Americans whose race consciousness was said to keep them from acknowledging Simpson's guilt. In his plea for an end to "racialist" liberalism, for example, Michael Lind has evoked Simpson to illustrate the presence of a "Creole right," for whom it does not matter "what color your skin is, long as you are wealthy." In Lind's view, "For most white Americans, O. J. Simpson was just a rich celebrity" without racial identity. But the very term *colorblindness,* as it applies to race, is a curious one. Hardly free of internalized race-thinking, it implies that whites have learned to *overlook* color, which is nevertheless apparent and real. Nowhere is the vexed history of such looking, overlooking, and looking again more fascinating than in Simpson's case.[4]

The Unmilitant: Black Revolt
and the Simpson Difference

So familiar is Simpson's commercial success, and that of the few African American athletes who followed him to advertising superstardom, that it is difficult to recall how spectacularly improbable such celebrity was. No Black athlete, no matter how great, had ever crossed over with anything like such appeal. In the late 1960s, contracts for paid commercial endorsements remained unavailable even to those who had had professional careers as the greatest in their sports, be they Willie Mays, Hank Aaron, Bill Russell, Oscar Robertson, Wilt Chamberlain, Jimmy Brown, or (above all) Muhammad Ali. Nor were African American stars who might have been marketed for their excellence and their youth deluged with offers—not Lew Alcindor, not Lou Brock, not Arthur Ashe, and not Tommie Smith, who in the late 1960s had perhaps the broadest claim ever to the title "world's fastest human." Superstars such as Russell and Bob Gibson faced slights and exclusion even in the relatively narrow local markets in which they were the dominant sports figures. Advertising firms, reacting to research demonstrating that commercials overwhelmingly focused on and appealed to whites, stridently maintained that characters in ads had to look like what white mainstream audiences supposedly thought America should look like. They listed products, such as razors and razor blades, for which African Americans were perceived as being too different-looking to endorse in ads pitched to those outside the Black community. More broadly, as Anne McClintock's work in cultural studies points out, mass advertising since 1900 or before had consistently used racist and racial imagery to sell to white markets. Black images on products were not unknown, but they were often demeaning, servile, and anonymous: Aunt Jemima, the Cream of Wheat man, Uncle Ben, the Gold Dust twins, and so on. Indeed, McClintock tellingly shows that such "commodity racism" was not just reflective of how the larger society's racism showed up in ads but also deeply constitutive of the very ways in which whites connected race, pleasure, and service.[5]

And then O. J. Simpson, two years out of junior college and never having played a down in the National Football League, suddenly entertained so many offers from advertisers that he could turn down any proposals that he appear in individual commercials, insisting on contracting only as an ongoing spokesperson for products. Money poured in from GM, from Royal Crown Cola (for whom Simpson had worked as a deliveryman until shortly before moving to the University of Southern California), and from so many other sponsors that, as one *Sports Illustrated* writer put it, he was busy just cashing checks. ABC made him a network sportscaster. He soon would impress Schick as not so different as to rule out his appearance in shaving ads. By 1977, he would win polls as the most admired person among U.S. fifth- to twelfth-graders and as the "most watchable man" in the world. He would garner *Advertising Age's* "Oscar" as the top celebrity spokesperson in the United States, and he would receive coverage not just as the Black athlete most successful in attracting money from beyond his sport but also as the most successful athlete of any color.[6]

That this phenomenal success began in 1969, after Simpson's Heisman Trophy–winning season, not in his record-breaking 1973 NFL year, is crucial to explaining his crossover appeal. Then, as now, winning the Heisman had little relation to future professional success, but corporations and the media took a chance on O. J. The sunlit 1968 season of Simpson's Heisman "campaign"—he had chosen Southern Cal in large part because its campaign machinery had functioned so well when Mike Garrett won the trophy—stands in stark contrast to the other dramas of that eventful year. But those stormy events constitute an indispensable context for any explanation of Simpson's commercial crossover. His triumph—not in the Heisman race, where he had no close rivals, but in the corporate world—lay in the distance Simpson put between himself and those momentous events, quite as much as in the ground he put between himself and would-be tacklers.[7]

Simpson's reception during and after his Heisman campaign unfolded amid revolt and repression. In 1968, from Paris to Prague to Mexico City to Chicago, protesters faced guns, clubs, and tanks as they campaigned for nothing less than a new society. Vietcong military campaigns reached their turning point in the bloody Tet offensive. The U.S. presidential campaign saw the assassination of Robert F. Kennedy and police riots at the Democratic National Convention. Richard M. Nixon won the White House, skillfully deploying a "southern strategy" of appealing to the "backlash" of white voters against civil rights. The campaign of Memphis sanitation workers for dignity and trade union rights called Martin Luther King, Jr., to that city and to his death.

Students, African Americans, Californians, and, to an unprecedented extent, athletes played central roles in the struggles of 1968. Thus Simpson's glorious football Saturday afternoons, his disdain for "politics," his ability to socialize one moment with Bill Cosby and the next with John Wayne, and his smiling California and American dreaming contrasted sharply with other televised images of campuses, of the Bay area, of southern California, of Black America, and of the world of sports. The Black Panther Party, whose roots lay in the Bay area, also became a significant force and a victim of savage COINTELPRO police repression in southern California. California's campuses, especially in the Bay area and Los Angeles, continued to be symbols of student revolt. California's Governor Ronald Reagan, Senator George Murphy, and San Francisco State University administrator S. I. Hayakawa joined Nixon (yet another Californian) as the most visible figures capitalizing on opposition to campus protests. So extensive was politicization across the ideological spectrum that even Nixon had an African American superstar as an active supporter: Wilt Chamberlain, drawn to Nixon's advocacy of Black capitalism, was the tallest delegate at the 1968 Republican National Convention.[8]

In sports, two symbols dominated what the California-based sociologist and activist Harry Edwards called the "revolt of the black athlete." The first, Muhammad Ali, faced jail in 1968 and suffered suspension from boxing for his refusal to regard the Vietcong as his enemy and to be inducted into the military as a draftee. Pretty, poetic, and seemingly invulnerable in the ring, Ali clearly enjoyed greater recognition, nationally and internationally, than any other American athlete. Just as clearly, he had what the advertisers call "high negatives."[9]

The second symbol of Black athletes' revolt—the protests surrounding the 1968 Mexico City Olympic games—hit far closer to home for Simpson. The entire summer games carried an immense political charge, from Cold War medal-counting to the gunning down of protesters that, more tellingly than the lighting of the Olympic torch, marked the beginning of the competition. The struggle against South

Africa's readmission to the games invigorated international protest against apartheid. Fighting for a host of demands, the topmost of which was an end to Ali's victimization and at the center of which were the rights of collegiate athletes, California's Edwards and others built the Olympic Project for Human Rights, which counted Dr. King among its supporters. For a time, the threat of an African American boycott of the games loomed. Lew Alcindor, Lucius Allen, and Mike Warren of UCLA's outstanding basketball team all declined to try out for the U.S. team. Alcindor's gracefully worded demurral did not stop threats against his life. Although he did not adopt the name Kareem Abdul-Jabbar until later, Alcindor converted to Islam in 1968. In Mexico City, sprinters Tommie Smith and John Carlos, both of San Jose State University, protested most visibly, memorably clenching their fists in Black Power salutes on the victory stand after the 200-meter race. Simpson, who had run a leg on a world-record-setting 4-by-110 yards sprint relay team earlier in 1968, might well have competed at Mexico City had he concentrated solely on track. Back in California, he publicly denounced the Olympic protests. This denunciation was of a piece with Simpson's generally oppositional stance vis-à-vis the revolt of the Black athlete, although his frequently noncombatant response of simply ignoring freedom struggles and his ability to tap into certain aspects of Ali's cultural style and of Chamberlain's Black capitalism also are vital in accounting for Simpson's ability to cross over.[10]

Southern Cal, in contrast to UCLA's limited but real progressivism, had an abysmal record on race relations. Even the *Sports Illustrated* reporters who were there to write about Simpson's football exploits commented on the tense, besieged-by-the-city whiteness of the campus. Dean Cromwell, the legendary track coach who engineered many of the school's most significant pre-Simpson triumphs, explained in the 1940s that "the Negro excels in the events he does because he is closer to the primitive than the white man." In the late 1960s, the school's enrollment of Black students who were not athletes was tiny, a fact the student newspaper complacently attributed to the tuition's being so high. At a time when football success had passed overwhelmingly to large public universities, USC was an oddity: an elite (in terms of tuition anyway) private college football power. When a necessarily small Black student movement took shape at Southern Cal, Simpson denounced it. He argued that its leaders were rich "Baldwin Hills" kids agonizing over a Black identity that they had just discovered, but one that he was "born with" by virtue of his poverty.[11] Aside from the doubtful merits of this analysis of USC's movement, it deserves noting that origins among the working poor hardly discouraged such leading figures as Tommie Smith from protesting. Simpson's main competitor for the Heisman, Purdue running back Leroy Keyes, proudly told reporters of his role in militant protests, including the hanging of a banner that read THE FIRE NEXT TIME. Simpson emphasized his "own philosophy" of positioning himself to be able to make charitable contributions and to offer himself as a role model of financial success to black youth.[12]

Simpson carried into his professional career an animosity toward politics, which meant for him both endorsing candidates and supporting protests. He offered to stay out of politics as long as politicians stayed out of football. At the time, as Nelson George puts it, "Brothers [in sports] were sporting huge Afros, bellbottom pants and gold medallions. They were reading Eldridge Cleaver's *Soul on Ice,* listening to the Last Poets and smoking marijuana instead of drinking beer." Simpson meanwhile disavowed drug use, kept private his feeling that it would be "crazy" to go to Vietnam, and made fun of bearded acquaintances to reporters, referring to them as H. Rap Brown. Buffalo's team had a hair and grooming code during his early career. That Simpson complied made him look different from many athletes of the time. In the late 1970s he again connected beards and politics in a remarkable, highly public campaign to be cast as Coalhouse Walker, the Black entertainer-cum-revolutionary in the film version of E. L. Doctorow's *Ragtime.* Not only did reporters note his sudden interest in African American culture and politics and his new, bearded look, but Simpson himself repeatedly announced that he was changing his image in a frank bid to get a role that would enable him to realize his central acting goal: to become a "bankable" star.[13]

Simpson also weighed in during the mid-seventies on an issue of great concern among antiracist sports activists, the nearly total absence of Black quarterbacks in the National Football League. Coaches continually steered Black quarterbacks to other positions—those for which speed and power, rather than intelligence and leadership, figured most prominently in the job description. Discouraged by many college coaches, Black quarterbacks were infrequently drafted as professionals and, when they were, needed to deliver solid results much more quickly than white signal callers. James Harris, a young Black quarterback who had performed successfully and yet had won no steady starting job, became a focus of the debate. Enter Simpson, who provoked strong opposition in the Black press in 1977 when he unaccountably offered the opinion that an aging and injured Joe Namath could quarterback the Rams better than Harris, who for a time played on the Bills with Simpson.[14] Only on the issue of greater mobility between teams for professional athletes did Simpson flirt with protest movements. But even on this matter, his retreats, and the grounds for them, were more spectacular than his self-interested advances.

In 1969 Simpson made plans to sue the National Football League—before he had ever played a down in it. Fresh off his Heisman Trophy–winning 1968 season at Southern Cal and just drafted by the Buffalo Bills, Simpson badly wanted to avoid going to a frigid city with a poor team and a small market. He came within an eyelash of emulating baseball's Curt Flood and risking his career to challenge restrictions on players' movement from team to team. Like Flood, a gifted St. Louis Cardinal centerfielder much influenced by the Black freedom movement, Simpson sometimes cast his personal contractual situation within a broader civil rights framework. His large contracts with General Motors and other corporations, Frank Deford observed in *Sports Illustrated,* made it possible for Simpson to finance legal action and to survive a delay in signing. But the corporate endorsements cut two ways. The negotiator for the Bills, a former union lawyer, pointed out to Simpson that the real money coming his way would be provided by advertisers, not football owners, and that such endorsements could continue only if he remained in football's limelight. Chevrolet, the negotiator argued, would not fork over another quarter-million dollars to a holdout. After much hesitation, Simpson signed for much less than he had demanded. He admitted that the agreement was a capitulation on his part, but he embraced the logic that his real future lay in advertising and "image." Looking around at all the things he had acquired, particularly his new home, and glorying in his relationship with Chevrolet division head John DeLorean left Simpson certain that he had done the right thing. He would again threaten legal action against the league in the middle 1970s when he charged the NFL with placing itself above the Constitution and supported the 1974 players' strike; he also predicted cooperative ownership of all franchises. But his flirtations with open challenges to the league typically stopped short of any decisive action. Simpson's first year with the Bills would be the subject of a book, which he wrote with the football journalist Pete Axthelm. Despite his disappointing contract, its title, *Education of a Rich Rookie,* was apt and significant.[15]

Locating Simpson's crossover success within the era of the revolt of the Black athlete illuminates two critical ironies of that crossover. The

first is that militants in and outside of sports both established the pre-
conditions for the advertising and media success of a Simpson and
ensured that the first athlete to cash in on new possibilities would be
anything but a militant. Black Power, as Robert Weems has shown,
brought sharply rising interest in African American markets among
advertising executives: The ferment of 1968 in particular generated an
unprecedented escalation in civil rights lobbying against racism in
advertising; mass pressure encouraged sports, media, and marketing
elites to search energetically for role models and to trumpet the myth of
sport as a "level playing field" loudly enough to deflect attention from
inequalities within athletics and from the realities of who owned and
ran the industry. The second irony is more subtle. As he made his
historic crossover breakthrough, Simpson's seeming transcendence of
color rested squarely on his racial identity. The epithet "white man's
Negro" is noteworthy in this connection, even though we are far more
interested in why Simpson's image sold, and in what he bought into,
than in the question of whether he sold out. Even the most assimilative
crossover strategies rested not only on pleasing the white (and in Simpson's case mainly male) public but also on pleasing that public as a
"Negro." Being a cheerful athlete who deflected attention from Black
revolt worked so powerfully in Simpson's case not because he crossed
over from Black to white. Rather, those attributes had meaning largely
because he remained an African American as they enabled him to move
from being an athlete to being an advertisement.[16]

Buying and Selling Houses:
Home and the Traffic in Style

Simpson's wealth underwrote a southern California existence that took
him far from his roots in inner-city San Francisco to fabulous homes in
overwhelmingly white areas. His "lifestyle of the rich and suburban"
image reinforced his seeming transcendence of color in a nation in
which upper-class whiteness is often cast as the normative experience.
However, not only did Simpson's pride in grand homes grow out of his
past, but white fascination with his lifestyle and with what flavor he
could bring to suburban blandness fundamentally hinged on Simpson's
racial identity. At fifteen, and just out of a short stay at a youth detention center, O. J. Simpson got to spend much of a day with Giants'
centerfielder Willie Mays. During this adventure, Simpson later and
often related, he was not awed. But the ease of Mays's manner and the
absence of any preaching about staying out of trouble deeply impressed
Simpson. Equally impressive was simply viewing Mays's house and

possessions. This visit showed Simpson what success could bring. He worshipped Mays not simply for being a great player but for having "a big house to show for it." Fiercely defensive of Mays when the latter was said to pay insufficient attention to using his fame to further African American causes, Simpson argued that his teenage encounter with Mays's superstardom provided a model for playing the role of celebrity. In Heisman-year interviews and later, he emphasized desire not only to fund a boys' club in the "old neighborhood" of Potrero Hill but also to build an impressive house for himself outside of it. He cast both acts in terms of aiding black youth. "I feel that it's the material things that count," he told reporters when explaining how to impress lessons on young people. To accusations that he played the "Establishment game" to acquire "the money [and] the big house," he replied that such acquisitions would "give pride and hope to a lot of young blacks." From his early *Sports Illustrated* interviews to the video he sold after his acquittal, Simpson has invited America to tour his houses. Indeed, prosecuting attorney Christopher Darden complained that Simpson gave such tours when the jury in the murder trial visited his Rockingham home.[17]

Simpson's passion for houses and homes as the symbols of success was not surprising, given his own youth as a resident in housing projects built as temporary shelter for World War II shipyard workers in the Bay area and his father's absence from the family. Simpson could gush, in an interview with *Playboy,* over the projects as "America the Beautiful" and as a "federally funded commune," but he seldom looked back after his move to Southern Cal. Although *Time* referred to him as "molded by the slums," reporters and biographers showed little interest in the facts of his youth. The mainstream press spelled Potrero Hill no fewer than four different ways—and usually wrong. His own autobiography, with Pete Axthelm doing the writing, offered the least plausible misspelling.[18] The "old neighborhood" became, not just for Simpson but also for the press, a handy source of legends, spun out as the occasion required and with much of the ambience of *West Side Story.* Nearly all the accounts centered on whether the "gangs" Simpson joined were or weren't tough and criminal. To a remarkable extent, Simpson managed to portray his gang activity both as hard and masculine and as playful and harmless. Even when he referred to cohorts as a "bunch of cutthroats," his half-seriousness enabled readers to interpret his youth charitably. He described his teenage encounter with marijuana with similarly wonderful ambiguity. Long before President Clinton professed not to have inhaled, Simpson offered virtually the same account of what happened when he was offered a joint after the "hippie invasion" of San Francisco. Like Clinton, he told the story with a savvy that mixed blamelessness with intimations of a thorough knowledge of the drug culture.[19]

In the main, Potrero Hill functioned simply as a backdrop to Simpson's real life of stardom. Even when he was just a year out of San Francisco, *Ebony* wrote of Simpson as a "once-tough youngster" who had become "a model of deportment, a B-minus student, a dedicated husband, and an interviewer's dream." Simpson's collaborator on his 1970 book described him as having succeeded in "running from the traps of his ghetto upbringing . . . towards new dreams and images of himself." Simpson married his high school sweetheart and hung out consistently at Southern Cal and elsewhere with Al Cowlings, a high school teammate. But his visits to Potrero Hill grew ever more infrequent. And they tended to be mediated by charitable contributions and commodities— most spectacularly when Simpson publicized fruit juices with ads revisiting his youth.[20]

The most significant omission from accounts of Simpson's youth is that of the 1966 rebellion against San Francisco police violence after Matthew Johnson, a Black teenager, was shot dead by a white patrolman in the Hunters Point/Potrero Hill area. For more than five days, "soft" and "hard" antiriot tactics failed to quell the resulting defiance, looting, arson, and vandalism. Damage caused by the rebellion was limited, but police intimidation of the community was not. The authorities' attempts to enlist the aid of former gang leaders—the foremost study of the neighborhood insists that gangs "no longer existed" in Hunters Point in the mid-1960s—failed dramatically, as did efforts to bring in middle-class "community leaders," largely from other neighborhoods. Police so aggressively "herded" Blacks from other public spaces in the city to Hunters Point that "moderate, responsible" adults feared that a plan was being implemented in which an aircraft carrier passing in the Bay would stage massive bombings of the neighborhood "like," as one resident put it, "they do in Vietnam." These extremely bitter relations with the police, and the passionate denunciation of "Uncle Toms" and "white Negroes" on Potrero Hill during and after the 1966 events, figure nowhere in accounts of Simpson's youth, although they are important aspects of the context from which emerged both his triumphs in the sixties and his trials in the nineties.[21]

Even more remarkable than the ways in which the desire to escape poverty, to enjoy the fruits of achievement, and to secure privacy led Simpson to concern himself so passionately with house and home was the extent to which his home hunting became a hugely publicized story on America's sports pages. The larger society's obsession with his personal obsession is another key to his crossover appeal and demands an explanation set in the context of the larger racial politics of the period. When Simpson showed reporters his first home as it was going up in Los Angeles's Coldwater Canyon, the focus was on color and housing, but in a way strikingly unfamiliar to readers. At a time when such idols of Simpson's youth as Bill Russell and Willie Mays had recently suffered through highly publicized incidents of racial discrimination in housing in California, and when NFL teams had just begun to break the color line in rooming assignments, Simpson's concern centered on the orange color of Los Angeles's smoggy air. His solution was a fully private one. The house sat, he proudly noted, above the "smog line."[22]

This same sense of the transcendence of concern about race via class and geographic mobility ran through the extended drama of Simpson's attempts to get out of his Buffalo Bills contract and to play "at home." From the start of his pro career, "home" was a wealthy section of Los Angeles, not his longtime boyhood home and not gritty Buffalo. Simpson's image was not simply that of a Californian, but that of a wealthy southern Californian. His world was warm, cosmopolitan, lavish, and upscale. Buffalo, known as ethnic and working-class as well as cold, had a team run as a "rinky-dink" operation, and it was a city with nothing going on. Its grime and grit contrasted with L.A.'s splendor and sparkle in a drama in which Simpson's race seemingly mattered little and his class and regional loyalties much. Indeed, in describing what made Buffalo rinky-dink, he told *Playboy,* "In college, I'd played at L.A. Coliseum, which you can see from half a mile away. In Buffalo, you'd be walking through a black neighborhood and suddenly, sixty feet in front of you, you'd see this old, rundown stadium."[23] Simpson so consistently criticized Buffalo that when his salary reached a (mis)-reported $2.5 million annually, the comedian Johnny Carson joked that the half-million was for playing football, the balance for living there. His decisions to renege on refusals to go back to the Bills consistently turned on dollars and on supporting his Bel-Air lifestyle. In 1973 he returned to Buffalo, for example, after a hard look at "the material things that I have" in Bel-Air. His symbolic value here went far beyond providing a hopeful scenario of fame and wealth as antidotes to racial division. Embodying and very visibly championing the lifestyle of the white upper-middle class in the very region in which its growth and pretensions were most spectacular, Simpson reassured a vital segment of audiences that what they had and what they wanted, along with the ways in which they related work to consumption, were everybody's dreams—notwithstanding the profound questions raised by the Black freedom movement, by hippies, and by the sixties generally. Simpson's race, even and especially when it went unmentioned, mattered greatly in his providing of this reassurance.[24]

A subplot of the "rescue O. J. from Buffalo" melodrama focused more directly on race. Nearly all of the many stories of his migrations and his threats to stay put mentioned his thorough consideration of family in all decisions. Because Marguerite, his first wife, neither liked Buffalo nor wished to uproot the children twice a year, joining and rejoining the Bills meant prolonged separation from his nuclear family (such separations from his mother and other extended-family members went unremarked). Coverage consistently stressed O. J. Simpson's role as a model father and husband who anguished over the decision and recalled his own father's estrangement from the household as Simpson grew up. "Home is always where the heart is," *Parents' Magazine* headlined in a Simpson profile, which admitted that it was often not where he was. The responsibility of O. J.'s decision contrasted sharply with his father's apparently unconsidered decision, just as the tremendous financial reward that O. J. reaped contrasted with the lack of support provided by his father. At a time, much like ours, when single mothers and absent fathers were indicted as the key to the "pathology" of Black families and communities, the "O. J., L.A., and Buffalo" stories did more than offer a positive role model. They portrayed African American success as overwhelmingly hinging on male responsibility, such that Simpson, and not Marguerite, became the model family member, even as his adulation of Willie Mays often crowded Simpson's mother out of the success story of Simpson's youth.[25]

However much Simpson marginalized racism and claimed a "colorless" appeal, his crossover success very much continued to rest on his race. This was true not only with regard to his anti–Black Power, suburban homeboy positioning, but also with regard to his ability to remix familiar racist marketing images and to sell new images of Black style. Although his later advertising image derived more or less strictly from the country club, Simpson's early appeals drew heavily on the marketing of Black athletic style for crossover purposes. This was at a time when African American "aesthetics" had begun to dominate images of professional basketball, when Maury Wills and Lou Brock had revolutionized base running, and when Muhammad Ali had brought to the public new styles in boxing and voluble reflections on those styles.[26]

Simpson's claims to symbolize stylistic innovation came from a relatively weak position, especially compared to basketball players, because football was not a game nurtured on playgrounds to anything like the extent that basketball was. Played mostly (at least after high school) before white coaches with white quarterbacks calling the signals, football was not so dramatically transformed by African American athletes, although running back was the most changed position. Nor, of course, was Simpson's style anywhere near as distinctive as Ali's. With neither the power of Jimmy Brown, who more than doubled Simpson's professional touchdowns in a significantly shorter career, nor the breakaway creativity of Gale Sayers, Simpson was a brilliant back largely because of his combination of gifts. But that combination did not rival Brown's.

Simpson, profiting greatly from the increased use of slow-motion photography in sports, did successfully cultivate public interest in his style, which he linked to African American expressive behavior. Although his Heisman campaign stressed the standard elements of grit, aggression, power, and speed, Simpson quickly developed a more distinctive rap about his style. Reporters referred to his use of "jive patter" in describing his own running, replete with references to music and dance. While other backs slashed and ground out yardage, his game plan involved fakes and feints—"juking the tough guys," as he put it, using in juke (or jook) a term that originated in West Africa and referred in African American slang to dance halls and evasive swerving as well as to sex. He told *Playboy* that "setting a cat down" with a convincing open-field fake and cut was his greatest football thrill. Stressing his own studied invulnerability, he claimed to have learned to tell the place on the field of all defenders as plays unfolded so that he could escape crippling hits. Nor, he bragged, even during the losing early years in Buffalo, did he hesitate to go out of bounds to avoid punishing tackles. He never let critics force him to squirm for the last bit of yardage, and therefore he offered star defenders such as Dick Butkus (the linebacker Simpson most delightedly talked of frustrating) few chances to hit him squarely. On his own description, he hit holes "like a coward" searching for seams.[27]

In his caginess, in his claims of an invulnerability born of intelligence and instinct, and in his ability to evoke comparisons with dancers, Simpson called to mind the ways in which Ali marketed his style. Like Ali, Simpson claimed to redefine and transcend his sport. Sportswriters accepted Simpson's claims and the connections to Ali. One major account argued that Simpson's appeal lay in his daring demonstration that "a man can play football just the way he lives." As early as 1968, *Senior Scholastic* clearly made the links to Ali, claiming that Simpson "changed direction like a butterfly and hit with the power of an oil truck."[28]

Echoing the champ's penchant for rhyming self-promotion, Simpson named his deceptive repertoire of fakes, shifts, starts, and pauses the *okey-doke,* again popularizing "jive" Black speech. The press bit hard on the term. His 1973 season, *Time* headlined, was the "Year of the Okey-Doke." When Simpson shared a story of fooling high school administrators with playful lies, he was portrayed as perfecting the verbal *"okey-doke."* Simpson nonthreateningly brought sprinklings of "the other's" slang to white Americans. He may also have had a sly, complicated laugh of his own in the case of *okey-doke,* which not only meant a "con game" but also sardonically referred to "white values."[29]

Simpson's nicknames offered a further opportunity for white fans to consume "the other." In reflecting on Michael Jordan, breakfast cereal, and McDonald's (which once named a sandwich after Jordan), Michael Eric Dyson has recently argued that the historical consumption of Black bodies by Western capitalism is recapitulated in a very different form today via athletics and athletic endorsements.[30] In Simpson's case, the tie between older and newer forms of such consumption was greatly facilitated by his nicknames. Called O. J. rather than Orenthal James since his youth, Simpson was, according to one journalist, nearly as famous for being dubbed Orange Juice as for his running at Southern Cal. "The Juice," connoting energy, appears to have been generated as a shorter nickname in Buffalo, where Simpson's blockers were the "Electric Company." As Orange Juice, Simpson came prepackaged as a breakfast staple, recapitulating the impressive history of Black advertising icons invited into homes to serve whites their morning pleasure. The Orange Juice image contributed to the sunny, cheerful "southern Californiazation" of Simpson. It also connected him to Aunt Jemima and to the Cream of Wheat man and offered, à la the McJordan sandwich, a direct opportunity for Simpson to be consumed. His runaway fame eventually made "O. J.," originally lunch counter shorthand used by waitresses, an almost universally recognized reference to orange juice. His earliest and some of his most lucrative endorsements came from juice contracts, especially the "teaming up of two great juices" in Tree Sweet ads. If his big contracts broke with advertising's powerful tradition of "commodity racism," his image was also very much a part of that tradition.[31]

Media-Made O. J.: Race, Speech, and Slow-Motion Supermanhood

As early as 1968, media projections of O. J. Simpson so insistently pegged him as Superman that his first wife felt compelled to remind the press that there's no such thing.[32] If not quite interplanetary, Simpson's aura of greatness and goodness was distinctly Supermanly, and that aura suffused accounts of his image as being above the racial fray. In his reflections on the trial, none of Simpson's anger runs more deeply than that directed against the press, which he portrays as suddenly seeing him in terms of race and making him regretfully see race in everyday life. The contrast that Simpson notes was stark. Before 1994 he enjoyed adulation from the sports media's star-making machinery and from a quarter-century's work as one of the boys in the booth of television sportscasting. After 1994, he became (literally, in the case of *Time* magazine's controversial doctored cover) a blackened figure. Executives, who had earlier held that his jobs would probably be waiting for him if a "not guilty" verdict came in, made no gestures toward such reemployment.[33] But to see such dramatic changes as simply a movement from "colorless" acceptance to race-thinking overlooks the large extent to which Simpson's Superman image was itself about race and the extent to which he remained the Black guy in the booth as well as one of the boys there.

Simpson's media image clearly derived from long-standing journalistic traditions and modern television innovations that influenced the public's view of both white and Black athletes, though in differing ways. When *Los Angeles Times* sportswriter Dwight Chapin flatly proclaimed, "Superman is Orenthal James Simpson" in 1968, he followed a tradition of monumentalizing football heroes that dates back almost a century. An 1891 *New York World* football story caught the spectacular flavor perfectly: "Surely, here were the old Roman kings circled about in their clattering chariots gloating over the running fight, and satiated with death. . . . Here were the lovely maidens of ancient days, turning down their pretty thumbs with every mangling scrimmage, and shrieking with delight at every thrust and parry. . . . Think of Ulysses as a center rush, of Menelaus as a guard or of Paris as a quarterback."[34]

The early twentieth century's Walter Camp–inspired reportage on All-American football role models, mostly from elite colleges, coexisted with, and by the 1920s gave ground to, emphases on spectacle, violence, and the alleged racial and ethnic characteristics of minority players. Nor did decades of print journalism on football resolve the tension between dwelling on manly, individual heroism and presenting the competing and equally masculine narrative of teamwork and male bonding in the trenches. Simpson—a ghetto kid at an elite private school and the breakaway Juice in the open field, as well as a back who depended on the blocking and loyalty of the Electric Company line in front of him—became the focus of these tensions and traditions, especially in *Sports Illustrated* reporting. Nowhere did his distance from the 1968 protest help him more than among sportswriters, whose opposition to the Olympic boycott was broad, unreasoned, and angry.[35]

Ironically, the media's fascination with Simpson's Supermanly body and spirit coexisted with emphases on the abuse that body took from tacklers and on the inevitability of injury. The "Superman for a day" narrative of so much media coverage of modern sports finds its best expression in highlight films of football, showing bodies that "can fly" but that also collide, writhe, break, and suffer paralysis. Not incidentally, these bodies are increasingly Black, and the audience that consumes images of their triumph and destruction is overwhelmingly white.

Having grown up with an ineffectively treated case of rickets that led to childhood taunts of "Pencil Pins," Simpson was acutely aware of disability. Sportswriters and opposing coaches often commented on his practice of getting up very slowly after being tackled, looking absolutely unable to continue, and then fully bouncing back. This habit, which was reminiscent of Jimmy Brown and designedly disheartening to defenses, dramatically suggested Simpson's vulnerability. His early Ali-like boasts regarding invincibility backhandedly raised the same concerns. In his many interview references to endorsements and films as necessary to ensure a career after football, Simpson increasingly broached the issues of the inevitable brevity of his career and the peril to his body. Sportswriters played on the same theme. Predictably enough, Simpson was in fact chronically hurt by his later years in the NFL. Reference in the murder trial to his joint problems only continued a long-running pattern of press coverage regarding the results of the "sacrifice" of Simpson's body. Nowhere was the obsession better reflected than in the *Naked Gun* film series, in which Simpson's acting career came pitifully to rest on the repetition of injuries, culminating in a pratfall from a wheelchair. Although part of the humor here arose from the contrast with Simpson's slow-motion grace in the field and in

Hertz commercials, the gags also recalled his long career of risking and receiving crippling injuries, of "sacrificing his body" before white audiences.[36]

Print journalists, who consistently emphasized his "mild, warm, and talkative" nature, as contrasted with the moodiness of Bill Russell and the cerebral qualities of Kareem Abdul-Jabbar, enhanced Simpson's crossover appeal by making him known as an affable and "inoffensive" Black football superstar.[37] But it was television coverage and corporate sponsorship that contributed most decisively to the polishing and preserving of his image of easygoing Supermanhood. Both as football-playing object of the television camera's attention and as sportscaster covering football and the whole "wide world of sports," Simpson found his fortunes consistently intertwined with those of the producer Roone Arledge. Arledge's technical innovations in the filming of sports and his studied blurring of the line between journalism and entertainment helped to make Simpson spectacular.[38] His reliance on Simpson as a broadcaster helped to ensure that O. J. would not leave the spotlight and would function as one of the boys in sports journalism, largely insulated from serious criticism.

The story of dramatic and seemingly race-neutral technical innovations in the world of televised sports is largely Arledge's story. Arledge began the transformation of television sports coverage seven years before Simpson entered USC. Hired at ABC's sports division in 1960, he immediately set out to cover sporting "events" as sets of spectacular happenings occurring off as well as on the field. In 1966, when ABC signed a contract with the NCAA granting it exclusive college football coverage, Arledge pioneered in the introduction of instant replay during live telecasts. He combined this technique with the extensive incorporation of slow-motion photography. The latter technology, which had been applied to the screening of sports since the early twentieth century and was used most effectively by the pro-Nazi director Leni Riefenstahl in the 1930s, had become a staple of Arledge-produced sports telecasts by the time Simpson played his most celebrated games at USC.[39]

The combination of slow motion and instant replay, along with Arledge's increased use of close-ups, stop action, and sidebar stories on individual athletes, transformed the ways in which sports, and Simpson, appeared. It suddenly became arguable that television viewers could take in more of the action than viewers attending the event. So thoroughly did Arledge come to regard the game as only the raw material from which he would fashion a "show" that his *Wide World of Sports* often featured esoteric sports such as curling and ski-jumping, with little worry that viewers would be lost.[40] Simpson profited greatly from Arledge's innovations. He smiled not only engagingly, as other athletes had, but also in stop action, as they largely had not. Above all, Simpson was among the first great backs to play his college ball with slow-motion instant replay in full use. The effect of such replays cut in two directions. On the one hand, it enabled couch-bound athletes of all races to imagine themselves "in his shoes," seeing the holes in the defense and the coming of contact in ways that live action could not produce. (Hertz's advertising men also exploited this opportunity in transforming Simpson into a slow-motion rusher through airports.) On the other hand, slow-motion replays became vital in the popularizing of specifically African American sports performance styles such as the one Simpson marketed with his "jive talk." As Riefenstahl appreciated, slow-motion photography let viewers linger over the "natural" bodies of athletes, making it an effective vehicle for her monumentalizing of Aryan supermen in sports. Before Arledge, slow motion had most frequently been used in the filming of boxing matches, contests in which racially and ethnically typed bodies clashed most nakedly and openly.[41] Slow motion also, as Arthur Ashe incisively observed, provided the medium that could best showcase highly improvised and visually exciting running styles that were increasingly seen as hallmarks of African American players, especially Simpson. So thoroughly were race, body, and style entwined in viewers' perspectives that the extent to which intelligence and judgment undergird such rushing went almost unremarked. Instead, the style was seen as natural and Simpson as not only Superman but also "supernatural."[42]

Beyond technical innovations, Arledge typified two other important trends in sports television, changes that would influence coverage both of Simpson as a player and by Simpson as a reporter. The first centered on Arledge's further blurring of the line between sports journalism and entertainment. Famously illustrated by Howard Cosell's bitter writings on the battle between professionals (Cosell) and "jockocrats" (everyone else) on Arledge's *Monday Night Football,* the threat to standards that was posed by Arledge's allowing stars to report sports was undoubtedly overblown. Ex-athletes had long announced games, and Cosell himself used celebrity rather than qualifications to branch out into reporting on sports about which his expertise was much in doubt. When Arledge's entertainment-first philosophy won him promotion to head of the news division, Cosell steamed because he was not hired to work on the news side, next to such Arledge discoveries as Geraldo Rivera. Print journalism's standards of objectivity in sports reporting hardly provided an impeccable professional model for television. The broader ethical problems of the cozy, contractual, and mutually rewarding relationships between the networks and the leagues, and between the networks and sponsors that employed celebrity spokespersons who were being reported on during the games, raise much more troubling issues than the presence of "jockocrats." Nonetheless, Arledge's use of players, including active professional athletes, on telecasts clearly set the stage for Simpson's crossover into media and abetted the sort of nonreporting that caused fraying in Simpson's Superman cape to go unremarked.[43]

The fraternity of jockocrats that Cosell ultimately hated was part of a second contribution of Arledge as a producer. He popularized a sports television style that crafted an appeal avowedly designed mainly around gender, rather than race or class. Comparing football to bullfights and heavyweight boxing, he hoped to capture some interest from women, but not because they appreciated either the subtleties of football or even the "deftness" of athletes generally. Instead, he hoped women would tune in to "see what everyone is wearing [and] watch the cheerleaders." He filmed the latter from "a creepy, peepy camera," knowing that "very few men have ever switched channels when a nicely proportioned girl was leaping into the air."[44] Before coming to sports programming, Arledge had hoped his pilot of *For Men Only,* described as a network version of *Playboy,* would move his career beyond the producing of *Hi, Mom,* a Shari Lewis puppet show. Much of his football programming could have also carried the "for men only" tag. Male camaraderie was especially at a premium in the antics of the "teams" of broadcasters, especially the road warriors covering *Monday Night Football.*[45]

Simpson joined the boys on ABC telecasts quite early in his career, very much as both a jockocrat and a Black voice. As in advertising, his crossover from the football field to television reporting was precocious and virtually without precedent. He had just left USC when Arledge signed him to a 1970 contract as a very visible freelancer with *Wide World of Sports.* That role, and his reporting on the 1972 Olympics, cast Simpson as an American, abroad and often at sea in the confusing variety of international athletic competitions.[46] But his race was far from irrelevant. Simpson's easygoing presence as a *Wide World* correspondent bespoke efforts to make the world forget the 1968 Olympics. His more durable career as a "color man" on football telecasts unfolded

squarely within a context of race. He succeeded where other great
Black athletes, such as Bill Russell, floundered. Racism plagued Russell's brief tenure as a superb network basketball commentator and was
charged when Fred Williamson was removed after a few pioneering
Monday Night Football telecasts.[47] However, the fact that Simpson
prospered and became the first African American to work regularly on
Monday night games hardly suggests a transcendence of race. His non-
standard English, so endearing to print reporters, became the object of
a running dialog among critics, who constantly anticipated improve-
ment. During his bitter 1983 feud with Simpson, Cosell began to doubt
that his partner's "deplorable diction" and "locution problem" would
ever be remedied.[48] Critics noted his bobbing head, mechanical deliv-
ery, and forced smile as well, but Simpson's highly publicized announc-
ing problems centered on his language, which was heard as insufficiently
white English. His 1985 demotion to pre- and postgame coverage of the
Super Bowl afforded a rare example of contact between Simpson and
a civil rights group; the National Association for the Advancement of
Colored People vigorously lobbied ABC on his behalf.[49]

Nor was race absent from the masculine and economically driven
dynamics that led to the failure of the press to investigate and cover
stories about Simpson's abuse of women and his use of drugs. After
the murders, long-standing allegations of cocaine use, violence toward
Marguerite Simpson and women at USC, and compulsive sexual conquests were reported.[50] That these stories had never before seen the
light of day, or at least had not been subjected to scrutiny, inspired no
significant self-criticism among journalists.[51] To raise this issue of nonreporting is not to encourage more sensationalist, censorious news
about the personal lives of athletes; less would be better. But in light of
the constant stories on Simpson as family man and role model, the
quite negative press on other athletes, and the mania for reporting
anything and everything about Simpson after 1994, his earlier insulation from bad press regarding violence, sex, and drugs requires some
explanation.

That insulation clearly reflected Simpson's role as a commodity valuable to his teams, to the NFL, to the networks, and to major corporate
sponsors of games and much else on television. Preserving his image
served also to protect the images and profits of powerful interlocking
forces. The silence of the press on the difficult, complex relationship of
football to male supremacy and to the battering of women suggests
how the media and the game protect each other. In Geraldo Rivera's

remarkably persistent attempts to combine utter sensationalism with worn-on-the-sleeve concern about domestic violence, you didn't hear, for example, the nuanced analysis of gender and football provided in James McBride's *War, Battering and Other Sports.*[52]

Simpson likewise benefited from a more intimate form of journalistic self-protection. When he reportedly interrupted filming of a sidebar story on "nightlife" and football to have semipublic sex in the back seat of a car, or when he sought out one-night stands during his marriages, Simpson scarely violated the norms of sports journalism. Arledge had married the personal secretary of RCA head David Sarnoff in 1953. She once typed Arledge's proposal for a pilot on Sarnoff's letterhead and forwarded it to the president of NBC, then an RCA subsidiary, as though it came from on high. This "different brand of cunning" failed. So did the marriage, when Arledge left his wife while on vacation. He subsequently wed his own secretary, a former Miss Alabama 17 years his junior.[53] Cosell, the professional on air at *Monday Night Football,* "joked" with network secretaries by unbuttoning their blouses "playfully." The ABC network had precisely one woman in an executive position.[54] Sexism was neither news nor a target for investigative reporting.

But as thoroughly structured by white elite male supremacy and economic self-interest as the nonreporting on O. J. was, the dynamics by which his image was propped up were hardly "colorless." The Black-star-as-role-model and Black-star-as-thug-on-drugs images had grown up absolutely in tandem in the press over the last quarter-century, so that there was little room to cast Simpson in a middle position. Reporters and athletes did not just fraternize via shared drugs, sex, and secrets, but such vices often specifically lubricated more extensive interaction between African American athletes and white journalists. And, of course, the black Superman media images of the 1970s were also those of Superspade and Superfly, icons in which violence, sex, and drugs were assumed to be prominent. Indeed, so important is the extent to which recent chatter about an allegedly colorblind common manliness across racial lines has in fact assumed, expressed, and reinforced racial stereotypes that this chapter concludes with an examination of Simpson, gender, and race that extends beyond the coverage of sports and forward to the present.

Hertz and the Buying of O. J.:
Company Man, Real Man, Black Man

In a 1994 *Business Marketing* article describing Simpson's genius, a top Hertz executive credited him with having transcended mere sport and "really taken on the persona of a businessperson" impressively "capable of speaking to another businessperson." Aside from its noteworthy assumption that moving from being among the greatest athletes of one's generation to being a businessperson represents a steep ascent, the executive's observation is of interest for its framing of Simpson's crossover as one from sports to commerce in a way that ignores race and also renders Simpson's rise in gender-free language.[55]

Such a claim both captures and obscures large parts of Simpson's appeal to the independent entrepreneurs and the corporate salesmen targeted by Hertz's rental car ads. Simpson consistently emphasized his desire to own businesses and to invest. In his initial Buffalo contract negotiations, the one significant concession he did manage to secure was a large bonus for investment purposes. He made films not only as an actor but also as the owner of a production company. His switch from ABC to NBC was much publicized as resulting from a desire to be a producer.[56] He acquired stakes in many of the corporations he endorsed—enough, as he put it, to be "a player." As time went by, his commitment to being an entrepreneur was increasingly colorless, divorced from any claims to his being a specifically African American role model in the realm of business, let alone from the sort of ideologically nationalist commitment to Black capitalism that became so much a part of Jimmy Brown's ongoing projects.[57]

By all accounts constantly busy, always moving about along with other men, risking family relationships amid anguish in order to be a good provider, Simpson served as a perfect symbol with which the business traveler could identify. However, given the fact that his business ventures were plagued by failures born of incredibly bad timing, and given his great prominence as a spokesperson for Hertz and a host of other corporations, Simpson actually wore the label "company man" more fittingly than "businessman." One of the nation's most sought-after motivational speakers at corporate dinners, Simpson could convincingly address his audiences on the importance of being a "team member" in the corporate world. Appealing both to the independent businessmen and to the company men who constituted the bulk of the rental car market, Simpson sent Hertz's sales and recognition skyward.[58]

But even Simpson's appeal to white men in meetings, airports, and offices ultimately turned on his status as an acceptable and exemplary Black man, not as a colorless fellow worker. In this connection, the recent study of race, gender, and sport by Lisa Disch and Mary Jo Kane illuminates how the notion of upper-middle-class white masculinity both entails the capacity to fantasize important connections with Black athletes and retains prerogatives to judge, type, and distance itself from such stars. Employed largely in physically passive jobs, such men cannot claim maleness on the basis of a working body and therefore base such a claim, to an unprecedented extent, on the "sovereign masculinity" of sport.[59] Thus the golf course's male foursome beckons as the reward for choosing Hertz's faster service. The passive experience of flying becomes an open-field dash through airports. Sporting performance by a few professionals becomes the property of many. As one white male professional puts it in a study by the sociologist Michael Messner, "A woman can do the same job as I can do—maybe even be my boss. But I'll be *damned* if she can go out on the football field and take a hit from Ronnie Lott." Forging pan-male unities, athletic striving particularly shores up male dominance in periods of forward political and economic motion by women. Hence women's liberation movements as well as Black Power form a critical context for Simpson's rise in the late 1960s.[60]

To imply that every male middle manager could "take a hit" from Lott is on one level ludicrous, but such a view expresses in shorthand the very real fact that professional team sports are largely places where women can neither play on the field nor participate in ownership and management. For Black men, during Simpson's career, sports were one of the few realms in which it was possible to be a "player," though the bars to their assuming managerial roles, let alone ownership, remained intact. Sport has functioned as a spectacle in which the male body and the white mind are at once exalted and in which white men feel especially empowered to judge, to bet on, and to identify vicariously with African Americans. Thus when Simpson, as early as 1969, boasted that his triumph lay in being seen as a "man" and not as Black, he was half right.[61] The white male target audience had a great interest in claiming his footloose power as male. But in so doing, they could also reserve the right to view his abilities as the natural, easy, and elemental traits of what Messner calls the "primitive other." Time and again, sportswriters, executives, and middle-level managers would credit him as a "real man." From fans at corporate dinners through the television executive commenting on why Simpson's "diction" did not get him fired, to the network official who explained why his 1989 domestic violence case did not doom his broadcast career, the judgment was that he was also a "nice guy." Such accolades were not conferred in a racial vacuum. At the height of his acceptance, Simpson was a "real Black man" and a "nice Black guy."[62]

Simpson's crossover success offered white viewers the opportunity to sit in judgment of Black manliness at the same moment when they claimed to have gotten past racial thinking. The irresistible appeal was not Simpson's supposed transcendence of race but rather the alleged transcendence of race among his audiences. The terrible force of much white reaction to the trial and to the verdict grew in no small part out of the dynamics described in this article. Such was most obviously the case with regard to the ease with which Simpson's image as a Black man could fully accommodate the renewed outbreak of racist stereotypes. But perhaps more telling was the outpouring of white rage against the "injection" of the issue of race into the trial—a rage that has consistently led to blaming a Black attorney rather than white police for the presence of race in the courtroom. Despite the wholesale change in attitudes toward Simpson himself, his image remained a vehicle through which white racial ideologies, and the pretense of their colorblind absence, could be spun out together.

TWO

Toward Nonwhite Histories

Nonwhite Radicalism

DU BOIS, JOHN BROWN,
AND BLACK RESISTANCE

Amid the empty rhetoric and commercialized hype over the millennium, we risked missing an anniversary of tremendous significance. The year 2000 marked the 200th anniversary of John Brown's birth. In his magnificent 1909 biography of Brown, the great African American scholar and activist W. E. B. Du Bois perfectly set the grand and workaday context of Brown's birth and of Brown's greatness: "Just at the close of the eighteenth century, first in Philadelphia and then in New York, small groups of [free Blacks] withdrew from white churches and established churches of their own, which still have millions of adherents. In the year of John Brown's birth, 1800, Gabriel planned his formidable uprising in Virginia." In *Black Thunder,* Arna Bontemps's remarkable novel on Gabriel's Rebellion, 1800 became the year that would "positively let no Virginian sleep." Herbert Aptheker, following Du Bois, has pronounced 1800 probably "the most fateful year in the history of American Negro slave revolts . . . ," emphasizing that it saw the birth of Nat Turner as well as of Brown and that Denmark Vesey, a third great strategist of revolt, bought his freedom at that time with lottery winnings. Indeed, as Douglas Egerton's recent study of Vesey reminds us, it was precisely the first moment of 1800 when Vesey drew his first free breath. Twenty-two years later, Du Bois wrote, Vesey would go "grimly to the scaffold, after one of the shrewdest Negro plots ever to frighten the South into hysterics." In 1859 Brown himself would plot a daring raid on the federal arsenal town of Harpers Ferry, Virginia, hoping to generate a vast freedom movement by slaves.

There is a temptation with Brown, as with other martyrs, to subordinate his life to a heroic act and a brave death. However, it is worth resisting such a temptation. In celebrating Brown's long life, not just his raid on Harpers Ferry and his hanging, vital matters are at stake. Connecting Brown with 1800 rather than with his 1859 death first of all links his magnificence with that of Turner, Gabriel, Vesey, and the resistance of slaves and Black workers generally. Du Bois insisted on this point, acknowledging that in his early life Brown's consciousness was only slightly touched by revolts, but adding that "in later years he learned of Gabriel and Vesey and Turner, and told of their exploits and studied their plans." Speaking more generally of Brown's contacts with African Americans, Du Bois wrote, "He sought them in home and church and out on the street, and he hired them in his business. He came to them on a plane of perfect equality—they sat at his table and he at theirs." What James Redpath had called Brown's "higher notion of the capacity of the Negro race"—his faith in "their fitness to take care of themselves"—was for Du Bois the key to Brown's genius.

The modern account that comes closest to approximating Du Bois's sense of how militancy and racial egalitarianism were one for Brown is Russell Banks's wise and tough-minded historical novel *Cloudsplitter.* The book roots pivotal and revealing chapters in the Brown family's working alongside Blacks and recounts direct actions of resistance to slavery and to the capture of runaway slaves. The Underground Railroad adventures of the Browns, Banks stresses, consistently expressed John Brown's preference for cooperating with rank-and-file African Americans rather than with white abolitionists. "In this work, it's their lives . . . on the line," Brown reasoned. "When it comes to a showdown, white people can always go home and read their Bibles if they want. . . . Who would you rather have at your side, a well-meaning white fellow who can cut and run if he wants, or a Negro man whose freedom is on the line?"

By virtue of his continued work with Black freedom fighters, Brown occupied a privileged position from which to see the possibilities of resistance. As Du Bois put it,

> Nowhere did the imminence of a great struggle show itself more clearly than among the Negroes themselves. Organized insurrection ceased in the South not because of the increased rigors of the slave system, but because the great safety-valve of escape northward was opened wider and wider. . . . The slaves and freedmen started the work and to the end bore the brunt of danger and hardship, but gradually they more and more secured the cooperation of men like John Brown.

The narrator of *Cloudsplitter*, Brown's son Owen, adds that knowledge of patterns of flight to freedom and of defense of such flight that already existed gave Brown's plans for insurrection their shape and foundation.

In crafting this portrayal of Brown, Du Bois contributed his part to a river of African American adulation of Brown, whose 1859 raid on Harpers Ferry, Virginia, and martyrdom established his willingness to fight and die even as it failed to liberate slaves. This willingness to confront slavery with force certainly accounts for some of the African American admiration of Brown. Such respect began with the Blacks who worked with Brown in 1851 in the League of Gileadites, with the five African Americans who helped besiege Harpers Ferry, and with the African American John Rock, who declared, "I believe in insurrections," just after the raid. It reached to Malcolm X and to James Baldwin, who, when asked what lackluster major-party presidential candidate he would be voting for, once declared "John Brown." Brown's revolutionary commitment and Christian martyrdom were much invoked by those who kept his flame alive. Such virtues also mattered in Du Bois's account of Brown as an Old Testament militant consecrated by righteous anger and innocent death. But in the end, Du Bois was equivocal concerning revolutionary violence and was far more impressed by Brown's life than by his death. The heroism Du Bois captured came from Brown's participating in a specifically African American abolitionism. If Du Bois did not go quite so far as Frederick Douglass, who found Brown "in sympathy a black man," he did surely regard Brown's greatness in light of the latter's clear perception that Black actions against slavery were the leading edge of antebellum freedom movements. As early as 1903, Du Bois had written that "the assertion of the manhood rights of the Negro by himself was the main reliance [of the antebellum years] and John Brown's raid was the extreme of its logic." Du Bois's *John Brown* fully elaborated this theme.

As Du Bois showed, Brown's commitment to struggling alongside Black freedom fighters did not—indeed, given the realities of day-to-day contact under tremendous pressure, *could not*—partake of a sentimentalism that would make him "blind to their imperfections." *Cloudsplitter* properly places Brown in awe of the Underground Railroad heroine Harriet Tubman, but he did not romanticize African Americans collectively or individually. Brown hated slavery and race prejudice because they exacted terrible human costs, especially in the realm of education. According to Du Bois, Brown saw African Americans complete with human weaknesses but sustained "perfect faith in their ability to rise above these faults."

The most direct expression of both Brown's critical edge and his faith in the ability of African Americans to liberate themselves was his remarkable 1848 essay "Sambo's Mistakes." In it, Brown wrote in the voice of an African American (though not in dialect), reflecting on lessons he had painfully learned. Partly a self-help manual and partly a revolutionary tract in blackface, "Sambo's Mistakes" encourages readers to study more, talk less, save, invest, disdain mainstream politicians, abstain from tobacco, and (above all) unite and resist. Du Bois found the essay "quaint," and certainly modern readers will see it as such, if not presumptuous and preachy. But Du Bois added that he also thought it "excellent," "delicately worded," and well worth rereading sixty years after its appearance. Such an assessment reflects how thoroughly Brown managed to become a comrade-in-arms, rather than a cheerleader or dictator, where Black resistance was concerned. To see him as a singular genius who rose and fell (and perhaps rose again) in 1859 slights the connections with ongoing Black militancy that enabled him to dream of and lead a rebel force and to demand that, when he was to be "publicly murdered," his "only religious attendants be poor little, dirty, ragged bare-headed slave boys and girls, led by some gray-headed slave mother."

Du Bois also strikingly argued against the view that Brown's martyrdom furthered emancipation only or mainly insofar as it inspired intellectuals and polarized political parties. Frederick Douglass's tribute, "If John Brown did not end the war that ended slavery, he did, at least, begin the war that ended slavery," led Du Bois into a deep inquiry regarding cause and effect. "The paths by which John Brown's raid precipitated the Civil War," he concluded, surely included the arousal of northern conscience and the lending of political ammunition to southern secessionist political leaders. But Du Bois was clear on Brown's central contribution: "In the first place he aroused the Negroes in Virginia" and thus helped to set into motion what Du Bois would later call the Civil War's "general strike" of slaves who fled to, and fought for, freedom. "Although John Brown's plan failed at the time," Du Bois wrote a century after Brown's death, "it was actually arms and tools in the hands of a half-million Negroes that won the Civil War." Indeed, Du Bois even suggested that the Civil War anthem "John Brown's Body" may have been based on African American music.

The other vital point preserved by dating John Brown's greatness from his birth rather than from his death concerns the remarkable internationalism of his campaigns and of the history of slave revolts generally. If Aptheker is right that 1800 was the "most fateful" year in such struggles, the pan-African resonances of the year certainly are the key to its centrality. Du Bois observed, "There was hell in Haiti in the red waning of the eighteenth century, in the days when John Brown was born." He added, "Ten thousand Frenchmen gasped and died in the fevered hills" of Haiti "while the black men in a sudden frenzy fought like devils for their freedom and won it." The Haitian revolution opened Du Bois's account of how Brown developed a "vision of the damned" not because its spirit was in the air at Brown's birth but because it so lastingly informed and emboldened rebels in the United States. What Du Bois called the "shudder of Haiti" was a context for Gabriel's Rebellion, along (as Bontemps so well shows) with echoes of the French Revolution. Vesey devoured written accounts of the events in Haiti, where he had lived for a time. His 1822 plot would promise that aid from Haiti could decisively help the rebels.

Likewise critical were the African dimensions of revolt. Indeed, Du Bois begins *John Brown* with a section titled "Africa and America." The turn-of-the-century church building that he saw as so pivotal in the development of a freedom movement featured churches that often took the name *African*. From the Stono and New York City revolts of the eighteenth century on, African-born slaves and African traditions played signal roles in rebellions. No leader more brilliantly marshaled African participation than Vesey. When Brown stayed at North Elba, New York, his revolutionary activity was in concert with members of the Black farming community that drew him there. The village had taken the name of Timbuctoo, "same as Timbuctoo in Guinea," as a character in *Cloudsplitter* puts it. In pledging after his fighting in Kansas to take the struggle much further, Brown promised, "I will carry the war into Africa."

Along with Bontemps's, the work that most fully captures the fateful turn of the eighteenth to the nineteenth century is Herman Melville's great novella of seagoing slave rebellion, *Benito Cereno*. Its hero, the African-born rebel leader Babo, leads a pan-African revolt in which the uniting of various African ethnicities into an African American freedom struggle (with return to Africa as its goal) is richly imagined. The novella, published four years before Brown's raid on Harpers Ferry, is based on an actual nineteenth-century revolt, but significantly, Melville switches the setting to 1799. The year and the ship's name, the *San Dominick*, resound with echoes of Haiti, but the U.S. captain Amasa Delano remains blind to the fact that the foundering ship he has boarded has been taken over by its slave cargo. After the uprising is put down, Babo is executed either—and here Melville is studiously vague—in the very last days of the eighteenth century or in the very first days of the nineteenth.

Much more could be said of Brown's internationalism and of his immersion in pan-African revolt. Inspired by British abolitionists, he studied not only Haiti, Gabriel, Vesey, and Turner but also the Napoleonic wars and the Spanish guerrillas under Mina in 1810, on whose methods of "cooking and discipline" Brown took notes. His ill-fated cooperation with the British journalist and self-described expert on guerrilla war, Hugh Forbes, rested on the latter's allegedly intimate knowledge of Garibaldi's revolt. Like Vesey's plot, Brown's promised the possibility of international pan-African resistance, in this case coming from Black communities in Canada.

Brown's life and death have long been of tremendous importance in informing and inspiring the actions of so-called traitors to the white race. Indeed, the recent research of Clarence Mohr, Randolph Campbell, and Ollinger Crenshaw shows that during the year after Brown's death, the slave system executed dozens of whites for real and alleged acts of solidarity with slave rebels. Even allowing for paranoia among the South's rulers, it is clear that Brown's raid had significant impact among whites. It did so not only because his courage set an example but also because his willingness to struggle alongside Black rebels of the world opened new possibilities.

Just after finishing *John Brown,* Du Bois read "Reconstruction and Its Benefits" to the American Historical Association. This article, published in 1910 in *American Historical Review,* joined *John Brown* in seeing African Americans as principal actors in the drama of their own liberation. A quarter-century later, Du Bois would expand "Reconstruction and Its Benefits" into perhaps his greatest book, *Black Reconstruction* (1935), where he introduced the idea of the "general strike" of the slaves—their flight to the Union Army and freedom—as the key to making the Civil War an emancipatory one. In 1962, when he republished *John Brown,* the occasion was no Brown anniversary at all. Instead, it marked the centenary of the Emancipation Proclamation, the fruit of what Du Bois called the "black worker's" resistance, of which John Brown was a part.

White Slavery, Abolition, and Coalition

LANGUAGES OF RACE, CLASS, AND GENDER

The rich historical literature on slavery and the idea of free labor, and the fine body of work on the roots of women's rights organizations and ideas in antislavery movements, fully establish the mid-nineteenth-century United States as illustrating Orlando Patterson's insight that Western ideas about freedom were "generated from the experience of slavery."[1] From "sex slavery" to "wage slavery" to "white slavery," slavery became what Barry Goldberg has called the "master metaphor" in the "language of social protest" and the *lingua franca* in which the women's, white labor, and abolitionist movements spoke to and past each other.[2]

But so pervasive was the slavery metaphor, and so balkanized is historical scholarship, that difficult issues surrounding its deployment remain unexplored. One such issue is timing. To regard, for example, the chattel slavery of Africans as unproblematically available as a touchstone against which to measure other oppression is to miss the accomplishment of mid-nineteenth-century antislavery movements, which helped to make it such a touchstone. As David Brion Davis writes, "For some two thousand years men thought of sin as a form of slavery. One day they would come to think of slavery as sin."[3] More-over, the view that there were many "slaveries"—to vice, to passion, to drink, to the bank, and in politics, for example—persisted well into the nineteenth century. For white workers and white women to contend so zealously that they were "no (or little) better off than slaves" was to enter into a dramatically changing and contested discourse that ultimately made chattel slavery into what Alice Felt Tyler called the "background for every crusade."[4]

In addition, our understanding of the slavery metaphor suffers from a tendency to study race, class, and gender separately (or, at best, in pairs) rather than in what Black feminist writers have called "their simultaneity."[5] Thus the very different grounds on which white, largely male, labor leaders and white, largely middle-class, women's rights spokespersons drew comparisons with Black slaves, the various conclusions that they drew from those comparisons, and their differing abilities to work in coalition with abolitionists—all go unexplored. The languages of social protest used by Black abolitionists and by militant working-class white women consistently fall through cracks in discussions of the slavery metaphor, examined neither for their own importance nor for what they can tell us about broader discourses and movements. When Davis writes that abolitionism was "always related to the need to legitimate free wage labor," we may wonder if he has fully considered whether such a claim could apply to Black abolitionist labor radicals such as Britain's Robert Wedderburn, to David Walker, to John Brown, to female labor abolitionists in the textile industry, or even to a Frederick Douglass.

This chapter centers instead on the positions taken by African American abolitionists in response to the claims that slavery described the positions of antebellum workers and of white women. It argues that Frederick Douglass and other such abolitionists displayed considerable tactical flexibility in sorting through such claims and in considering possibilities of coalition. In specifically rejecting wholesale application of the word *slavery* to the plight of white workers, Douglass and other ex-slave abolitionists did not simply argue that race was more important than class. Rather, they spoke (and moved much of the abolitionist movement, Black and white, to speak) of labor's condition on both sides of the color line, drawing close comparisons and showing why the abolition of slavery was the central labor question of the day.[6]

Considering more broadly the varied rhetoric of slavery and freedom also calls into question a tendency of existing scholarship to accept the premises of the discourse it describes. One excellent study of abolition and women's rights describes their symbiosis as "natural," whereas most treatments of white labor and abolition are inordinately sympathetic to the antebellum view that reformers, "trapped in a zero-sum game," were bound to give precedence to one cause over the other.[7] But if we set the "sex slavery" and the "wage slavery" metaphors alongside each other, a more complicated picture emerges: The seemingly natural affinity of movements promoted by the former metaphor, like the "inevitable" hostility promoted by the latter metaphor, is precisely what needs to be explained. Indeed, if we carry our examination of the trajectories of these languages of social protest through 1870 rather than stopping in 1860, the difficulties inherent in regarding any coalitions as "natural" emerge clearly, as abolitionist-feminist alliances fall apart and as former abolitionists lend significant support to radical labor movements.[8]

To initiate a discussion of what a "simultaneous" consideration of the slavery metaphor across lines of gender, race, and class might mean for our historical understanding of visions of freedom; of how those visions are related to the terms of labor, to white terror, and to party politics; and of the dynamics of coalition among the oppressed, I would like to begin modestly. This chapter turns on an examination of several moments involving Frederick Douglass, using each as a point of departure to broader issues. It may be true that comparison of other oppressions with chattel slavery, whether that comparison involved the wage system or conventional marriage, necessarily "diluted the charge that Negro slavery in the South was a system of exceptional and intolerable oppression."[9] However, the *logic* of discourse was not all that was at issue, and for a variety of reasons, labor reformers' use of the slavery metaphor sparked explosive opposition from abolitionists, whereas use of the same metaphor by women's rights advocates did not always do so. What follows is an attempt to survey and account for the various patterns of resistance and accommodation to the slavery metaphor by Douglass and other abolitionists. It seeks to locate those patterns only partly in the idealization of free wage labor by abolitionists. Opposition to slavery, and the need to build effective coalitions and arguments against it, undergirded both the questioning and the toleration of use of the slavery metaphor. That opposition was most insistently expressed and most effectively organized and articulated by African Americans, especially former slaves. Their strategies and arguments consistently bespoke a knowledge of the slave as worker.

Douglass, Abolition, and the Challenge to "Wage Slavery" Metaphors

In 1846, on an extended speaking tour in Britain, Frederick Douglass had substantial contact with Chartist radicals—masters in the use of the language of political slavery, and to some extent wage slavery, to describe the plight of the British masses. In a marvelous account that flirts with the idea of a "natural" but tragically missed connection between labor radicals and abolitionists, Douglass's biographer William McFeely details the patterns and limits of contacts between Douglass and the Chartists. In the course of this discussion, McFeely pauses to make the vitally important observation that in the corpus of Douglass's writings and speeches, the "metaphoric" use of slavery is largely absent. Indeed, after Douglass's bitter 1845 comparison of the fawning "slaves" of political parties with plantation slaves who curried favor from overseers and masters, such rhetoric is almost wholly absent from his writing.[10]

This silence was not Douglass's alone. Although free Blacks in the North were, by 1840, among the ranks of those denied the republican liberty of political participation, African American protests seldom employed the slavery metaphor without carefully circumscribing it to describe this denial. In the appeal for political rights in the "Address of the New York State Convention to Their Colored Fellow Citizens," for example, the goal was to avoid "political slavery" by building on the fact of having been "relieved" from "chains and slavery," to continue progress to the "exalted privileges of a freeman," although the document briefly referred to Black New Yorkers as "political slaves". A similar 1848 appeal in Pennsylvania emphasized that "we are not slaves," as it framed the struggle historically: "Our fathers sought personal freedom—we now contend for political freedom." In an 1855 letter to Douglass, the abolitionist Uriah Boston went so far as to provide an annotated list of the free Blacks' advantages over slaves. Although the idea that free Blacks were often only "nominally" so ran through the antebellum African American state convention movement and early Black nationalism, the slavery metaphor appeared far less frequently than in women's movement and white labor movement literature.[11] Firm distinctions between enslavement and prejudice recurred. Douglass even argued at times that the "low condition" of free Blacks in the North ought to claim abolitionists' attention because it was used to argue against emancipation and thus stood as a "stumbling block [to] the slave's liberation."[12]

This care to portray southern slavery as *sui generis,* even while agitating against northern oppression, must be seen as part of an abolitionist strategy properly designed to make chattel slavery the focus of moral outrage. But it is likewise important to stress that Black abolitionists, and especially runaway slaves who became abolitionists, occupied positions that enabled them to contribute to the shaping of such a strategy most forcefully. C. L. R. James's characterization of such figures as the "self-expressive presence ... embodying in their persons the nationally traumatic experience of bondage and freedom [without whom] antislavery would have been a sentiment only,"[13] captures much. It suggests the monumental import, as matter of fact and as political statement, of a Frederick Douglass regarding his life as being divided into two distinct parts. In one he "experienced slavery;" in the other he became a "part of this living, breathing world."[14]

The remarkable 1850 "Letter to the American Slaves from Those Who Have Fled from American Slavery" made the same point more self-consciously. Slavery, its authors wrote in terms that find echoes in recent scholarship, was not just death but the experience of being "killed all the day long." It stood as "the curse of curses, the robbery of robberies, and the crime of crimes." The fact that, especially after 1850, runaways necessarily feared capture and return to slavery sometimes made for a feeling, as Harriet Jacobs put it, of being still a "slave" in the North. But such realities, as well as the reality of racial discrimination in the North, also made all the more impressive and vital the more common drawing of a sharp distinction between Southern bondage and the Northern "liability to be seized and treated as slaves."[15]

In July of 1843, John A. Collins, a white advocate of land redistribution and utopian socialism who was the general agent of the American Anti-Slavery Society (AASS), scheduled an "antiproperty" meeting in Syracuse at the same time that Douglass, Abby Kelley, and Charles Lenox Remond were to speak at an abolitionist gathering. When challenged, Collins agreed to appear at the abolition event and cancel the antiproperty one. But what he said at the meeting distanced him from Remond and Douglass. Collins "quickly turned the audience's attention from the 3,000,000 of his countrymen held in slavery to the 800,000,000 people worldwide whom he described as living with the evils deriving from property." Abolition, in this view, was "a mere dabbling with effects." Remond, who just two years before had collaborated with Collins and Irish activists in drawing up an ambitious address designed to win Irish Americans to abolitionism, responded to the 1843 events by furiously reasserting the primacy of the evil of chattel slavery. Douglass more coolly pledged to leave the projected tour on which he and Collins were to speak under AASS auspices, if Collins were not prevented from repeating his performance. As they waited for support from the AASS leadership in Boston, Douglass and Remond showed signs of implementing such a boycott, attending the National Convention of Colored Citizens, not a scheduled AASS convention, in Buffalo. The national leadership, after threatening to dock Douglass's pay, ultimately but hesitantly did side with Douglass and Remond, removing the unrepentant Collins as general agent.[16]

The Douglass-Collins conflict was an early exchange in an increasingly fierce battle. In the middle and later 1840s, labor and land reformers attempted to show that landlessness and wage labor amounted to a "slavery" as vile as, and more pervasive than, southern slavery. Abolitionists fiercely rejected "metaphoric uses" of slavery in such ways. The term white slavery, and labor reform contentions that at most a "shade" of difference separated it from chattel slavery, had existed in the United States since the 1830s; William Lloyd Garrison had unsympathetically parried charges of abolitionist insensitivity to the white poor's plight during his 1840 trip to Britain for the World's Anti-Slavery Convention. "Have We No White Slaves?" read one leaflet he was handed there.[17] But the initial U.S. clash leading to an open rupture between abolitionists and those who styled themselves as opponents of "all slavery" had Douglass and Collins at its center. By 1847 Garrison was publishing words reflecting the "Down with all slavery, both chattel and wages" position in his abolitionist publication the *Liberator*. However, they appeared only in its "Refuge of Oppression" column, which sourly reprinted proslavery propaganda. However strenuously such reformers as George Henry Evans, William West, and Horace Greeley insisted that they did not "hate chattel slavery less [but] wages slavery more," abolitionists insisted otherwise.[18]

The major exceptions—cases in which Douglass and fellow abolitionists suggested that they might see white laboring people as being in a state of semislavery—lay on the other side of the Atlantic. Wendell Phillips, for example, held out the possibility that political powerlessness and driven work made some British workers unfree. But in his case and that of others, when lack of freedom within aristocratic nations was admitted, it was usually in the context of making the point that white American workers, enfranchised and mobile, could not be considered enslaved.[19] Reflections on the oppression of increasingly landless, politically disempowered, and colonized Ireland fit this pattern. In an antebellum autobiography, Douglass recounted a visit to Ireland in which the sorrowful music he heard convinced him that Irish peasants and American slaves were trapped inside the same "wail." He credited a speech on "Catholic emancipation" in Ireland, which he had read while he was still a slave in Baltimore, with giving a "tongue" to his antislavery dreams. In attempting to recruit support for abolitionism in Ireland and among Irish Americans (with considerable success in the former case and little in the latter), abolitionists preached a double "repeal": that of U.S. slavery and that of British oppression in Ireland. In an 1846 letter to Garrison, Douglass wrote of his need, as a person "identified with one class of outraged, oppressed and enslaved people," to speak out against the "misery and wretchedness of the Irish people."[20]

In praising the 1848 risings in Europe, Douglass singled out "Ireland, ever chafing under oppressive rule," for its heroic determination to "be free or die." After the Civil War, with the need to placate British antislavery opinion no longer in force, Douglass was even more emphatic, welcoming the jeering of the "besotted" English royal family on tour in Ireland as "a very natural and genuine exhibition of the feelings of the Irish people" reacting to the "oppression and despotism" of the English government. Writing at a time when the land question was especially posed in the American South as well as in Ireland, Douglass skewered British reformers who had taken "safe and harmless pleasure" in agitating for abolition while ignoring Ireland. He singled out for praise the Irish revolutionary Jeremiah O'Donovan Rossa, connecting Rossa's exploits with those of the anti-British rebels who mounted the Sepoy insurrection in India from 1857 to 1859 and the Gordon conspiracy in Jamaica in 1865.[21]

Nonetheless, Douglass and other abolitionists stopped well short of characterizing British oppression of Ireland as enslavement, although the analogy between such oppression and that of free Blacks in the United States did have its appeal. After such prolabor papers as the *Voice of Industry* counted Irish famine deaths as proof that wage slavery caused greater horrors than Black slavery, and after recruitment of Irish Americans to abolition had proved a failure, Douglass was firm in his warning against loose comparisons. "The Irishman is poor," he reasoned in 1850, "but he is not a slave. He is still the master of his own body." The Irish multitude could assemble, press grievances, write, speak, and emigrate. American slavery, that "grand aggregation of human horrors," rendered its victims mute, the "silent dead." The escaped slave Harriet Jacobs added, "I would ten thousand times rather that my children should be the half-starved paupers of Ireland than . . . the most pampered among the slaves of America."[22]

Accounting for the often splendid rage that energized abolitionist reaction to agitation using the term *white slavery* is made difficult by the consistent expressions of common ground by enemies of chattel slavery and those who extended the metaphor to white labor. Douglass termed land reform a "great project," for example, and responded to pleas from supporters in a factory town that he pay more attention to poverty among whites by declaring deep sympathy for their cause.[23] He specifically lauded workers' mobilizations during the 1848 revolutionary upsurge in France, and at times he verged on proclaiming what the historian Waldo Martin has called a "utopian, quasi-Marxist unity" of Black and white workers. Phillips meanwhile insisted that "wages slavery [and] white slavery would be utterly unintelligible" to a typical audience of laboring people. But he added that "crowded cities" and "manufacturing towns" provided some exceptions and that the absence of women's rights especially burdened women workers. Garrison signed an 1858 letter of sympathy to a radical labor meeting with the salutation "Yours to break every yoke."[24]

Abolitionists, and especially Black abolitionists, did not deny the possibility of white slavery but rather searched for literal instances of it (for example, in the history of "Saxon slavery" and in much-debated contemporary southern cases in which whites claimed that they had been racially redefined and kidnapped into chattel slavery) that undermined complacency about certain races being "fit" for slavery. Political slavery fostered by the "slave power" and the degradation of slaveholding women and nonslaveholding poor whites in the South were evoked in abolitionist writing well before their use by the Republican party. But such "white slavery" did not rest on wage labor.[25]

Conversely, land and labor reformers often avowed a hatred of slavery. Indeed, recent scholars such as Eric Foner and Alan Dawley have found in the very "rhetoric of wage slavery" evidence of a critique of all slavery and even an "identification" of free workers with slaves. In the British case, appeals to and by the working class often turned on the inattention of some abolitionists to the problems of workers domestically. However, as Seymour Drescher and others have shown, there were also deep connections, at the levels of discourse and mutual support, between labor and abolitionist mobilizations.[26] Some who used the white slavery metaphor, especially in areas with large numbers of organized women workers, took considerable care to specify that "chattel slavery is the worst degree of slavery" though "far from the only one." The *Voice of Industry,* the labor paper of the Lowell factory women and others, printed poems in homage to Garrison and careful analyses of the unsurpassed "depth of slavery" suffered by Douglass and his fellow slaves, alongside contentions that abolitionists needed to reserve at least "a tear" for white slaves. The great shoe strike at Lynn in 1860 was fought under the banner AMERICAN LADIES WILL NOT BE SLAVES, but a worker at a strike meeting there maintained, "We know we are not a quarter as bad off as the slaves of the South," who could not vote, complain, or strike.[27] Urban artisans participated actively, out of proportion to their number in the population, in supporting abolition campaigns, although their unions did not. Moreover, large sectors of the land reform and abolitionist movements did join eventually in political coalition under the Republican banner.[28]

Indeed, so great are the overlaps between labor reform and abolition that we might well wonder why the two movements did not amicably agree to view the wage slavery metaphor, as some modern scholars have, as a "rhetorical device" not to be taken literally in any case. Why did the 1845 hopes of the radical reformers at *The Harbinger* that the "Land and Labor Reform movements" and the "general Anti-Slavery movement" would come to see themselves as one so consistently go unrealized amid contention over the slavery metaphor?[29]

A key to the abolitionist opposition to wage/white slavery metaphors has already been suggested. It lies in the insistence of Black leaders, often escaped slaves or the children of runaways, that the line between slavery and wage labor—a difference central to their own life experiences—be kept distinct. The Douglass-Remond-Collins episode illustrates a broader tendency for Black abolitionists to criticize forcefully the extension of discourse regarding chattel slavery to other forms of economic oppression. When militants from Douglass to William Wells Brown directly challenged such metaphors—at times by advertising the job vacancy created by their having fled slavery and asking if any white workers wanted to fill the position—they functioned not just generically as abolitionists intervening in an important debate but also specifically as Black ex-slave abolitionists reflecting on their own and their families' life histories. Often their experience was transatlantic; the daring runaway William Craft could report that he never met a poor person in Britain who "did not resent it as an insult" when his or her circumstances and those of American slaves were compared.[30]

The land and labor reformers' penchant for reporting their own life histories also complicated matters. George Henry Evans and Horace Greeley, the most prominent such reformers, openly described their evolution from a focused opposition to Black slavery to the realization that many slaveries needed to be fought. They, and others, often added plainly that this realization made chattel slavery a less pressing issue. Indeed, they insisted that the allegedly more radical reforms they championed had to precede abolition in time. Lacking such prior changes, abolitionism was mere "substitutionism." Emancipation would leave the Black southerner as "a slave still, though with the title and cares of a freeman" and as "a great loser by such a change." Evans opposed "the slavery of property" and "the slavery of the lash," but he and his followers were certain that the former would have to end first. They even held that land reform would set an egalitarian example for slaveowners to follow.[31] Liquidation of the struggle for the immediate abolition of slavery was thus not just an abolitionist charge but was often the stated policy of labor and land reformers. On both sides, issues of timing and priority were openly debated. To regard, as Bernard Mandel does, Evans and his followers as "in favor of emancipation" but as adopting "tactics which required the subordination of the slavery question to the labor question" is to see the abstract position that land reformers championed and to miss the fact that the implications of their position were anything but abstract.[32]

The forceful abolitionist rejection of the wage/white slavery metaphor also grew out of a history and a context in which calling white workers in the North slaves was promoted not only by those who opposed "all slavery" but also by those who supported southern slavery. It was not merely that proslavery southerners, including such very visible figures as John C. Calhoun, James Hammond, and George Fitzhugh, found northern workers utterly degraded, but also that proslavery northerners, including such labor reformers as Ely Moore, Theophilus Fisk, and Mike Walsh, did likewise.[33] The inability of opponents of "all slavery" to separate themselves from supporters of southern slavery deepened abolitionist suspicions of the idea of white slavery. It was not just that an Evans and a Walsh shared rhetorical habits but also that northern groups decrying all slavery often hosted proslavery advocates and at times entered into political alliances with them. That the record of support for abolition by labor groups institutionally was spotty and that trade union racism against Black workers was egregious also undermined claims of labor's universal opposition to oppression.[34]

The association of those who avowedly employed the slavery metaphor to attack all forms of oppression with those who did so to deflect attacks on chattel slavery did more than raise questions regarding hypocrisy, however. In republican America, working men and women did not relish being termed slaves or being called females "without virtue" by outsiders, even though they themselves and their leaders might use such rhetoric.[35] Thus abolitionists who rejected the white slavery metaphor did not simply refuse to see the world as workers saw it. Douglass, after all, practiced his abolitionist appeals early on by trying various "whispered" arguments out on white workers. He carefully crafted appeals to the republican pride and the aspirations of such workers, who were perhaps more eager to hear of their distance from slavery than of their proximity to it. Those who rejected the white slavery metaphor were particularly well positioned to argue in defense of the reputation of white workers against proslavery southerners whose disdain for degraded factory women and "greasy mechanics" was clear.[36]

Finally, the division between abolitionists and those opposing "white slavery" was ensured by the grounds on which labor and land reformers pressed comparisons designed to make the slavery metaphor plausible. Both of the two major comparisons made by opponents of "white slavery" flew fully in the face of abolitionist ideas, at the levels of facts and values. The case for "white slavery" was first of all narrowly materialistic. White workers in the North, it was argued (from decidedly partial evidence), worked harder, for longer hours, and at a higher rate of exploitation then did slaves. Sometimes the alleged evidence came anecdotally and rhymed: "The niggers have their tasks, and when done they may spree it, But the jers [journeymen] they were asked to work as long as they could see it." At other junctures, mathematical precision seemed possible, as in the contention that capital kept $9/11$ of the northern white worker's product and far less of the slave's. Abolitionist arguments, strongly made by Douglass, for the much greater efficiency of free labor, became grist for the "white slavery" mill; they could be flipped over to suggest proportionally more exploitation in the North. The most widely used analogy about working conditions held that the slave resembled the horse owned by one owner, who took care not to work the animal to death, whereas the free laborer was like a horse for hire, whose renters cared nothing about his or her welfare in the long run.[37]

It was not simply that such material comparisons were wrong, from an abolitionist point of view, but also that the narrow grounds for making these comparisons undercut the indictment of chattel slavery. Focusing on narrowly material concerns obscured the systematic terror of slavery, a theme that always framed abolitionist descriptions of bondage.[38] When labor reformers did stray beyond speculations about

the hours and conditions of work and the return on labor, they curiously emphasized that slaves enjoyed the relative advantage of "mutual
dependence" in their relationship to owners. According to this fully
unrepublican distinction, slavery was preferable because it provided
"protection," whereas wage labor did not. Here again, it was not just
conclusions that were at issue, but also the labor reformers' adoption of
a terrain of comparison that did not sharpen attacks on "all slavery"
but instead mitigated indictments of chattel slavery.[39] In its essentials,
the extension of the slavery metaphor to white labor found its premises in the same view of slavery that was current in another venue
in which white workers have been said to "identify" with slaves: the
minstrel stage.[40]

Abolitionism, Feminism and the Limits of "Sex Slavery"

In 1848 Douglass stood up for women's rights at the first national convention held in the United States on that subject. Reportedly the only
African American man in attendance—no Black women participated—
Douglass was also, according to Eleanor Flexner, the first and for a
time the most significant male leader to support Elizabeth Cady Stanton's insistence that the Seneca Falls gathering stand unequivocally for
women's suffrage.[41] During the twenty years before the Black aboli-
tionist/women's rights alliance fell apart during Reconstruction debates
over women's suffrage and constitutional change, Douglass enjoyed a
deserved reputation as a leading male advocate of women's rights. If he
occasionally wavered on women's property rights, he did not do so on
the franchise. If he once suggested that earlier abolitionist splits over
women's rights amounted to destructive contention over a "side issue,"
he also placed blame for the split squarely on abolitionists who made
the "judgment [that] the American slave system, with all its concom-
mitant horrors, is less to be deplored" than public reform activities by
women.[42]

Douglass's feminism has drawn considerable attention from historians as a living embodiment of the historical connection between abolition and women's rights. That connection is so well known that it is not
surprising that it is at times seen as "natural." But when viewed in comparison to Douglass's (and other abolitionists') reaction to white labor
reformers' use of the slavery metaphor, Douglass's position seems more
in need of historical explanation. Although he rose to combat notions
of the "white slavery" of workers, he abstained from condemning the
usage of "sex slavery" metaphors by women's rights campaigners.

Such usages pervaded reform discourse quite as insistently as did land and labor reformers' fixation on the "slavery" of some white workers. From very early in abolitionism, when the Grimké sisters signed their letters "Thy sister in the bonds of women and the slave," and when Margaret Fuller decried as akin to slavery "even well-meant restrictions" placed on women by men, women's rights leaders frequently used comparisons with chattel slavery to describe their oppression. As Blanche Glassman Hersh observes, the "woman and slave" comparison was both an "effective rhetorical device" and a favorite one. Susan B. Anthony found a wife "the slave of the man she marries." Taking of a husband's name was seen as akin to the fastening of masters' names onto slaves.[43] Stanton's eloquent defense of a mother who took her child away from an abusive husband challenged abolitionist men to see the case as like the defense of runaway slaves. To Sarah Grimké, "the very being of a woman, like that of a slave, is absorbed in her master." For Stanton, the "free" woman resembled "the slave on the Southern plantation" in that she could "own nothing, sell nothing."[44]

The comparison of white women with slaves was surely open to charges of overstatement, just as the white slavery metaphor was.[45] Nonetheless, the former metaphor thrived. It could explain why men opposed women's rights. Like slaveowners, they could not see their own roles as oppressors. It could explain why, as Douglass put it, "women have more and stronger prejudices" against women's rights than men. Like slaves, such white women allegedly had "been oppressed so long that [they] cannot appreciate the blessings of Liberty." Such a woman, as Lucretia Mott held, had learned the slave's lessons in subservience: "she hugs her chains."[46]

Douglass registered no objection to the slavery metaphor when white women's rights advocates applied it to themselves. It is true that during the late 1830s and early 1840s, bitter debates over women's rights and over women's speaking to "promiscuous audiences" rocked abolition and called into question Angelina Grimké's contention that "the rights of the slave [and] woman blend like the colors of the rainbow." Indeed, Grimké's husband, the militant abolitionist Theodore Weld, sharply warned against mixing the "lesser work" of women's rights with the "greater work" of abolition. But after these early clashes, as women's rights advocates elaborated the slavery metaphor in the 1840s and 1850s, abolitionists could rarely be found insisting on giving priority to one of the two struggles. Despite a considerable record of exclusion and segregation of Black women by white feminists, and notwithstanding biting criticism from Sojourner Truth and others regarding the racial and class blindnesses of the women's movement, the slavery metaphor went increasingly unchallenged by abolitionists when it was applied to white women. This was true even though, as Kristin Hoganson's important work shows, abolitionist appeals to conventional gender roles in indicting slavery existed in considerable tension with feminist attempts to challenge such roles among whites in the North. To understand why no sharp abolitionist opposition to the idea of "sex slavery" arose is to see how differently the metaphor was employed by women's rights advocates than by labor reformers and to appreciate how different were the relations of the two reform movements to abolitionism.[47]

A first major contrast between women's rights usage and labor reform usage of the slavery metaphor lay in context. Whereas labor reformers lacked a substantial record of ongoing practical activity on behalf of slaves, the women's rights movement grew in large part out of abolition. This historical reality, as Hersh shows, was as much a part of the logic of woman/slave metaphors as any specific set of comparisons.[48] Much early argument for the extension of women's rights rested squarely on recognizing and enhancing their activities as fighters against slavery. In *History of the Condition of Women,* Lydia Maria Child used the same methods and much of the same material as in her earlier comparative studies in *Appeal in Favor of That Class of Americans Called Africans.* Indeed, as Carolyn Karcher argues in her stirring biography of Child, the antiracist agenda of *History of the Condition of Women* remained more explicit than the feminist one.[49] Discussion of white women's oppression often unfolded alongside, not instead of, detailing of the horrors experienced by slave women. Meanwhile, as Nancy Hewitt reminds us, a substantial number of female abolitionists eschewed advocacy of women's rights altogether and did not press comparisons between slaves and themselves.[50]

At times, women's rights advocates bragged, as labor reformers did not, of being "more fully identified with the slave," not just of being in a similar plight.[51] Rarely, but significantly, they also argued for affinities between their own oppression and that of free Blacks, as did Stanton when she pronounced "skin and sex" the "scarlet letters" of the antebellum United States. Nor, of course, did alliances with proslavery political forces undermine women's rights organizations' usage of the slavery metaphor as they did in the case of labor reformers. Not only did women bring no voting strength to the table, but proslavery ideologues clearly tied the defense of patriarchy with their defense of slavery.

Proslavery attacks on women's rights, seen as a symptom of northern degeneracy, were at times repaid in kind. Thus when women's magazine editor Jane Grey Swisshelm forcefully opposed the Fugitive Slave Law, the proslavery editor George D. Prentice accused her of being wrong on slavery and branded her as "a man for her outspoken views." Swisshelm began her reply with

> Perhaps you have been busy
> Horsewhipping Sal or Lizzie
> Stealing some poor man's baby
> Selling its mother, maybe.[52]

The content and the terrain of comparisons employed by women in using the slavery metaphor also mattered greatly. Unlike white labor reformers, who often convinced themselves that their own oppression was more harsh than that of slaves, feminists nearly always acknowledged significant differences. Women, especially wives, were degraded (all emphasis is my own) "*almost* to the level of the slave," were in "*about* the same legal position [as] the slave," and suffered disabilities "*not very unlike* the slave laws of Louisiana." Women's legal status was "pathetically *suggestive*" of slavery. When Lucy Stone's use of the slave metaphor to describe married white women once underwent mild challenge, she immediately allowed that chattel slavery "is a still lower depth."[53]

Thus, in the use of slavery as a metaphor by women's rights advocates, there was far less to challenge the hard-won insights of a Douglass into the differences between chattel slavery and other forms of oppression than there was in the rhetoric of those who discussed "white slavery." Nor did women's rights discourse include anything like the labor reformers' strong implication that abolition was a cause necessarily fated to wait until other "slaveries" ended before it could be addressed.

Finally, the terrain on which women's rights advocates claimed comparability to chattel slavery was far more compatible with abolitionist appeals than were the arguments developed by land and labor reformers. This was largely because feminists and abolitionists both idealized what C. B. McPherson has called "possessive individualism," whereas land reformers idealized the individual's possessions. The inability of white women and of slaves to possess and control their individual labor, wages, property, and bodies made possessive individualism's advocacy of such control powerfully appealing to abolitionists and to women's rights advocates. The parallels between laws regarding slavery and those regarding married white women's property were substantial. In evoking the slavery metaphor, the advocates of women's rights consistently addressed such parallels. But these comparisons, unlike those made by land and labor reformers, utterly eschewed the construction of ersatz measures of relative exploitation. Indeed, when connections to slavery were made, there was little specific discussion of the labor, as opposed to the property, of married white women. Nor was the alleged protection of ill, disabled, and aged slaves advanced as evidence that slaves were like, or even better treated than, married white women. Abolitionists and women's rights supporters both sought to disarm such references to patriarchal beneficence. In short, the land and labor reformers wanted the slavery metaphor to concentrate on paternalist protection and on bloodless considerations of rates of return on labor. The feminist writers, by contrast, left intact the abolitionists' insistence that stark realities of property and terror set slavery apart from free labor.[54]

On the issue of terror, the women's rights argument accommodated abolitionism in a particularly interesting and intricate way. As a number of feminist scholars have shown, the antebellum white women's movement tended not to make control over the physical bodies and the sexuality of married white women a public issue, although its leaders at times privately insisted on the centrality of just such control to women's freedom. This silence, and at times self-censorship, left much space in women's rights discourse for the slave woman's imperiled body to stand in for consideration of white women's vulnerability to sexual coercion and terror. Consider, for example, S. E. P.'s remarkable 1839 poem "Appropriate Sphere of Woman," published in the *Liberator:*

> Tell me not of Woman's station,
> Tell me not we leave our "sphere,"
> When we urge by mild persuasion,
> Rights to every woman dear.
> When her back is stained and gory,
> When her tears in anguish flow,
> Shall we then not heed her story—
> Her sad tale of grief and wo?
> When her tend'rest ties are riven,
> For the sordid love of gold;
> And her children from her driven,
> "Human chattels" to be sold . . .

Evoking the slavery metaphor and then concentrating solely on the bodies of slave women, feminists made, and refused to give flesh to, a critical comparison. Thus Karen Sanchez-Eppler observes that abolitionist-feminist literature could "emphasize the similarities in the condition of women and slaves" even as its frequent use of the image of "the sexually exploited female slave betray[ed] an opposing desire to deny any share in this vulnerability."[55] Such psychological projection rightly has been read as evidence of a desire to avoid speaking, if not thinking, directly about the politically and personally difficult issue of sexual terror, but it may also have reflected a desire to avoid making claims that would have rendered the slavery metaphor explicit and put abolitionist-feminist cooperation at risk. In any case, the concentration of attention on the bodies of *slave* women in white feminist literature raised issues of slavery and terror that labor reformers' use of the slavery metaphor thoroughly suppressed.

The Burden of Slavery and the Roots of Division

This close consideration of the differences between labor reform and women's rights where the slavery metaphor is concerned has emphasized putting the discourse of each movement into counterpoint with abolitionism, and particularly with the African American abolitionism of Frederick Douglass. It suggests that although the abolitionists claimed chattel slavery as the greatest American evil, they did not reject out of hand all other claims of "enslavement." From the plight of the Irish to women's rights, Douglass and his colleagues could accommodate limited use of the slavery metaphor, if doing so promised to serve the interests of political coalition and if the particulars of the comparison did not vitiate the argument against slavery and/or cast abolition as a secondary reform that must wait its turn behind "more fundamental" ones. The existence of ongoing coalitions, or their absence, could also structure the ways in which the slavery metaphor was articulated, was tolerated, and was attacked. The stark distinction between the abolitionists' acceptance of the slavery metaphor as used by women's rights advocates and their fierce opposition to its use by land and labor reformers also suggests that some coalitions were more viable than others while slavery existed in a society taking off toward industrial capitalist expansion. Because both slavery and patriarchy violated the sanctity of property in one's own person, the meshing of abolitionist and women's rights arguments was far less difficult than making abolitionism square with labor reform ideas.

Nonetheless, this comparison of interactions between abolitionism and land reform and between abolitionism and women's rights around the slavery metaphor does not support the extension to the antebellum

United States of David Brion Davis's arguments concerning antislavery's contributions to the legitimation of wage labor. To argue that abolition and women's rights could find common ground because they were both bourgeois reform initiatives that validated capitalist labor relations misses the mark in several ways. The women's rights movement, in its evocations of the slavery metaphor and elsewhere, spoke little of the question of wage labor, and it was by no means clear in 1850 that the logic of capitalist social relations could successfully undergird even limited appeals for women's freedom. More critically, if we take Douglass (rather than an atypical capitalist reformer such as Lewis Tappan) as central to abolitionism, it becomes properly difficult to suppose that idealizing the wage relationship formed any significant part of the core of the abolitionist political project. Certainly, Douglass could be found singing the praises of "free" wage labor in the North. But he did so largely in response to proslavery, labor reform, and minstrel arguments that held chattel slavery to be less onerous and perilous than free labor. His goal, and that of abolitionists generally, was manifestly the ending of slavery, not the perpetuation of wage labor. When emancipation came, abolitionists often moved dramatically to positions critical of the wage system.[56]

The abolitionists' wholesale rejection of labor reformers' use of the slavery metaphor might, of course, be said to have had powerful consequences in legitimating wage labor, no matter what its strategic antislavery impetus. But one could easily counter that it was labor reform provocations and exaggerations in deploying the slavery metaphor that forced the abolitionists into strong defenses of wage labor. That the issue admits none but very highly subjective resolutions indicates how difficult it would have been to find an ideal middle position that effectively criticized wage labor while also acknowledging chattel slavery as the greater evil. No significant U.S. thinker or group managed to strike such a balance. The Black abolitionists most familiar with both systems, and the broader abolitionist movement that they profoundly shaped, could nurture some coalitions built on a rhetoric of shared "slavery," but not one structured around the notion that white workers were literally slaves.

The Pursuit of Whiteness

PROPERTY, TERROR, AND
NATIONAL EXPANSION, 1790–1860

Paul Gilroy, holding acerbically forth in the collection *Black British Cultural Studies,* warns that attempts to write in an interdisciplinary way about identity "can send the aspirant practitioners of cultural studies scuttling back toward the quieter sanctuaries of their old disciplinary affiliations, where the problems and potential pleasures of thinking through identity are less formidable and engaging." Behavior after the scuttling back, he adds, follows disciplinary lines: "Anthropologists utter sighs of relief, psychologists rub their hands together in glee, philosophers relax [and] literary critics look blank and perplexed. Historians remain silent."[1]

In discussing matters of identity, privilege, and the consolidation of the United States as a white nation, historians have been far less silent than Gilroy's model implies. The major review essays on what has lamentably been named "whiteness studies" consistently place social history at the center of a burgeoning multidisciplinary literature, citing the work of Alexander Saxton, Theodore Allen, and Noel Ignatiev, among others.[2] Most ambitious accounts of white identity by (in terms of formal departmental affiliations) nonhistorians, including those of Karen Brodkin, Susan Gubar, Eric Lott, and Michael Rogin, frame their material historically. Moreover, I will argue, a too often "lost" historical literature on American Indians, nation-building, and white identity anticipated many of the insights of more recent work and deserves rereading in the light of cultural studies.[3]

Nonetheless, tensions surround the place of history in investigations of white identity. Some theoretical work in the area lacks historical grounding and ignores or misconceives the emphasis on class relations that is common among historians of whiteness. Conversely, not a few historians of race disdain theory and view with suspicion inquiries into race and cultural representation more generally, regarding them as ethereal and frivolous. One goal of this chapter is therefore to expose an audience of historians to critical insights from those not formally or entirely in the history business. Implicit throughout, that agenda is made explicit at the outset in a prelude that brings together the writings of the legal analyst and critical race theorist Cheryl Harris and the American studies scholar Saidiya Hartman around the themes of property, happiness, and terror in the formation of white nationhood and white identity.[4] The main section of the chapter then uses a dramatic moment in the 1858 Lincoln-Douglas debates as a window through which to survey the strengths, weaknesses, and gaps in recent writings on whiteness, expansion, and terror in the early national and antebellum periods. In arguing that relatively neglected older studies offer promising approaches to deepen understanding of that moment in the Lincoln-Douglas confrontation, this section emphasizes the necessity of considering white racial formation in the context of a settler colonial nation, as well as a slaveholding one. Looking at the state of the art in studies of whiteness that cover the crucial first decades of the making of a white U.S. nation offers the further advantage of introducing key themes in the broader scholarship on white identity in a delimited and focused context.

White Pursuits: A Prelude

Political theorists tell us that when the founding fathers used the wonderful phrase *the pursuit of happiness,* some of the happiness seekers had in mind largely the pursuit of property. The fascinating connections between property and happiness hinge not only on the vocabulary of John Locke's political philosophy and its influence on American revolutionaries, but also on the ways in which both property and happiness found meaning in their relationship to whiteness and white privilege.[5] In some ways these relationships are familiar. Herman Melville's 1850 novel *White-Jacket,* the most extended antebellum exploration of the differences and affinities between white labor's "slavery" and racial slavery makes the jacket/skin of the sailor at the center of its plot a piece of property, an obsession, a protection, and a source of misery.

From Edmund Morgan's study of race and liberty in colonial Virginia to the recent work of the political philosopher Charles Mills, it has been clear that ideas of freedom for the mass of white males developed in tandem with notions and practices that ensured that those who were not white could not pursue happiness effectively in political, social, and economic realms.[6] What Mills calls a "racial contract" served as a fundamental part of the bourgeois social contract. "European humanism," Mills wryly observes, all too consistently "meant that only Europeans were human" and rewrote history as a struggle to extend both the property- and happiness-producing rights of Europeans and the hegemony of white, "civil" spaces over nonwhite, "wild" spaces.[7] The most sophisticated and celebrated bringing together of property and enjoyment as benefits of whiteness remains W. E. B. Du Bois's discussion of the financial as well as the "public and psychological" wages accruing to whites that appears in his *Black Reconstruction,* a study that undergirds much recent scholarship on whiteness.[8]

But even given that they draw on so rich a tradition, Cheryl Harris and Saidiya Hartman sharpen our understanding of whiteness, property, and happiness in startling ways. In her massive *Harvard Law Review* article "Whiteness as Property," Harris's deeply historical work far transcends the commonplace observation that whiteness has carried, and still carries, disproportionate access to property in the United States. She argues instead that whiteness has been so intimately tied to the right to own property that it has itself come to constitute a legally recognizable, usable, and cherished form of property *possessed by all whites*. The attempted reduction of Blacks, but not whites, to "objects of property" in slavery and the expropriation of Indian land via legal mechanisms that "established whiteness as prerequisite to the exercise of enforceable property rights" created, in Harris's view, an enduring set of expectations that whiteness had a value as property.[9]

In addition to its ability to ground whiteness both within and beyond binary Black-white dynamics, Harris's approach offers great insight into the complexity of the label *white*. Far from denying the existence and import of poverty among whites, Harris establishes the grounds on which poor whites became chained to both their poverty and their anticipation of property benefits as whites—often a bad check, but just as often the only one they had.[10] Harris specifically notes that whiteness fits legal definitions of property in that those categorized as white had the "right to use and enjoy" their racial position. She adds tellingly that "as whiteness is simultaneously an aspect of identity and a property interest, it is something that can both be experienced and deployed as a resource,"—that is, it has utility in both the pursuit of happiness and the pursuit of property and forms part of the connective tissue between the two.[11]

Hartman's cultural history originates at a point very near to Harris's legal/historical observations regarding whiteness, property, and enjoyment. Indeed, Hartman begins *Scenes of Subjection* with a long section of linked chapters titled "Formations of Terror and Enjoyment." In her specific discussion of "the property of enjoyment," she subtly connects the white pursuits of property and of happiness. Her excerpting of *Black's Law Dictionary* on what it means to "enjoy" drives home her (and Harris's) points dramatically: "to have, possess, and use with satisfaction; to occupy or have the benefit of . . . the exercise of a right, privilege or incorporeal hereditament. Comfort, consolation, ease, happiness, pleasure and satisfaction."[12] Holding that white "hereditament" created expectations that relations with Black people would create "delight" as well as wealth, Hartman "re-places" popular culture within economic structures, state policies, and practices of terror. Of blackface minstrelsy and melodrama, she writes, "The punitive pleasures yielded through figurative possession of blackness cannot be disentangled from the bodily politics of chattel slavery." She continues, "The terror of pleasure—that violence that undergirded the comic moment in minstrelsy—and the pleasure of terror—the force of evil that propelled the plot of melodrama and fascinated the spectator—filiated the coffle, the auction block, the popular stage, and plantation amusements in a scandalous equality."[13]

Hartman's study builds on a substantial African American tradition that regards terror and complicity in terror as the glue binding together those who think that they are white.[14] Hartman's contribution, among much else, is to capture the terror in what she calls "liberal" moments, such as Abraham Lincoln's chilling racialized reflections on what he called the "effect of condition on human happiness." As Lincoln observed twelve slaves on a steamboat, "'strung together like so many fish on a trot-line" and being separated from home and kin, his attention fell on fiddle playing, singing, dancing, and joking among the twelve. His conclusion bespeaks the ways in which, as Hartman puts it, "white self-reflection" used the supposed "elasticity of blackness . . . as a vehicle for exploring the human condition," expecting at once to know happiness and to come to terms with misery by looking on Blacks. After his description of the utterly inhuman conditions of the slaves, Lincoln ended by evoking the slaves' mirth and musing that God "renders the worst of the human condition tolerable, while He permits the best to be nothing but tolerable."[15]

If Harris's locating of whiteness *within* the very conception of property productively complicates attempts to arrive at a materialist account of race and class in the antebellum United States, Hartman's study demolishes to the surprisingly insistent recent attempts to rehabilitate minstrelsy and other racist entertainments. Going far beyond Eric Lott's useful insistence that both "love and theft" were involved in minstrel appropriations of African American music, David Grimsted and William Lhamon have argued that present-minded scholars have been so eager to brand such entertainments as racist that they have missed the real core of the stagecraft. For Grimsted that core was humor; for Lhamon, it was a subversive lumpenproletarian cultural exchange across the color line, "a racial project more radical even than abolitionism."[16] Hartman elaborates on the firm and wise position staked out by Alexander Saxton on this issue a quarter-century ago: "The ideological impact of minstrelsy was programmed by its conventional blackface form. There is no possibility of escaping this relationship because the greater the interest, talent, complexity and humanity embodied in its content, the most irresistible was the racist message of its form." *Scenes of Subjection* illustrates reasons for the irony Saxton identifies. At once about pleasure, humor, and property (Minstrel question: "Why is we niggas like a slave ship on de Coast of Africa?" Answer: "Because we both make money by taking off the negroes."), minstrelsy "reiterated racial subjection." The "love" on which blackface bodysnatching traded was, for Hartman, as terrifying as the "theft" its performance implemented. Furthermore, it was utterly inseparable from that theft. Both joined to constitute "the illusory integrity of whiteness." For reasons that Kalpana Seshadri-Crooks develops in her recent and rich psychoanalytic account of the dynamics of racial jokes, minstrel scenes of subjection and their punch lines required endless repetition. They could never quite exorcise the threat, subversive to both white pleasure and white supremacy, of being laughed at in ways that threatened to expose the lie of whiteness.[17]

Shouting White Men

If historical reenactors want to get it just right, reprises of the 1858 Lincoln-Douglas debates will need not only the eloquent starring principals but also a large cast of extras to swell the audience, whose belligerent interventions at Freeport were an anthem to a burgeoning white identity. Among the lines for Stephen A. Douglas's backers were "White men, white men," and the echoing "White, white." These eerie interventions, delivered at the Freeport debate amid Douglas's far-fetched but powerful denunciations of Lincoln as a race mixer alleged to have accepted advice from the African American abolitionist Frederick Douglass, gave voice to the popularity of white identity in the late antebellum United States.[18] In many ways, the recent and much celebrated historiography on whiteness between the Revolution and the Civil War effectively positions us to understand that shouting crowd and the ways in which Douglas (and Lincoln) played to it. The base of support for the Democratic party, in Illinois and in the national arena where Douglas's larger ambitions lay, depended on the incorporation of Irish and other immigrants as white voters. Ignatiev's *How the Irish Became White* shows why Douglas's insistence on moving beyond an Anglo-Saxon whiteness to posit a pan-white "American race" could resonate dramatically. The homosocial habit of affirming white maleness in public provides the subject matter for recent analyses of minstrelsy that go to the heart of how Douglas's auditors rehearsed their chants and knew their lines. The utility of white identity in forging cross-class alliances and in providing real and psychological payoffs to the poorest Douglas Democrats is central to the agenda of studies showing what it meant to be "not a slave" in an increasingly class-divided and proletarianized labor force.[19]

However, the reverberating shouts and the debates they punctuated also signal ways in which a focus on "whiteness studies" risks prematurely cutting off historical exchanges, leaving critical dimensions of the workings of race, property, and terror unexamined and encouraging neglect of classic older studies (and exciting new ones) when whiteness is investigated. The white noise at Freeport ought immediately to alert us to large gaps in even the best of the "whiteness studies" recently produced by historians of the nineteenth century. If cross-class alliances cemented by white consciousness are at issue, our knowledge of working-class motivations for joining such an alliance runs far ahead of what is known, even after James Brewer Stewart's intelligent opening up of the issue, about middle-class white identity. Whiteness among midwesterners, and among rural populations generally, is so understudied as to make any generalizations about Douglas's backers debious. As well as the process by which the Irish "became white" is understood—and even here some amendments are likely to be required in light of Catherine

Eagan's revisionist analysis of awareness of race in nineteenth-century Ireland and fascinating recent work on Irish immigrant men and women who in some ways resisted becoming white—studies of other immigrant groups are lacking.[20] German Americans are the largest and most interesting such group. Bruce Levine's able investigations of radical immigrant Germans and the growth of "black Dutch" participation in the antislavery cause heads a slim body of scholarship. German immigrants also surely found their way into the ranks of Douglas's militantly white Democrats.[21] That religious fissures conditioned differing stances among Germans only reminds us of another large gap: the absence of discussion of religious faith, particularly among antebellum Protestants, by historians of whiteness.[22]

As Dana Frank has eloquently shown, the new literature on white identity, especially among workers, overwhelmingly focuses on white male identity. Although this emphasis might superficially seem apt as we try to understand chanting white men, it leaves so much out as to imperil understanding even of the gender on which it concentrates. The chanters in Freeport responded specifically to Douglas's charge that the city had recently been sullied by Frederick Douglass's appearance in a "magnificent" carriage on which a "beautiful young [white] lady" sat while her mother "reclined" with Douglass inside. Although some opponents of Douglas in the crowd shouted, "What of it?" Lincoln took such appeals to white purity seriously. He fended them off by attempting to capture the race-mixing issue as his own, arguing that it was the spread of slavery that threatened to bring whites and Blacks together sexually in the Midwest. As my recent research on affinities and differences between the antebellum feminist metaphor of "sex slavery" and the (white) labor movement's metaphor of "wage slavery" shows, consideration of white women's identity throws relations between masculinity and property into new relief. Dana Nelson's *National Manhood: Capitalist Citizenship and the Imagined Fraternity of White Men,* which is discussed at the end of this chapter, squarely focuses on the study of white masculinity, but its subtle analysis crosses and recrosses gender lines, making it also the best account yet of white womanhood in the antebellum United States.[23]

Nonetheless, the need for gendered accounts that make white womanhood their central subject remains acute, especially because women's history of the early national and antebellum periods brilliantly links gender, property, and citizenship in ways that cry out for comparison with and connection to the property of whiteness. Indeed, Nancy Isenberg grounds her *Sex and Citizenship in Antebellum America* in the idea that a "disinvestment" of women's rights to property and liberty was central to nation-building in the United States. Jeanne Boydston's remarkable *Home and Work* reminds us that whiteness became a much more common male public performance precisely in the context of a widening and deeply gendered ideological split between the private and the public. Moreover, this split denied the fact that white women's labor was critically and increasingly tied to the market economy. Even as white masculine identity could be used to paper over contradictions between the "free labor" ideology of economic independence and the reality of increasing proletarianization, white true womanhood could shore up perceptions of women's isolation from the world of power and money.[24]

Superb recent studies of slavery and white womanhood in the South by Martha Hodes, Ariela Gross, Nell Painter, and others suggest that we are poised for a sweeping new interpretation of race and gender, one that will also draw on Karen Sanchez-Eppler's important *Touching Liberty*. The latter study includes telling observations on terror, arguing that antebellum women's rights advocates used narratives regarding slave women's bodies as a means to both broach and evade the ways in which sexual violence touched their own bodies. Appropriately enough, Cheryl Harris has initiated the synthetic investigations so badly needed by considering whiteness and gender within both systems of production and system of reproduction in her recent and provocative "Finding Sojourner's Truth."[25]

White Race, Power, and Representation

Stephen A. Douglas's performance in debating Lincoln suggests critical issues much in need of exploration by historians of whiteness who emphasize the roles of property and of terror in making race. Douglas characterized the overwhelmingly white and avowedly white supremacist state of Illinois in terms of a racial spectrum. The Lincoln-Douglas debates toured the state, whose political/racial geography Douglas summed up as follows: ". . . pretty black in the north end of the state, about the center it is pretty good mulatto and it is almost white when you get down to Egypt [southern Illinois]."[26] In his positing of an imperiled "white politics" (and of "black" deviations from it) even in areas nearly all white, Douglas raises a particularly vexed issue: the extent to which white identity grew in face-to-face contact with people of color (crudely, in the realm of social history) or in the context of representation and symbolism (crudely, in the realms of cultural theory and cultural history). Because property and terror so closely imply power relationships, it is tempting to think that sites where such power was exercised, or resisted, most immediately ought to be the focus of the research. Rich accounts that attend more closely to the labor process and to race relations in neighborhoods underline the force of calls for a finely grained social history of whiteness. Studies, such as those by James Brewer Stewart, Lois E. Horton, and Joanne Pope Melish, that are well grounded in the histories of free Blacks in the North likewise demonstrate the value of textured scholarship that crosses the color line. So too do fine recent inquiries, including Lacy K. Ford's work, regarding race and whiteness in the South, an oddly underemphasized site of white racial formation where opportunities for face-to-face transracial contacts were most extensive.[27]

Given the excellence of such scholarship and the common-sense association of property and of terror with direct social experience, the assumption that white identity is always best studied as the local product of immediate social relations across racial lines has its appeal. However, such an assumption can generate quite naïve positions, which neglect Saidiya Hartman's reminders about the "filiation" of slavery, discrimination, and cultural representations of race. As Douglas and his chorus of supporters demonstrated, white racial identity could function, largely in the absence of people of color, to position white voters in national, partly race-based political coalitions; could shore up exclusionary efforts in the face of real and perceived threats of in-migration of those not categorized as white; and could produce pleasure as well as unity. As Stuart Hall has forcefully shown, posing representations of race as outside of and opposed to concrete lived experience clarifies little. If starkly and consistently contradicted by day-to-day direct experiences, racist representations could not in the end survive intact. But in the shorter run, there was ample space for patterns of racist representation to structure how such interactions would unfold and would be understood.[28]

Two very recent works make especially noteworthy and materially grounded assaults on questions involving race, representation, and day-to-day interactions. Joanne Pope Melish's *Disowning Slavery: Gradual Emancipation and "Race" in New England, 1780–1860* argues against locating white identity in the region mainly in the context of Yankees' contemplation of the slave South. The New England experience of slaveholding, and of a gradual, oppressive emancipation designed to serve the interests of order and property among whites, mattered greatly in racial

formation, according to Melish. However, in restoring this social experience to the important position it deserves in white racial formation in
the Northeast, Melish evokes great complexity. She shows that it was
not just the history of New England slavery that influenced white identity but also the process by which slavery was forgotten ("disowned")
and that a vision of a "free white republic" without significant African
American presence was propagated in various cultural and political
forums. Melish's apt discussion of the fascination with the terror accompanying the enslavement of whites in the Barbary States in the 1780s
and 1790s details an important chapter in the prehistory of ideas about
"white slavery," a chapter based on the direct social experience of a relatively tiny number of victims.[29]

John Kuo Wei Tchen's monumental *New York before Chinatown:
Orientalism and the Shaping of American Culture, 1776–1882* also
serves as a model of a healthy refusal to imagine a choice between experience and representation in accounting for white racial formation. In
his early chapters Tchen fleshes out a U.S.-based orientalism honed in
the presence of very few Asian people but out of highly property-
inflected relationships to Asian commodities such as porcelain and tea.
However, later sections place Chinese migrants squarely in the wildly
diverse and freewheeling "port culture" of New York City, where they
worked with, worked for, sold to, cohabited with, and (representation
never being absent) performed before white New Yorkers.[30]

Expanding Pursuits of Whiteness

Another of Stephen A. Douglas's arresting appeals went out to white-
thinking veterans of the Mexican War who lived in Illinois. They could,
Douglas argued, corroborate his views on the need to defend "white
blood" against threats of racial "amalgamation." In the war, they had
seen the results of mixing "white men, Indians and negroes" in the
faces and the degradation of the Mexican population. Douglas explicitly defined white manhood as superior to both African American and
Indian others. At another juncture, Douglas took the debate further
abroad. When Lincoln held that the Declaration of Independence
applied to African Americans, Douglas fretted that if such arguments
were countenanced, white men would be reduced to parity with Fiji
Islanders.[31]

Douglas's expansion of the racial terrain far beyond a Black-white
binary identifies an area of weakness in recent histories of white racial
formation. Nearly all the most-cited historians of whiteness are authors
whose earlier writings are in labor history, or whose analyses are much

influenced by Marxism, or (usually) both. This materialist bent remains a rather well-kept secret, and the study of whiteness is sometimes criticized as though it emanated entirely from the most airy expanses of cultural studies. But materialist influences characterize the work of Alexander Saxton, George Lipsitz, Noel Ignatiev, Theodore Allen, Dana Frank, and myself.[32] The focus, not too surprisingly, has often fallen on labor systems and property, with slavery looming large as a race-making response to class conflict, as a barrier to working-class unity, and as a counterpoint against which notions of free labor and white identity took form. Whatever insights it has offered, this line of thought has clearly contributed to the tendency to see racial formation in Black and white.

In the case of *Wages of Whiteness,* an emphasis on the history of the white worker made it especially tempting to oversimplify matters. Important as they were, so the argument went, Indian-white relations were about land and not labor, and, in any case, Indians were seen as disappearing, not as an ongoing other against which whiteness could be defined and mobilized. (Minstrel pun: "The Indian's race is almost run.") The result was that my work relegated settler colonialism and the terror attending it to the "prehistory" of white racial formation among workers, repeating an error made in even some of the best accounts of race in the colonial period. Even on their own terms, these particular arguments in *Wages of Whiteness* collapse utterly. Early- and mid-nineteenth-century labor politics often hinged precisely on land. Waged Indian labor, as excellent recent studies show, was itself significant and widespread. In parts of the antebellum North, there thrived a wishful pretense that African Americans, not just Indians, were disappearing. Moreover, as Lora Romero's and Jean O'Brien's superb investigations show, the very act of "disappearing" still-existing Indian populations mattered greatly in the formation of local, national, and racial consciousness in antebellum New England, even as the region also "disowned" its slaveholding past.[33]

Very recent work and neglected older studies move us decisively beyond a Black-white binary and toward consideration of settler colonialism in structuring Douglas's expansive commentary on Indians, Mexicans, and Fiji Islanders. Philip Deloria's impressive *Playing Indian,* for example, uses the history of Indian impersonation to pose broad questions of race and nation. Deloria writes, "Blackness, in a range of cultural guises, has been an essential precondition for American whiteness, [and] the figure of 'the Indian' holds an equally critical position in American culture." Susan Scheckel, in her *Insistence of the Indian,* makes similar arguments where connections between race and nation are drawn. Darlene Wilson and Patricia Beaver point out that the ignored history of ethnically mixed "Melungeon" people in Appalachia raises large questions about Native American identity, coercion, gender, whiteness, and property in that region and the nation at large.[34] Paul Foos's ambitious "Mexican Wars: Soldiers and Society in an Age of Expansion," offers a sophisticated study of the social history of "the phenomenon of [white] working class manifest destiny" in war and politics. Despite a certain overeagerness to transcend race, Foos illuminates the position of Douglas and that of the chanters—and even the possible tension between their positions.[35] Recent books on race in California and the Southwest before and during the nineteenth century, especially those by Tomás Almaguer, Ramon Gutiérrez, and Lisbeth Haas, bear strongly on questions regarding who became categorized as white and what it meant to enter a white nation. Strongly attentive to questions of property as well as to religion, gender, and racial ideas within subordinated groups, these studies signal rising sophistication and provide models for future work. Likewise important for studies of whiteness, and of race generally, are the friendly challenges by leading Asian Americanists to the tendency of some marxists to assume that the categories as "labor" and "reserve army" of the unemployed are abstract and raceless except in peculiar instances when race obtrudes.[36]

As impressive as this emerging scholarship is proving to be, it is perhaps the rereading of older classic studies of race, nation, and U.S. expansion that holds the greatest promise in moving the study of whiteness beyond a Black-white axis and in ensuring that the experience of settler colonialism will not be seen as unrelated to the history of white identity. The most exciting such contributions include Richard Drinnon's *Facing West,* Michael Rogin's *Fathers and Children,* Reginald Horsman's *Race and Manifest Destiny,* Richard Slotkin's *The Fatal Environment,* and Ronald Takaki's more broadly pitched *Iron Cages.*[37] These books, most of them written as investigations of racism and nationalism in the context or the wake of antiwar and anti-imperialist movements of the Vietnam period, offer especially apt points of departure for historical reflections that place questions about when and why white identity came to be embraced within the context of anti-Indian violence, capitalist expansion and U.S. nationalism. With some exceptions, these American-studies-influenced works suffer from a focus, however critical, on conquest, on the conquerors, and on sources generated by victors. Not only is the agency of Indian people (so well invoked in the work of James P. Ronda and Daniel K. Richter) typically underplayed, but so too are Indians' critical reflections on race and whiteness, topics that have begun to be charted in the fine works of Nancy Shoemaker and R. Keith Basso. In probing what Herman Melville called "the metaphysics of Indian hating," Drinnon, Slotkin, and others often greatly emphasize cultural history over social history and develop class differences in racial ideology hesitantly.[38] All that said, however, the freshness and force of this older literature remain nothing short of remarkable when it is read as part of the history of whiteness.

The work of Rogin, Takaki, and others reveals why direct social experience with "others" cannot be the only focus of research on the generation of white identity. When Douglas debated Lincoln, much of the crowd had not consistently encountered Indians, but they knew something of Lincoln's record of soldiering, the folklore of conquest, and arguments regarding the relationship of free labor and "free" land. Some may have been Mexican War veterans; many more had heard the stories of those veterans. Indeed, hard by its discussion of "the metaphysics of Indian-hating," Melville's *The Confidence-Man* adds another ambiguity, drawing a masterful portrait of a "soldier of fortune" who begs as a disabled Mexican War veteran but whose misfortunes probably grew out of class and political conflicts in New York City.[39]

The older literature, centered largely on the ways in which the "civilized" white American took the "savage" Indian as his or her counterpoint, deserves attention for several additional reasons. The first involves the considerable extent to which these studies concentrate on matters of importance in shaping property relations far beyond the confines of the (shifting) frontier. In Chapter 31 of *Capital,* Marx's account of the "dawn" of capitalism in processes of so-called primitive accumulation of capital emphasized "the extirpation, enslavement and entombment in mines of the aboriginal population" of the Americas as one key to such accumulation. He made this point, however, in a chapter titled "Genesis of the Industrial Capitalist," refusing to imagine separate histories for metropoles and peripheries.[40]

In doing justice to Marx's insight, Slotkin, Rogin, and Takaki have probed white identity not just in zones of contact and conquest but also far more generally. Slotkin subtitles *The Fatal Environment* as *The Myth of the Frontier in the Age of Industrialization.* He lays the groundwork for his postbellurn discussions of convergences between anti-Indian and anti-(white) labor radical stereotypes with a close treatment of how antebellum thinkers as different as Theodore Parker and George Fitzhugh developed "a racialist reading of social class" among whites by drawing on American Indian as well as African American counterpoints. Most astoundingly, in terms of Douglas and the shouts of "White men," Slotkin offers a surprising reminder that the Kansas-Nebraska conflict—the linchpin of Douglas's career and a set of events nearly always discussed in terms of freedom and slavery—also included insistent charges that Douglas's Democratic party had attempted to create and manipulate an "Indian vote" in Kansas. Party organizers brought "savages" to the polls there, so the charges went, even as they rallied racially and religiously suspect Irish voters in urban areas.[41]

In a key early chapter of *Iron Cages,* Takaki gracefully moves "Beyond Primitive Accumulation," making the treatment and imagination of Indians by whites central in shaping individualism, asceticism, enterprise, and acceptance of alienation nationally.[42] Rogin, who begins *Fathers and Children* with long sections explicitly titled "Whites" and "Whites and Indians," patiently develops dialectical relationships among primitive accumulation, liberal capitalism, and the "market revolution." He further elaborates and historicizes an argument on the role of projection of desires onto Indians and into "wild" spaces by whites uneasily internalizing new disciplines. His views strikingly parallel George Rawick's seminal insights into the ways in which white bourgeois anxieties were projected onto Africans and African Americans. Rogin writes:

> Disastrously for the liberal self-conception, however, its distance from primitive man was not secure. At the heart of ambitious expansionism lay the regressive impulse itself. Indians were in harmony with nature; lonely, independent liberal men were separated from it. Liberalism generated a forbidden nostalgia for childhood—for the nurturing, blissful, primitively violent connection to nature that white Americans had to leave behind.[43]

Noteworthy too is the great extent to which the older literature brings questions of gender and terror to the foreground. This is true not only within Rogin's explicitly family-centered and psychoanalytic framework but also, for example, in Takaki's brilliant commentary on just why Melville took care to have a "western" character describe his model Indian hater, Colonel John Moredock, as "no cold husband or cold father" but a warm, patriarchal protector whose anti-Indian rage allegedly never moved to other realms. (*The Confidence-Man,* published just as the Lincoln-Douglas debates were taking shape, remembers Moredock as being so beloved popularly that he "was pressed to become candidate for governor" of [note well!] Illinois, an honor he declined as possibly "incompatible" with his Indian hating).[44] In conjunction with more recent work regarding the social history of race and gender in the early Old Northwest and West, and regarding the cultural meaning of widely circulating "captivity narratives" describing life among Indians, the older literature challenges assumptions that contemplation of African Americans was the central process that shaped ideas concerning white gender roles.[45]

It is the very comprehensiveness of the consideration of race, class, and expansion in the works written in the 1970s and early 1980s that offers the most food for thought. For example, these writers were far more likely than recent practitioners of "whiteness studies" to move beyond Black-white binary approaches to white racial formation. Drinnon's *Facing West* follows expansion from colonial Indian removals to Indochina, tracing its contributions to racism and bureaucratic forms of social control. His chapter on the South Carolina writer William G. Simms joins anti-Indian and anti-Black racism in especially revealing counterpoint.[46] Takaki's *Iron Cages* alternates chapters on Indians and Blacks. It demonstrates, for example, how Richard Henry Dana's whiteness, so central to his celebrated indictment of the "slavelike" treatment of white sailors, was inflected by experiences with Mexicans and Hawaiians and how Hinton Rowan Helper's whites-only attack on slavery partook of his earlier distress at living in California, where he came to fear and to hate the "motley crowd [including] the tattooed islander, the solemn Chinaman and the slovenly Chilian [sic]."[47] Horsman's *Race and Manifest Destiny* ranges widely in time and place. He develops the history of the drawing of a vital distinction between an invigorated "mixed" white "American" race (Douglas told his listeners, "Our ancestors were not all of English origin . . . we inherit from every branch of the Caucasian race") and nonwhite "mongrel" offspring, especially in the wake of the Mexican War. It is not an accident, given his spanning of older and newer studies, that Alexander Saxton's *Rise and Fall of the White Republic* so thoroughly surpasses other recently published accounts in its encompassing narrative and in its ability to address questions of whiteness, property, and national political power.[48]

Perhaps the greatest and most instructive tribute that can be paid to this older body of scholarship is to observe that the very best of the newest work on racial identity stands on it shoulders. Dana Nelson's stunning *National Manhood: Capitalist Citizenship and the Imagined Fraternity of White Men* sets a new standard for the synthetic treatment of white racial formation in the early national and antebellum periods. Nelson describes and dramatizes a series of failed attempts to create fellowship among white men who were set in fierce competition by capitalist expansion, who feared women's work and sexuality, and who worried over the possibilities of democracy. She shows, in analyses of subjects ranging from gynecology to Egyptology, how African Americans, women, Indians, and "primitives" functioned as the "others" necessary to forge white masculinities that were as powerful as they were "melancholy," and that promised fraternity but delivered atomized racial identities.[49] No book better positions us to understand the chants from Douglas's supporters.

For all of its insights from postcolonial theory, from critical race theory, from recent interventions in feminist psychology, and from the history of gender and work, *National Manhood* resonates equally with the work of Rogin, Takaki, and others of their cohort. It frames events within capitalist transformation and the alienation attending liberal obsessions with pursuing social happiness via individual gain and racial privilege. It moves deftly from "Inindianation" as a key to white national symbolism to anti-black racist science, from the explorations of Lewis and Clark to the abolitionism of Lydia Maria Child. Herman Melville moves through Nelson's pages, as he does through Rogin's and Drinnon's. Above all, the emphasis on the production of white manhood in private as well as in public is sure. Indeed, what is perhaps Nelson's most vigorous exposition of her position comes precisely in her effort to supplement Rogin's use of "a psychoanalytic model of 'regression'—a forbidden nostalgia for childhood—to explain the energy at the heart of the United States' westward expansion and its murderous consequences." Nelson writes of the need to locate white masculinity within "that ideological fiction of the 'peaceful competitiveness' of early U.S. capitalism (the providentially soothing logic of the 'invisible hand') versus its experientially anxious, potentially vicious cultural and material results." She continues, in ways that as much complement as contest Rogin, by arguing that newer formations of manhood, tied in a complex manner to national ideals and emerging capitalist practices, effectively and ideologically isolated men, setting them at far remove from the "thick network of obligation and duty within family and community" that had characterized older masculine ideals. White identity, she shows, perpetually promised to build a bridge (back) to the eighteenth-century ideals of mutuality and fraternity but succeeded only in supplementing the fictions of the liberal marketplace with its own fantasies.[50]

The existing literature does not contain final answers to the riddles of U.S. nation-building and of white racial formation. But it does demonstrate that in addressing Gesa Mackenthun's call to "add empire" to the study of history, we build on substantial foundations where racial identity is concerned.[51] Moreover, looking back to fine older works ought to alert us to the fact that many themes addressed in recent scholarship are not exotic concerns driven by recent trends in cultural studies but rather, long-standing concerns of historians. Nelson's insights, and those of the scholars on whom she draws, position us to see the extent to which whites sought happiness and power in interactions with African Americans, South Sea Islanders, American Indians, Mexicans, Cape Verdeans, and others. Such work connects us to critical literatures on race, property, empire, and nation beyond the United States and to studies on the role of the astonishingly diverse international maritime proletariat in spreading and challenging ideas about race. These connections will help us immeasurably in identifying what is exceptional about white identity in the United States. and what is shared with a larger white world.[52] Those of us who believe, with Theodore Allen, that whiteness in the United States is a "peculiar institution," formed in a unique conjuncture of anticolonial/bourgeois revolution, industrial takeoff, and continuing slavery, can make the case for such peculiarity only if these dramas are discussed along with the scenes of subjection, racializations of property, and pursuits of white happiness that accompanied U.S. expansion.[53]

Inbetween Peoples

RACE, NATIONALITY, AND THE
"NEW-IMMIGRANT" WORKING CLASS

WITH JAMES BARRETT

By the eastern European immigration the labor force has been cleft
horizontally into two great divisions. The upper stratum includes
what is known in mill parlance as the "English-speaking" men;
the lower contains the "Hunkies" or "Ginnies." Or, if you prefer,
the former are the "white men," the latter the "foreigners."

John Fitch, *The Steel Workers* (1910)

In 1980 Joseph Loguidice, an elderly Italian American from Chicago,
sat down to tell his life story to an interviewer. His first and most vivid
childhood recollection was of a race riot that occurred on the city's near
north side. Wagons full of policemen with "peculiar hats" streamed
into his neighborhood. But the "one thing that stood out in my mind,"
Loguidice remembered after six decades, was "a man running down the
middle of the street hollering . . . 'I'm White, I'm White!'" After first
taking him for an African American, Loguidice realized that the man
was a white coal handler covered in dust and was screaming for his life,
fearing that "people would shoot him down." He had, Loguidice concluded, "got caught up in . . . this racial thing."[1]

Joseph Loguidice's tale might be taken as a metaphor for the situation of millions of eastern and southern European immigrants who
arrived in the United States between the end of the nineteenth century
and the early 1920s. The fact that this episode made such a profound
impression is in itself significant, suggesting both that this was a
strange, new situation and that thinking about race became an important part of the consciousness of immigrants such as Loguidice. At issue

in this chapter is the development of racial awareness and attitudes and an increasingly racialized worldview among new immigrant workers themselves. Most did not arrive with conventional U.S. attitudes regarding "racial" difference, let alone its significance and implications in the context of industrial America. Yet most, it seems, "got caught up in . . . this racial thing." How did that happen? If race was indeed socially constructed, then what was the raw material that went into the process?

Another central concern of this chapter is how these immigrant workers were viewed in racial terms by others: employers, the state, reformers, and fellow workers. Like that of the coal handler in Loguidice's story, their own ascribed racial identity was not always clear. A whole range of evidence—laws, court cases, expert opinion on race, social conventions, and popular culture in the form of slang, songs, films, cartoons, ethnic jokes, and popular theater—suggests that the native-born and older immigrants often placed these newer immigrants not only *above* African and Asian Americans, for example, but also *below* "white" people. Indeed, many of the older immigrants, and particularly the Irish, had themselves been perceived as "nonwhite" just a generation earlier. As labor history, this chapter examines the ways in which Polish, Italian, and other European artisans and peasants became American workers, but it is equally concerned with the process by which they learned what it meant to be "white" in the U.S. context. Indeed, in the United States, racial and national identities intertwined and together helped to structure persistent divisions within the working-class population. What, the chapter ultimately asks, did it mean to live "inbetween"?

Such themes have not typically been central to immigration history, which has largely been the story of newcomers becoming American, of their holding out against becoming American, or, at its best, of their changing America in the process of discovering new identities. To the extent (and it is a very considerable extent) that theories of "American exceptionalism" have intersected with the history of immigration, the emphasis falls on the difficulty of enlisting heterogeneous workers into class mobilizations or, alternatively, on the unique success of the United States as a multiethnic democracy.[2] But the immigration history Robert Orsi has recently called for, one that "puts the issues and contests of racial identity and difference at its center," has only begun to be written. Proponents of race as an explanation for American exceptionalism either have not focused on European immigrants or have regarded their racialization as a process completed by the 1890s.[3]

Even with the proliferation of scholarship on the social construction of race, it is sometimes assumed that such immigrants really were "white" long before they were fully American. And being white, largely poor, and self-consciously part of imagined communities with roots in Europe, they were therefore "ethnic." If social scientists referred to "national" groups as races (the "Italian race") and to southern and eastern European pan-nationalities as races ("Slavonic and Mediterranean races"), they did so because they used *race* promiscuously to mean other things. If the classic work on American exceptionalism, Werner Sombart's 1906 *Why Is There No Socialism in the United States?*, has a whole section on "racial" division with scarcely a mention of any group that modern Americans would recognize as a racial minority, this is a matter of semantic confusion. If Robert Park centered his pioneering early-twentieth-century sociological theory of assimilation on the "race relations cycle," with the initial expectation that it would apply to African Americans as well as to European immigrant "races," he must not have sorted out the difference between race and ethnicity yet.[4] So certain are some modern scholars of the ability of "ethnicity" to explain immigrant experiences described by contemporaries largely in terms of race and nationality that a growing literature seeks to describe even the African American and Native American experiences as "ethnic."[5]

Racial identity also clearly followed and shaped gender lines in important ways, and historians are just beginning to understand the gendered quality of racial language, conventions, and identity. Such processes are apparent even in the sorts of public spheres emphasized in this chapter, which include citizenship, the state, the union, and the workplace. But we are most apt to find the conjunctions between gender and race in places that are not probed here, at those points where more intimate relations intersect with the rule of law. The taboo against interracial sex and marriage was one obvious boundary between low-status immigrant workers and people of color with whom they often came in contact. As Peggy Pascoe has noted, ". . . although such marriages were infrequent throughout most of U.S. history, an enormous amount of time and energy was spent in trying to prevent them from taking place . . . the history of interracial marriage provides rich evidence of the formulation of race and gender and of the connections between the two." Yet we have little understanding of how this taboo was viewed by immigrant and African American or Asian American workers. One obvious approach is to look at laws governing interracial marriage and court cases aimed at enforcing such laws. Native-born women who became involved with immigrant men could lose their citizenship, and if the immigrant was categorized as nonwhite, they could be prosecuted for "race-mixup." "Race mixing" occurred in spite of all this, of course. Chinese men, who lived under particularly oppressive conditions because of restrictions on the immigration of Chinese women, tended to develop relationships either with African Americans or with Poles and other "new-immigrant" women.[6] Here we have not attempted to unravel this fascinating and complex problem or the racial identity of immigrant women. Except where clearly indicated, we are describing situations where racial identity was informed and shaped by—often even conflated with—notions of manhood.

This chapter fully acknowledges the inconsistency with which "race" was used, by experts and popularly, to describe the "new immigrant" southern and eastern Europeans who dominated the ranks of those who came to the United States between 1895 and 1924 and "remade" the American working class in that period. That inconsistency counts as important evidence of the "inbetween" racial status of such immigrants.[7] The story of Americanization is vital and compelling, but it took place in a nation also obsessed by race. For immigrant workers, the processes of "becoming white" and "becoming American" were intertwined at every turn. The "American standard of living," which labor organizers alternately and simultaneously accused new immigrants of undermining and encouraged them to defend via class and neighborhood organizations, rested on "white men's wages." Political debate turned on whether new immigrants were fit to join the American nation and on whether they were fit to join the "American race." The argument here is emphatically not that eastern and southern European immigrants were in the same situation as nonwhites. Stark differences between the racialized status of African Americans and the racial inbetween-ness of these immigrants meant that the latter *eventually* "became ethnic" and that their trajectory was in broad contours predictable. But their history was messier and more interesting than their trajectory, and they did not know its end. From day to day they were, to borrow from E. P. Thompson, "proto-nothing," reacting and acting in a highly racialized nation.[8]

This overly ambitious chapter is also deliberately disorderly. It aims to destabilize modern categories of race and ethnicity and to capture the confusion, inbetween-ness, and flux in the minds of native-born Americans and the immigrants themselves. Entangling the processes of Americanization and of "whitening," it treats a two-sided experience: New immigrants underwent racial categorizing at the same time they developed new identities, and the two sides of the process cannot be understood apart from one another. Similarly, the categories of state, class, and immigrant self-activity, used here to explain how race is made and to structure the chapter, can be separated at best arbitrarily and inconsistently. Expect therefore a bumpy ride, which begins at its bumpiest—with the vocabulary of race.

Inbetween in Popular Thought and Language

America's racial vocabulary had no agency of its own but, rather, reflected material conditions and power relations—the situations that workers faced on a daily basis in their workplaces and communities. Yet the words themselves were important. They were not only the means by which native-born and elite people marked new immigrants as inferiors but also the means by which immigrant workers came to locate themselves and those about them in the nation's racial hierarchy. In beginning to analyze the vocabulary of race, it makes little sense for historians to invest the words themselves with an agency that could be exercised only by real historical actors or with meanings that derived only from the particular historical contexts in which the language was developed and employed.

The word *guinea,* for example, had long referred to African slaves, particularly those from the continent's northwest coast, and to their descendants. But from the late 1890s onward, the term was increasingly applied to southern European migrants, first and especially to Sicilians and southern Italians who often came as contract laborers. At various times and places in the United States, *guinea* has been applied to Greeks, Jews, Portuguese, Puerto Ricans, and perhaps any new immigrant.[9]

Likewise, *hunky,* which originated, probably in the late nineteenth and early twentieth centuries, as a corruption of Hungarian, eventually became a pan-Slavic slur connected with perceived immigrant racial characteristics. By World War I the term was frequently used to describe any immigrant steelworker, as in *mill hunky.* Opponents of the Great 1919 Steel Strike, including some native-born skilled workers, derided the struggle as a "hunky strike." Yet Josef Barton's work suggests that for Poles, Croats, Slovenians, and other immigrants who often worked together in difficult, dangerous situations, the term could be embraced as expressing a remarkable, if fragile, sense of prideful identity across ethnic lines. In *Out of This Furnace,* his 1941 epic novel based on the lives of Slavic steelworkers, Thomas Bell observed that the word *hunky* bespoke "unconcealed racial prejudice" and a "denial of social and racial equality." Yet as these workers built the industrial unions of the late 1930s and took greater control over their own lives, the meaning of the term began to change. The pride with which second- and third-generation Slavic American steelworkers, now women as well as men, wore the label in the early 1970s seemed to have far more to do with class than with ethnic identity.[10]

Words and phrases employed by social scientists to capture the inbetween identity of the new immigrants are a bit more descriptive, though a bit more cumbersome. As late as 1937, the social scientist John Dollard wrote intriguingly of the immigrant working class as "our temporary Negroes." More precise, if less dramatic, is the designation *not-yet-white* offered by Barry Goldberg. This term not only reflects the popular perceptions and everyday experiences of such workers but also conveys the dynamic quality of the process of racial formation.[11] The examples of Greeks and Italians particularly underscore the new immigrants' ambiguous positions with regard to popular perceptions of race. When Greeks suffered as victims of an Omaha "race" riot in 1909, and when eleven Italians died at the hands of lynchers in Louisiana in 1891, their less-than-white racial status mattered alongside their nationalities. As in the case of Loguidice's coal handler, their unclear racial status put their lives in jeopardy. As Gunther Peck shows in his fine study of copper miners in Bingham, Utah, the Greek and Italian immigrants were "nonwhite" before their tension-fraught cooperation with the Western Federation of Miners during a 1912 strike ensured that "the category of Caucasian worker changed and expanded." Indeed, the work of Dan Georgakas and Yvette Huginnie shows that Greeks and other southern Europeans often "bivouacked" with other "nonwhite" workers in western mining towns. Pocatello, Idaho, Jim-Crowed Greeks in the early twentieth century, and in Arizona they were not welcomed by white workers in "white men"s towns" or "white men's jobs." In Chicago during the Great Depression, a German American wife expressed regret over marrying her "half-nigger" Greek American husband. African American slang in the 1920s in South Carolina counted those of mixed American Indian, African American, and white heritage as "Greeks." Greek Americans in the Midwest showed great anxieties about race and were perceived not only as Puerto Rican, mulatto, Mexican, or Arab but also as nonwhite *because of* being Greek.[12]

Italians, who were involved in a spectacular international diaspora in the early twentieth century, were racialized as the "Chinese of Europe" in many lands.[13] But in the United States, their racialization was pronounced and, as the evolution of the epithet *guinea* suggests, more likely to connect Italians with Africans. In a celebrated 1922 case in Alabama, an African American male was acquitted on miscegenation charges because his Sicilian partner was, as Matthew Jacobson summarizes the court's position, not "conclusively" white. During the debate at the Louisiana state constitutional convention of 1898, in discussions concerning how to disfranchise Blacks, and over which whites might lose the vote as well, some acknowledged that the Italian's skin "happens to be white" even as they argued for his disfranchisement. But others held that "according to the spirit of our meaning when we speak of "white man's government," [the Italians] are as black as the blackest negro in existence."[14] More than metaphor intruded on this judgment. At the turn of the century, a West Coast construction boss was asked, "You don't call the Italian a white man?" The negative reply assured the questioner that the Italian was "a dago." Recent studies of Italian and Greek Americans make a strong case that racial, not just ethnic, oppression long plagued "nonwhite" immigrants from southern Europe.[15]

The racial categorization of eastern Europeans was likewise striking. While racist jokes mocked the Black servant who thought her child, fathered by a Chinese man, would be a Jew, racist folklore held that Jews, inside out, were "niggers." In 1926 Serbo-Croatians ranked near the bottom of a list of forty "ethnic" groups whom "white American" respondents were asked to order according to the respondents' willingness to associate with members of each group. They placed just above Negroes, Filipinos, and Japanese. Just above them were Poles, who were near the middle of the list. One sociologist has recently written that "a good many groups on this color continuum [were] not considered white by a large number of Americans."[16] The literal inbetweenness of new immigrants on such a list suggests what popular speech affirms: The state of whiteness was approached gradually and controversially. The authority of the national government both smoothed and complicated that approach.

White Citizenship and Inbetween Americans:
The State of Race

The power of the national state gave recent immigrants both their firmest claims to whiteness and their strongest leverage for enforcing those claims. The courts consistently allowed "new immigrants," whose racial status was ambiguous in the larger culture, to be naturalized as "white" citizens and almost as consistently turned down non-European applicants as "nonwhite." Political reformers therefore discussed the fitness for citizenship of recent European immigrants from two distinct angles. They produced, through the beginning of World War I, a largely benign and hopeful discourse on how to Americanize (and win the votes of) those already here. But this period also saw a debate on fertility rates and immigration restriction that conjured up threats of "race suicide" if this flow of migrants were not checked and the fertility of the native-born increased. A figure like President Theodore Roosevelt could stand both as the Horatio warning of the imminent swamping of the "old stock" racial elements in the United States and as the optimistic Americanizer to whom the play that originated the assimilationist image of the "melting pot" was dedicated.[17]

Such anomalies rested not only on a political economy that at times needed and at times shunned immigrant labor but also on peculiarities of U.S. naturalization law. If the "state apparatus" told new immigrants both that they were and that they were not white, it was clearly the judiciary that produced the most affirmative responses; U.S. law made citizenship racial as well as civil. Even when much of the citizenry doubted the racial status of European migrants, the courts nearly always granted their whiteness in naturalization cases. Thus the often racially based campaigns against Irish naturalization in the 1840s and 1850s and against Italian naturalization in the early twentieth century aimed to delay citizenship, not deny it. The lone case that appears exceptional in this regard is one in which U.S. naturalization attorneys in Minnesota attempted unsuccessfully to bar radical "red" Finns from naturalization on the ethnological grounds that they were not Caucasian and therefore not white.[18]

The legal equation of whiteness with fitness for citizenship significantly shaped the process by which race was made in the United States. Whereas southern and eastern European immigrants remained "inbetween people" because of broad cultural perceptions, Asians were in case after case declared unambiguously nonwhite and therefore unfit for citizenship. This sustained pattern of denial of citizenship provides, as the sociologist Richard Williams argues, the best guide to who would be racialized in an ongoing way in the twentieth-century United States. It applies, with complications, in the case of Native Americans. Migrants from Africa, although they were nominally an exception in that Congress in 1870 allowed their naturalization (with the full expectation that they would not be coming), of course experienced sweeping denials of civil status both in slavery and in state-sanctioned segregation. Nor were

migrants from Mexico necessarily exceptional. Despite the natural-
izability of such migrants by treaty and later court decisions, widespread
denials of citizenship rights took place almost immediately—in one
1855 instance in California as a result of the "Greaser Bill," as the
Vagrancy Act was termed.[19]

Likewise, the equation of legal whiteness with fitness for naturaliz-
able citizenship helps to predict which groups would *not* be made nonwhite in an ongoing way. The Irish, whose whiteness was under sharp
question in the 1840s and 1850s, and later the "new immigrants,"
gained the powerful symbolic argument that the law declared them
white and fit. They also held the power of comprising significant numbers of voters, although naturalization rates for new immigrants were
not always high. During Louisiana's disfranchising constitutional convention of 1898, for example, the bitter debate over Italian whiteness
ended with a provision passed that extended to new immigrants protections comparable—even superior—to those that the "grandfather clause"
gave to native white voters. New Orleans's powerful Choctaw Club
machine, already the beneficiary of Italian American votes, led the campaign for the plank.[20] When Thomas Hart Benton and Stephen Douglas
argued against Anglo-Saxon superiority and for a pan-white "American race" in the 1850s, they did so before huge blocs of Irish voters.
When Theodore Roosevelt extolled the "mixture of blood" constituting the American race, a "new ethnic type in this melting pot of the
nations," he emphasized to new immigrant voters his conviction that
each of their nationalities would enrich America by adding "its blood
to the life of the nation." When Woodrow Wilson also tailored his
thinking about the racial desirability of the new European immigrants,
he did so in the context of an electoral campaign in which the "foreign"
vote counted heavily.[21] In such a situation, Roosevelt's almost laughable proliferation of uses of the word *race* served him well, filling his
various needs as reformer, imperialist, debunker and romanticizer of
the history of the West, and political candidate. He sincerely embraced
seemingly contradictory principles: Darwin *and* Lamarck's insistence
on the heritability of acquired characteristics, melting pots *and* the
threat of Anglo-American white "race suicide," an adoring belief in
Anglo-Saxon and Teutonic superiority *and* in the grandeur of a "mixed"
American race. Roosevelt, like the Census Bureau, thought in terms of
the nation's biological "stock," a term that by then evoked images of
Wall Street as well as the farm. That stock was directly threatened by
low birth rates among the nation's "English-speaking race." But races

could also progress over time, and the very experience of mixing and clashing with other races would bring out, and improve, the best of the "racestock." The "American race" could absorb and permanently improve the less desirable stock of "*all* white immigrants," perhaps in two generations, but only if its most desirable "English-speaking" racial elements were not swamped in an un-Americanized Slavic and southern European culture and biology.[22]

The neo-Lamarckianism that allowed Roosevelt to use such terms as *English-speaking race* ran through much of Progressive racial thinking, though it was sometimes underpinned by appeals to other authorities.[23] We are likely to regard whether one eats pasta or meat, whether one speaks English or Italian, whether one lives in ill-ventilated or healthful housing, whether or not one comes to work on religious holidays, and whether one votes Republican or Socialist as decisions based on environment, opportunity, and choice. But language loyalty, incidence of dying in epidemics, and radicalism often defined race for late-nineteenth- and early-twentieth-century thinkers, making distinctions among racial, religious, and antiradical varieties of nativism messy. For many, Americanization was not simply a cultural process but an index of racial change that could fail if the concentration of "lower" races kept the "alchemy" of racial transformation from occurring.[24] From its very start, the campaign for immigration restriction that was directed against "new" Europeans carried a strong implication that even something as abstract as "moral tone" could be inherited. In deriding "ignorant, brutal Italians and Hungarian laborers" during the 1885 debate over the Contract Labor Law, its sponsor framed his environmentalist arguments in terms of color, holding that "the introduction into a community of any considerable number of persons of a lower moral tone will cause general moral deterioration as sure as night follows day." He added, "The intermarriage of a lower with a higher type certainly does not improve the latter any more than does the breeding of cattle by [mixing] blooded and common stock improve the blooded stock generally." The extremist adherents to the restrictionist cause saw mixing as always and everywhere disastrous. Madison Grant's *The Passing of the Great Race* (1916), a racist attack on recent immigrants that defended the purity of "Nordic" stock, the race of the "white man par excellence," against "Alpine," "Mediterranean," and Semitic invaders, is a classic example.[25]

Professional Americanizers and national politicians who courted to immigrant constituencies seemed able for a time to marginalize those

who racialized new immigrants. Corporate America generally gave firm
support to relatively open immigration. Settlement house reformers and
others taught and witnessed Americanization. The best of them, such
as Jane Addams, learned from immigrants as well and extolled not
only assimilation but the virtues of ongoing cultural differences among
immigrant groups. Even progressive politicians reined in their own
most racially charged tendencies. As a southern academic, Woodrow
Wilson wrote of the dire threat to "our Saxon habits of government"
by "corruption of foreign blood" and characterized Italian and Polish
immigrants as "sordid and hapless." But as a presidential candidate in
1912, he reassured immigrant leaders that "We are all Americans,"
offered to rewrite sections on Polish Americans in his *History of the
American People,* and found Italian Americans "one of the most interesting and admirable elements in our American life."[26]

Yet Progressive Era assimilationism, and even its flirtations with cultural pluralism, could not save new immigrants from racial attacks.
Racial prejudice against new immigrants was more provisional and
nuanced than anti-Irish bias in the antebellum period, but political
leaders also defended *hunkies* and *guineas* far more provisionally.
Meanwhile, the Progressive project of imperialism and the Progressive
nonproject of capitulation to Jim Crow systems of segregation ensured
that race thinking would retain and increase its potency. Even though
corporate leaders backed immigration and funded Americanization
projects, the corporate model emphasized standardization, efficiency,
and immediate results. This led many Progressives to support reforms
that called immigrant political power and voting rights into question, at
least in the short run.[27] In the longer term, big business proved by the
early 1920s an unreliable supporter of the melting pot. Worried about
unemployment and about the possibility that new immigrants were
proving to be "revolutionary and communistic races," business leaders
equivocated on the openness of immigration, turned Americanizing
agencies into labor spy networks, and stopped funding the corporate-
sponsored umbrella group of professional Americanizers and conservative new-immigrant leaders, the tellingly named *Inter-Racial Council.*[28]

Reformers, too, lost heart. Because mixing was never regarded as an
unmitigated good but rather as a matter of proportion with a number
of possible outcomes, the new immigrants' record was constantly under
scrutiny. The failure of Americanization to deliver total loyalty during
World War I and during the postwar "immigrant rebellion" within U.S.
labor made that record one of failure. The reformers' prediction that

race mixture would inject "virility," "manhood," and "vigor" into the American stock had long coexisted with emphasis on obedience and docility in Americanization curricula.[29] At their most vigorous, in the 1919–1920 strike wave, new immigrants were most suspect. Nationalists, and many Progressive reformers among them, were, according to John Higham, sure that they had done "their best to bring the great mass of newcomers into the fold." The failure was not theirs, they believed, but a reflection of the "incorrigibly unassimilable nature of the material on which they had worked."[30]

The triumph of immigration restriction in the 1920s was in large measure a triumph of *racism* against new immigrants. Congress and the Ku Klux Klan, the media and popular opinion all reinforced the inbetween, and even at times nonwhite, racial status of eastern and southern Europeans. Grant's *Passing of the Great Race* suddenly enjoyed a vogue that had eluded it in 1916. The best-selling U.S. magazine, *Saturday Evening Post,* praised Grant and endorsed Kenneth Roberts's massively promulgated fears that continued immigration would produce "a hybrid race of people as worthless and futile as the good-for-nothing mongrels of Central America and Southeastern Europe." When the National Industrial Conference Board met in 1923, its director allowed that immigration restriction was "essentially a race question." Congress was deluged with letters of concern for preservation of a "distinct American type" and of support for stopping the "swamping" of the Nordic race. In basing itself on the first fear and setting quotas pegged squarely on the (alleged) origins of the current population, the 1924 restriction act also addressed the second fear, because the U.S. population as a whole had come from northern and western parts of Europe to a vastly greater extent than had the immigrant population for the last three decades. At virtually the same time that the courts carefully drew a color line between European new immigrants and nonwhite others, the Congress and reformers reaffirmed the racial inbetween-ness of southern and eastern Europeans.[31]

Americanization thus was never just about nation but was always about race and nation. This truth stood out most clearly in the Americanizing influences of popular culture, in which mass-market films socialized new immigrants into a "gunfighter nation" of westerns and a vaudeville nation of blackface; in which popular music was both "incontestably mulatto" and freighted with the hierarchical racial heritage of minstrelsy; in which the most widely advertised lures of Americanized mass consumption turned on the opportunity to harness the energies of Black servants (such as the Gold Dust twins, Aunt Jemina, and Rastus, the Cream of Wheat chef) to household labor. Drawing on a range of anti-immigrant stereotypes as well, popular entertainments and advertisements cast newcomers as nationally particular and racially inbetween, while teaching the all-important lesson that immigrants were never so white as when they wore blackface before audiences and cameras.[32]

Occasionally, professional Americanizers taught the same lesson. In a Polish and Bohemian neighborhood on Chicago's lower west side, for example, social workers at Gads Hill Center counted their 1915 minstrel show a "great success." Organized by the center's Young Men's Club, the event drew 350 people, many of whom at that point knew so little English that they could only "enjoy the music" and "appreciate the really attractive costumes." Young performers with names like Kraszewski, Pletcha, and Chimielewski sang "Clare De Kitchen" and "Gideon"s Band." Settlement houses generally practiced Jim Crow, even in the North. Some of their leading theorists invoked a racial continuum that ended "farthest in the rear" with African Americans, even as they goaded new immigrants toward giving up particular Old World cultures by branding the retention of such cultures an atavistic clinging to "racial consciousness."[33]

"Inbetween" Jobs: Capital, Class, and the New Immigrant

Joseph Loguidice's reminiscence of the temporarily "colored" coal handler compresses and dramatizes a process that went on in far more workaday settings as well. Often while they themselves were begrimed by the nation's dirtiest jobs, new immigrants and their children quickly learned that "the worst thing one could be in this Promised Land was 'colored.'"[34] But if the world of work taught the importance of being "not black," it also exposed new immigrants to frequent comparisons and close competition with African Americans. The results of such clashes in the labor market did not instantly propel new immigrants into either the category or the consciousness of whiteness. Instead, management created an economics of racial inbetween-ness that taught new immigrants the importance of racial hierarchy, while leaving open their place in that hierarchy. At the same, time the struggle for "inbetween jobs" further emphasized the importance of national and religious ties among immigrants by giving those ties a crucial economic dimension.

The bitterness of job competition between new immigrants and African Americans has rightly received emphasis in accounting for racial hostility, but that bitterness must be *historically* investigated. Before 1915, new immigrants competed with relatively small numbers of African Americans for northern urban jobs. The new immigrants tended to be more recent arrivals than the Black workers, and they came in such great numbers that, demographically speaking, they competed for jobs far more often with each other than with African Americans. Moreover, given the much greater "human capital" of Black workers in terms of literacy, education, and English language skills, immigrants fared well in this competition.[35] After 1915, the decline in immigration that resulted from World War I and restrictive legislation in the 1920s combined with the Great Migration of Afro-southerners to northern cities to create a situation in which a growing and newly arrived Black working class confronted a more settled but struggling immigrant population with massive competition. Again, the results were not of a sort that would necessarily have spelled bitter disappointment to those whom the economic historians term SCEs (southern and central Europeans).[36]

The ways in which capital structured workplaces and labor markets contributed to the idea that competition should be both cutthroat and racialized. New immigrants suffered wage discrimination when compared to the white native-born. African Americans were paid less than immigrants for doing the same jobs. In the early twentieth century, employers preferred a labor force divided by race and national origin. As the radical cartoonist Ernest Riebe understood at the time, and as the labor economists Richard Edwards, Michael Reich, and David Gordon have recently reaffirmed, work gangs segregated by nationality as well as by race were made to compete against each other in a strategy designed not only to undermine labor unity and depress wages in the long run but also to spur competition and boost productivity every day.[37]

On the other hand, management made broader hiring and promotion distinctions that brought pan-national and sometimes racial categories into play. In some workplaces and areas, the blast furnace was a "Mexican job"; in others, it was a pan-Slavic "hunky" job. "Only hunkies," a steel industry investigator was told, worked blast furnace jobs that were "too damn dirty and too damn hot for a white man." Management at the nation's best-studied early-twentieth-century factory divided the employees into "white men" and "kikes." Notions about the genetic "fit" between immigrants and certain types of work were buttressed by the "scientific" judgments of scholars like the sociologist E. A. Ross, who observed that Slavs were "immune to certain kinds of dirt . . . that would kill a white man." "Scientific" managers in steel and in other industries designed elaborate ethnic classification systems to guide their hiring. In 1915 the personnel manager at one Pittsburgh plant analyzed what he called the "racial adaptability" of thirty-six different ethnic groups to twenty-four different kinds of work and twelve sets of conditions and plotted them all on a chart. Lumber companies in Louisiana built what they called "the Quarters" for Black workers and (separately) for Italians, using language very recently associated with African American slavery. For white workers they built company housing and towns. The distinction between "white" native-born workers and "nonwhite" new immigrants, Mexicans, and African Americans in parts of the West rested largely on the presence of "white man's camps" or "white man's towns" in company housing in lumbering and mining. Native-born residents interviewed in the wake of a bitter 1915 strike by Polish oil refinery workers recognized only two classes of people in Bayonne, New Jersey: "foreigners" and "white men." In generalizing about early-twentieth-century nativism, the historian John Higham concluded, "In all sections native-born and Northern European laborers called themselves 'white men' to distinguish themselves from Southern Europeans whom they worked beside." As late as World War II, new immigrants and their children, lumped together as "racials," suffered employment discrimination in the defense industry.[38]

There was also substantial management interest in the specific comparison of new immigrants with African Americans as workers. More concrete in the North and abstract in the South, these complex comparisons generally, but not always, favored the former group. African Americans' supposed undependability "especially on Mondays," intolerance for cold, and inability to do fast-paced work were all noted. But the comparisons were often nuanced. New immigrants, as Herbert Gutman long ago showed, were themselves counted as unreliable, "especially on Mondays." Some employers counted Black workers as more apt and skillful "in certain occupations" and cleaner and happier than "the alien white races." An occasional blanket preference for African Americans over immigrants surfaced, as at Packard in Detroit in 1922. Moreover, comparisons had a provisional quality, because ongoing competition was what was desired. In 1905 the superintendent of Illinois Steel, threatening to fire all Slavic workers, reassured the immigrants that no "race hatred" [against Slavs] motivated the proposed decision, which was instead driven by a factor that the workers could change: their tardiness in adopting the English language.[39]

The fact that recent immigrants were relatively inexperienced vis-à-vis African American workers in the North in 1900 but were relatively experienced by 1930 makes it difficult for economic historians to measure the extent to which immigrant economic mobility in this period derived from employer discrimination. Clearly, timing and demographic change mattered alongside racism in a situation in which the immigrant SCEs came to occupy rungs on the job ladder above African Americans and below those who were fed into the economic historians' computers as NWNPs (native-born whites with native-born parents). Stanley Lieberson uses the image of a queue to help explain the role of discrimination against African Americans in leading to such results.[40] In the lineup of workers ordered by employer preference, as in so much else, new immigrants were inbetween.

In a society in which workers did in fact stand in lines to seek jobs, the image of a queue is wonderfully apt. However, the Polish worker who stood next to an African American on one side and an Italian American on the other as an NWNP manager hired unskilled labor did not know the statistics of current job competition, let alone what the results would be by the time of the 1930 census. Even if the Polish worker had had this information, the patterns of mobility for his group would probably have differed as much from those for the Italian Americans as from those for the African Americans (who in some cities outdistanced Polish immigrants in intra-working-class mobility to better jobs from 1900 to 1930).[41] Racialized struggles over jobs were fed by the general experience of brutal, group-based competition and by the knowledge that Black workers were especially vulnerable competitors who fared far less well in the labor market than any other native-born American group. The young Croatian immigrant Stephan Mesaros was so struck by the abuse of a Black co-worker that he asked a Serbian laborer for an explanation. "You'll soon learn something about this country," came the reply, "Negroes never get a fair chance." The exchange initiated a series of conversations that contributed to Mesaros's becoming Steve Nelson, an influential radical organizer and an antiracist. But for most immigrants, caught in a world of dog-eat-dog competition, the lesson would simply have been that African Americans were among the eaten.[42]

Even though immigrants did not know the precise order of the job queue or their prospects in it, they did have their own ideas about how to get into the line, their own strategies about how to get ahead in it, and their own dreams for getting out of it. These tended to reinforce a sense of the advantage of being "not nonwhite" but to also emphasize specific national and religious identifications rather than generalized white identity. Because of the presence of a small employing (or sub-contracting) class in their communities, new immigrants were far more likely than African Americans to work for one of "their own" as an immediate boss. In New York City in 1910, for example, almost half of the sample of Jewish workers studied by Suzanne Model had Jewish supervisors, as did about 1 Italian immigrant in 7. Meanwhile, "the study sample unearthed only one industrial match between laborers and supervisors among Blacks."[43]

In shrugging at being called *hunky,* Thomas Bell writes, Slovak immigrants took solace in the fact that they "had come to America to find work and save money, not to make friends with the Irish." But getting work and "making friends with" Irish American foremen, skilled workers, union leaders, and politicians were often very much connected, and the relationships were hardly smooth. Petty bosses could always rearrange the queue.[44] But over the long run, a common Catholicism (and sometimes common political machine affiliations) gave new immigrant groups access to the fragile favor of Irish Americans who were in positions to influence hiring—an access that African Americans could not achieve. Sometimes such favor was organized, as through the Knights of Columbus in Kansas City packinghouses. Over time, as second-generation marriages across national lines but within the Catholic religion became a pattern, kin joined religion in shaping hiring in ways that largely excluded African Americans.[45]

Many of the new-immigrant groups also had distinctive plans to move out of the United States wage labor queue altogether. From 1880 to 1930, fully one-third of all Italian immigrants were "birds of passage" who in many cases never intended to stay. The same was true of 46 percent of Greeks entering between 1908 and 1923 and of 40 percent of Hungarians entering between 1899 and 1913.[46] Strong national (and subnational) loyalties obviously persisted in such cases, and saving money to send or take home was probably a far higher priority than sorting out the complexities of racial identity in the United States. Similarly, those many new immigrants (especially among the Greeks, Italians, and Jews) who hoped to (and did) leave the working class by opening small businesses set great store in saving and often catered to a clientele composed mainly of their own group. But immigrant saving itself proved highly racialized, as did immigrant success in small business. Within U.S. culture, African Americans symbolized prodigality and lack of savings, whereas the Chinese, Italians, and Jews symbolized fanatical obsession with saving. Popular racist mythology held that if they were paid a dollar and a quarter, Italians would spend only the quarter and African Americans would spend a dollar and a half. Characteristically, white racial common sense construed both patterns as pathological.[47] Moreover, in many cases, Jewish and Italian merchants sold to African American customers. Their "middleman minority" status revealingly identifies an inbetween position that, as aggrieved southern "white" merchants complained, rested on a more humane attitude toward Black customers and on such cultural affinities as an eagerness to participate in bargaining over prices. Chinese merchants have traditionally, and Korean merchants more recently, occupied a similar position. Yet, as an 1897 New York City correspondent for a national newsweekly captured in an article remarkable for its precise balancing of anti-Black and anti-Semitic racism, the middleman's day-to-day position in the marketplace reinforced specific Jewish identity and distance from Blacks. "For a student of race characteristics," the reporter wrote, "nothing could be more striking than to observe the stoic scorn of the Hebrew when he is made a disapproving witness of the happy-go-lucky joyousness of his dusky neighbor."[48]

Other immigrants, especially Slovaks and Poles, banked on hard labor, home ownership, and slow intergenerational mobility for success. They too navigated in very tricky racial cross-currents. Coming from areas in which the dignity of hard, physical labor was established, both in the countryside and in cities, they arrived in the United States eager to work, even if in jobs that did not take advantage of their skills. They often found, however, that in the scientifically managed industries of the United States, hard work was driven and alienating.[49] It was, moreover, often typed and despised as "nigger work"—or as "dago work" or "hunky work" in settings in which such categories had been freighted with the prior meaning of "nigger work." The new immigrants' reputation for hard work and their unfamiliarity with English and with American culture generally tended to lead to their being hired as an almost abstract source of labor. *Hunky* was abbreviated to *hunk,* and Slavic laborers in particular were treated as mere units of work. This had its advantages, especially in comparison to Black workers;

Slavs could more often get hired in groups, whereas skilled workers and petty bosses favored individual "good Negroes" with unskilled jobs, often requiring that they exhibit a familiarity with tasks and a subservience that were not expected of new immigrants. But being valued mainly as brute force also involved eastern Europeans in particularly brutal social relations on the shopfloor.[50]

Hard work, especially when closely supervised, was likewise not a certain badge of manliness in the United States, as it had been in eastern Europe. Racialized, it was also demasculinized, especially because its extremely low pay and sporadic nature ensured that new-immigrant males could not be breadwinners for a family. The idea of becoming a "white man," unsullied by racially typed labor and capable of earning wages that a family could live on, was therefore extremely attractive in many ways, and the imperative of not letting one's job become "nigger work" was swiftly learned.[51] Yet no clear route ran from inbetweenness to white manhood. "White men's unions" often seemed the best path, but they also erected some of the most significant obstacles.

White Men's Unions
and New-Immigrant Trial Members

Although organized labor exercised little control over hiring outside of a few organized crafts during most of the years from 1895 to 1924 and beyond, its racialized opposition to new immigrants did reinforce their inbetween-ness, both on the job and in politics. At the same time, the American Federation of Labor (AFL) also provided an important venue in which "old-immigrant" workers interacted with new immigrants, teaching important lessons in both whiteness and Americanization. As an organization devoted to closing skilled trades to any new competition, the craft union's reflex was to oppose outsiders. In this sense, most of the AFL unions were "exclusionary by definition" and marshaled economic, and to a lesser extent political, arguments to exclude women, Chinese, Japanese, African Americans, the illiterate, noncitizens, and the new immigrants from organized workplaces and, whenever possible, from U.S. shores. So clear was the craft logic of AFL restrictionism that historians are apt to regard it as simply materialistic and to note its racism only when direct assaults were made on groups traditionally regarded as nonwhite. John Higham, for example, argues that only in the last moments of the major 1924 debates over whom to restrict did Gompers reluctantly embrace "the idea that European immigration endangered America's racial foundations."[52]

However, Gwendolyn Mink and Andrew Neather demonstrate that it is far more difficult than Higham implies to separate appeals based on craft from those based on race in AFL campaigns to restrict European immigration. A great deal of trade unions' racist opposition to the Chinese stressed the connection between their "slave-like" subservience and their status as coolie laborers, indoctrinated in the Chinese social system and willing to settle for being "cheap men."[53] Alleged dietary practices (rice and rats rather than meat) symbolized Chinese failure to seek the "American standard of living." All of these are cultural, historical, and environmental matters. Yet none of them prevented the craft unions from declaring the Chinese "race" unassimilable and supporting exclusionary legislation based largely on racial grounds. The environmentalist possibility that over generations, Asian "cheap men" might improve was simply irrelevant. By that time the Chinese race would allegedly have polluted America.[54]

Much of the anti-Chinese rhetoric was applied as well to Hungarians in the 1880s and was incorporated in AFL campaigns against new immigration after 1890. Pasta, as Mink shows, joined rice as an "un-American" and racialized food. Far from abjuring arguments based on "stock," assimilability, and homogeneity, the AFL's leaders supported literacy tests designed specifically "to reduce the numbers of Slavic and Mediterranean immigrants." They endorsed the nativist racism of the antilabor Senator Henry Cabot Lodge, hoped anti-Japanese agitation could be made to contribute to restrictions on new immigration, emphasized "the incompatibility of the new immigrants with the very nature of American civilization," and both praised and reprinted works on the peril of "race suicide."[55] They opposed immigration by "the scum" from "the least civilized countries of Europe" and "the replacing of the independent and intelligent coal miners of Pennsylvania by the Huns and Slavs." They feared that an "American" miner in Pennsylvania could thrive only if he "Latinizes" his name. They explicitly asked, well before World War I: "How much more [new] immigration can this country absorb and retain its homogeneity?" (Those wanting to know the dire answer were advised to study the "racial history" of cities.)[56]

Robert Asher is undoubtedly correct in arguing both that labor movement reaction to new immigrants was "qualitatively different from the response to Orientals" and that AFL rhetoric was "redolent of a belief in racial inferiority" of southern and eastern Europeans. Neather is likewise on the mark in speaking of "semi-racial" union arguments for restriction directed against new immigrants.[57] Gompers's characterization of new immigrants as "beaten men of beaten races" perfectly captures the tension between fearing that southern and eastern Europe was dumping its "vomit" and "scum" in the United States and believing that Slavic and Mediterranean people were scummy. Labor sometimes cast its ideal as an "Anglo-Saxon race . . . true to itself." Gompers was more open but equivocal. He found that the wonderful "peculiarities of temperament such as patriotism, sympathy, etc.," which made labor unionism possible, were themselves "peculiar to most of the Caucasian race." In backing literacy tests for immigrants in 1902, he was more explicit. These tests would leave British, German, Irish, French, and Scandinavian immigration intact but would "shut out a considerable number of Slavs and other[s] equally or more undesirable and injurious."[58]

Such "semi-racial" nativism shaped the AFL's politics and led to the exclusion of new immigrants from many unions. When the iron puddlers' poet Michael McGovern envisioned an ideal celebration for his union, he wrote:

> There were no men invited such as Slavs and "Tally Annes,"
> Hungarians and Chinamen with pigtail cues and fans.

The situation in the building trades was more complicated. Some craft unions excluded Italians, Jews, and other new immigrants. Among laborers, organization often began on an ethnic basis, although such immigrant locals typically were eventually integrated into a national union. Even among craftsmen, separate organizations emerged among Jewish carpenters and painters and other recent immigrants. The hod carriers union, according to Asher, "appears to have been created to protect the jobs of native construction workers against competing foreigners." The shoeworkers, pianomakers, barbers, hotel and restaurant workers, and United Textile Workers likewise kept out new immigrants, whose lack of literacy, citizenship, English-language skills, apprenticeship opportunities, and initiation fees also effectively barred them from many other craft locals. This "internal protectionism" apparently had lasting results. Lieberson's research through 1950 shows that new immigrants and their children had far less access to craft jobs in unionized sectors than did whites of northwestern European origin.[59]

However, southern and eastern European immigrants had more access to unionized work than did African Americans, and unions never supported outright bans on their migration, as they did with Asians.

Organized labor's opposition to the Italians as the "white Chinese," or to recent immigrants generally as "white coolies," usually acknowledged and questioned whiteness at the same time, associating whites with nonwhites while leaving open the possibility that contracted labor, and not race, was at issue. A strong emphasis on the "brotherhood" of labor also complicated matters. Paeans to the "International Fraternity of Labor" ran in the *American Federationist* within fifteen pages of anti-immigrant hysteria such as A. A. Graham's "The un-Americanizing of America." Reports from Italian labor leaders and poems like "Brotherhood of Man" ran close to fearful predictions of race suicide.[60]

Moreover, the very things that the AFL warned about in its anti-immigrant campaigns encouraged the unions to make tactical decisions to enroll southern and eastern Europeans as members. Able to enter the country legally in large numbers, secure work, and become voters, *hunkies* and *guineas* had social power that could be used to attack the craft unionism of the AFL from the right or, as was often feared, from the left. To restrict immigration, however desirable from Gompers's point of view, would do nothing about the large proportion of the working class that by 1910 was already of immigrant origins. Nor would it change the fact that many new immigrants were already joining unions—in the AFL, in language and national federations, or under socialist auspices. If these new immigrants were not to undermine the AFL's appeals to corporate leaders as an effective moderating force within the working class, the American Federation of Labor would have to consider becoming the Americanizing Federation of Labor.[61]

Most important, changes in machinery and the growth of scientific management made real the threat that crafts could be undermined by expedited training of unskilled and semiskilled immigrant labor. This threat gave force to labor's nativist calls for immigration restriction, but it also strengthened initiatives toward a "new unionism" that crossed skill lines to organize recent immigrants. Prodded by independent, dual-unionist initiatives such as those of Italian socialists and the United Hebrew Trades, by the example of existing industrial unions in its own ranks, and by the left-wing multinational, multiracial unionism of the Industrial Workers of the World, the AFL increasingly got into the business of organizing and Americanizing new-immigrant workers in the early twentieth century. The logic, caught perfectly by a Lithuanian American packinghouse worker in Chicago, was often quite utilitarian: ". . . because those sharp foremen are inventing new machines and the work is easier to learn, and so these slow Lithuanians and even green [inexperienced] girls can learn to do it, and the Americans and Germans and Irish are put out and the employer saves money . . . This was why the American labor unions began to organize us all." Even so, especially in those unions where new-immigrant women were the potential members and skill dilution threatened mainly immigrant men, the Gompers leadership at times refused either to incorporate dual unions or to initiate meaningful organizing efforts under AFL auspices.[62]

However self-interested, wary, and incomplete the AFL's increasing opening to new-immigrant workers remained, it initiated a process that much transformed "semi-racial" typing of recently arrived immigrants. Unions and their supporters at times treasured labor organization as the most meaningful agent of democratic "Americanization from the bottom up," what John R. Commons called "the only effective Americanizing force for the southeastern European."[63] In struggles, native-born unionists came to observe not only the humanity but also the heroism of new immigrants. Never quite giving up on biological/cultural explanations, labor leaders wondered which "race" made the best strikers, and some comparisons favored the recent arrivals over Anglo-Saxons. Industrial Workers of the World leader Covington Hall's reports from Louisiana remind us that we know little about how unionists, and workers generally, conceived of race. Hall took seriously the idea of a "Latin race," including Italians, other southern Europeans, *and Mexicans,* all of whom put southern whites to shame with their militancy.[64] In the rural west, labor investigator Peter Speek wrote, "a white man is an extreme individualist, busy with himself," a "native or old-time immigrant" laborer, boarded by employers. "A foreigner," he added, "is more sociable and has a higher sense of comradeship" and of nationality. Embracing the very racial vocabulary to which he objected, one socialist plasterer criticized native-born unionists who described Italians as *guineas.* He pointed out that Italians' ancestors "were the best and unsurpassable in manhood's glories; at a time when our dads were running about in paint and loincloth as ignorant savages." To bring the argument up to the present, he added that Italian Americans "are as manly for trade union conditions as the best of us; and that while handicapped by our prejudice."[65]

Although such questioning of whiteness was rare, the "new unionism" provided an economic logic for progressive unionists who wished to unite workers across ethnic and racial lines. With their own race less open to question, new immigrants were at times brought into class-conscious coalitions, as whites and with African Americans. The great success of the packinghouse unions in forging such unity during World War I ended in a shining victory and vastly improved conditions. The diverse new immigrants and Black workers at the victory celebration heard Chicago Federation of Labor leader John Fitzpatrick hail them as "black and white together under God's sunshine." If the Irish American unionists had often been bearers of "race hatred" against both new immigrants and Blacks, they and other old immigrants also could convey the lesson that class unity transcended race and semi-race.[66]

But even as they offered more openings to new unionism and new immigrants, labor organizations taught very complex lessons regarding race. At times, overtures toward new immigrants coincided with renewed exclusion of nonwhite workers, underlining Du Bois's point that the former were mobbed to make them join unions and the latter to keep them out. Western Federation of Miners (WFM) activists, whose episodic radicalism coexisted with nativism and a consistent anti-Chinese and anti-Mexican racism, gradually developed a will and a strategy to organize Greek immigrants, but they reaffirmed exclusion of Japanese mine workers and undermined impressive existing solidarity between Greeks and Japanese, who often worked similar jobs.[67] The fear of immigrant "green hands," which the perceptive Lithuanian immigrant quoted above credited with first sparking the Butcher Workmen to organize recent immigrants in 1904, was also a fear of Black hands; one historian has suggested that the desire to limit Black employment generated the willingness to organize new immigrants.[68] In 1905 Gompers promised that "caucasians are not going to let their standard of living be destroyed by negroes, Chinamen, Japs, or any others."[69] Hearing this, new-immigrant unionists might have reflected on what they as "caucasians" had to learn regarding their newfound superiority to nonwhites. Or they might have fretted that *guineas* and *hunkies* would be classified along with "any others" undermining white standards. Either way, learning about race was an important part of new immigrants' labor education.

Teaching Americanism, the labor movement also taught whiteness. The scattered racist jokes in the labor and socialist press could not, of course, rival blackface entertainments or the "coon songs" in the Sunday comics in teaching new immigrants the racial ropes of the United States, but the movement did provide a large literature of popularized racist ethnology, editorial attacks on "nigger equality," and (in Jack London) a major cultural figure who taught that it was best to be "first of all a white man and only then a socialist."[70] But the influence of organized labor and of the left on race thinking was far more focused on language than on literature, on picket lines than on lines on a page. Unions that opened the door to new immigrants more readily than to "nonwhites" not only reinforced the "inbetween" position of southern and eastern Europeans but also attempted to teach immigrants intricate and spurious associations of race, strikebreaking, and lack of manly pride. Even as AFL exclusionism ensured that there would be Black strikebreakers and Black suspicion of unions, the language of labor equated scabbing with "turning nigger." The unions organized much of their critique around a notion of "slavish" behavior that could be employed against ex-slaves or against Slavs, but they indicted the former more often than the latter.[71] Warning all union men against "slave-like" behavior, unions familiarized new workers with the ways in which race and slavery had gone together to define a standard of unmanned servility. In objectively confusing situations, with scabs coming from the African American, immigrant, and native-born working classes (and with craft unions routinely breaking each others' strikes), Booker T. Washington identified one firm rule of thumb: "Strikers seem to consider it a much greater crime for a Negro who had been denied the opportunity to work at his trade to take the place of a striking employee than for a white man to do the same thing."[72]

In such situations, whiteness had its definite appeals. But the left and labor movements could abruptly remind new immigrants that their whiteness was anything but secure. Jack London could turn from denunciations of the "yellow peril" or of African Americans to excoriations of "the dark-pigmented things" coming in from Europe. The 1912 Socialist party campaign book connected European immigration with "race annihilation" and the "possible degeneration of even the succeeding American type." The prominence of Black strikebreakers in several of the most important mass strikes after World War I strengthened the grip of racism, perhaps even among recent immigrants, but the same years also brought renewed racial attacks on the immigrants themselves. In the wake of these failed strikes, the *American Federationist* featured disquisitions on "Americanism and Immigration" by John Quinn, the national commander of the nativist and antilabor American Legion. New immigrants had unarguably proven the most loyal unionists in the most important of the strikes, but the AFL now supported exclusion based on "racial" quotas. Quinn brought together biology, environment, and the racialized history of the United States, defending American stock against Italian "industrial slaves" particularly and the "indigestion of immigration" generally.[73]

Inbetween and Indifferent:
New Immigrant Racial Consciousness

One Italian American informant interviewed by a Louisiana scholar remembered the early twentieth century as a time when "he and his family had been badly mistreated by a French plantation owner near New Roads where he and his family were made to live among the Negroes and were treated in the same manner. At first he did not mind because he did not know any difference, but when he learned the position that the Negroes occupied in this country, he demanded that his family be moved to a different house and be given better treatment." In denouncing all theories of white supremacy, the Polish-language Chicago-based newspaper *Dziennik Chicagoski* editorialized, ". . . if the words 'superior race' are replaced by the words 'Anglo-Saxon' and instead of 'inferior races' such terms as Polish, Italian, Russian and Slavs in general—not to mention the Negro, the Chinese, and the Japanese—are applied, then we shall see the political side of the racial problems in the United States in stark nakedness."[74] In the first instance, consciousness of an inbetween racial status led to a desire for literal distance from nonwhites. In the second, inbetween-ness led to a sense of grievances shared in common with nonwhites.

In moving from the racial categorization of new immigrants to their own racial consciousness, it is important to realize that ". . . Europeans were hardly likely to have found racist ideologies an astounding new encounter when they arrived in the U.S.," although the salience of whiteness as a social category in the United States was exceptional. "Civilized" northern Italians derided those darker ones from Sicily and the mezzogiorno as "Turks" and "Africans" long before arriving in Brooklyn or Chicago. And once arrived, if they spoke of "little dark fellows," they were far more likely to be describing southern Italians than African Americans. The strength of anti-Semitism, firmly ingrained in Poland and other parts of eastern Europe meant that many immigrants from these regions were accustomed to looking at a whole "race" of people as devious, degraded, and dangerous. In the United States, both Jews and Poles spoke of riots involving attacks on African Americans as "pogroms." In an era of imperialist expansion and sometimes strident nationalism, a preoccupation with race was characteristic not only of the United States but also of many European regions that experienced

heavy emigration to the United States.[75] Both eager embraces of whiteness and, more rarely, flirtations with non-whiteness characterized
these immigrants' racial identities. But to assume that new immigrants
as a group clearly saw themselves as sharing an identity with nonwhites
or clearly fastened on differences from them is to miss the confusion of
inbetween-ness. The discussion of whiteness was uncomfortable terrain
for many reasons, and even in separating themselves from African
Americans and Asian Americans, immigrants did not necessarily become
white. Indeed, they often were curiously indifferent to whiteness.

Models that fix on one extreme or the other of immigrant racial
consciousness—the quick choice of whiteness amid brutal competition
or the solidarity with nonwhite working people based on common
oppression—capture parts of the new-immigrant experience.[76] At times
southern and eastern Europeans were exceedingly apt, and not very
critical, students of American racism. Greeks who were admitted to the
Western Federation of Miners saw the advantage of their membership
and did not rock the boat by demanding admission for the Japanese
American mine workers with whom they had previously been allied.
Greek Americans sometimes battled for racial status fully in the context
of white supremacy, arguing that classical civilization had established
them as "the highest type of the caucasian race." In the company town
of Pullman and adjacent neighborhoods, immigrants who were sharply
divided along national and religious lines coalesced impressively as
whites in the 1920s to keep out African American residents.[77] Recently
arrived Jewish immigrants on New York City's lower east side resented
reformers who encouraged them to make a common cause with the
"schwartzes" on the other side of the color line. In New Bedford, "white
Portuguese" angrily reacted to perceived racial slights and sharply drew
the color line against "black Portuguese" Cape Verdeans, especially
when preference in jobs and housing hung in the balance.[78] Polish
workers may have developed their very self-image and honed their reputation in more or less conscious counterpoint to the stereotypical *niggerscab*. Theodore Radzialowski reasons that Poles "who had so little
going for them (except their white skin—certainly no mean advantage
but more important later than earlier in their American experience),
may have grasped this image of themselves as honest, honorable, non-
scabbing workers and stressed the image of the black scab in order to
distinguish themselves from . . . the blacks with whom they shared the
bottom of American society."[79] Many new immigrants learned to
deploy and manipulate white supremacist images from the vaudeville

stage and the screens of Hollywood films where they saw "their own kind" stepping out of conventional racial and gender roles through blackface and other forms of cross-dressing. "Facing nativist pressure that would assign them to the dark side of the racial divide," Michael Rogin argues provocatively, immigrant entertainers such as Al Jolson, Sophie Tucker, and Rudolph Valentino, "Americanized themselves by crossing and recrossing the racial line."[80]

At the same time, immigrants sometimes hesitated to embrace white supremacy and even to adopt a white identity. Houston's Greek Americans developed, and retained, a language that set them apart from *i mavri* (the Blacks), from *i aspri* (the whites), and from Mexican Americans. In New England, Greeks worked in coalitions with Armenians, whom the courts were worriedly accepting as white, and Syrians, whom the courts found nonwhite. The large Greek American sponge-fishing industry based in Tarpon Springs, Florida, fought the Ku Klux Klan and employed Black workers on an equal, share-the-catch system. Nor did Tarpon Springs practice Jim Crow in public transportation. In Louisiana and Mississippi, even when they were legally accepted as whites, southern Italians learned Jim Crow so tardily that native whites fretted and Black southerners "made unabashed distinctions between Dagoes and white folks," treating the former with a "friendly, first name familiarity." In constructing an anti-Nordic-supremacist history series based on "gifts" of various peoples, the Knights of Columbus quickly and fully included African Americans. Italian and Italian American radicals "consistently expressed horror at the barbaric treatment of blacks," in part because "Italians were also regarded as an inferior race." Denouncing not only lynchings but also "the republic of lynchings," and branding the rulers of the United States as "savages of the blue eyes," *Il Proletario* asked, "What do they think they are as a race, these arrogant whites?" and ruthlessly wondered, "and how many kisses have their women asked for from the strong and virile black servants?" The Jewish press at times identified with both the suffering and the aspirations of African Americans. In 1912 Chicago's *Daily Jewish Courier* concluded that "in this world . . . the Jew is treated as a Negro and [the] Negro as a Jew" and that the "lynching of the Negroes in the South is similar to massacres of Jews in Russia."[81]

Examples could, and should, be piled higher on both sides of the new immigrants' racial consciousness. But to see the matter largely in terms of which stack is higher misses the extent to which the exposed position of racial inbetween-ness could generate both positions at once, and sometimes a desire to avoid the issue of race entirely. The best group with which to compare new-immigrant racial consciousness is the Irish Americans in the mid-nineteenth century. Especially when they were not broadly accepted as such, Irish Americans insisted that politicians acknowledge them as part of the dominant race. Changing the political subject from American-ness and religion to race whenever possible, they challenged anti-Celtic Anglo-Saxonism by becoming leaders in the cause of white supremacy.[82] New-immigrant leaders never approximated that path. With a large segment of both parties willing to vouch for the possibility of speedy, orderly Americanization and with both parties unwilling to vouch unequivocally for their racial character, southern and eastern Europeans generally tried to change the subject from whiteness to nationality and loyalty to American ideals.

One factor in such a desire not to be drawn into debates about whiteness was a strong national/cultural identification as Jews, Italians, Poles, and so on; at times, the strongest tie might even be to a specific Sicilian or Slovakian village. The first sustained contact between African Americans and "new immigrants" occurred during World War I when many of these immigrants were mesmerized by the emergence of Poland and other new states throughout eastern and southeastern Europe. Perhaps this is why new immigrants in Chicago and other riot-torn cities seem to have abstained from early-twentieth-century race riots to a far greater extent than theories connecting racial violence and job competition at "the bottom" of society would predict. Important Polish spokespersons and newspapers emphasized that the Chicago riots were between the "whites" and "Negroes." In this view, Polish immigrants had—and should have had—no part in them. What might be termed an *abstention from whiteness* also characterized the more general practice of rank-and-file eastern Europeans. Slavic immigrants played little role in the racial violence spread by Irish American gangs.[83]

Throughout the 1919 Chicago race riot, so vital to the future of Slavic packinghouse workers and their union, Polish American coverage was sparse and occurred only when editors "could tear their attention away from their fascination with the momentous events attending the birth of the new Polish state." Even then, comparisons with pogroms against Jews in Poland framed the discussion. That the defense of Poland was as important as analyzing the realities in Chicago emerges starkly in the convoluted expression of sympathy for riot victims in the organ of the progressive, prolabor Alliance of Polish Women, *Glos Polek:* "The American Press has written at length about the alleged pogroms of Jews in Poland for over two months. Now it is writing about pogroms against Blacks in America. It wrote about the Jews in words full of sorrow and sympathy, why does it not show the same today to Negroes being burnt and killed without mercy?"[84]

Both "becoming American" and "becoming white" could imply coercive threats to European national identities. The 1906 remarks of Luigi Villiari, an Italian government official investigating Sicilian sharecroppers in Louisiana, illustrate the gravity and interrelatedness of these processes. Villiari found that "a majority of plantation owners cannot comprehend that . . . Italians are white" and instead considered the Sicilian migrant "a white-skinned negro who is a better worker than the black-skinned negro." He patiently explained the "commonly held distinction . . . between 'negroes,' 'Italians,' and 'whites' (that is, Americans)." In the South, he added, the "American will not engage in agricultural, manual labor, rather he leaves it to the negroes. Seeing that the Italians will do this work, naturally he concludes that Italians lack dignity. The only way an Italian can emancipate himself from this inferior state is to abandon all sense of national pride and to identify completely with the Americans."[85]

Both 100 percent whiteness and 100 percent Americanism carried overlapping and confusing imperatives for new immigrants in and out of the South, but in several ways the former was even more uncomfortable terrain than the latter. The pursuit of white identity, so tied to competition for wage labor and to political citizenship, greatly privileged male perceptions. But identity formation, as Americanizers and immigrant leaders realized, rested in large part on the activities of immigrant mothers, who entered discussions of nationality and Americanization more easily than those of race.[86] More cast in determinism, the discourse of race produced fewer openings to inject class demands, freedom and cultural pluralism than did the discourse of Americanism. The modest strength of herrenvolk, or "master race," democracy, weakened even in the South at a time when huge numbers of the white poor were disfranchised, paled in comparison to the opportunities to try to give progressive spin to the idea of a particularly freedom-loving "American race."

In a fascinating quantified sociological study of Poles in Buffalo in the mid-1920s, Niles Carpenter and Daniel Katz concluded that their interviewees had been "Americanized" without being "de-Polandized." Their data led to the conclusion that Polish immigrants displayed "an absence of strong feeling so far as the Negro is concerned," a pattern "certainly in contrast to the results which would be sure to follow the putting of similar questions to a typically American group." The authors therefore argued for "the inference that so-called race feeling in this country is much more a product of tensions and quasi-psychoses born of our own national experience than of any factors inherent in the relations of race to race." Their intriguing characterization of Buffalo's Polish community did not attempt to cast its racial views as "pro-Negro" but instead pointed out that "the bulk of its members express indifference towards him." Such indifference, noted also by other scholars, was the product not of unfamiliarity with, or distance from, the U.S. racial system but of nationalism compounded by intense, harrowing, and contradictory experiences inbetween whiteness and non-whiteness.[87] Only after the racial threat of new immigration was defused by the racial restriction of the Johnson-Reed Act restricting immigration in 1924 would new immigrants haltingly find a place in the ethnic wing of the white race.

Plotting against Eurocentrism

Eurocentrism, the dictionaries tell us, came into usage as a critical term as recently as thirty years ago. However, the struggle against the fraudulence and terror that accompany and proceed from the habit of placing the so-called white so-called West at the center of the world has a far longer and prouder history. Naming the enemy is all to the good, but it is an act of remarkable hubris—and indeed of Eurocentrism—to suppose that critiques of putting Europe at the center of everything developed recently, with academics in European and United States universities taking the lead. Such institutions have thrown, and still throw, their oppressive weight behind Eurocentric notions of the most bizarre sort. Perhaps the oddest of these fictions is the very idea that the tiny outcropping of land called Europe somehow counts as a continent, on the order of, for example, Asia or Africa.

Although they are only beginning to be explored, most searchingly in dissident publications such as the radical geography journal *Antipode,* the connections among imaginations of place, imperialism, and mapping remain deeply impressed on the unconscious of most of us. What Martin Lewis and Karen Wigen call "the myth of continents" is a fiction that helps to rule our world. Thus we grow up knowing that longitude begins and ends with the prime meridian. We are less encouraged to consider how it came to pass through England, the leader of the plundering nations in 1884 when an international agreement established the system. And if we read Joseph Conrad's *The Secret Agent* (written in 1907 but set in 1886 and based loosely on events occurring in 1894), we have no idea why it is appropriate that much of the tale turns on anarcho-police agent fascinations with blowing up Greenwich Observatory, the epicenter of imperialist mapping and standardization of time. In the United States, children mature staring to the front of classrooms at world maps that grossly overstate the size of northern nations and that center on the Atlantic Ocean—and therefore on the United States and Europe as land masses. Thus, in looking at the 1929 surrealist map on which this article focuses, my eleven-year-old son noted its "Océan Pacifique"–centeredness by asking, "How come it's backwards?"

If students later see less distorted maps such as those based on the Peters Projection, the land masses seem bunched around the equator, with Africa remarkably large and the United States surprisingly tiny. Maps are passed off as replications of the land (and, less often, of the oceans), not of how humans imagine their relationship to nature. As Robert Harrison's *Eccentric Spaces* argued in 1977, "On the kind of maps most people use, one feature is exaggerated at the expense of everything else, the system of roads." And yet these are seen simply as objective maps, rather than as plottings tailored to a civilization whose relationship to the natural world is utterly and perhaps fatally mediated by automobiles. Churches, national forests, colleges, and tiny drawings of oil wells occasion little comment when they crop up on authoritative maps. If toxic waste dumps, areas redlined by banks and insurance companies, union halls, and bird populations are mapped, however, the project is surely exotic and peculiar.

Geographers often refer to attempts to provide alternatives to imperialist projecting not as mappings but as "countermappings." The tradition is a venerable one. Just over a century after Christopher Columbus carried getting lost to world-historical proportions, colonists at Jamestown, Virginia, encountered an ambitious map drawn by members of Chief Powhatan's confederacy. The map placed the land which the Native Americans inhabited at the center of a flat world. Near the map's edge, a small pile of sticks represented England. In the early 1720s, remarkable Chickasaw and Catawban maps came into the possession of British officials in Charlestown, South Carolina. One Chickasaw map placed the "Chickasaw Nation" in Northern Mississipi at its center, and one produced by a member of a Catawban group enlarged the Piedmont dramatically. Both the Chickasaw and Catawban maps represent Native American groups with circles of various sizes. "The Catawban mapmaker," the archaeologist and historian Greg Waselkov writes, "expanded the metaphor of the social circle when he drew a rectangular grid plan of Charlestown and a square representing Virginia." Charlestown's grid on the map may have plotted the actual pattern of the streets or rice fields in the area, but the depictions of Virginia signaled to Waselkov a clear commentary. In contrast to recognition of even enemy tribes as "circular people," he writes, "the British are square."

More self-consiously anti-imperialist countermaps of the recent past include the frontispiece of Kwame Nkrumah's *Class Struggles in Africa* (1970). Within the confines of Africa, Nkrumah's map inserts the whole of Europe and the United States, as well as Japan, all shaded gray, and the British Isles blackened. India, like Africa unshaded, is added for good measure, and there remains plenty of room to spare. Philippe Rekacewicz's beautiful recent "Towards a New African Geopolitics: Africa Redrawn," which appeared in the journal *Public Culture* in 2000, applies ideas on space developed by Achille Mbembe. Zones on that lavishly colored map include "Pillaged Territories" and "States Undergoing a Process of Implosion." The collaborative "indigenous counter-maps" produced recently by the Kek'chi and Mopan Maya peoples of southern Belize, recently collected in the strikingly beautiful *Mayan Atlas* (1998), came into being as part of a struggle to resist deforestation and to secure land rights. Making land claims and claims about how people do and should interact with the land, these intensely local maps represent the results of collaborative deliberations. The cartographers are popularly elected.

It is within such traditions that the 1929 "Surrealist Map of the World" ought to be considered. Originally published in Belgium in the special "Surrealism in 1929" issue of the review *Variétès* under the title "Le Monde au temps des surréalistes" ("The World in the Time of the Surrealists"), the map almost certainly represented a collaboration. Thus it was included as a "collective declaration" in José Pierre's *Tracts surréalistes et déclarations collectives, Tome I, 1922–1939* (1980). In a 1999 talk on "Surrealism: The Caribbean Connection," Michael Stone-Richards emphasized that the map reflects the surrealists' "explicit engagement" with the poet Paul Valéry. More specifically, the map responds to Valéry's 1919 text "The Crisis of the European Mind," in which he had asked whether Europe "will become what it is in reality?—that is to say, a little tip of the continent of Asia." To this question, Stone-Richards added, "the Surrealist Map of the World says yes."

The Surrealist Map of the World. 1929. Collective declaration of the Surrealist Movement.

Probably drawn by the French surrealist painter Yves Tanguy, who assembled the rescaled world as collage, the map retains charming enigmas.

For some, the project defies explanation. Indeed, the British leftist David Widgery, in his article on the 1978 "Dada and Surrealism Reviewed" exhibition at London's Hayward Gallery, reported overhearing the following conversation there:

> WOMAN: "Surrealist map" what's it all mean?
>
> MAN: Well, I suppose that it is trying to portray, er it's like a child would draw a map you know, a childlike drawing. See the United States is missing.
>
> WOMAN: Oh, yes, and England's missing too.
>
> MAN: Yes, I don't understand that at all.

Less uncomprehending, if not fully sympathetic, is Patrick Waldberg's *Surrealism* (1965), which echoes the idea of the map as "childish," while casting the project as emblematic of surrealist enmity to "Western Christian civilization" and of the movement's readiness to sacrifice "all Romanesque art, the cathedrals, the chateaux of the Loire, and Versailles, in favor of the statues on Easter Island." Waldberg adds that the drawing creates "an imaginary world" that is "considered to be the only desirable one."

However puzzled and distant Widgery's overheard exchange and Waldberg's history are, on one level they together suggest what cannot be missed as striking qualities of the "Surrealist Map of the World." Reconnecting mapmaking with imagination, and frankly posing cartography as a matter of political and creative choice, the map does uncompromisingly disappear England (which may be a tiny, nameless dot near Ireland) and the United States. Indeed, with the exception of a much-enlarged Soviet Russia, at that time by no means unequivocally considered "Western," the 1929 map literally belittles Europe. It anticipates Richard Wright's 1957 reminder, in his *White Man, Listen!* that "It is difficult for white Western Europe to realize how tiny Europe is in the minds of the people of the earth." If, as the surrealist poet Ted Joans has recently put it, the United States and Europe, those "two too-white places," are merely "meeting places for humankind to do technological and monetary jive," the map is drawn to human scale.

Although brief, Gérard Legrand's discussion of the map under the entry "Carte géographique" in the *Dictionnaire Générale du surréalisme et ses environs* (1982) makes two vital points. Calling the drawing an "imaginary planisphere," Legrand insists that it is at once a "humorous provocation" and a reflection of the "spirit as well as the artistic and political tendencies of the group at a given moment." To miss its playfulness—the intricacies of its production may preclude our crediting it with childishness—in order to linger over the meaning of each detail invites the sort of misunderstanding all too typical of today's humorless academic studies of surrealism generally. But neither would it do to miss the clear political and artistic messages, at a given moment, that it contains.

The example of the rendering of Soviet Russia helps to clarify interpretive matters. Russia's aggrandizement moves the map's center dramatically northward in a way so discomfiting to those of us accustomed to seeing global inequality mapped on a North–South rather than an East–West axis that we risk missing the novelty of a map that directs the viewers' attention to the Bering Straits and the Pacific. Moreover, as Gérard Durozoi has recently written in his *Histoire du mouvement surréaliste* (1997), this positioning of the Stalinizing Soviet Union exists in counterpoint with the inclusion of Constantinople—then the place of the anti-Stalinist militant Leon Trotsky's exile—as the only named city in addition to Paris. Moves following surrealism's trajectory toward far more explicit critiques of Stalinism would have made for a much different surrealist mapping in the mid-1930s than in 1929. Similarly, it is easy to imagine a much larger Latin America and Caribbean quickly replacing the small renderings of those places on the 1929 map, as West

Indian and Brazilian influences changed the racial politics and world-view of surrealism.

Although Durozoi rightly observes that the map "affirms that [surre-alist] interest in communism did not in the least diminish their interest in nonWestern cultures," it is fair to add that the interest focused in this instance on Oceania and on Eskimo and Northwest Coast Indian terri-tories—those areas least in contact with colonizing powers and known for the unspoiled wildness of their land and animals. The communist and surrealist activist André Thirion observed in his later recollections (*Revolutionaries without Revolution,* 1975) that the 1929 map imag-ined a world in which "half the globe is reduced in favor of New Guinea and Easter Island." Thirion emphasized that this resizing stemmed from both aesthetic and political commitments. The Afro-visionary novelist Ishmael Reed used related aspects of the 1929 map, in his 1990 collec-tion *Writin' Is Fightin',* to question the idea of pure and monolithic "Western civilization." He asked, "And what of the cubists, through whom the influence of African art changed modern painting; or the sur-realists, who were so impressed with the art of the Pacific Northwest Indians that, in their map of North America, Alaska dwarfs the lower forty-eight in size?"

Africa, somewhat surprisingly, shrinks in the rendering of Tanguy. In this specific case, the bourgeois and "avant-fraud" vogue for things African in 1929, in and outside of France, may have played a role. Dawn Ades overdraws her insistence (in the catalog of the 1978 "Dada and Surrealism Reviewed" exhibition in London) that the 1929 world map downsized Africa out of a conviction that the art of that continent was "too terrestrial in its themes, too concerned with rendering the human figure in a more or less realistic way, and with beauty and pro-portion in form." Surrealist admiration for African art, and for what André Breton called its "explosive contribution" to the modern spirit, before and after 1929, cuts against so sweeping a judgment. However, as Ades and Ishmael Reed both suggest, it is true that passion for African art among Europeans was more long-standing and widespread than the celebration of Oceanic, Eskimo, and Northwest Coast art, which was more apt to be considered a surrealist "discovery." More-over, the grounds on which African art found admiration in the years after World War I sometimes took forms that could only have appalled surrealists, as in Apollinaire's naïve appreciation of "Negro sculpture" as a precursor of the Greek and as "able to compete perfectly well with the beautiful works of European sculpture."

Haifa Zangana's *Destruction of a Map*. Collage. 1978. With
permission of the artist.

But it remains vital not to overinterpret the map. The surrealists' collective mapping project encouraged and even cultivated idiosyncrasy
and inconsistency. In that sense the prominence of Paris (included as the
capital of Germany, although France is omitted) ought to be read not as
Francophilia but as provocation, reminding viewers that the map is a
production imagined and made in a specific place, time, and context,
not a reproduction of reality. The attack launched by the map centered
not only on challenging the specifics of imperialist, capitalist, and tech-
nocratic mapping but also on blowing the cover of exactitude and science that the idea of mapping as reproduction gives to the acceptance
of a world of misery.

In this sense, as well as others, the "Surrealist Map of the World"
bears strong affinities to the brilliant "Destruction of a Map," a 1978
collage by the female Iraqi-born surrealist, pharmacist, novelist and
anti-imperialist militant Haifa Zangana. Zangana's work boldly suggests that the labored and manly forces none too successfullly attacking

the map are so musclebound by the trappings of a classical, Christian, and nationalist logic as to undermine their own effects.

Finally, and critically, it deserves emphasizing that, like the best of the whole utopian tradition of which it is a part, the 1929 surrealist remapping of the world does not invite our assent to its particular imagination. Rather, it demands our active imagination of new worlds. Marx's injunction that the point is not merely to understand the world but to transform it finds apt literal impression in the 1929 map, but as an anti-Eurocentric work in progress, not as a last word. Ted Joans's 1984 invocation of the "Map of the World," in reprinting the Nkrumah volume's African map, stands as a powerful example. Writing in the Berlin-based surrealist journal *Dies und Das* (*This and That*), which he coedited with the German surrealist poet Richard Anders, Joans offered the reprint from the Nkrumah book not only in order "to demonstrate the immensity of the continent" but also "to update the true surrealist point of view of Africa."

THREE

The Past/Presence of Nonwhiteness

What If Labor Were Not White and Male?

Before becoming the greatest historian of race and class of his generation, Alexander Saxton was a young activist working in the railroad industry. In a lengthy article for the *Daily Worker* during World War II, he captured the complexity of racial discrimination among railway unions. The brotherhoods that organized railroad labor included several unions that historically had the worst records of attempting to enforce what one commentator called the "Nordic closed shop" in their crafts. By the time Saxton wrote, however, the railway unions had joined in campaigns against the poll tax and against lynching. What they avoided was agitation against "alleged" racism in their own workplaces. When the Fair Employment Practices Committee canceled hearings inquiring into discrimination in railroad employment, the unions rejoiced. Their newspaper observed that in any case, such hearings would be illegitimate if African Americans joined in the deliberations. "There should be on the Committee," according to *Labor*, "no representative of any race or special interest." Saxton wryly added, "Apparently white men belong to no race."[1]

Bernice Anita Reed's fine 1947 study of racial "accommodation" in a West Coast aircraft factory during the second world war likewise lay bare contradictions. Using plant records and hundreds of formal interviews to reconstruct how white and Black workers "harmonized" after the latter group gained entry into wartime aircraft industry jobs, Reed found that open opposition to working with African Americans was immediate and significant, but not at all simple. Frequent voluntary

terminations of employment by whites greeted integration. In about
1 case in 20, exiting white workers gave the relaxing of color bars as
the reason why they left. However, 86% of the foremen who were
interviewed reported an equally significant pattern, in which white
workers announced their intention to quit if required to work with
African Americans but relented and then became much more amenable
to working in interracial groups. Reed describes extensive change in
white, often southern-born, workers' attitudes and notes the growth of
exchanges of pleasantries, and even of on-the-job friendships, across
the color line. She finds that a curious kind of pride in knowing and getting along with Black workers developed among whites working in the
industry. But the distinction between interracial "plant friendships"
and "socializing" beyond the factory gate remained clear, and any
closeness that evolved was confined to the workplace. What Reed does
not much note is the further complexity raised by the fact that Black
workers were being brought into, and kept in, the four low-wage occupations in the factory, no matter what their skills. Thus Reed unproblematically writes of a kind of "harmonizing" behavior among white
employees that may say more about how thoroughly bosses and white
workers continued to regard "whiteness as property" than about liber-
alizing changes wrought by the war:

> Frequently the white employee aided in the accommodation of Negro
> employees with superior backgrounds, when such Negroes were assigned as
> helpers to white employees with inferior qualifications. Often the white
> sensed the Negro employee's difficulty in adjusting to the situation and
> avoided giving him direct orders or instructions. He attempted in innumer-
> able ways to ease the situation by making the Negro employee less aware of
> his subordinate position. When this occurred, accommodation was eventu-
> ally achieved and tended to permit development of genuine affection . . .
> between the two employees.[2]

These two examples illustrate the extent to which whites have been
seen to occupy not only a central position in American labor but also a
natural one. Their privileges—and sometimes the very fact that they
have a racial identity—go un(re)marked. As one observer of labor in
the 1940s put it, "Because few Negroes have been promoted to the better paying jobs in the past, white workers have come to regard white
priority as the established order of things." Toni Morrison has brilliantly argued that one huge achievement of white racial identity in the
United States has been to make the very word *American* imply *white
American,* so that only so-called "nonwhites" have needed to have their
racial identities as Americans specified.[3] The same logic has applied to

labor, which in iconography, public discourse, and historical writing has often been assumed to be white and male. The labor movement and the working class were so strongly identified with whiteness by the founding fathers of labor studies in the United States that the passage of Chinese exclusion legislation was portrayed by the Commons School as *the* historic triumph of American labor, one that allegedly ensured that U.S. labor history would unfold as a story of class and not of race. The union label and the "white label" were used almost interchangeably in some late-nineteenth-century crafts that were attempting to use boycotts to enhance unionism's strengths.[4]

Nor are such assumptions buried in the distant past of conservative craft unionism. The very language and the (il)logic of attacking "discrimination in reverse" was precociously developed in the industrial unions in the steel and auto industries, as the bureaucracies in those bodies fought attempts to increase black representation in leadership positions and defended mechanisms of internal promotion that much favored whites. The AFL-CIO accused A. Philip Randolph of reverse racism when, in 1961, he proposed a moderate set of policies to end white privileges in unionized sectors. When the AFL-CIO gave conditional support to Title VII antidiscrimination legislation in 1964, a major condition was that it not interfere with "seniority rights already obtained by any employee."[5] Seniority and layoff policies that took race, gender, and past discrimination into account were manifestly "unjust to white workers." The AFL-CIO argued for strict adherence to seniority as a "colorblind" policy, ignoring the ways in which seniority systems on separate departmental lines had long been used to keep skilled and high-paying jobs as a white preserve. When the union federation insisted that Title VII "take away nothing from the American worker which he has already acquired" it perfectly illustrated Morrison's point about the conflation of *white* and *American* and perpetuated the deep connections between whiteness and the "natural" expectation of property advantages so tellingly detailed in Cheryl Harris's recent analysis of the long roots of opposition to affirmative action.[6]

Those who coded "American labor" as white and male in the past at least had on their side the fact that the wage-earning population, like the rank-and-file of organized labor, did in fact fit into those categories, if we specify that southern and eastern European immigrants were at least on some level classified as white in the early twentieth century. For the past twenty years, white women and male and female workers of color have gone to wage-earning jobs in greater numbers than have white men, however. In 1982 white men constituted 47% of the U.S.

labor force. By 2005, according to *Monthly Labor Review,* that figure will drop to just over 1 worker in 3 (37%). That same year, 1 worker in 4 will be Black or Latino. White males are likewise becoming a minority among trade union members. In 1995 the Bureau of Labor Statistics counted 8.33 million white male union members. Unionized Black and Hispanic men and women, along with unionized white women, totaled 8.93 million.[7]

This chapter attempts to come to grips with these demographic changes, particularly where race is concerned. It asks how a working-class history written with the changed labor force and labor movement "in mind" might change the field. An initial section argues that, quite beyond simple demographics and in ways far more profound than the much-discussed recent changes in top AFL-CIO leadership, the face of organized labor is changing and that this transformation is likely to open fresh avenues of inquiry into the past. A second section broadly outlines how recent work in labor history has begun to respond to changes in the composition of the working class and of organized labor. The chapter then considers how one specific debate—that over the record of organized labor in combating racism—might be transformed as historians write for a changed labor audience and react to the fact that the coding of labor as white and male cannot be sustained. It concludes still more concretely, with a consideration of the labor movement during and after Reconstruction, arguing that Du Bois's critique of the assumption that white workers constituted the center of class struggles after the Civil War speaks profoundly to the ways in which labor history might be recentered and rewritten.

Seeing Change

In his useful study of organized labor and civil rights, Alan Draper contextualized AFL-CIO head George Meany's refusal to endorse the 1963 Black freedom movement's March on Washington. Draper attributed Meany's abstention to political pragmatism, not racism or callousness. According to Draper, Meany "was reluctant to associate labor with tactics that might damage the image of middle-class respectability he sought for it." The "desire for respectability" made Meany "disavow such political tactics as street demonstrations that might associate labor with such crude and vulgar activities." Much recent writing on race, whiteness, and organized labor would suggest that Draper's sharp distinction between race-thinking and hankering for respectability as possible motivations for Meany's inaction needs further examination.

To what extent was the imperative to be middle-class and respectable itself colored by a long-standing desire to be disassociated from "dirty work" and from the nonwhite "lower classes"? Why was a peaceful, dignified, and largely African American demonstration for justice and jobs considered "crude and vulgar"? In what ways were Meany's white-centered refusals to learn, tactically and morally, from the civil rights movement constitutive of what Draper later called "the insecure, obsequious personality of the American labor movement during his tenure," rather than simply a result of such insecurities?[8]

Such questions are very much posed by the course of the contemporary labor movement. With the exception of the conservative core of the antiabortion organizations, perhaps no social movement in the United States more strains to identify with the movements of the 1950s and 1960s for racial justice than organized labor. The 1989 insurgencies during the Pittston coal strike in southwest Virginia, for example, featured United Mine Workers leader Cecil Roberts frequently referring to his reading of Taylor Branch's classic history of the "King years," *Parting the Waters,* as inspiration for calls to nonviolent direct action. Roberts, (later president of the mine workers union) and current AFL-CIO vice-president Richard Trumka continually make this connection in agitational speeches. In the recent Detroit *News* and *Free Press* strikes, unionists began with evocations of Dr. King and moved to quoting Malcolm X, who has in at least one instance been memorialized in the trade union press as a "friend of labor." In the "war zone" strikes and lockouts among auto workers, miners, and corn syrup processors in the area of Decatur, Illinois, overwhelmingly white strike supporters sang "We Shall Overcome" and chanted "No Justice, No Peace" in militant street demonstrations. When strikers want national publicity, the first call is usually to request a visit from civil rights leader Jesse Jackson. When the AFL-CIO seeks to enlist college students as organizers, it restages the civil rights movement's Freedom Summer as "Union Summer."[9]

Such developments reflect the pervasiveness of the influence of the Black freedom movement in U.S. political culture generally and the relative absence of ongoing traditions of struggle within organized labor. But they also coincide with a profound development that labor historians and labor activists have yet to address: the demographic shift to a labor movement no longer predominantly white and male, except in its leadership. This important change receives little attention in writings that seek to situate organized labor's current weakness historically. Thus comparisons are made between the 1990s and the 1920s, a decade in which the American Federation of Labor was not only over-whelmingly white and male but also given to racist appeals against even "white" workers from southern and eastern Europe. "Lessons of his-tory" are certainly worth seeking in this regard, but the deeply altered context needs as much emphasis as continuities and cycles of historical development. Similarly, when intellectuals discuss whether organized labor has changed, the debate frequently centers on rehashes of the record of new AFL-CIO president John Sweeney. The role of rank-and-file initiatives in structuring changes at the top is given its due in the best writings on labor's recent history, but treatment of the implications of demographic shifts in the ranks of labor remains rare. Pessimists even entertain the notion that the working class itself is disappearing. This view is, of course, deeply connected with the coding of labor as white, European, and male—a coding whose influence on the historiog-raphy of labor is acutely discussed in the fine recent work of Iain Boal and Michael Watts.[10]

The failure to acknowledge that we write labor history in a new con-text is partially understandable, in that labor's leaders remain over-whelmingly white, male, and inept at forging links among the unions, women's groups, and communities of color. The change in race and gender of union membership obviously does not in and of itself guaran-tee policy change, as Herbert Hill's historical work on the International Ladies' Garment Workers Union and other unions amply demonstrates. Moreover, the demographic shift in labor's base has resulted as much from the loss of white men as members as from dynamic organizing among white women or among minority workers, male and female. But whatever the source of the shift in membership, the lag in leadership, and the precarious position of unions generally, the recomposition of the labor movement raises unprecedented possibilities, especially if we take seriously the growing historical literature that argues that defense of "whiteness as property," especially when combined with male supremacy, has shaped a conservative, narrow, and weak labor move-ment in the United States.[11]

One personal example and one based on *Wall Street Journal* report-ing—both admittedly suspect sources—will further suggest some of the ways in which working-class struggles and antilabor initiatives might be transformed by demographic changes in organized labor. In early April of 1996, my wife and I went to a demonstration in Las Vegas that had been called to protest the videotaped and much publicized police beat-ings of immigrant workers in southern California. The loud gathering of perhaps 200 people surged from the Federal Building's sidewalks onto Las Vegas's famous "strip," stopping traffic and provoking a blare of horns. Convened by the community group Action Latino, the demonstration featured scores of Latino workers in red "Culinary Workers Union" t-shirts. Members of the largely white Bartenders Union joined the protest. All the speeches were by union activists, who were also identified with Action Latino.

The *Wall Street Journal* example is more troubling and suggests ways in which a labor movement unmoored from the burdens and privileges of race and gender respectability will be subject to new attacks, even—and especially—as it achieves successes. Nearly three years after workers at Youngstown, Ohio's Carrington South Health Care Center voted to join Local 627 of the Service Employees International Union (SEIU), the large nursing home corporation that employed them was still contesting the election. The delay followed on a National Labor Relations Board complaint typical of a spate of similar ones files by management in other union elections. Local 627 was charged with "playing the race card." The "racist propaganda" that Carrington South charged the local with illegally using to win Black workers' votes consisted of three cartoons in union literature. In one of them, a white boss, with cigar, was near to an integrated group of workers. He flipped a dime forward, saying, "I'll take a dozen." In the second cartoon, workers of "indeterminable race" were flogged as they strained to pull a wagon. The third and most dramatic image featured a white employer who directed a Black employee toward an electric chair. Its caption read, "You don't need your union rep. Just have a seat and we'll discuss your grievances like two rational human beings." Carrington South maintained that the cartoons showed the white management of the company in "the most despicable light to black employees." The firm's lawyer, paraphrased by the *Journal,* warned that the cartoons "could remind the workers of slavery" and insisted that an appeals court decide whether the cartoons "could be seen as glaring, graphic appeals to racial prejudice."[12] In this alarming case, the labor movement's contributions to the development of a rhetoric of "reverse racism" came fully home to roost. As labor comes more and more to be, and to be seen as, a social movement of white women and people of color, it will risk being singled out for new attacks, presaged by the Carrington South case; by Yale University's fierce initiatives against its clerical, dining hall, and maintenance workers; and, most broadly, by the intense campaigns against organized public employees, who are among the most diverse and pro-gender-equity of the unionized sectors in the U.S. labor force.[13] Moments of flux, promise, and peril coincide, in ways that we are only beginning to realize, encouraging—necessitating—the rethinking of labor history.

Recentering Labor History

Imagining how a historian's friend-of-the-court brief for the SEIU's position in Carrington South might read is troubling in instructive ways. Certainly it would be easy to demonstrate, especially using the fine research of Barry Goldberg, that labor organizations historically made ample use of comparisons of "free labor" with slavery, typically without being hauled before labor boards and judges. But in these instances, the critiques of "wage slavery" or "white slavery" were pitched overwhelmingly to a white audience. Moreover, some of the labor literature on white slavery strongly implied that the wrongs being indicted were unconscionable precisely *because* whites were the victims. In other cases, labor's whiteness was simply assumed. Because the Carrington South representation election did in fact turn on the votes of Black workers, who constituted a large majority of the labor force, the more pressing historical issue may be the precedent for references to slavery in attempts to organize African American workers. In any case, we know too little about the impact of what Lawrence Levine calls "slave consciousness" on postbellum class consciousness among Black workers, and much of what we do know comes from disciplines outside labor history.[14]

Such a gap, and its potential importance in a case such as *Carrington South,* opens onto one of the three areas in which I will argue that the writing of working-class history is likely to change, and is already changing, partly in response to changes in the composition of the working class and of the labor movement. First, we are seeing an accelerated appreciation of the fact that the American working class was never nearly so white or so male as has been assumed. This point emerges from recent labor historiography in a variety of ways. Most obvious, of course, is the remarkable outpouring of work on the history of working white women and of workers of color. The important scholarship of Mary Blewett, Thomas Dublin, Nan Enstad, Alice Kessler-Harris, Christine Stansell, and (above all) Susan Porter Benson has, for example, demonstrated the centrality of women workers at key junctures in the evolution of new industries and services.[15] Recent studies by Robin D. G. Kelley, Earl Lewis, Chris Friday, Joe Trotter, A. Yvette Huginnie,

Zaragosa Vargas, and many others have immeasurably advanced the study of "nonwhite" workers.[16] The hitherto unappreciated extent of wage labor among American Indians recently has found its historians. The history of the international and racially mixed maritime working class has received expert treatment, especially in the work of Marcus Rediker and Peter Linebaugh, who emphasize the centrality of that proletariat to the rise of capitalism, and of resistance to it, globally.[17] Studies that consider commonalities and differences among various groups of nonwhite workers have been undertaken in the work of Neil Foley, Tomas Almaguer, and Ronald Takaki, among others.[18] Accounts of the history of working women of color, especially those by Vicki Ruiz and Tera Hunter, are groundbreaking in their sophistication and scope. Those by Hunter and Kelley draw deeply on scholarship on slavery, which contributes greatly to the unparalleled methodological facility that marks their work. Elsa Barkley Brown's studies of working class women in postbellum Richmond provide another striking example in this regard.[19] Indeed there is some indication that slavery will at last become central to labor history and there is even some debate about whether slaves labored in a capitalist social system.[20] The history of the relationship between nonwhite workers and white women workers is an especially salient issue at this juncture; it is brilliantly treated in the work of Kevin Boyle, Eileen Boris, and Dolores Janiewski.[21]

Many recent studies of workers who were not white and male usefully move beyond the point of production and beyond questions of trade union organization to discuss leisure, family, and consumption. But these same studies also frequently reveal that their subjects were deeply involved in class organizations, including unions. To the extent that scholars such as Jacqueline Dowd Hall, Robert Korstad, Dana Frank, Earl Lewis, Lisa Norling, and Elizabeth Faue appreciate the importance of studying working-class communities, families, and patterns of consumption, the idea of a working-class that was historically mostly white and male becomes still more open to question.[22]

The second broad change that can already be glimpsed in the writing of working-class history lies in the "problematizing" of white and male identities. Rather than assuming that whiteness and masculinity describe "natural" identities with which most wage earners are born, much recent scholarship asks when, how, and why such categories as *workingmen* and *white worker* came to be invested with such importance. This curiosity, linked to changing demographics that challenge assumptions that "naturally" connect white/male/worker/trade unionist, is perhaps most fully realized in the work of such feminist-influenced scholars as Ava Baron, Paul Taillon, Joshua Freeman, and Patricia Cooper, whose case studies of the history of printers, machinists, railroad workers, construction workers, and cigar makers go far toward delineating a changing class experience "lived" in what Stuart Hall and Paul Gilroy call the "modalities" of race and gender. Robert Lee's searching account of the roles of family, class, and ideology in the drama of "the coolie and the making of the white working class" marks another significant advance. George Chauncey's *Gay New York,* much admired broadly but too little claimed by labor historians as a classic in working-class history, offers perhaps the most challenging interrogation of the dynamics of gender, sexuality, and class.[23]

Work that begins with a focus on historicizing and problematizing working-class whiteness, rather than masculinity, has been less successful at incorporating gender as a category of analysis than scholarship that begins with a focus on gender and class has been at incorporating race. Eric Lott's study of minstrelsy and working-class formation remains a notable exception.[24] Even so, studies of whiteness in the working class have pushed the boundaries of labor history significantly. Particularly challenging have been the very recent works on how immigrant workers learned race in the United States, often coming to claim white identity tragically and successfully. Noel Ignatiev's *How the Irish Became White,* Karen Brodkin's study of Jewish Americans and whiteness, and Rudolph Vecoli's suggestive essay on Italian American racial identity are all noteworthy in this regard. My own research, with James Barrett, on how "new immigrant" males from various areas encountered race in the United States would have been impossible even a decade ago, both because of the absence of secondary literature and because of the presumed naturalness of white identity among European workers.[25]

The Trials of White Labor

The third area of possible dramatic change in the writing of working-class studies involves the historical record of labor unions where racism and exclusion are concerned. Because this hotly contested area is one in which the signs of changes are far less evident in recent scholarship, I want to move beyond simply sketching the historiography and to suggest in more detail how the recomposition of the working class and of the unions might be shifting lines of inquiry and debate. In this instance, I will include a concrete example of how historical debate can productively be shifted: the policies of the National Labor Union and other working-class organizations following the Civil War.

The most noteworthy fact about historians' writings on race and labor lies in the extent to which the records of the unions regarding racism have been put on trial. The most passionate recent incarnation of debates on this score are those sparked by Herbert Hill's 1987 article "Race, Ethnicity and Organized Labor" and by his still more controversial 1988 polemic against Herbert Gutman's alleged "myth-making" in the latter's writing on the late-nineteenth-century career of the Black union organizer Richard L. Davis. Hill, a former labor secretary for the National Association for the Advancement of Colored People, has long experience contributing to legal arguments by constructing a record of labor's racism. In responding to Hill's 1987 article, historian Nick Salvatore observed that it at times resembled a "legal brief (more) than reasoned analysis." Hill countered by defending the brief as an apt model for writing about labor and race. When Stephen Brier responded to Hill, he too alluded at length to the differences between legal argument and "critical, analytical and appropriately nuanced" historical writing. That Brier's response carried the title "In Defense of Gutman: The Union's Case" suggests that it marked a less than total break from the pattern of indictment and defense that has characterized debate on Hill's scholarship.[26]

The particular acrimony surrounding these very recent controversies should not obscure the fact that serious accounts of the history of race and labor have long been dominated by frank consideration of whether unions have mainly and inevitably functioned as "white male job trusts" or have been and may further become appropriate vehicles for mobilizing and satisfying the demands of workers of color.[27] This framing of issues is clear in the works of the African American scholars who have so powerfully contributed to writings on labor and racism. In 1935, when W. E. B. Du Bois published *Black Reconstruction,* one of the first historical works to inquire deeply and explicitly into the role of the "white worker" in the U.S. past, he was enmeshed in a series of debates with Black intellectuals who argued that the rise of industrial unionism provided a historic opportunity for Black-white labor unity. Arguing from history, Du Bois warned against placing hope narrowly in the labor movement. Although he wanted to "keep in close touch" with new trends in organized labor, he reminded readers of a long record of exclusion and suggested that many unions and most white workers were sure to be loath to "unite in any movement whose object was the uplift of the masses of Negroes to essential equality with them."[28] Horace Cayton read past and present differently from Du Bois in his enthusiastic endorsement of the early Congress of Industrial Organizations, only to express sharp disappointment and revised views later. The fullest account to date of the history of organized labor and Black workers, an important volume by the white Marxist Philip S. Foner, was similarly clear in linking its historical narration with political questions.[29]

The debate over whether labor has a "usable past" where antiracism and the addressing of the interests of workers of color are concerned is one that scholars have been able neither to settle nor to transcend in the context of a labor movement largely and, it would seem, naturally white and male. Even the useful recent scholarship emphasizing nuance, contradiction, variety, and the need for further research on labor's past where race is concerned might properly be asked whether the instances of interracial unionism that it has described are significant and unambiguous enough to permit a more optimistic *overall reading* of the history of race and labor.[30] Several impressive students of race and class, including Du Bois himself, took widely different positions on labor's racism at various stages of their careers.[31] Very often the judgment has boiled down to a reckoning, as Bert Cochran put it in the 1950s, of how many swallows make a spring. And in making such judgments, calculations of possibilities in the present and in the future have inevitably mattered as much as dispassionate inquiries into the past.[32]

Often, both pessimists and optimists on the issue have argued from the same evidence and assumptions. Thus Hill emphasizes the considerable record of interest and success in organizing among nonwhite workers themselves when he measures the enormity of the betrayal of egalitarianism by union racism. His opponents, at times wrongly assuming that there is no room in Hill's arguments for prounion initiatives by workers of color, count such initiatives as evidence that the record of the labor movement on race is more varied and less abysmal than its critics allow.[33] The Marxist idea that material interests have structured the exclusionary tendencies of white workers as capitalism has created (and capitalists have exploited) racial divisions among workers can be used to argue for the improbability of meaningful interracial labor unity or to mitigate the record of racism by white workers and their unions. The other major Marxist generalization about race and material conditions, often held in some tension with the contention that capitalism fosters racial division, holds that the common experience of class exploitation unifies workers across racial lines. It too undergirds both optimistic and pessimistic arguments. In the former case, instances of Black-white unity are treated not merely as conjunctural but also as evidence of the motion of history. In the latter case, the tragically protracted tendency of white workers to accept elite concessions of racial privileges rather than combating (or even seeing) common class exploitation, receives attention.[34]

Although the question of whether interracial labor unity has been "successful often enough" to support optimism regarding the future has been unwieldy, vexed, subjectively answered, and in many ways unproductive, it has also been central to labor history in the United States. It will remain so to the degree that union leadership remains disproportionately white and male and that high-paying trades continue to largely exclude nonwhite workers. But the changing demographics of the working class and of the ranks of organized labor alter the stakes of the debate greatly, permitting more dispassionate inquiry as well as the posing of new questions.[35] If labor is going to be less and less a "white thing," the record of trade union racism can be examined without an all-consuming search for *direct* historical lessons. Indeed, a full acknowledgment of the weight of the fetters that labor stands to shake off as it loses its whiteness may arguably come to be seen as the optimistic position, one that can examine past failures and envision future successes.

Signs that a more broadly sophisticated scholarship on race and labor may be emerging include an increasing emphasis on the specific factors that encourage interracial unity on the one hand and those that foster exclusion on the other. The long tradition of considering the role of union leadership on racial matters (Were the communists better?) continues to inform productive work, as does the issue of the extent to which organization along industrial lines fostered more egalitarian policies.[36] But recent studies, especially those by Eric Arnesen, Ronald Lewis, Joe Trotter, Michael Honey, Rick Halpern, Daniel Letwin, David Wellman, and Roger Horowitz, also underscocre the importance of the density of nonwhite workers in the industry and area studied and their social power to limit production. Such studies suggest that it is precisely in the situation in which we increasingly find ourselves (in highly mixed and white-minority workplaces) that white workers are most apt to move in racially egalitarian directions.[37] The increasing influence of Alexander Saxton's and Gwendolyn Mink's research is of special importance, because they demonstrate not only that racism was accentuated by organized labor's narrow craft traditions and lack of political independence but also that racism contributed to those very tendencies.[38] Recent investigations also illuminate the ways in which state-sanctioned terror against African Americans at times came to be used against white workers and their unions.[39] The "costs" of labor's racism appear not to be as simple to reckon as we had thought. If full studies of just how some white workers in particular times and places have reached antiracist conclusions remain sadly rare, at least we know something of the ways in which solidarities based on gender, and not just class, undergirded crossings of the color line.[40]

This optimistic view does not imply that the changing base of union membership will automatically call new scholarship into being. Indeed, in the short run, organized labor's new diversity coincides with an interesting consolidation of what might be called a "new, old labor history" that discusses the racism of the labor movement less than urgently or not at all as it builds a case for the tactical wisdom and practicality of Samuel Gompers and other craft union leaders. When articulated seventy and more years ago by the pioneering labor historian John R. Commons, such a view was accompanied by an endorsement of the racial policies of the American Federation of Labor. To its credit, the "new, old labor history" offers no such endorsement, but it does support the idea of the AFL's supposed strategy of "doing what we can" in a way that closes off the question "Doing what we can *for whom?*"[41] Thus labor and urban historian Richard Schneirov has recently called for sympathetic reconsideration of Selig Perlman's "old labor history" position, which held that, far from witnessing defeats, the 1890s represented a time of consolidation and even triumphs for labor. Schneirov applauds Perlman's "optimistic, prodevelopment portrayal of labor history" for its emphasis on the acceptance of the "trade agreement" and of participation in "liberal politics," as well as the rejection of "the less fruitful alternatives of insurrectionary strikes and independent politics," as the keys to the AFL's success. That the 1890s saw the AFL unions in wholesale retreat on the question of building integrated unions and in full cry for racially exclusionist immigration policies does not enter into the calculus of such praise for labor's realism.[42]

Michael Kazin's recent homage to Samuel Gompers is more interesting still in that it comes in a *New Labor Forum* article squarely designed to bring history to bear on current strategies for labor. Kazin's aim in this article is to defend labor's ongoing ties to the Democratic party. He portrays the practical politics of "doing what we can" as a positive heritage of Gompers. Race and gender suddenly appear and are quickly dismissed. Kazin writes of the American Federation of Labor,

"The organization that Gompers led has been roundly condemned as the exclusive preserve of male officials from northern European backgrounds who patronized or actively despised a long list of their fellow workers—blacks, Latinos, East Asians, women, the unskilled and those who came from peasant backgrounds. . . ." The dismissal, on rather different grounds from the charge, immediately follows: "The real federation never resembled this baleful portrait. Among its two million members in 1910 were thousands of waitresses and immigrant seamstresses [and] black and Slavic coal miners."[43]

Dan Letwin's summary of what he sees as the conclusions to be drawn from recent studies of race and labor in the U.S. South perfectly captures the tone of recent writings that see this history as complicated and edifying rather than tragic:

> For one, interracial labor campaigns were seldom conceived as civil rights enterprises (although over time black unionists grew more and more inclined to merge the two), and most took care to leave the social boundaries of race undisturbed. In explaining why black and white workers tested Jim Crow in some settings and acknowledged (or endorsed) its hegemony in others, material considerations were often pivotal. Where an equal rights agenda threatened the tangible fruits of segregation (such as white domination of skilled positions), white workers were unlikely to subordinate their ingrained racism to a (usually quixotic) venture in interracialism; that latter impulse prevailed only where collaboration across the color line advanced prospects for better wages and conditions, job security, and the right to organize. [New scholarly works] leave the racial dynamics of Dixie's labor movement looking more fluid than ever.

The matter-of-factness with which Letwin allows that white self-interest set the broadest contours of the labor movement in the South coincides with glib dismissal of historians who offer a sterner judgment of labor's racism. The standards of such historians, Letwin suggests, "align more closely with current sensibility than with historical circumstance."[44]

Kazin phrases far more dramatically his insistence that sharp criticism of racial exclusion in labor history is ahistorical. In a rejoinder to Nikhil Singh's acute response to his *New Labor Forum* essay, Kazin begins with "Dear Nikhil" and then delivers an accusation: "You regard labor's past like a hanging judge peering down at a homicide suspect: Samuel Gompers, George Meany, and any other erstwhile leaders, who, in their time, failed to come up to the egalitarian and class-conscious standards of today get swiftly convicted as villains, pure and simple."[45]

The logic of the new old labor history tends to rule out firm judgments concerning the historical record of trade union racism, branding
such assessments as anachronistic and ahistorical. In an almost perfect
example of what Bruce Nelson calls the effort of "scholars and labor
activists to envelop race in the language of class," Kazin calls for "an
anticorporate politics that acknowledges race and gender but transcends them." Such a line of argument is surely timeworn, but as Singh
suggests, the new openings in the labor movement may ironically give it
a temporary new lease on life. Singh sees in Kazin's analysis "an 'aw
shucks' teleology in which all the nasty things work themselves out in
the end," so long as labor is not utterly defeated. To the extent that
labor's changing membership can be used to imply that things "work
themselves out in the end," writings about trade union racism can be
branded as increasingly quaint and irrelevant. It seems unlikely that
such logic can triumph in the long run, given that activists increasingly
know that unsparing clarity on the history, impact, and persistence of
trade union racism is necessary to labor's organizing around affirmative action and to its building coalitions with communities of color.
Indeed it is possible that labor historians will move to a position like
that recently spelled out by the labor educator and militant Fernando
Gapasin, who holds that a defining feature of class-conscious labor
leadership is that it "recognizes that workers have multiple identities
that are given meaning by their occupation, gender and race" and
adopts "activist strategies that create internal union coalitions aimed
at increasing democratic participation." However, the Letwin/Kazin
stance ought to remind us that it is not enough to chronicle exclusion
without also tackling the central question of who and what labor has
been in the U.S. past. To do so sends us back to Reconstruction and to
Du Bois's insistence that understanding that critical period and its aftermath required a frontal challenge to the myopic focus on white workers
and white-led unions in labor history.[46]

Du Bois, Reconstruction, and the
Origins of Nonwhite Labor History

Perhaps no period in working-class history inspires more debate about
whether Black-white unity amounted to a few stray swallows or to the
coming of a new spring than the years immediately following the Civil
War. Before the war, instances of interracial solidarity in organized labor
were sufficiently rare to justify Michael Goldfield's recent contention
that labor leaders were "more concerned with freedom *from* African

Americans than freedom *for* them."[47] The postwar period featured the first sustained examples of Black-white cooperation in strikes and the first significant participation by African American representatives at national labor conventions organized by white unionists. Leaders such as William Sylvis and Andrew C. Cameron developed forceful arguments for interracial labor unity based on a recognition that in the wake of emancipation, African American men had become both producers and citizens; objections that Black workers lacked the requisite independence were muted. Cameron wrote hopefully in 1867 that the "moral influence," as well as the votes of freedpeople, would be of "incalculable value" to labor. It was, Sylvis argued, "impossible to degrade one group of workers without degrading all." Labor organizations courted prominent former abolitionists, with some success.[48] At its 1869 convention, the National Labor Union (NLU) resolved that it knew "no north, no south, no east, no west, neither color nor sex on the question of the rights of labor." The African American ship caulkers' leader Isaac Myers gave the convention's most eloquent address.[49]

The debits were every bit as impressive. Hate strikes proliferated to drive Black workers from jobs, North and South. Even if the historian Rayford Logan was wrong to claim that unions were the first private institutions systematically to apply Jim Crow race separation in the postbellum years, they were surely among the first. Sylvis rightly characterized "whites striking against the blacks" as a recurring debilitating pattern at the NLU convention in 1867. In 1869 a *New York Times* investigation found that trade unions in New York City had successfully kept Black workers from all unionized workplaces, both by refusing to integrate their own organizations and by taking direct action against African Americans. Although it opened its conventions to a few Black delegates, the NLU never pressed for integrated workplaces or trade unions. Indeed, Isaac Myers rose to prominence as a labor leader when he organized a Baltimore shipyard cooperative after a massive 1865 hate strike by white caulkers and ship carpenters drove Black workers from shipyard work there.[50] Openly racist labor appeals to ban Chinese immigration likewise came to the fore after the Civil War, providing a focus for labor politics in California and beyond.[51] Despite inviting Black leaders to its convention, the NLU refused to endorse integrated unionism. Sylvis did not press on this issue. Moreover, his published 1869 letters from a tour of the South promised to unite "black and white" in the region but also ridiculed "mixed juries," denied the very existence of the Ku Klux Klan, and excoriated white

parents who allowed their daughters to "entertain young negro gentle-
men in their parlors." The aftermath of Myers's speech to the NLU in
1870, according to a contemporary biographer of the labor leader, was
his being forced "back over the railing" to avoid physical attack.[52]

When they do treat such deep contradictions, labor historians have
often been of several minds within the same study. Philip S. Foner
praises Sylvis's "insight" on race and class and then details, in a footnote, how Sylvis's views were "marred by racism." "Even though the
NLU was the first American union to admit black representatives to its
conventions," he writes in a work coauthored with Ronald Lewis, "it
nevertheless remained silent on the sensitive issue of member unions
barring black workers from their ranks." This reverses a page-earlier
formulation holding that "although [the NLU] did not go on record
as favoring integration," its 1869 convention "marked the first occasion in which a national organization of white workers authorized the
admission of black unionists as affiliated union representations and
advocated the organization of black trade unions." The same tensions
run through my writing on the NLU.[53]

In accounting for such jarring shifts, historians have emphasized
good and bad leadership, even seeing Sylvis's death as something of a
turning point. They have explained how the very different experiences
that Black and white workers had with the Republican party caused
insurmountable obstructions to meaningful joint action between the
NLU and the Colored National Labor Union (CNLU). And they have
stressed the role of the racism of rank-and-file white workers in con-
straining NLU initiatives toward Black workers. The pioneering
African American historians Sterling Spero and Abram Harris were
particularly direct on the last score. In an account generally quite sympathetic to NLU positions, they argued that the organization, "while
desirous of uniting Negro and white labor, did not wish to alienate
the support of delegates from trade unions that excluded Negro workingmen by continually harping on racial discrimination, for the loss
of trade-union support meant the downfall of the National Labor
Union."[54]

Du Bois decisively differed from any assessment of NLU racial policy
that stresses its pragmatism and the ability to make progress in a regret-
tably narrow field. He further denied that such policies were so complex, contradictory, and multidetermined that they could not reveal any
one "fatal flaw" bound to disfigure future attempts at interracial cooperation. Du Bois began, as no other account so penetratingly has, with

"The Black Worker" and then moved to discussion of "The White Worker" in *Black Reconstruction*. The latter category requires explanation for Du Bois. Why, and with what results, he asked, would some workers think it vital to identify as white? Because Du Bois's prose is so striking, because his points were so subtly made in the very form of the study rather than didactically, because he intricately critiqued together the assumptions of historians writing about Reconstruction and those of white workers living through it, and above all because the centrality of white workers to the history of American labor has seemed so "natural," historians have not been in a position to measure the full force of his analysis. When he wrote of the tragic inability to "discern" in African Americans' action during slavery and Reconstruction any "part of our labor movement," Du Bois did not include just historians among the "blind and [those] led by the blind." In specifically portraying the inability of white labor to see in "black slavery and Reconstruction the kernel and meaning of the labor movement in the U.S.,"[55] he attempted to move debate from an obsession with whether white labor was irredeemably racist to an examination of whether white labor was really the center of the labor movement's story. Utterly ahead of its time, this leap opens up a host of new ways to look at the history of unions and race, in and after Reconstruction.

Black Reconstruction's emphasis on the ongoing "White Blindspot," as well as on white racism, enabled Du Bois to speak with unmatched clarity about the pattern of recurring bursts of antiracist resolve by leaders of national federations of unions, coupled with continued racial discrimination by many individual unions and locals. The labor economist Herbert R. Northrup captured this dynamic in 1948:

> But whatever one may think of the ethics of trade union discrimination, there is a fundamental inconsistency between the racial policies of most of the [individual unions] and the oft-repeated principles of their parent body, the American Federation of Labor, the spokesmen for which never tire of "reiterating, re-endorsing and reaffirming" the fact that the AFL has no color bar, and of proclaiming that the "workers must organize and unite under its banner, without regard to race, color, or national origin."[56]

Whereas other scholars have acknowledged the presence of such inconsistency in the post-Civil War period, Du Bois portrayed the pattern then and after not as contradictory, hypocritical, or conjunctural but as the logical result of a bedrock assumption of the NLU and the white labor movement. This assumption was that white male workers *were* the labor movement. Du Bois pointed out that the arguments for inclusion of African American workers and those for their exclusion rested on a shared assumption that the defense of the distinct interests of a white working class and white labor movement necessitated the framing of strategies on interracial unity. The logic of Sylvis and other prominent advocates of organizing Black workers, Du Bois held, was strictly white-centered and utilitarian. This white utilitarianism sounded the "first halting note" presaging disaster. "Negroes were welcomed to the labor movement," Du Bois wrote, "not because they were laborers but because they might be competitors [of whites] in the labor market." Sylvis could hardly have been more clear on this—or less sensitive in his language—when he advocated strategic overtures toward Black workers: "the time will come when the Negro will take possession of the shops if we have not taken possession of the Negro."[57]

That the most principled-sounding of labor's statements affirming the need for Black-white cooperation were from the start based on a rationale in which white interests were given and paramount had far-reaching implications during and after Reconstruction. If a trade was overwhelmingly white, or if racism was deeply entrenched, then the logic of utilitarian egalitarianism simply did not apply. As the early twentieth-century reformer Elmer Carter put it, the field was open for white labor leaders to demand that Black workers do all of the "co" while white-dominated unions did all of the "operating." As Du Bois observed, "competition" could logically be stemmed not only by organizing Black workers but also by "guarding" against their entry into jobs—an alternative to which, according to Du Bois, "white American labor almost unanimously turned" whenever possible.[58]

Indeed, to decide that in this NLU convention, in that industry, or in most localities, the forces of racial separation were too strong to be challenged did not even require that a union accept that it was racist. When Lewis Douglass was embroiled in a bitter postbellum fight over his membership in the International Typographical Union (ITU)—a dispute that brought his father, Frederick Douglass, into direct conflict with the union and threatened labor's ties to ex-abolitionists—the ITU easily rationalized its position. Just as the NLU left to individual unions the responsibility for racial exclusion, the ITU shifted responsibility to the locals and the rank and file: "That there are deep-seated prejudices against the colored race no one will deny; and these prejudices are so strong in many local unions that any attempt to override them will almost inevitably lead to . . . disintegration . . . and surely no one who has the welfare of the craft at heart will seriously contend that the

union [of] thousands of white printers should be destroyed for the purpose of creating a barren honor of membership to a few Negroes."[59] In
1870 the carpenters' union offered a similar combination of egalitarian
rhetoric and exclusionary practice in a perfect illustration of the "White
Blindspot": "Resolved that we are ever willing to extend the hand of
fellowship to every laboring man, more especially to those of our own
craft; we believe that the prejudices of our own members against the
colored people are of such a nature that it is not expedient at present to
admit them."[60]

The lynchpin of NLU (and later of the Knights of Labor and AFL)
pragmatism regarding race was the ability to develop economistic arguments for what was later called "stomach equality" while rejecting the
notion that such trade union unity implied any support for "social" or
full political equality. Sylvis's public disapproval of cross-racial socializing, his criticism of the seating of Blacks on juries, and his denial of the
very existence of the Klan, even as he battled for a level of African
American inclusion in unions, was of a piece with a host of later efforts
to draw a clear line between economic cooperation (necessary because
capital forced mixing at work) and "intermingling." It long seemed wise
to preserve this distinction as a tactic to keep racial hatred from making
it impossible for unions to grow. Indeed, one of the earliest Black delegates to an NLU convention disavowed any desire to focus on "parlor
sociabilities" between whites and African Americans.[61] Even left-wing
union organizers have generally accepted this logic, regarding too crusading an antiracism as a threat to the survival of the union, which
itself was taken to be a bulwark of long-term progress toward racial
justice.[62] Within inclusive unions, it has often seemed needlessly divisive to push for equal access to skilled jobs.[63]

But the walling off of social/political equality from "stomach equality"—a distinction invented, not merely continued in the Reconstruction years—constituted common-sense tactical wisdom for organized
labor only if the labor movement's key constituency was assumed to be
white. As Isaac Myers maintained at the time, social "intermingling"
and agitation for political rights for African Americans were precisely
what the working-class movement needed. As a strategy to organize all
workers, the "stomach equality but not social/political equality" stance
was profoundly out of touch with the real world. It ignored, for example, the obvious fact that the brotherhoods and other "uplift unions" of
the late nineteenth century were clearly organizations in which mutual
aid and interaction off the job were deeply important. As Spero and

Harris observed, in such instances the "social and moral features" were "quite as much in evidence as the economic," so that unions felt "as much justified in eliminating the Negro from membership as the Elks, Masons [or] Odd Fellows."[64]

Workplaces likewise were intensely social, often crowded spaces, and labor at times involved sharing everything from water buckets to dining areas. The glass blowers' union based exclusion on the grounds that the "pipe on which the glass is blown passes from mouth to mouth and no one would use it after a Negro." The intimacy of labor on trains enabled exclusionary railroad unions to base their public appeals on the notion that common work by Blacks and whites was *ipso facto* "social equality." Where Black men and white women worked together, questions of inappropriate "intermingling" divided workers and weakened unions.[65] The inevitably social nature of work and of unions found eloquent expression, if to no good end, in the remarks of a Michigan craftsman who responded to requests for debate on the race question by the editors of the journal of the International Brotherhood of Electrical Workers. Capturing why social discrimination inevitably had economic and trade union consequences, he wrote, "If we allow a colored man to come into our union, we would not feel so disposed to do good turns for him as we would for a white man, and we could not expect them to stick to our union in case of trouble when we did not use them 'white.'"[66]

Where political equality is concerned, the impracticality of speaking about purely economic struggles is clearer still. In criticizing the Freedmen's Bureau as a fraud for which (white) workers paid, Sylvis did not avoid political controversy but took a side in it, giving credence to the worries of President Andrew Johnson, who pioneered the notion of "reverse racism" during those years. Sylvis's opposition to Blacks on juries raises more concrete issues in that he ridiculed not just the exercise of a basic democratic right but that of a right with significant implications for labor. In north Florida during Reconstruction, for example, African American jurors returned acquittals in important cases that expanded the tactical options open to Black strikers.[67] Sylvis's wishing away of the existence of the Klan and the broader NLU refusal to understand Black workers' support for the Republican party in the context of terror and of the necessity to preserve fundamental rights were equally naïve if organizing Black workers was the goal.[68]

The grounds on which Du Bois stakes claim for the centrality of Black labor during Reconstruction are so visionary and so extraordinary in their breadth that a fair share of labor historians will regard them as suspect or as beside the point where discussion of working-class organization is concerned. He holds that a significant share of the slave population mounted a "general strike" that had a decisive impact on the coming of emancipation. Moreover, in various times and places during Reconstruction, the Republican party expressed profound material *and moral* longings of freedpeople, functioning in effect as a labor party. Thus small white unions, which Du Bois derided as "craft and race unions," subordinated an epochal social movement to their petty concerns.[69] The CNLU, in Du Bois's view, was more politically advanced than its white counterpart, and it fought over working-class issues, including redistribution of land, that were clearly posed and central to Reconstruction politics. The CNLU also took more enlightened positions than the NLU on Chinese exclusion, on the vital issue of the rights of working women, and above all on Black-white unity.[70] The moral example and the rhetoric of "jubilee" inspired by freedpeople undergirded the dynamism that the white labor movement did possess.[71] And the "moral impetus" provided to all labor by emancipated slaves was no after-the-fact figment of Du Bois's imagination, but rather a feature of the period, commented on by figures ranging from Cameron to Karl Marx.[72] Similarly, it was not just Du Bois later, but also Frederick Douglass and white Haymarket martyr Albert Parsons, who made a postbellum case for the Republicans in some southern states as a labor party.[73]

A narrower, workplace-based argument will perhaps be more telling among labor historians. White labor leaders (usually in the North) often justified exclusionary policies by pointing out the necessity of taking "southern" labor's opinion into account.[74] By this they naturally meant white southern opinion. But the white population was not the more union-supporting one in the South from the Civil War until the late 1890s. State labor conventions, militant strikes, and Knights of Labor organizing all drew more consistent African American than white support in the late-nineteenth-century South.[75] As late as 1912, the great student of immigration and labor Isaac Hourwich produced arresting figures on race and union density among wage-earners. For whites with a native-born father, whites with a foreign-born father, and the foreign-born, essentially the same percentage of workers, between 13.4% and 14.1%, had joined unions. For African Americans, it was 17.9%. The clearest illustration of our lack of appreciation of such possible patterns lies in the history of strikebreaking. In his recent study of such activity, the economist William Whatley counts thirty-six cases of African American strikebreaking between 1865 and 1891. Only two

of these occurred in the South, the region Du Bois saw as key to
the evolution of a genuinely national postbellum labor movement.
A cursory review of the secondary literature for those years shows at
least fifteen cases of strikes by Afro-southern workers in which white
workers scabbed or white militias and mobs attacked the strike
(as well as two more cases of the sort Whatley has studied).[76] That
this pattern has attracted so little attention from historians, and that
it attracted none from a white labor movement avowedly bent on
courting (white) "southern labor," is a perfect example of the "White
Blindspot's" effects.

I make no claim that the extent of white-on-Black strikebreaking as
compared to its opposite (or to the many muddier situations) can be so
easily discerned. But I do argue that we now know not only that whites
broke strikes of other whites but also that they often broke strikes of
Blacks. If we look at strikes historically and regionally, we discover that
the question "Were Negroes strikebreakers?" is not necessarily the best
historical question to pose about race and strikebreaking. Nor, of
course, do I claim that Du Bois said the last word about race and labor
in *Reconstruction* six decades ago. The important recent work on gender and labor after the Civil War greatly complicates Du Bois's account.
But I do argue that Du Bois said brilliant things sixty years ago because
he had moved past seeing labor as white. With the help of changing
demographics, we can begin to see the depth of his insight and to
deepen it further. Thirty-five years ago, David Montgomery wrote
Beyond Equality: Labor and the Radical Republicans, 1862–1872.
Despite his subtitle, and though deeply influenced by Du Bois, Montgomery did not discuss the Colored National Labor Union. A decade
and a half ago, Philip S. Foner and I, also deeply influenced by Du Bois,
nonetheless supposed that the history of the working day in the United
States could be told without devoting attention to what we called "the
very different labor system of Afro-American slavery."[77] A decade from
now, labor historians will tell different, fuller, and better stories, not
because a new working class changes the facts of the past but because
new opportunities for seeing that past are being opened.

Mumia Time or Sweeney Time?

In February 1995, Bay Area Typographical Union Local 21, what labor historians are used to calling a conservative craft union, resolved to advocate full freedom for the African American journalist and political prisoner Mumia Abu-Jamal. Convicted in a speedy and irregular 1982 trial for the 1981 murder of a Philadelphia policeman, Abu-Jamal faced, and faces, the death penalty. In a letter to Pennsylvania's governor, Local 21 argued that Abu-Jamal was "an innocent victim of a racial and political frameup" and branded his possible execution a disgrace.[1]

Still more remarkable was what transpired during the filming of a recent segment on Abu-Jamal's case by the ABC television newsmagazine *20/20*. ABC let Abu-Jamal know of its plans to ask prison authorities to arrange an on-camera interview with him from Death Row. The feature promised to break the scandalous silence of the national media regarding the case and the still more comprehensive blackout of Abu-Jamal's side of the story. Offered this opportunity to make what would probably a last public appeal to save his own life, Abu-Jamal replied that he would of course be delighted to speak to ABC. He specified, however, that no interview could take place while the network's technicians, organized in the National Association of Broadcast Employees and Technicians (NABET), remained on strike. He added with brave precision, "I'd rather die than cross that picket line." Those who produced the report, from star reporter Sam Donaldson on down, apparently had no qualms about scabbing on the strike. Nor did they choke on presenting a more or less pat recapitulation of even the most discredited police testimony in the case. Helping to sign the death warrant of a fellow journalist, 20/20 exemplified the utter decay of "crusading journalism" in the United States—crusading for network management, crusading for the police, crusading for the death penalty.[2]

Although it will probably never grace the infotainment airwaves, the story symbolized by Local 21's support of Abu-Jamal and by his incredible support of NABET is a blockbuster that demands the serious attention of those of us who are trying to build a new labor movement. Abu-Jamal's prolabor journalism and activism, from Death Row with his days and columns grimly numbered, has been extraordinary. It has included not only a penetrating analysis of the importance of the recent strike by Philadelphia's transit workers but also support for U.S. longshore unionists under threat of repression because of their militant refusal to service the *Neptune Jade,* a job action undertaken in solidarity with beleaguered British dockworkers in Liverpool.[3]

Impressive labor support for Abu-Jamal has likewise developed, especially in the Bay Area, Chicago, and New York City. In the April 1999 demonstrations around Abu-Jamal's case in Philadelphia, New York City's Workers to Free Mumia mobilized labor contingents, and Local 1199 of the Health and Hospital Workers appeared in force. In the San Francisco march on the same day, 200 to 300 International Longshore and Warehouse Union members headed the crowd of 20,000, wearing union caps and carrying an ILWU banner. They chanted, "An injury to one is an injury to all. Free Mumia Abu-Jamal." The San Francisco Labor Council endorsed the April action, as did that of Alameda County and the California Federation of Labor. The Labor Council's resolutions specifically referred to Abu-Jamal's "refusal to be interviewed by ABC's scab crews." Organized teachers, postal workers, writers, transit workers, carpenters, hotel and restaurant workers, and boatmen have likewise raised protests on Abu-Jamal's behalf. So have the Coalition of Black Trade Unionists (Region Six); the Madison, Wisconsin Central Federation of Labor; the Coalition of Labor Union Women; and the recently formed Labor party. Internationally, "Justice for Mumia" endorsements have arrived from the Congress of South African Trade Unionists and its powerful food and metal workers affiliates; the Transport and General Workers Union in London; a section of the General Confederation of Workers in France; organized German, British, and Irish journalists; the Ontario Federation of Labor; and the Canadian Auto Workers Council, as well as from organizations of public employees in Canada and of Australian telecommunications workers. Recent resolutions of support have come from the King's County Labor Council (Seattle), the United Farm Workers, the Farm Labor Organizing Committee, and United Auto Workers locals. The Labor Conference for Mumia, held in May 2000 in Oakland, received endorsements from five central labor councils in California, from Pride at Work, from several Communications Workers of America (NABET's parent international) locals, from Hotel and Restaurant Employees Local 2850, from Service Employees International Union Locals 616 and 1877, from Plumbers and Fitters Local 393, from Teamsters Local 315, from United Transport Workers Local 1741, from National Writers Union Local 3, from the A. Philip Randolph Institute, from the United Electrical Workers, from the California Nurses Association, and from officers of steelworkers', auto workers', postal workers', transit workers', and longshore workers' locals. That same month, the 1100 delegates at the international convention of the Service Employees International Union unanimously approved a resolution demanding justice for Abu-Jamal. The December 2000 Labor for Mumia delegation seeking to see Attorney General Janet Reno on Abu-Jamal's behalf included representatives of the teachers' union in Frankfurt, Germany; the Race Relations Committee of the Trades Union Congress in Britain; the Workers' Party in Brazil; the Haitian Coalition for Immigrant Rights; and the AFL-CIO Civil Rights Department. The national leadership of the All Pakistan Trade Union Federation sent its support.[4]

Most important by far, on April 24, 1999, the ILWU shut down all Pacific Coast ports—thirty of them—from Seattle to San Diego, in solidarity with Abu-Jamal and in support of the demonstrations on his behalf. The work stoppage, which came as a result of rank-and-file initiatives, occurred over heated management opposition and lasted the entire day shift. It was, according to ILWU president Brian McWilliams, the first officially sanctioned coastwide "stop-work" on the behalf of a U.S. political prisoner ever. Messages of solidarity with the ILWU's job action came from longshore workers in England, Cyprus, Sweden, Denmark, Finland, and Japan. Rio de Janiero's 100,000-member teachers' union, which had itself stopped work in a two-hour show of support for Mumia on the previous day, also sent greetings.[5]

The extent of two-way solidarity between Abu-Jamal and the labor movement deserves publicity for the ways in which it gives the lie to recent slanders against the Free Mumia movement. According to these slanders, retailed by sources from 20/20 to *The Nation* magazine,

Abu-Jamal has irrationally attracted the support of a cultlike following of naïve musicians, New Leftovers, and Internet geeks who find it easier to champion the cause of a charismatic former-Black Panther than to agitate around "real" class issues. In an uncharacteristically overwrought *Nation* column, the populist film director Michael Moore offered a particularly distressing version of the charge that Mumia supporters are not serious, a view recently seconded by "good leftist" journalist Marc Cooper via the website of *Mother Jones* magazine. Cooper, who brands Free Mumia efforts as a "collective affliction" and who himself wishes to be "Free of Mumia," frets loudly over the danger that mobilizations for Abu-Jamal distract attention from the broader issue of the death penalty.[6] In fact, as Rebecca Hill's fine studies of the history of left defense campaigns show, the Free Mumia movement is virtually unique in its thorough integration of a defense of a political prisoner with efforts to abolish capital punishment generally. Adolph Reed, Jr.'s *Class Notes* echoes the line that Abu-Jamal may well be guilty and warns against elevating his status politically merely because he may be a "victim of injustice." In a passage especially disturbing because Reed parades his own Labor party activism throughout *Class Notes,* he writes, "All that most of us know about his politics, apart from his speaking out against police brutality, is that he has some connection to MOVE—a group with pretty wacky ideas." Surely it is incumbent on a Labor party activist writing about the case to learn something of Abu-Jamal's politics, especially where workers are concerned.[7] That the Free Mumia forces enjoy significant labor support cuts against any such efforts to characterize the campaign as superficial and sentimental.

Moreover, labor support often finds its justification in the clear realization that police violence and race/class-based justice are workers' issues and in hardheaded analyses of the importance of building community/labor coalitions. Larry Adams, president of Local 300 of the National Postal Mail Handlers Union, has written: "Mumia is us. We are Mumia. . . . Trade unions exist for the right to defend democratic rights of working class people, due process, fair and equal treatment, freedom from police brutality—all of which is being denied Mumia in this effort at a legal lynching." ILWU Local 10 executive board member Jack Heyman has emphasized that support for Abu-Jamal connects his union to both "the struggles of minorities here and the dockworkers' movement internationally." At the pro-Mumia demonstration in the Bay Area, he asked the 20,000 assembled, "If the ILWU goes on strike, will you be there for us?" "The response was resoundingly affirmative.[8]

However, the point that I wish to make in the balance of these pages goes quite beyond the argument that labor support for Abu-Jamal is significant, inspired, and inspiring. My further claim is that labor's solidarity with Mumia, and his with labor, best locate the terrain on which our boldest hopes for a new labor movement ought to be grounded. My friend George Lipsitz, inspired both by hiphop and by rhythm and blues, has insisted that "What time is it?" ought to be a central question for anyone writing and thinking about class and race. For me it is "Mumia Time," a time when new potentialities for the U.S. labor movement are under consideration. This position is admittedly a pretty lonely one. For intellectuals writing about, and to some extent struggling alongside, U.S. labor, there has been little hesitancy over the last several years in telling what time it is. It is, for most, John Sweeney Time. From the 1996 Teach-In with the Labor Movement at Columbia University, to the founding of Scholars, Writers and Artists for Social Justice as a labor support group, to Stanley Aronowitz's *From the Ashes of the Old*, Sweeney's accession to the presidency of the AFL-CIO has been seen as the symbol of change, the source of new space for progressive activity in the labor movement, and the basis for a return to solidarity with labor by left-liberal academics. Thus *Audacious Democracy*, the volume of essays that grew out of the Columbia Teach-In, proclaims in its introduction that Sweeney's election constitutes the "best sign that the labor question is alive and well."[9]

If such a view restores hope and encourages the growth of concrete acts of solidarity with labor struggles, it is all to the good. Moreover, it is plain that Sweeney is nothing like as backward as his immediate predecessors at the top of the AFL. Nonetheless, the "It's Sweeney Time" position remains a problematic one. Sweeney's "America needs a raise" platform turns out to be pretty thin gruel if we want to maintain that the AFL-CIO is headed by an insurgent. Deeply nationalistic, Sweeney's demand harks back to Samuel Gompers at his most economistic and narrow, not to the labor heroes who have held that workers need freedom, justice, and time to live.[10] Even Aronowitz's *From the Ashes of the Old*, the best of the "Sweeney Time" writings, partly reflects this narrowness. The labor anthem on which the book's title plays envisioned the bringing forth of a "new world" from the old world's ashes, but Aronowitz instead describes the possibilities of building a somewhat stronger and more influential union movement from the ruins of the Meany-Kirkland leadership. Sweeney's poor record on union democracy has meanwhile tempted some of his supporters to toy with the idea that workers' democracy is perhaps overrated and expendable, in a move that underlines long-standing connections among despair regarding transformation of rank-and-file workers, racial division in unions, and acquiescence to leadership by vanguards and bureaucracies.[11]

Using Sweeney to mark labor's transformation and possibilities also coincides with a troubling nostalgia. Eric Foner and Betty Friedan, for example, in their *Audacious Democracy* essays, voice hopes for a relatively unproblematic return to labor's former glories. In Foner's words, the unions are poised to be "once again a voice both for the immediate interests of . . . members and the broader needs of of working- and middle-class Americans." At their most expansive, such backward gazes fix on a long, mythic period in which, as Steve Fraser and Josh Freeman put it, class was the "primordial social question"—one whose "capacious embrace" could "absorb . . . the fate of women and children, racial and ethnic hatred."[12]

What if we instead took the solidarity between Mumia Abu-Jamal and the labor movement as the symbol of what a new labor movement promises? What if it is Mumia Time rather than Sweeney Time? Such a choice would mean several things. Most significant initiatives on Abu-Jamal's behalf have been local ones, although there has been great awareness of international connections. In most cases, pro-Abu-Jamal activities have been undertaken as a result of rank-and-file initiatives within locals, not as projects of the labor leadership. To think in Mumia Time rather than in Sweeney Time thus challenges us to entertain the possibility that the promises of a new labor movement cannot be imagined if the focus stays on national institutions and labor's officialdom.

To emphasize that it is Mumia Time also opens critical questions concerning the state and labor. Whereas the largest initiatives and greatest claims of success by the Sweeney leadership have centered on the election of more Democrats to national office, significant labor support for Abu-Jamal registers a deepening suspicion of state power. These mobilizations identify with an accused cop killer who is utterly unsparing in his excoriation of the corruption and crimes of the government and of its complicity with corporate power.

Most impressively, the extent to which Abu-Jamal knows that he needs to identify with the labor movement, and to which some in the labor movement know that they need to support him, signals what the working-class movement is becoming and what it can be. In 1995, in a demographic shift that escaped the attention of mainstream, labor, and radical journalists, organized labor became for the first time a movement in which white males are a minority. The Bureau of Labor Statistics counted 8.33 million white men in unions and 8.93 million African American, Latino, and white female members. According to 1995 statistics, 14.2% of whites in the nonfarm labor force were in unions, whereas 19.9% of African American workers were members. Latinos as were likewise more highly unionized than white workers. Crossing the 50% threshold produces no magical transformation, of course, especially while the leadership remains overwhelmingly white and male. Nonetheless, the trend is of real significance. With African Americans among the most prounion segments of the U.S. population, and with white males projected to constitute just 37% of the labor force by 2005, unions cannot grow as an institution dominated by white men.[13]

The white-male-identity politics—which has historically taken many forms including hate strikes against the employment of workers of color, anti-Asian rioting, making a "family wage" for male workers the watchword of organizing drives, and the more pervasive inability to see that a "class" politics articulated so largely by white men could neither "absorb" nor even consistently recognize questions of racial and gender justice—need not so crushingly burden the labor movement of the future. White workers will often be a minority or nearly so in workplaces and in union locals. This minority position is the one from which white workers have historically moved in the most egalitarian directions. In this context, the recent and nostalgic call by Ruy Teixeira and Joel Rogers for a refocusing of attention away from race and toward "America's forgotten majority" of white workers could hardly be more ill-timed and counterproductive. Their argument that the white working class "still matters" is as irreproachable as their failure to weigh the changed circumstances in which it matters is regrettable. With demographic changes, the sharply limited but real protections that a white male membership base accorded the unions may come to apply less and less. The draconian attacks on organizing by undocumented workers and on the diverse, pro-gender-equity public employee unions may well presage a time when labor will represent those who are, in terms of class and of other forms oppression, outsiders.[14]

Where change in official AFL-CIO policy has emerged most dramatically, a top-down Sweeney Time perspective cannot explain the transformation. In no area has the changing base of organized labor led to a more astonishing change in organized labor's policy than immigration reform. In 1986, as Chicano farm workers in Watsonville, California, achieved a rare strike victory in the teeth of Reaganism, the AFL-CIO busied itself backing Immigration Reform and Control Act language that imposed "sanctions" on the employers of undocumented workers. In effect, as David Bacon has shown, the law made "working illegal for [the] undocumented." At that time, subjecting immigrant workers to intimidation was seen as a justifiable means to the end of limiting the supply of immigrant labor. Although, as William Flores and Peter Kwong have observed, substantial numbers of Latino/a and Asian American workers shared in a desire for immigration restriction, the AFL-CIO strategy also drew on long traditions of white nativist and white supremacist opposition to immigration. The repressive results of the legislation for individuals, families, and unions were predictable.[15]

However, in February 2000 the Executive Council of the AFL-CIO did an about-face on immigration, calling for amnesty for the undocumented, for initiatives to educate immigrant workers regarding their rights, and for an end to employer sanctions. This critical shift cannot be understood without reference to the increasing organization of immigrant workers (with and without documents) and their heroism in, for example, the campaigns of Latino drywall workers, Asian American sweatshop workers, and the Justice for Janitors initiatives. Immigrants have, according to historian and labor activist David Montgomery, increasingly brought "new vigor and new ideas" into the labor movement, as well as strong community support for union struggles. The timeworn AFL-CIO view that "illegals seldom join unions and they almost never go on strike or otherwise complain about their wages or working conditions" certainly survived into the 1990s and beyond, but it clashed jarringly with reality. The AFL-CIO's new departures on immigration demonstrate what Farm Labor Organizing Committee leader Baldemar Velasquez calls "the power of Latino workers" and of other immigrants. Its central logic grows out of bitter experience with employers repeatedly using the Immigration and Naturalization Service and other agencies to punish and deport militant undocumented workers and to attempt to silence both "legal" and "illegal" immigrant workers. The change, however hesitantly implemented to date, bespeaks the ways in which organization and self-activity by immigrants have encouraged the perception that such workers are a key constituency, rather than a problem, for labor.[16]

New possibilities for imagining and creating working-class solidarity emerge, though by no means automatically, out of the recomposition of the labor movement. If labor is mainly not white and male, but the unions decidedly have been, then what Bill Fletcher, Jr., and Richard Hurd have recently called "the internal transformation required to build a labor movement of all working people becomes an urgent priority." Indeed, Fletcher and Hurd's challenging "Is Organizing Enough? Race, Gender and Union Culture" and Alicia Schmidt Camacho's equally astute "On the Borders of Solidarity: Race and Gender Contradictions in the 'New Voice' Platform of the AFL-CIO" both reflect an exhilarating sense of new possibilities and a sober knowledge of the weight of history and the cost of white business unionism-as-usual. Fletcher and Hurd show how race and gender matter not just in picking organizing targets but at every turn. They question the "sanctification of organizing," the planning of which often remains in the hands of an all-white and all-male coterie of staff members who mobilize new members only "symbolically" as "bodies for a rally."[17] Schmidt-Camacho, writing about recent San Diego-based union solidarity efforts with strikers at the Han Young factory in Tijuana, sounds a similar cautionary note on the necessity to break out of a pernicious "old labor" script: "The voiceless Mexican workers perform the physical labor of the movement—the sit-ins, work stoppages, and strikes-off-screen, while the U.S. labor movement assumes the role of the 'head' or consciousness of the movement, its tactician." Fletcher and Hurd portray a pattern of symbolic organizing that weds business unionism—current union members hear organizing drives justified as increasing the union's "market share"—to a white (often left) male organizing culture that separates leaders from the rank and file. Their article shows just why, as one activist puts it, such "white male dominance," however well-meaning and self-sacrificing, "alienates working people." They show how hard and how vital it is to create "a movement that embraces, attracts, and promotes women, people of color, immigrants, and lesbians and gays" and that builds solidarity among these groups.[18]

If it is Sweeney Time, rebuilding a Democratic party majority and refurbishing labor's image as a voice that represents the U.S. middle class will give us a clear and circumscribed agenda and plenty to do. If it is Mumia Time, we will enter far less familiar territory, in which we acknowledge that the labor movement cannot simply be rebuilt but must and can be built on new foundations. We will search, locally and internationally, for ways to embrace and nurture workers' organizations that draw their poetry from the future and that express what Abu-Jamal has set out to capture in his journalism—"the voice of the voiceless."

In Conclusion

ELVIS, WIGGERS, AND CROSSING OVER
TO NONWHITENESS

Director Aimee Sands's forthcoming film attempts to bring the insights of the critical study of whiteness to a broad audience. Its title, *Crossing Over*, captures much, including the move from academic discourse to the popular and the possibility of breaching color lines. It conjures up the image of what Susan Gubar has studied as "racechange"—the assumption of another racial identity, whether in art or life. It echoes both meanings of the music-business term *crossover*. On the one hand, *crossover* in that industry describes a product's achieving popularity outside its original marketing niche, as when a country record hits the popular charts. On the other hand, *crossover* also connotes a move by musicians of one race into genres and markets associated with those of another race. Finally, and most important, *crossing over* repeats the language of African American spirituals, which used the term to mean the salvation and liberation to be found on the other side of the River Jordan biblically and, secularly, on the other side of the Ohio River or another boundary symbolizing freedom and escape.[1]

It is tempting to confuse the crossover of CD sales, and the crossover of individual impersonators of other races, with the prospects of crossing over into freedom. Gubar's superb historical study of racechanges in U.S. culture, for example, adopts a hard-nosed stance in assessing the crossing of color lines in art, film, and music. Her language is difficult, but the meaning is clear. Despite "the anarchic potential of racechange," she argues, "epidermal fungibility . . . almost always seems historically to have resulted in the subordination, muting, or obliteration of [people of color]." Moreover, the "conscious aims of performers" usually have made little difference in the dire outcomes of racechange. And yet five pages later, Gubar allows herself to hope for a different future: "In terms of its most liberating potential and despite its history, . . . transracial transgressions can crack open any monolithic notion one might have about the coherent racial self."[2] For others, most notably W. H. Lhamon in his ambitious rehabilitation of the blackface minstrel tradition and appreciation of its modern inheritors, even racial impersonation's history gives little pause, becaue that history is alleged to have been consistently subversive of the racial order.[3]

Such investments in the accomplishments and possibilities of racial crossover coexist with various political conclusions. At their worst, they dovetail with the neoconservative/neoliberal agreement described in this book's opening chapter—that if nothing is fixed racially, then nothing needs fixing. Those who want to "rearticulate" white identity in a positive direction, most capably Howard Winant, also take heart in the extent to which white Americans already are culturally African American in many ways.[4] Nor have those of us who want to abolish whiteness—or, as I will put it here, to create the conditions for a non-white society—failed to embrace racial crossover as a telling sign of the dissatisfaction of white youth with whiteness.[5] On the other side, white supremacists have also treated racial crossovers in the culture industry as matters of great import and portent.[6]

Such crossover dreams and fears are not altogether misplaced. As Martin Luther King, Jr., himself at times a harsh critic of popular music, told an audience of African American disc jockeys shortly before his assassination, ". . . you have paved the way for social and political change by creating a powerful, cultural bridge between black and white. School integration is much easier now that [students] have a common music, a common language, and enjoy the same dances."[7] The importance of the "language of soul" that King evoked, and of the bridge he described, cannot be denied, especially in the context of segregation. The best accounts of the positive role of crossover emphasize, like King, the way in which ordinary cultural workers and fans built the local connections between crossover and pleasure.[8] However, to imagine that the bridge King described can bear all the weight of transforming racial capitalism and white investments in it is to court disaster. In considering the most widely studied crossover success, Elvis Presley, and the almost entirely unexamined contemporary phenomenon of the "wigger," this conclusion seeks to show both why cultural crossover matters and why it cannot *by itself* generate a crossing over into nonwhiteness. The final pages suggest how the vision of a nonwhite society can help us to transcend crossover and build a better bridge.

An Elvis Retrospective

In a special 1997 issue titled "America's Changing Colors," the formerly sort-of radical *Mother Jones* magazine perfunctorily evoked the changing demographics of race in the United States to argue that the politics of racial justice, and particularly affirmative action, were doomed. But while *Time* magazine embraced Eve, the computer-generated multiracial symbol of a new United States, *Mother Jones* featured the conservative-cum-populist Michael Lind's very different analysis. Lind predicted and welcomed the "end of the rainbow" (and of race) in U.S. liberal politics by way of a circuitous scenario. He haplessly foresaw a political right-turn by Hispanic and Asian American voters, making up a "rainbow right." In response, the "native" electorate would be mobilized around underspecified economic demands, the defense of Judeo-Christian culture, and the desire sharply to limit immigration. In so uniting, the natives would realize the inconsequentiality of racial differences among themselves and see that the color line had already been decisively crossed. An old "vernacular culture hero" would symbolize the new departure, which would achieve politically what was alleged to already exist culturally. That hero was a "mixed race, white/Cherokee prole who sang like a black man." Lind's liberalism thus came pre packaged with its rallying cry. "ONE NATION," the subheadline ran, "UNDER ELVIS."[9]

Lind's use of Elvis as a larger-than-life symbol of unproblematic inclusions and as a rallying figure for new exclusions suggests something of the complexity of the racial position Presley held and of the difficulties of rooting hopes for racial justice in the alleged "crossover" of cultural figures from white to Black forms. I encountered Lind's piece shortly after badgering my sons to come with me to a small Elvis museum that doubled as a greasy spoon restaurant in tiny Wright City, Missouri. The hamburgers took forever and a large Elvis-dressed man at the next table punctuated the wait with repeated threats to beat his children. We uneasily shifted our attention to the "Elvis Is Alive" video playing on a big-screen TV in one corner of the room. After solemnly showing the special certificate given to Elvis by President Richard M. Nixon, and after quoting Elvis's resolve to use his acceptance in the counterculture to spy for the federal police, the film argued that its hero was forced to fake his own death. He had so decisively contributed to the struggle against the antiwar left, against the "drug culture," and particularly against Black militants, that his own life was in danger from a broad, dark conspiracy.[10]

With Lisa Marie Presley's 1994 marriage to the African American pop star and racechanger Michael Jackson, popular humor had its proof that Elvis was really dead: Otherwise, he would have put a stop to the ceremony. The joke signaled the extent to which Elvis, the great white racial cross-dresser of the '50s, could be pressed into service as the white father, prohibiting his daughter's marriage to the great African American racial cross-dresser of the '80s and '90s. The joke may have had some basis in fact. The evidence authenticating Presley's famous (alleged) racial slur that "niggers" could only shine his shoes and buy his records is weak. And his supposed stating of a preference for kissing multiple African American women rather than one Mexican woman—the point was the undesirability of kissing women from either group—rested on a mistranslation of his remarks or, as some accounts have it, on a plot by Mexican government officials. But the evidence that he pronounced himself dead set against his daughter marrying across the color line is relatively strong.[11]

Elvis tried much—and had much tried on him—where racial identity was concerned. Elaine Dundy's 1985 biography pronounced Presley "quite a mixture, genetically speaking." She credited his genius not only to French Norman and Scots Irish "blood" but also to "the [American] Indian strain supplying the mystery and the Jewish strain supplying spectacular showmanship." Albert Goldman's biography-as-hatchet-job made Elvis the "victim of a fatal hereditary disposition," rooted in an unfortunate family tree and in Presley's membership as a poor white youth in a "distinctive branch of Southern yeomanry."[12] A noted country singer attacked him as a "white nigger."[13] A recent supermarket tabloid's historical expose of the Presley family posited a kinship between Elvis and Oprah Winfrey. However, the details were fudged. Elvis's Old South forefathers, the story improbably revealed in the ultimate memorialization of Presley as white patriarch, *owned* Oprah's ancestors. There may or may not, the article sheepishly added, have been some race mixing along the line (or, more exactly, along *her* line.)[14]

Born in a house of African-influenced "shotgun" design but built by his impoverished white father, Elvis grew up in the "poor white" section of East Tupelo, Mississippi. Presley matured into a South where those two adjectives defined a group that has been both aggressive in claiming racial supremacy and victimized by suspicions of its own biological stock. His own youthful contacts with the music of the Black "Shake Rag" community in Tupelo were perhaps exaggerated in his later accounts, but Presley clearly lived around African Americans. The family's brief move up was into a "respectable colored neighborhood" in Tupelo. As a teen in Memphis, Elvis appeared in his high school's minstrel show and sneaked from the white First Assembly of God Church to "the colored church" where the "music was out of this world." He learned, at a series of working-class jobs, that white workers had bosses too. He had found a Jim Crow-building trades union in which he might apprentice as an electrician when his apprenticeship in Beale Street's blues clubs and as a listener to Black-oriented radio stations in Memphis and Nashville gave him a look and a sound that made record labels specializing in "race" and "hillbilly" records believe he might transcend such categories. When he hit, he mused that "the colored folk been singing it and playing it just the way I'm doing now man, for more years than I know." His slicked hair looked like processed African American styles, and his electric "nigger outfits" came from stores catering to Memphis's Black community.[15] For a time he commanded a substantial and enthusiastic "reverse crossover" audience of African American concert goers and record buyers. He sang songs (and took part of the composing royalties) of the African American genius Otis Blackwell (including "All Shook Up" and "Don't Be Cruel") on the one, rocking hand, and of the Ink Spots on the mellow other. To cast him, as did the video, as spying on Black culture fits the facts, but for a time his espionage was studious and enamored. Furthermore, as Dave Marsh has observed, while deeply partaking of Black music, the young Presley sought to create a "new form," not merely to imitate.[16]

The utter indispensability of contact with African American music and with the minstrel tradition to Elvis's early triumphs is recognized by worshippers and detractors alike. Even so stern a Presley critic as Nelson George has allowed that the young Elvis somehow managed to "inhale [Black performers'] passion into his soul" and "scared white parents and the guardians of separation just as if he were black." Explaining why Presley's substantial African American following, especially among young women, was not still more visible, soul's godfather, James Brown, said, "Do you think a black girl could run up and kiss him? The system wouldn't let us be together."[17] Even given this pressure, Presley for a time appeared in Black shows in Memphis and drew white supremacist protest against race-mixing, "voodoo" music, and African sounds in rock like a lightning rod. Only in the longer run, as George argues, did Elvis exhale and prove a "derivative" artist, a "package," and "a damned lazy student" of African American music. It is possible to be less harsh, and even to admire some of Elvis's later work, without missing George's point: Presley's career came to be less and less about creative contact with African Americans. However unforgiving, George's account makes the critical move toward treating the evolution of Presley musically and racially, rather than a rehash of timeless debates about the intent and quality of his borrowings, as the most interesting issue.[18]

Presley's rise came at the moment when the literal act of a paid entertainer putting on blackface makeup to perform the stereotyped minstrel roles of African Americans had dramatically waned. Certainly, such performances by amateur groups in schools, churches, lodges, and even PTAs continued, and minstrel traditions undergirded African American performances on television and in films. But professional blacking-up was on the run. Civil rights pressure helped to account for the change. However, less noticed is the extent to which a transformation in the character of white claims to cross racial boundaries also made blackface superfluous in the 1950s. Presley's persona symbolized such a new "postminstrel" claim, one based on sharing not simply the craft of African American musicians but also the soul. Elvis was blackened by coal dust and then whipped in *Jailhouse Rock,* but his racecrossing generally proceeded along other lines. Whereas blackface was traditionally elaborate and epidermal, Presley's "blackness" famously came from below the waist and below the skin. Clothing, following on the zoot suit of the '40s, enabled "racial cross-dressing" to be much more gestural than blacking-up. The white Catholic radical John Howard Griffin's early 1959 use of chemicals to change color and to experience wrenching soul-changing lessons regarding racism, recounted in *Black Like Me,* was so arresting precisely because it was anomalous. By the time of the 1990s attempt at a progressive minstrelsy in *Bulworth,* Warren Beatty's politician-turned-rapper emerged as a reclothed, but not very much darkened, hiphopper.[19]

Presley thus did not imitate blackface performers who reminded audiences of their whiteness beneath the soot, sometimes comparing themselves to widows who only wear black for a little while, sometimes putting on blackface in front of the audience, and, in the case of vaudeville star Sophie Tucker, sometimes donning blackface but then removing a glove to show, as she put it, that she was white. Elvis did, however, "take off" blackness in another time-honored entertainment tradition, that of achieving success through imitation of African American forms and then moving on, as many blackface performers did, to something else.[20]

Like so many other performers who managed to inhale, or at least to market, African American culture, Presley began on the margins of whiteness and in his later career patrolled racial margins from a much more commanding racial position. Elvis was *King Creole* on film; he was the "half-breed" renegade of *Flaming Star*, a film banned in South Africa for its race-mixing. His Navajo role in *Stay Away Joe* earned him a Golden Turkey nomination from critics as the "Most Ludicrous Racial Impersonation in Hollywood History"—Presley's Cherokee "great-great-great-grandmother" notwithstanding. He went native having *Fun in Acapulco* (or seemed to, although lingering fears of Mexican resentment ruled out his being filmed on location there) and in Hawaii.[21] The Asian American sociologist turned film star Beulah Ong Kwoh once played Elvis's adoptive mother. *Kissin' Cousins* found Elvis a hillbilly. In *Harem Scarum* he reprised Rudolph Valentino's famous role as a dark white in Arab disguise. He wore the turban and makeup home, through dinner and until bedtime. The casting was appropriate in that Presley had long looked to Valentino (who, like Elvis, played across gender as well as racial boundaries) as a hero and a model. Elvis almost took a serious role in a film commemorating the life of the great traitor to whiteness, John Brown.[22] Often playing a "greasy" white character initially without money, Presley seemed more at home in many ways with racialized, exotic background characters than with his Scandinavian and white South African leading ladies. Presley's passion for karate led him to cast about for a film vehicle that would enable him to tell the story of Asian martial arts as a "philosophy." In one scenario, the planned film closed with Presley performing "a middle punch with a kee yap" and then rendering "the Lord's Prayer in Indian sign language."[23] Presley's involvement with the disciples of Indian yogi Parahansa Yogananda, self-parodied in his singing of "Yoga Is As Yoga Does" in *Easy Come, Easy Go*, was more brief but equally intense. Late in his life, Elvis attempted faith healings wearing a bejeweled turban. In India, his racial ambiguities helped to make him almost as much the king as he was in the United States. Similar dynamics applied in Japan, in Egypt, and eventually in Mexico as well.[24]

In films and in life, Presley's multiple racial positionings proved entirely compatible with his securing a position as fully white. This achievement was far from an entirely happy one, and Greil Marcus's image of Presley (fatally) taking on a "white whaleness" is illuminating in some ways.[25] Certainly Presley continued acutely to feel slights based on his class origins and rightly to fear that his acting in particular was being ridiculed. However, his fantastic wealth and his removing himself from lived contact with African American culture ensured Presley's whiteness even amid his exotic adventuring. During Presley's early years, a major New York television critic identified the racecrossing appeals and vulnerabilities of Presley's "gyrating" by acidly comparing it to "an aborigine's mating dance."[26] By the time of Presley's 1960 discharge from the army, the Dutch-immigrant-become-southern gentleman, Colonel Tom Parker, could confidently play with the images of Elvis and indigenous people. Parker, who presided over the sanitizing of Presley's image with consummate care, nonetheless energetically lobbied studios to set Elvis's first post-GI movie in Hawaii, where the hero would flee from too-adoring fans and the demands of the music industry by "disappearing in disguise into the bush of the tropics." There he would fall victim to bootleg record producers who would record his joyous singing with the "natives." An alternative scenario had Elvis raised by gypsies.[27]

The symbol of Presley's sad arrival into fuller whiteness was Graceland, the neoplantation *Playboy* mansion into which he moved with his parents in 1957. The suburban whiteness Elvis lived in the early Graceland years did not utterly reject his earlier life. Donkeys lived in the dream home's swimming pool, Presley's father kept pigs, and watermelon-seed-spitting contests occurred in the yard. But the life of Presley's youth, close to African Americans in spite of segregation, gave decisive way to a far greater separation. Graceland sat in the aptly named Memphis suburb of Whitehaven, a name that Parker and Presley would also apply to one of their business ventures. Just being developed in subdivisions, Whitehaven's railroad stop was reportedly a grass field with a signpost reading only "White."[28]

Of course, Graceland did not utterly sequester Presley from African Americans. The phonograph played his old idols, especially the extraordinary R and B performers Roy Hamilton and Jackie Wilson, and some new ones. Elvis apparently warmed to Bob Dylan's work by hearing the great Black gospel and folk singer Odetta sing Dylan on a record. When on the road, especially in Los Angeles and Las Vegas, Presley listened to and socialized with African American performers. In one memorable late-1960s instance, he sat in with Hamilton at a small

Memphis studio. His Los Angeles meeting with Wilson was another such event. Both the Wilson and the Hamilton meetings were central to his middle-aged bursts of creativity and to his gearing up for comeback attempts. However, as Peter Guralnick writes, high spots such as the meeting with Wilson were also memorable because they "happened so seldom." Figures like B. B. King and Rufus Thomas, so central to Presley's early development and to African American music in Memphis, simply disappear after 1958 in Guralnick's encyclopedic account of Presley's life. Sam Cooke apparently failed to register on Elvis's radar at all.[29]

The ways in which Presley grew and descended into full whiteness complicate one part of Erika Doss's fascinating analysis, in her *Elvis Culture*, of the fans who still make pilgrimages to Graceland. Doss rightly observes that the cult following of Presley adorers "deny Elvis' self-conscious racial synthesis in favor of an ahistorical myopia" that makes their hero "all-white." It should be added that Elvis's own later life, his marketing, and even his playing with racial lines invite such conclusions. For example, Doss particularly decries popular culture's association of Presley with the Confederate flag and lingers over the artist Fred Stein's interesting hand-colored photographic merging of Elvis and Dr. Martin Luther King, Jr., into "The Kings." But surely the fact that Presley did not ever directly associate himself with major campaigns for civil rights, even after King's assassination in Memphis (and even though his heroes Roy Hamilton and Jackie Wilson were regulars at movement benefits), mattered in fixing his distance from King. Just as obviously, Elvis's associations with the arch-segregationist George Wallace helped to wrap the Confederate flag around him.[30]

Considerations of the ways in which Presley's case illuminates the possibilities and limits of racial crossover are best left until after we examine the quite different case of wiggers. However, the ways in which Elvis's life demonstrates that we need to think about different types of crossovers deserve early mention here. First, limiting the meaning of *crossing over* to traversing the Black-white divide, or even boundaries separating musical genres, fails utterly to capture the complexities of Elvis's racechanges. Hawaii, Mexico, India, and Japan all intruded on Presley's story, as did cross-fertilization with Latino music, claims of Native American ancestry, and the place of poor whites in the U.S. racial order. Second, crossover by Elvis, and by white entertainers generally, typically involved the possibility of crossing back with age and with success. To consider only half of this dynamic obscures a great deal, including the possibility of returning to whiteness but to a different location within it. Crossover was thus both a multi-lane highway and a two-way street.

As he whitened, for example, Elvis became closer and closer with the very embodiment of ethnic white superstardom, Frank Sinatra. Indeed, Sinatra, who had once derided Presley's music as "deplorable, a rancid-smelling aphrodisiac," came to be both his champion and his model. As Presley entered the Army, Sinatra albums were being offered as prizes in "Why I Hate Elvis" contests. When he came out, much less "black" and much more respectable, he debuted on Sinatra's television show. The gossip columns might contrive to make them romantic rivals or speculate that Sinatra was loath to give up his claim as the "king" of popular music, but the relationship matured. Sinatra had gone precariously from a young singer/actor victimized both as a racialized *guinea* and as an antiracist activist who worked in concert with leftists, to a top-of-the-heap White House guest. He did so without losing his aura of otherness and sexual danger. The two were America's most successful *greasers*—Elvis by virtue of his hairstyle and Sinatra by virtue of his ethnicity and supposed Mafia ties. Elvis, Mae Axton observed, "was almost in awe of Sinatra—and Sinatra was almost in awe of him." Long before "the king" and the "King of Pop" dynasties were united in the wedding of Lisa Marie Presley and Michael Jackson, Elvis was rumored to be romantically linked to Nancy Sinatra, Frank's daughter. Had *they* married, everyone could have worn white.[31]

What to Make of Wiggers

Elvis Presley was a lone individual born into a Jim Crow system of integation and navigating the crosscurrents of the entertainment industry, and his racial crossings were perhaps inevitably troubled. In turning from this celebrated individual case to a contemporary group of avowed, accredited, or accused racechangers, who are not typically marketing their transformations, we might expect to find a wider field for transformative actions. Indeed one point of juxtaposing Presley with "wiggers"—that group of white youth said to be, or claiming to be, imitating African Americans today—is to show that white racial transgressions have histories and social geographies. Across time and place, would-be white racechangers do not share an existential predicament but rather face particular dilemmas, possibilities, and illusions. In the absence of an antiracist politics, as this conclusion emphasizes, all reliance on racial impersonation to change the racial order is likely to end in disappointment. However, the ways in which such imperson-ations might connect to antiracism and deepen cracks within white identity change and vary in a complex manner.

If Elvis needed no introduction, wiggers surely do, and that introduc-tion must stress complexity, potential, and peril. Charles Murray, that well-paid worrier about the alleged "black underclass," frets these days too about those white kids described by the "popular neologism *wig-ger*"—that is, white niggers. Taking in U.S. society from his comfortable vantage point at the far-right tail of what he regards as the all-important "bell curve" of IQ, Murray argues, "If the dominant culture deems you a misfit, then you plug away." But, he adds, "If there is an alternative culture that says, 'Who needs that shit?' then dropping out becomes an option. And that alternative culture is the black underclass." According to Murray, female-headed households among the white population and the very presence of the Black poor have produced—the dominant cul-ture and patriarchal families that brand kids as misfits get no blame—a spate of wiggers who "mimic black dress, walk or attitudes." But such mimicry, largely male, masks a deeper reality: what wiggers are "really imitating is black-underclass attitudes toward achievement."[32]

Fashion writer Robin D. Givhan likes wiggers. Pronouncing them, as of the early 1990s, "perhaps the fastest growing group among teenagers," she finds these "white kids who want to be black" open to "new worlds and different ideas." Her informant, a youth marketing consultant whom "companies such as Pepsi pay big bucks," describes wiggers as white kids "wearing Cross Colors and oversized baggy jeans . . . watching Spike Lee movies, 'Soul Train' and 'Yo! MTV Raps.'" Givhan holds that "these folks have absorbed" Black culture, making it "their own." Their interest in "what makes some African Americans groove can only be helpful to improved race relations." Wiggers "are crossing cultural lines. And that's a lot more stylish than anything you can buy off the rack." Covering "Style" for the *New York Times,* Molly O'Neill echoes Givhan: "Hip-hop has unbalanced the cultural compass . . . When white girls wear dreadlocks . . . another distinction is being teased apart, hair by hair." The "tattoos and baggy tatters" of hiphop fashion, O'Neill concludes, are "weaving together formerly polarized segments of society." Focusing on music, *Spin* writer Charles Aaron concurs, musing that "Black Like Them" white kids may be the "last best hope for healing America's racial divide.[33]

In the inaugural 1992 issue of *VIBE,* the slick magazine of "hip-hop culture," James Ledbetter dismissed or maybe just dissed wiggers.

They were "desperate . . . parodies," "rip-offs," and "suckers." They had failed to do more than "play at being black." Ledbetter wrote in the same issue of *VIBE* in which Greg Tate improbably denounced rappers for having failed to denounce "commodity fetishism." They had not been "willing to renounce, up front, the systematic abuses of the white order."[34]

Neil Bernstein, writing in *West Magazine,* world-historicizes wiggers. They, along with "white cholitas," "white skaters and Mexican would-be-gang-bangers [who] listen to gangsta rap and call each other 'nigga' as a term of endearment," "blond cheerleaders" who stress their Cherokee ancestry, and "children of mixed marriages [who] insist that they are whatever race they say they are," are the world. They are "facing the complicated reality of what the 21st century will be," and "inching toward . . . the dream of what the 21st century should be," each time that they treat racial identity as a voluntary claim rather than as a biological or cultural inheritance.[35]

My own notes on wiggers can claim nothing like the conclusiveness of any of these journalistic accounts. In these pages, wiggers will be marching neither toward dystopia nor toward a utopian, integrated and corporate-sponsored community. Wiggers here will be seen neither as reincarnating minstrelsy nor as miraculously waving away both centuries of racism and current inequalities in money and power. They will be seen neither as just more of the same old past nor as the guides in our safe passage to a multicultural future.

What I have called the "Ellison question" frames my remarks. It provides a sharp reminder that in a society in which an imagination of blackness so thoroughly frames both what attracts and what repulses whites, discussions of white identity will turn as often on a question as on an answer. Two decades ago, Ralph Ellison posed that question as extremely and precisely as anyone had yet done: "What, by the way, is one to make of a white youngster who, with a transistor radio, screaming a Stevie Wonder tune, glued to his ear, shouts racial epithets at black youngsters trying to swim at a public beach?" In the early 1990s, while I was first trying to research the word *wigger* and come to grips with its larger meanings, life in mid-Missouri caused me to see the phenomenon very much in terms of Ellison's question. The first sign of wiggerdom I detected in that area was the "X" cap that white kids began to wear, backwards. Some of them had another "X"—the Confederate flag— on their belt buckles, t-shirts, or trucks. Part of a larger pattern in which racism chronically seems to be getting better and getting worse simultaneously, such jarring images suggested that Ellison had asked a question with not only profound cultural ramifications but also immediate political import: What can be "made of" the impulses that at once and often in the same person lead to tremendous attraction toward Malcom X and "nonwhite" cultures and toward hideous reassertions of whiteness as what the theorist and activist A. Sivanandan has called a "political color"?[36]

The following brief sketch of the varied explanations of the origin of the word *wigger*, and of its meanings, is not meant to answer exactly how and where the word was coined or what its most common use has become. Instead, the argument is that *wigger* is of interest precisely because of the messiness surrounding its meanings and because of the ways in which that messiness gives us some entry into the tragic and dramatic complexities of Ellison's question. *Wigger* first came to my attention as a slur used at Cabrini High School in a Detroit suburb in about 1989. When white Detroiters enrolled at the school, bringing with them "black-influenced" styles and friendships with African Americans, some of the suburban white students caused a stir by calling the newcomers wiggers, meaning "white niggers" or whites acting "too black." Similar recent uses of wigger as a slur against whites by whites have been reported in Madison, Wisconsin, and in Warren, Ohio. What brought the term briefly to the nation's attention were dramatic 1993 events in very rural Morocco, Indiana, where the hiphop fashions and musical tastes of two young white sisters resulted in their being called wiggers, suspended from their virtually all-white school, and spat upon and threatened with death by white male students who demanded that they "dress white" (or paint themselves another color and move to "the slums of Chicago"). The resulting discussions of the controversy on *Montel Williams,* and other major talk/outrage shows, as well as in the pages of *Esquire* and *VIBE,* catapulted the Moroccans into notoriety. By December 1993, after an *Oprah* show centered on *wiggers, The Source,* a leading hip-hop magazine, declared the term and the controversy "officially played and over." It wasn't.[37]

The sense of *wigger* described above is consistent with uses of *white nigger* as a white-on-white epithet (*like smoked Irishman, guinea, black Dutch, nigger lover,* and *Black Republican*) dating back at least to the nineteenth century, although *white nigger* was then more likely to be applied to a white either accepting "nigger work" or politically breaking with what was seen as proper behavior for whites than to a suspected cultural dissenter from whiteness. In 1868, for example, a

Confederate veteran who voted with the Republican opponents of white supremacy was seized by a Tennessee mob, placed on a mock auction block, and sold as a "white nigger." Closer to modern uses was the branding of Johnny Cash as a "white nigger" during his rockabilly days. Wigger as a culturally based white-on-white slur existed in Buffalo in the early 1970s. The white rapper MC Serch, heard it in the early 1980s when white classmates reacted to his adoption of hiphop clothing by calling him a wigger or a "black wanna-be"—shortly before many of them adopted the style themselves.[38]

However, at the same time that Serch was called a *wigger* derisively by whites, another young East Coast hiphopper, Gary Miles, was being called one affectionately by African Americans. Miles, self-described as only "phenotypically white," was when I contacted him a University of California-Los Angeles graduate student who forcefully argued that *wigger* originated among African Americans to denote whites who seriously embraced African American cultural forms and values, in contrast to "wannabe" dabblers in the external trappings of rap. The meaning was still "white nigger," but *nigger* in the rehabilitated sense proliferating in rap. Often pronounced *wigga,* the term signals the same sort of inclusion as a greeting "That's my nigga" might. In this sense, wigger would echo earlier African American uses of words such as *hillbilly cat* in early rock and roll and some Latina uses of "Whatina" for white women who share their struggles. Miles allowed that the approbation implied by *wigga* could sometimes change on short notice, however.[39]

In Milwaukee, another usage of *wigger* appeared. Although one young white informant there saw it as used in his inner-city high school as a flat (neither friendly nor mocking) description of those whites who "want to identify with black culture," another account found black Milwaukee high schoolers using it to discuss with contempt white suburban school kids who "wear the jackets . . . and try to talk black [but] who wouldn't last a minute" in the city. This comports with long-standing African American uses of *white nigger* as a derogatory term for "a white person with Negro affectations."[40]

The case for *wigger* as a coinage of African Americans—this does not rule out whites independently creating the term at another place and time—is buttressed by two further considerations. As both Miles and Sundiata Cha-Jua have pointed out, substituting *w* or *wh* at the beginning of existing words to create new words to describe whites or white institutions is not infrequent in African American speech— hence *witch* for *"white bitch"* and *whitianity* for "white Christianity."

Second, and here the tremendous hybridity of American slang complicates easy racial distinctions, *wigger* clearly gestures toward earlier uses of *wig* and *wigged out* by both Black and white jazz musicians and beat poets. *Wigged,* variously connoting overstimulated, intellectualized, laudably crazy, and stressed, could hardly have failed to strike Black-influenced musical subcultures as an apt cousin for *wigger.*[41]

Further variations exist. Youth culture journalist Charles Aaron reports *wigger*'s use by "whites who embrace black culture to call out whites who defame black culture." In a letter to *VIBE,* one reader adopted this "calling-out" usage in criticizing the "ignorant, redneck pieces of racist white trash" in Morocco, Indiana, as the "real *'wiggers'*" and as a "disgrace to the white heritage they fight so desperately to protect." Where my older son went to junior high school, *wigger* was at the same time acceptingly applied by Blacks to whites, disparagingly applied by racist whites to other whites, dismissively applied by whites adopting Black styles to whites who were seen as doing so inauthentically, and used approvingly by white would-be-hiphoppers to describe each other. One high schooler in the north suburbs of Chicago, who had recently moved there from the city, proudly saw herself as a wigger—as one of the white students who "wished they were black"— but had never thought of the term as derived from *nigger.*[42]

This is not the place to evaluate fully the political importance of wiggers, let alone their wisdom. The broader white hiphop audience is rather easily ridiculed. Hiphop magazines, marketed in large part to white audiences, who now are estimated to buy from 50% to 70% of rap recordings sold, often themselves ridicule wiggers and wannabes as middle-class, superficial, voyeuristic, apolitical, consumerist, dumb, and even racist. There is little reason to doubt these charges or to suppose that white fans are underrepresented among those whom Greg Tate derides as "all the B-boy wannabes who like to say *ho!*"[43]

When Italian American youth in New York City in the 1980s chose to identify themselves with elements of African American style, they at times proudly called themselves guineas. In doing so, they rehabilitated a term used earlier in the century to slur Italian immigrants and to connect Italians with Blacks. But those guineas, as Donald Tricarico writes, "resist[ed] identification" with African Americans on other levels and bit "the hand that feeds them style." For whites to easily appropriate a form of *nigger* is likewise fraught with difficulties. Venise Wagner's excellent San Francisco *Examiner* article on "wiggas" concluded with the words of a chastened white convert to Islam, formerly a wigger:

"They [wiggers] would like to imagine themselves as not part of the problem. But we are all part of the problem." Moreover, being a wigger is often an adolescent phase, calling to mind Leslie Fiedler's remark that white American males spend their early years as imaginary Indians and their teens as imaginary Blacks before settling into a white adulthood (not to mention Janis Joplin's curious hope that "being black for a while will make me a better white").[44]

As the courageous high schoolers of Morocco, Indiana, show, wiggers are by no means all male, but they often are aggressively so and identify with violence, scatology, homophobia, and sexism in rap rather than with Black music and culture more broadly. Indeed, Robin D. G. Kelley's fine work on hiphop reminds us that one impetus toward sexual violence in the lyrics is precisely that it sells well to white adolescent males. Bay area hiphop DJ Davey D's recent warning that some of the music and marketing leaves the impression that "calling a woman a . . . 'ho' is black culture," reveals the stakes involved in such a marketing approach. Recent controversies over the misogyny and homophobia of the white megastar Eminem raise the larger threat that such hatred will be the lowest common denominator uniting young male audiences across color lines. In her inspired rant "Owed to Eminem," the great poet June Jordan writes that she is "tired of wiggas that whine as they squeal/about bitches and faggots and little girls too." Brent Staples's *New York Times* opinion piece "Dying to Be Black," roots the wigger's embrace of gangsta rap in the feeling that blackness has the "power to generate fear," a power "particularly seductive to adolescent boys in the suburbs." One expert recently explained to *American Demographics* that marketers hope to reach white suburban consumers, and middle-class Black youth, precisely by developing the "hardest-core element" in hiphop. Consumerism, sexuality, and male supremacy can hardly be separated in either the music or the fan magazines, not when Benetton uses the center spread of the inaugural issue of *VIBE* to gesture toward both *Playboy* and *National Geographic* with a large photo of topless African women, including one who is albino to make the advertisement somehow subversive of racial boundaries.[45]

But the very matters that warn us against romantically mistaking wiggers for the vanguard of antiracism ought also to allow us to see that the proliferation of wiggers cannot simply be dismissed. The dynamics of cultural hybridity have long featured much that is deeply problematic on the white side. From minstrelsy to the blackfaced antebellum mobs who victimized African Americans, to the insidious recent film *Soul Man,* the superficial notion that blackness could be put on and taken off at will has hounded hybridity. Aggressive male posturing, sexual and otherwise, accompanied fascination with Black culture long before rap. Surely no wigger has gone further over the top in this regard than Norman Mailer's 1950s essay "The White Negro," which squarely premised an admiration for Black culture on that culture's capacity to produce orgasms in white males. Nor is the commodification of Black cultural forms by white promoters, artists, and audiences new. A century and a half ago, minstrels likened themselves to dealers in slaves on the African coast, joking that both made money by "taking off the niggers." Not only individual Black artists, but also whole genres have been impoverished in the process the minstrels began. When Elvis "discovered" Big Mama Thornton, Amiri Baraka reminds us, she was "dis'd" and her music "covered."[46]

Crossover, in a manifestly unequal society, has as often been the product of tragic, tawdry, and exploitive forces as of romantic ones. Whether we judge the beauty and solidarity created by the crossing of cultural color lines in the interstices of racial capitalism to outweigh the associated slights and tragedies is on one level immaterial. The process goes on, superficially and at times deeply. If to abdicate studying it were to abdicate only understanding that mythical thing called "white culture," the consequences would be bearable. But such an abdication also entails giving up on understanding the astonishing variety within U.S. culture and within African American culture, the latter having as one of its essential elements the ability to borrow creatively from others and to engender mixed and new forms.[47]

The specific perils, and openings, created by whites trying on and taking off African American culture change profoundly, even amidst continuities. In the case of wiggers, for example, the tendency to essentialize Blackness as male, hard, and violent is considerably more pronounced than was the case in earlier white attachments to rhythm and blues and to soul. Not only does violence loom larger in the marketing and mythmaking of hiphop than in the case of the older forms, but romance has, until recently, tended not to be for sale, even as sex surely has been. (The overlap of categories complicates matters here. Contemporary "rhythm and blues," which includes the inheritors of soul as well as some "pop-sounding" rappers and does market romance, at times outsells both hiphop and rock.) The physical separation of the races in the ultrasegregated United States combines with the seeming intimacy of MTV and videos to give a large field for adolescent fantasies of sex and violence. One 1997 student paper at Bowling Green State University aptly suspected that "because they listen to violence in the music," wiggers come to think "that they are a part of it." The student added, "In a way they are right."[48]

Indeed any serious account of wiggers must come to grips with place of fantasy and of electronically disseminated culture in their emergence. Most studies to date emphasize their presence in what the anthropologist Matthew Durington calls "suburban space." The most revealing film on wiggers, *Whiteboyz*, sets its tragicomedy in whitest Iowa. There Danny Hoch's rural wannabe character can develop, in total isolation from lived experiences with urban African Americans, the notion that his mole defines his real skin color and all else is just a huge white birthmark. In her superb reporting on Indiana wiggers, Farai Chideya casts MTV as the "cultural common denominator" fueling their imaginations and actions.[49] On the other hand, from Charles Murray's phantasms of the wigger to the uses of the word at Cabrini High, wiggers are also at times portrayed as emerging, and in fact do emerge, from racially mixed neighborhoods and from poverty shared with people of color. As former wigger Brendan Rogers described his own background, "If you don't have a lot of money, and you live in place that isn't predominantly white, you have trouble identifying with other white people."[50]

The challenges of disentangling the imaginary and the lived are great, and thinking in terms of either/or (and still less in terms of authentic/inauthentic) does not help us. For example, in the case of two white teenagers branded wiggers (or "wannabe gangsters") and victimized as such in the tiny, 98 percent white town of North Branch, Minnesota, in 1996, the temptation is to see young, video-driven imaginations run wild in a replay of events in Morocco, Indiana. However, the boys had recently moved from the Twin Cities and were ultimately exiled by authorities to St. Paul rather than sent to jail. Moreover, as Rose Farley's reporting on the case shows, the Black population of North Branch, though tiny, was a focus of surveillance and fear in the town. Even in the Indiana case, the area was not all-white, and proximity to the city of Gary clearly shaped intolerance in the town.[51] Nor, of course, does lived urban experience inoculate against vivid imaginations regarding the ease of racial crossings. William Upski Wimsatt, a bright, middle-class Chicagoan, is deservedly among the most often cited writers on wiggers. In 1993 he described his own transformation. "My school was predominantly black," Wimsatt wrote, "so I became black too."[52]

Likewise intricate and important are the changed ways in which white interpretations of music developed mainly by African American artists have found a market. Except perhaps for the very young, white hiphop consumers do not seek out music made by white entertainers who claim to be authentically Black or who endeavor to sanitize rap. The preference is for African American artists. There is little room for the sorts of pale, safe imitations provided in Elvis's time by Pat Boone. Nor is claiming to be a wigger viable in the long run. When white rappers attack each other, the charge of "wannabe" is routinely leveled. Here is Everlast, who sometimes answers to the name "Whitey Ford," on MC Serch: ". . . he might as well have been wearing a T-shirt that said I WISH I WAS BLACK . . . nobody's gonna really respect that." And Everlast on House of Pain (featuring Everlast): "We came out, 'Yo, we're peckerwoods, we're white trash . . . and we love hip-hop.'" Eminem's breakthrough Rolling Stone cover sported the huge headline "LOW DOWN AND DIRTY WHITE BOY RAP."[53]

From Crossover to Crossing Over

In 1993, moved by white young people's enthusiasm for a music that honored Malcolm X and that frequently offered unsparing criticism of the racism and corruption in U.S. society, as tough-minded an observer as the criminologist Zaid Ansari raised the possibility of significant numbers of whites "becoming X." By that, Ansari meant being and becoming much more than they were by losing that quality in whiteness that "keeps them accepting oppression, including their own oppression."[54]

Whether or not we believe that wiggers are part of anything like as grand a future transformation as that envisioned by Ansari, we ought to realize that the little things they do in the present reflect the racialized hierarchies that have so shaped U.S. culture. In identifying with hiphop, for example, white rap fans drew largely unconsciously on the African heritage of the United States. The hip in hiphop, like so much else in modern U.S. culture, was put there by Africans. As the extraordinary research of David Dalby and others has shown, enslaved Wolof speakers carried *hipi* from what is now Senegal to the New World perhaps as early as the late seventeenth century. In Wolof the word meant "to open one's eyes" and to "be aware of what's going on." In the welter of African ethnicities that slavery and creative self-activity melded into an African American people, *hip* survived and prospered. Nearly three centuries later, it was there for the white mainstream to pick up from the jazz subculture. Even the beatnik/jazz insider ideal of the *hep-cat* echoed the Wolof *hipi-kat,* which meant "someone with . . . eyes open." When the term hippie came to name the masses of young people who sought out eye-opening experiences in the 1960s, it did so because those young people were steeped in African influences, however little they were aware of the origins of those influences.[55]

A striking number of early *wiggers* (and of Black hiphoppers) sported oversized t-shirts and backwards baseball caps featuring the image of the hippest and hopping-est figure in U.S. popular culture, Bugs Bunny. Sometimes it was a dark Bugs with rasta braids and hiphop clothes. Sometimes it was standard-issue Warner Brothers Bugs. Some kids wore a "Black" Bugs one day and a gray one the next. This crossing of colors on Bugs Bunny shirts was perfectly, although again largely unconsciously, in tune with long-standing dramas in U.S. cultural history. Bugs's heritage is anything but "all-white." The verb *bug,* meaning "annoy" or "vex," helped to name the cartoon hero. The verb's roots, like those of *hip,* lie partly in Wolof speech.[56]

Moreover, the fantastic idea that a weak and vulnerable rabbit could be tough and tricky enough to menace those who would menace him entered U.S. culture, as the historian Franklin Rosemont observes, largely via the Brer Rabbit tales. Such stories were told among various ethnic groups, especially along the West African coast. They were developed further by American slaves before being popularized and bastardized by white collectors such as Joel Chandler Harris. They were available both as literature and as folklore to the white southern cartoonist Tex Avery, whose genius decisively helped to give us Bugs. Joe Adamson's forceful connection of African folklore with Bugs cut in two ways. Brer Rabbit inspired creators of Bugs and prepared us for his arrival.[57]

For all of their significance in reminding us how real and pervasive crossover has long been, neither Brer Rabbit nor Bugs Bunny has led us to cross over from white supremacy to racial justice. Indeed, they themselves got caught in the briar patch of racism often enough. Given this reality, it is not surprising that many commentators want to consign questions of representation, culture, and racial performance to the realm of the frivolous and to get back to the "real" business of politics. But because party politics in the United States so seldom allows for the frank discussion of racial oppression, let alone of the possibility of crossing over into freedom, we should perhaps not be too hasty in abandoning cultural struggles and in overlooking their political edges.

In charting a way out of this impasse, it is appropriate that we should return to, but also update, the wisdom of Fiedler and of Ellison. Fiedler's observation that his people are "born theoretically white" but are "permitted to pass our childhood as imaginary Indians, our adolescence as imaginary Negroes, and only then are expected to settle down to being what we really are: white once more" is so frequently quoted and so cleverly phrased that it can sometimes be read as a familiar throwaway line acerbically commenting on racial imaginations among U.S. whites. It does that, but it also describes social and political economic realities as well as life cycles. The commodity of blackness is hawked most insistently in youth markets. Barbie Doll ads feature hiphop, as do those for breakfast cereals. Bazooka Joe bubble gum comics include fifty separate "Bazooka Joe RAPS" cartoons, (w)rapping the gum. Serious and even subversive hiphop attracts an older, but still young, white audience.[58]

The identification with African American culture continues to be overwhelmingly mediated through commodities. Indeed, we might supplement Anne McClintock's intelligent theorizing about "commodity racism" with a discussion of "commodity antiracism" and its own dialectics and limits. In the 1990s, for example, Raisin Bran offered cereal buyers the chance to send in for "Hip Hop Gear," which it declared "official." The tag line for the clothing was "Statements of Social Consciousness," which the company *copyrighted*. (One such meaningful social statement featured on the very multicultural back of the box was "I'll be on the move 'cause I've got things to do!") Clearly, such commodification cannot utterly contain protest and creativity. Young people find their ways to, and help to create, Public Enemy, Mos Def, The Coup, Digible Planets, and Bahamadia. For teenagers to buy Timberland footwear under the slogan "GIVE RACISM THE BOOT" is not without significance. It is clearly better than their buying an Atlanta Braves hat. But commodity antiracism may remain so superficial that young people purchase both the the shoes and the hat.[59]

Moreover, if we are to take Fiedler's point fully seriously, we must add that buying into whiteness, and in particular into segregated housing markets, often emerges as a grownup, life-altering, and government-subsidized investment with which commodity antiracism cannot compete. The danger in such a situation is that identification with other races becomes, by definition, immature and ephemeral. At the level of lived experience, oral testimony and other sources tell us, feelings of strong interracial friendship often persist until adolescence, when they are outgrown. The onset of dating is rightly offered as one explanation for such a change, and the changing job patterns that young white workers encounter as they leave their early service-industry work surely matter as well. So do the ways in which youthful brushes with commodity antiracism give way to adult "possessive investments in whiteness." If Elvis's white fans could not all move into Gracelands, they did in great numbers move into Whitehavens, and their memories of an "all-white Elvis" hinge on the moves *they* made as adults.[60] In the absence of struggles for fair housing and lending, wage justice, and reparations, the cultural trajectory that Fiedler charts with regard to growing out of racial transgressions will continue to have powerful material underpinnings.

Ellison's white supremacist, transitorized Stevie Wonder fan usefully fixes our attention on the fact that infatuation with African American and African American-influenced music is too often a separate matter from loving and respecting African Americans. One of arch-segregationist Alabama Governor George Wallace's chief advisers was the lawyer Seymore Trammell. Even in a tough field, Trammell stood out; some considered him the "meanest son of a bitch" around Wallace. He was also the manager of a Black gospel group, the Harmony Jubilee Quartet.[61]

The most celebrated example of a recent political leader connecting African American culture with pleasure and excellence but responding on different wavelengths where racial politics was concerned is the late Lee Atwater. Atwater, who chaired the Republican National Committee (RNC) during George Herbert Walker Bush's presidency, arranged for blues and R and B greats such as Willie Dixon, Sam Moore, Albert Collins, Koko Taylor, and Percy Sledge to put in appearances at a Bush inaugural party. The critic Greg Tate, who described the festivities in "The GOP Throws a Mammy-Jammy," rightly insisted that Atwater was not just prospecting for African American votes but also wanted to pay "homage to his beloved rhythm and blues." Atwater grabbed a guitar and played himself, joining Moore on "Hi-Heel Sneakers." Tate judged the performance "more than competent" and "impassioned," concluding that "the white boy can play." Atwater, he added, "coulda been a contender," among hot white bluesmen, "maybe even on the order of a Stevie Ray Vaughn," who also played the event.[62]

Of course, Atwater is best remembered in a much different way. He masterminded the most famous use of race-coding in modern U.S. political advertising. In the 1988 Bush-Dukakis presidential campaign,

Atwater pledged that he would "strip the bark off that little bastard [Dukakis]" and "make Willie Horton his running mate." Advertisements featuring Horton, an African American prisoner who committed a rape and stabbing while on a prison furlough through a program authorized by Dukakis, did just that. An apology from Atwater, stricken with cancer and agonizing that he would probably "never play the guitar . . . again," came long after the damage was done.[63]

Nor should we imagine that the active racism of Ellison's young man or of Atwater as an individual represents the only problem here. White corporate control of the music business often rests in the hands of hip young white executives and editors who are very skilled at negotiating and selling cultural difference. Their credentials as what have been sometimes called (like a briefly successful white hiphop group) "Young Black Teenagers" are usually impeccable. Confidence that their cultural knowledge and commitment place them beyond criticism also dulls any possibility of self-criticism and justifies the absence of inquiries into ownership and control in the industry and into its responsibility to African American communities. Martha Bayles observes aptly that "homage" and "resentment" can be two sides of the same coin where white admiration of Black music is concerned. It is worth remembering, for example, that destructive discussions of so-called "reverse racism" against whites began in the jazz world among white musicians, critics, and fans who felt aggrieved that their love for and contributions to the music were not sufficiently acknowledged. They threw the term *Crow Jim* (that is, the opposite of Jim Crow segregation) around so wildly that in 1964, Charles Mingus was moved to reply, "Well, until we start lynching white people, there is no word that can mean the same as Jim Crow. Until we own Bethlehem Steel and RCA Victor, plus Columbia Records and several others industries, the term Crow Jim has no meaning."[64]

The Atwater and Mingus examples suggest, in very different ways, that struggles over cultural meaning are not neatly separable from those over property and political power. Ellison's young, white beach brawler is one useful point of departure here. He is, given our image of those who act directly on racist impulses, presumptively poor and not a suit-and-tie racist. Indeed, Tate conjured up this image even for the RNC official Atwater, writing that the blues-soaked Republican honcho was a "redneck" and "white trash" who "likes being licked by the tarbrush." Elsewhere he found that Atwater "reminds me of anybody." Understandable as such views of the mass and class bases of whiteness may be, such imprecision does not serve us well in answering Ellison's question about what is to be done with the young racist. If the "redneck" is a top Republican leader, what to do will remain a problem. If he is among the white working poor, the question can at least be addressed in the context of building a new labor movement, of developing reparations campaigns that promise structural improvements to devastated urban areas in ways that benefit all residents and of supporting mobilizations against environment racism, which are often led by people of color. In the absence of such movements, appeals to poor whites to give up privileges—however miserable those petty privileges are—will seem abstract and remain ineffectual.[65]

Indeed, expanding Ellison's question beyond music and beaches is urgent if the mutually reinforcing connections between whiteness and property are to be challenged. (As Ellison probably knew, in the era of Elvis African American popular music in the South was often called "beach music" to associate it with play and especially with proto–Spring Break sex and college partying, as well as to signal its divorce from everyday "adult" realities).[66] The close connections in our minds between racial crossovers and commodities—mostly music and clothes and sometimes also drugs—define one arena, but hardly the only arena, where transgressions of racial lines occur. In his excellent article "Why Be White?" the Chicago journalist Peter Leki does not invoke wiggers as models of racechange. Instead he introduces Scott, an Irish American factory worker and trade unionist. During a layoff, the foreman summoned the fifteen most junior workers at the plant to announce that they were out of a job. He later took Scott aside to say that actually the layoff would not apply to him. Scott immediately found an African American worker who was senior to him, but had been laid off, and the two confronted the foreman. Scott, with two kids and with a house payment due, was soon out of work but not out of principles.[67] Among the critical tasks before us is expanding the idea of crossover to cover Scott and also to include the building of institutions that validate Scott's individual heroism and ultimately render it unnecessary.

Our thinking about crossover and crossing over from whiteness also must be pushed in other directions. Ellison gives us a young white male, but we must also remember that the transitor radio—now the portable CD player—has often hooked up young white women to music. From early blackface minstrelsy's sex-segregated troupes (and often male-only audiences), to Elvis, to the Beastie Boys, crossover into a marketed encounter with Black culture has been largely a male privilege. In 1939 in the jazz journal *Downbeat,* Ted Toll argued for prohibiting white "gal yippers" from working in bands on the grounds that jazz was rooted in African American culture and was therefore no place for white women. As Gayle Wald puts it in her acute study of John Howard Griffin's racial impersonation in his *Black Like Me,* white men have "enjoyed a greater liberty than others to play with racial identities and to do so in safety, without permanent loss or costs." The exceptional white female players—Sophie Tucker, Mae West, Janis Joplin—have made spectacular, but often brief and anomalous, appearances in dramas that both challenge and reinforce racial lines.[68] The space for such figures to operate within hiphop remains tightly circumscribed.

And yet, if we are to think intelligently about the dynamics of crossover and the possibility of crossing over into a nonwhite society, gender must structure our analysis. In my 1950s and 1960s youth, transitor radios generated music not only at beaches but also in bedrooms, where late-night broadcasts of Black music played softly enough so that parents would not hear. The purpose of putting radios under a pillow was to keep mothers and fathers from knowing what was playing and how late it continued. To imagine that such nocturnal experiences were not deeply gendered is impossible. Similarly, as Randy McBee's work suggests, dancing was experienced very differently, and far more often, among young white women than among young white men. The emphasis on the more extravagant posturing of men involved in crossover leads us to forget that early rock lyrics were often "as sugary as they were salty," to overlook girl bands, and especially to minimize white attraction to the music of the women of Motown. To the extent that Aretha Franklin's soulful "R-E-S-P-E-C-T" is a much fitter anthem for second-wave feminism than Helen Reddy's "I Am Woman," missing such cultural connections also impoverishes our understanding of political struggles. Wini Breines's pioneering work of reminiscence and sociology, *Young, White and Miserable,* describes "growing up female" in the 1950s. In it, Breines persuasively argues that the appeals of early racecrossing rock and roll were gendered and that through fandom plus dance, young white women could begin to disentangle the last two adjectives in the book's title. For Breines, crossover specifically made possible an attack on sexual double standards, and soul music "blew a huge hole in *Leave It to Beaver*-land."[69]

However, possessive adult investments in whiteness also have continually reconstituted *Leave It to Beaver*-lands as sprawling white spaces. At almost the same moment in 1993 that *Time* discovered Eve as the "new woman" of the twenty-first century, the mass-market press lavished attention on the "angry white male," hurt and allegedly victimized by affirmative action. In the context of campaigns against that policy, alliances between white women and people of color have been fragile at best.[70] Such alliances, built around affirmative action, sexual harassment, and other issues, are indispensable to any strategy for creating a nonwhite society.

Finally, what if we step a little further beyond the comfort zone of imagining racial crossover as neatly situated on a Black-white divide? What if Ellison's white youth thinks he is Bruce Lee or another Asian martial artist as he unleashes "fists of fury"? What if we instead imagine crossover as a young Latina hooking up to Fred Ho's Afro-Asian Music Ensemble? What about a young Haitian American kid connecting with Cypress Hill, or with Big Pun, or with Kid Frost singing "La Raza"? What of a Hmong immigrant who falls in love with the Native American rhymes of Without Rezervation? And then again, what about the reservation teenagers who buy an Apache Indian CD and keep listening after they find it to be British Asian Indian music profoundly influenced by hiphop and by dancehall rhythms from the West Indies? Or what about the ethnic Korean already all about rap before immigrating to Los Angeles from Japan?[71]

Once such multiple questions are posed, it becomes clear that crossover, even more now than in Elvis's time, is plural and international. Such complexities do not in any simple way show us how to cross over into racial justice. For example, the fact that whites cross over to take on racial identities other than African American may only add problems. Certainly, as Rachel Martin's work has demonstrated, the presumption that hippies showed three decades ago in claiming American Indian identities was nothing short of astonishing. One satirist has modestly suggested that wigger suburbanites ought now to give up their "extravagantly protective hand gestures and pseudo-ebonics" to become "Weskimos." There is little guarantee that improvements would follow. Yvonne Tasker's deft work on race, representation, and martial arts cinema holds that the white male privilege of racechanging is especially pronounced in the attraction to Asian forms of self-defense.[72] In any case, so large a proportion of the white population now engages in some form of wholesale crossracial cultural borrowing and/or impersonation—hiphop nationalism, salsa, Asian martial arts, Internet-based racial crossings, Latin American martial arts, "Eastern" religion and meditation, powwow, rooting "reverently" for sports teams with racist mascots, "being like Mike," being Tiger Woods, and so on—that positive changes ought already to be showing up if such borrowings really chart the way forward. The "white cholitas" and the blonde cheerleaders calling themselves Indians in Bernstein's writings may in some cases be harbingers of a brave new century, but they also have had plenty of precursors who left the nation white and who often returned to whiteness themselves.[73]

The cases of racial crossovers among people of color have different dynamics but also define no surefire path to unity and liberation. Sunita, a young informant in Sunaina Maira's arresting ethnography of Indian American youth subculture in New York and New Jersey, describes the identification with hiphop by some Asian Indian young people in the United States as somewhat "rebellious" in that middle-class parents oppose it. The youth realize that hiphop is "not the norm associated with white culture," but Sunita adds that "at the back of their minds they are thinking, this is not long term." Maira endorses Sunita's views as broadly capturing the reality that "bhangra remix youth culture" in New York combines African American forms with Punjabi music and dance but is not seen by participants as engaged in "resistance to a system of economic and racial stratification." In that sense, "New York Mix" approximates the tendency of white youth culture sometimes to adopt the styles of others, but only temporarily. If we consider also the extent to which, as Michael Rogin has shown, crossing racial lines via impersonation was central to the Americanization and the whitening of Jewish immigrants, we might question where contemporary mixes with African American culture lead.[74]

However, Maira perceptively adds that for a layer of Asian Indian immigrant youth, New York Mix's cultural politics do more closely resemble those of politicized bhangra remix innovations in Britain, where "new Asian dance music" has " reemphasized an 'Asian identity' as a possible racial location [that] continues to be intimately tied to rethinking the possibilities of the . . . anti-racist project."[75] Such a view is concentrated in New York among the "more recent wave of lower-middle- and working-class South Asian immigrants" and second-generation youth politicized by growing up in diverse urban neighborhoods and by knowing "what it is to be racially harassed and . . . sometimes mistakenly identified as black or Latino." For all classes, she continues, "antiblack prejudices" imported from the Indian subcontinent are "reinforced by the black-white lines of U.S. racialization."[76]

Further complexities emerge when we juxtapose the comment of a Filipina student with Deborah Wong's powerful essay "The Asian

American Body in Performance." The student, writing at California State University in Fullerton in 1998, reported being besieged by a question from other Asian American students: "Why are Filipinos the blacks among Asians?" She then registered her own view that Filipino American youth had betrayed their Asian identities by embracing Black music and styles.[77] Wong, on the other hand, glories in highly politicized crossovers by Asian American performers. "As Asian American jazz musicians and rappers move toward Blackness," she insists, "their self-conscious movement away from Whiteness is unequivocal." According to Wong, such moves are "lateral" ones, with no echoes of the past hierarchies that structured either minstrelsy or passing. Although she briefly allows for some problematic areas, Wong sees a very promising "moving toward color" afoot. Far from betraying Asian identities, she argues, such "bridge-building" deepens Asian identities through "class-conscious cultural work of social and political transformation."[78]

In thinking about the possibility of crossing over from whiteness, it would be dangerous to conclude that the student is simply right and Wong is mistaken, or vice versa. Critiques of white identity emerge from various locations. As Hung C. Thai's work on second-generation Vietnamese Americans reveals, such critiques can in fact develop without embracing mixed, pan-Asian, Latina, or Black identities.[79] Even the attempt to "become white" can generate such critiques. When demographers tell us that in 2100 there will be 77 million "pure" Latinos among 261 million U.S. residents who are partly Latino, they frankly admit that they do not know how many people will identify as Latino. Some will identify as Latino, some as "21st century mestizas," mixed but not white, some as white, some as indigenous, some with specific national origins (such as Mexican, Salvadoran, or Brazilian), and some in ways we can only begin to imagine. Class, location, color, age, religion, country of emigration, time in the United States, gender, and language will all influence, but not neatly structure, choices of identity. Similarly, how police, judges, schools, realtors, employers, churches and other institutions categorize the people of 2100 is a political question that will be settled over time but *unevenly*.[80] I have watched, for example, the useful but West Coast-centered debates over the "triangulated" identities of Asian Americans, and over whether their "becoming white" was in the offing, from Minneapolis/Saint Paul. There poverty, language questions, and racism keep Hmong Americans very far from model minority status, let alone whiteness, in the eyes of authorities, and that local drama has reminded me constantly of the futility of glib generalizations.[81]

In the midst of such fluidity and complexity, it would be foolhardy to predict the precise racial future of the United States and counterproductive to lecture people about what their identities must "progressively" become. Identities that serve as rallying points for social justice movements at one juncture may resonate slightly, or be put to reactionary purposes, at others. To take the power of even the most inspiring crossover culture seriously is not to demand that it do all the work of social and political transformation. Indeed, many times, as recent work on Black-Latino musical interchanges shows, political movements help to create the opportunity for artists to borrow and recreate. Wong observes that the name of Jon Jang's Pan-Asian Arkestra echoes the late Horace Tapscott's Pan Afrikan People's Arkestra. Both grew from, and contribute to, political ferment. Jang's *Reparations Now!* (referring to reparations for Japanese American internment camp victims) suite gestures toward Max Roach's African American tribute to South African liberation, *We Insist! Freedom Now Suite.* As victories by Japanese Americans inspire reparations campaigns among African Americans, further overtures might be anticipated.[82] Such crossovers must be inspiring for us, and part of what they inspire must be the sort of movement building that makes more crossovers possible.

Above all, crossing over still requires the steady, everyday work of organizing to fight against white privilege and against the miseries that make whites settle for those privileges and encourage others to aspire to whiteness. There is a temptation to regard the opening up of whiteness in the twentieth century as on balance a positive thing, and certainly as preferable to continuing anti-immigrant racism against Greeks, Italians, Jews, Poles, and others. The hope that further openings in the ranks of privilege can now occur animates the faith, found in recent historical writings on race and immigration, in the ultimate triumph of an inclusive civic nationalism. However, the process of inclusion into whiteness has always been predicated on accepting the exclusion of others. What James Baldwin called the "vast amount of coercion" that went into ensuring that the marginalized "new immigrants" from Europe would choose whiteness during the twentieth century will operate likewise in the new century if whiteness and property stay yoked and if whiteness is the only property that many of the poor and many of the poor in spirit can aspire to obtain.[83]

Notes

Chapter 1

1. All citations here and in nn. 2, 3, and 4 below are in *Time* 142 (Fall 1993), a special issue not in weekly sequence. On the "universal nation" and "open door," see Editors, "America's Immigrant Challenge," 3, quoting Ben J. Wattenberg; Pico Tyer, "The Global Village Finally Arrives," 87, quoting Federico Mayor Zaragoza on "superpower"; Cathy Booth, "The Capital of Latin America: Miami," 82; Robert Eaton in Chrysler advertisement at 13. On "special issues" of popular magazines, nativism, and gender, see Lauren Berlant, *The Queen of America Goes to Washington City: Essays on Sex and Citizenship* (Durham: Duke University Press, 1997), 196.

2. Tyer, "Global Village," 87; James Walsh, "The Perils of Success," 55; Bruce W. Nelan, "Not Quite So Welcome Anymore," 10–13; Michael Walsh, "The Shadow of the Law," 17; Richard Brookhiser, "Three Cheers for the WASPs," 78–79; Editors, "America's Immigrant Challenge," 6. On efforts to end "birthright citizenship" in the United States in the 1990s, see Dorothy E. Roberts, "Who May Give Birth to Citizens: Reproduction, Eugenics, and Immigration," in Juan F. Perea's important collection *Immigrants Out! The New Nativism and the Anti-Immigrant Impulse in the United States* (New York: New York University Press, 1997), 208 and 205–19 passim.

3. "Rebirth of a Nation, Computer-Style," 66; James Gaines, "From the Managing Editor," 2; Jill Smolowe, "Intermarried . . . With Children," 64–65.

4. Front cover, Editors, "America's Immigrant Challenge," 5; "Rebirth of the Nation," 66. On *The Birth of a Nation*, see Michael Rogin, "'The Sword Became a Flashing Vision': D. W. Griffith's *The Birth of a Nation*," in Robert Lang, ed., *The Birth of a Nation* (New Brunswick, NJ: Rutgers University Press, 1994), 250–93; Toni Morrison, "On the Backs of Blacks," 57; William A. Henry III, "The Politics of Separation," 73–74. For Michael Rogin, see his

Blackface, White Noise: Jewish Immigrants in the Hollywood Melting Pot (Berkeley: University of California Press, 1996), 7–8 and 76–79.

5. Orlando Patterson, "Race Over," *New Republic* 222 (January 10, 2000), 6.

6. See the Interracial Voice website for September-October 1996 at **http://www.com/~intvoice/**.

7. Neil Bernstein, "Goin' Gangsta, Choosin' Cholita," as reprinted in *Utne Reader* (March–April 1995), 87–90, from *West*, a supplement to the *San Jose Mercury News*.

8. Molly O'Neill, "Hip-Hop at the Mall," *New York Times Magazine* (January 9, 1994), 43; Stanley Crouch, "Race Is Over: Black, White, Red, Yellow— Same Difference," *New York Times Magazine* (September 29, 1996), 170–71.

9. Alexander Saxton, *The Rise and Fall of the White Republic: Class Politics and Mass Culture in Nineteenth-Century America* (London and New York: Verso, 1990), 390; Smolowe, "Intermarried . . . With Children," 64–65 and the Interracial Voice website; Steven Masami Ropp, "Do Multiracial Subjects Really Challenge Race? Mixed-Race Asians in the United States and the Caribbean," *Amerasia Journal* 23 (1997), 1–16. On the peculiar mixture of race-transcendent claims with crudely essentialist notions of race, see also Josephine Lee's insightful "Disappointing Othellos: Cross-Racial Casting and the Baggage of Race" (Asian American Studies Workshop Series, University of Illinois, Urbana-Champaign, April, 2001).

10. See Lydia Chávez, *The Color Bind: California's Battle to End Affirmative Action* (Berkeley: University of California Press, 1998), esp. 36–37; George Lipsitz, *The Possessive Investment in Whiteness* (Philadelphia: Temple University Press, 1998), 211–34; George Fredrickson, *The Black Image in the White Mind: The Debate on Afro-American Character and Destiny, 1817–1914* (Middletown, CT: Wesleyan University Press, 1987, originally 1971), 120–22.

11. See Chapter 5 below; Smolowe, "Intermarried . . . With Children," 65; Stanley Lieberson, "Unhyphenated Whites in the United States," *Ethnic and Racial Studies* 8 (January 1985), 159–80 explores the most extreme case of this identification with whiteness to the exclusion of "any clearcut identification with, and/or knowledge of, a specific European origin" (159); Stanley Lieberson and Mary C. Waters, "The Ethnic Response of Whites: What Causes Their Instability, Simplification, and Inconsistency?" *Social Forces* 72 (December 1993), 421–50; see also Mary C. Waters, *Ethnic Options: Choosing Identities in America* (Berkeley: University of California Press, 1990); Ruben Rumbaut, "The Crucible Within: Ethnic Identity, Self-Esteem and Segmented Assimilation," *International Migration Review* 18 (1994), 748–94.

12. Barry Edmonston, Sharon M. Lee, and Jeffrey Passel, "Recent Trends in Intermarriage and Immigration and Their Effects on the Future Racial Composition of the U.S. Population," paper presented at the "Multiraciality: How Will the New Census Data Be Used?" conference at Bard College (September 2000) and available on webcast at **http://www.levy.org**; Cherrie Moraga, *The Last Generation: Prose and Poetry* (Boston: South End Press, 1993), 128. See also Joel Perlmann, "Reflecting the Changing Face of America," *Levy Institute Public Policy Brief*, Number 35 (1997); Mia Tuan, *Forever Foreigners or Honorary Whites: The Asian Ethnic Experience Today* (New Brunswick, NJ, and

London: Rutgers University Press, 1998), 152–67, and Clarence Page, "Piecing It all Together," *Chicago Tribune* (March 14, 2001).

13. Gaines, "From the Managing Editor," 2; Lee Svitak Dean, "Recipe for a New Betty Crocker," *Minneapolis Star-Tribune* (March 20, 1996), 1.

14. Priscilla Labovitz, "Immigration—Just the Facts," *New York Times* (March 25, 1996); Nelan, "Not Quite So Welcome," 10–12; Editors, "America's Immigrant Challenge," 3–9; Walsh, "Shadow of the Law," 17.

15. Yochi J. Dreazen, "U.S. Racial Wealth Gap Remains Huge," *Wall Street Journal* (March 14, 2000), A-2 and A-22; Unsigned (Doug Henwood, editor), "Race and Money," *Left Business Observer* 69 (September, 1995), 4–5. Melvin Oliver and Thomas Shapiro, *Black Wealth/White Wealth: A New Perspective on Racial Inequality* (New York: Routledge, 1995); David Savran, "The Sado-masochist in the Closet: White Masculinity and the Culture of Victimization," *differences: A Journal of Feminist Cultural Studies* 8 (1996), 137. More broadly, see Mary C. Waters and Karl Eschbach, "Immigration and Racial Inequality in the United States," *Annual Review of Sociology* 21 (1995), 419–46.

16. Douglas A. Massey and Nancy A. Denton, *American Apartheid: Segregation and the Making of the Underclass* (Cambridge, MA: Harvard University Press., 1993); john powell, "Sprawl, Fragmentation and the Persistence of Racial Inequality: Limiting Civil Rights by Fragmenting Space," forthcoming; Alejandra Marchevsky and Jeanne Theoharis, "Welfare Reform, Globalization, and the Racialization of Entitlement," *American Studies* 41 (Summer-Fall 2000), 235–65. Marc Mauer, *Race to Incarcerate* (New York: New Press, 1999), esp. 20, 118–20, 125, and 168–69; Joy James, ed., *States of Confinement: Policing, Detention and Prisons* (New York: St. Martin's Press, 2000). The category "Hispanic" is used in official statistics on concentrated poverty and on prison populations.

17. Unsigned, "Race and Money," 4–5.

18. john a. powell, "The Colorblind Multiracial Dilemma: Racial Categories Reconsidered," *University of San Francisco Law Review* 31 (Summer 1997), 790; Neil Gotanda, "A Critique of 'Our Constitution Is Color-Blind,'" *Stanford Law Review* 44 (November 1991), 2.

19. Stephan Thernstrom and Abigail Thernstrom, *America in Black and White: One Nation Indivisible* (New York: Simon and Schuster, 1997); Paul Sniderman, *The Scar of Race* (Cambridge, MA: Harvard University Press, 1993); Paul Sniderman and Edward G. Carmines, *Reaching Beyond Race* (Cambridge, MA: Harvard University Press, 1997); Ruy Teixeira and Joel Rogers, *America's Forgotten Majority: Why the White Working Class Still Matters* (New York: Basic Books, 2000), 40 [emphases original].

20. Don Hayner and Mary A. Johnson, "In the Workplace: Most Whites See No Hiring Bias, But 82% of Blacks Disagree," *Chicago Sun-Times* (January 12, 1993), 16.

21. Alexander Star, "Dumbskulls," *The New Republic* 4163 (October 31, 1994), 11; Richard J. Herrnstein and Charles Murray, *The Bell Curve: Intelligence and Class Structure in American Life* (New York: The Free Press, 1995). Among several devastating critiques of *The Bell Curve*, see Joe Kincheloe, Shirley R. Steinberg, and Aaron D. Greeson, eds., *Measured Lies: The Bell Curve Examined* (New York: St. Martin's Press, 1996). On the continuing

stereotyping of Blacks, especially as lazy, see Martin Gilens, *Why Americans Hate Welfare: Race, Media and the Politics of Antipoverty Policy* (Chicago: University of Chicago Press, 1999), 68–72 and passim, and Joe R. Feagin, *Racist America: Roots, Current Realities, and Future Reparations* (New York and London: Routledge, 2000), 110–11 and 116–17.

22. Editors, "The Issue," *The New Republic* 4163 (October 31, 1994), 9.

23. Ward Connerly, "*Loving* America," Interracial Voice website at **http://www.web.com/~intvoice/**. On Connerly, see Lydia Chávez, *The Color Bind*, esp. 24–34, 63–65, and 73–76; Randall Kennedy, "My Race Problem—And Ours," *Atlantic Monthly* 279 (May 1997), 55–66; Jim Sleeper, "Toward an End of Blackness," *Harper's* 294 (May 1997), 35–44. Cf. Margaret Talbot, "Getting Credit for Being White," *New York Times Magazine* 42 (November 30, 1997), 6.

24. Paul Gilroy, *Against Race: Imagining Political Culture Beyond the Color Line* (Cambridge, MA: Harvard University Press, 2000). For an acute commentary on Walter Benn Michaels's attempts to move beyond race, see Avery Gordon and Christopher Newfield, "White Philosophy," *Critical Inquiry* 20 (Summer 1994), 737–57. Cf. David Hollinger, *Postethnic America: Beyond Multiculturalism* (New York: Basic Books, 1995), esp. 84–86.

25. Rogin, *Blackface, White Noise*, 8; "Rebirth of a Nation," 66–67.

26. Martin Luther King, *Why We Can't Wait* (New York: Harper & Row, 1964).

27. Foxx as quoted in Christopher Porterfield, "The New TV Season: Toppling Old Taboos," *Time* 100 (September 25, 1972), 49.

28. Frantz Fanon, *Black Skins, White Masks*, trans. Charles Lam Markmann (London: Pluto Press, 1986, originally 1952), 110–11; Elazar Barkan, *The Retreat of Scientific Racism: Changing Concepts of Race in Britain and the United States Between the World Wars* (Cambridge, England: Cambridge University Press, 1992); Micaela di Leonardo, *Exotics at Home: Anthropologists, Others, American Modernity* (Chicago: University of Chicago, 1998), esp. 199–204; James B. McKee, *Sociology and the Race Problem* (Urbana and Chicago: University of Illinois Press, 1993), esp. 55–102; Lee Baker, *From Savage to Negro: Anthropology and the Construction of Race, 1896–1954* (Berkeley: University of California Press, 1998).

29. In the increasingly bitter debates over the history of racism in organized labor, charges of presentmindedness are traded by both sides. Cf. Stanford Lyman, "The 'Chinese Question' and American Labor Historians," *New Politics* 28 (Winter 2000), 113–14, and Eric Arnesen, "Up from Exclusion: Black and White Workers, Race, and the State of Labor History," *Reviews in American History* 26 (1998), 147 and 156–57.

30. Franklin Rosemont, "Notes on Surrealism as a Revolution Against Whiteness," *Race Traitor* 9 (Summer 1998), 29; Alice Walker, as quoted in David Wellman, "Minstrel Shows, Affirmative Action Talk, and Angry White Men: Marking Racial Otherness in the 1990s," in Ruth Frankenberg, ed., *Displacing Whiteness: Essays in Social and Cultural Criticism* (Durham and London: Duke University Press, 1997), 328.

31. W. E. B. Du Bois, as quoted in Herbert Aptheker's introduction to a reprint of Du Bois, *The Gift of Black Folk* (Millwood, NY: Kraus-Thomson Organization, 1975, originally 1924), 5.

32. Carl Swanson, "The White-Boy Shuffle," *Spin* 13 (October 1997), 54; Peter Erickson, "Seeing White," *Transition* 67 (1996), 166–85; David W. Stowe, "Uncolored People: The Rise of Whiteness Studies," *Lingua Franca* (September/October 1996), 68–77; Judith Levine, "The Heart of Whiteness," *Voice Literary Supplement* (September 1994), 11–16; the *Minnesota Review* special issue is Number 47 (Spring 1997); Frankenberg, ed., *Displacing Whiteness*; Michelle Fine, Lois Weis, Linda C. Powell, and L. Mung Wong, eds., *Off White: Readings on Race, Power and Society* (New York and London: Routledge, 1997); Vron Ware and Les Back, eds., *Outside the Whale: Essays on Whiteness, Politics and Culture* (forthcoming from University of Chicago Press); Chris J. Cuomo and Kim Q. Hall, eds., *Whiteness: Critical Philosophical Reflections* (Lanham, MD: Rowman and Littlefield, 1999); Mike Hill, ed., *Whiteness: A Critical Reader* (New York: New York University Press, 1997); Richard Delgado and Jean Stefanic, eds., *Critical White Studies: Looking Beyond the Mirror* (Philadelphia: Temple University Press, 1997); Joe L. Kincheloe, Shirley R. Steinberg, Nelson M. Rodriguez, and Ronald E. Chennault, eds., *White Reign: Deploying Whiteness in America* (New York: St. Martin's Press, 1998).

33. Richard Dyer, *White* (London and New York: Routledge, 1997); Vron Ware, *Beyond the Pale: White Women, Racism and History* (London and New York: Verso, 1992); Ware and Back, *Outside the Whale*, forthcoming; Jeremy Krikler, "Lessons from America," *Journal of Southern African Studies* 20 (December 1994), 663–69; Alastair Bonnett, *White Identities: Historical and International Perspectives* (Harlow, England: Prentice-Hall, 2000); Bronwen Walter, *Outsiders Inside: Whiteness, Place and Irish Women* (New York and London: Routledge, 2000); Ghasson Hage, *White Nation: Fantasies of White Supremacy* (New York: Routledge, 2000); Gillian Cowlishow, *Rednecks, Eggheads and Blackfellas: A Study of Racial Power and Intimacy in Australia* (Ann Arbor: University of Michigan Press, 1999); note also the focus on whiteness in recent conferences in Japan (Kyoto American Studies Seminar, 2000), Canada (University of Toronto, 2000), and South Africa (History Workshop, 2001).

34. Quentin Hardy, "School of Thought: The Unbearable Whiteness of Being," *Wall Street Journal* (April 24, 1997); "Nationline," *USA Today* (April 7, 1997); Peter S. Goodman, "Conference Seeks to Clear Up What It Means to Be White," *Washington Post* (April 12, 1997).

35. Angie Chabram-Dernersesian, "On the Social Construction of Whiteness Within Selected Chicana/o Discourses," in Frankenberg, ed., *Displacing Whiteness*, 110; Clinton's remarks are from a reception in Portland, Oregon, *Weekly Compilation of Presidential Documents, William J. Clinton* 341 (June 1998), 1114–19.

36. Margaret Talbot, "Getting Credit for Being White," *New York Times Magazine* (November 30, 1997) 116–18, which includes the photos.

37. Waldo E. Martin, Jr., *The Mind of Frederick Douglass* (Chapel Hill and London: University of North Carolina Press, 1984), 112; Editors of *Ebony, The WHITE Problem in America* (Chicago: Johnson Publications, 1966). See also the introduction to my edited volume, *Black on White: Black Writers on What It Means to Be White* (New York: Schocken, 1998); Crispin Sartwell, *Act Like You Know: African American Autobiography and White Identity*

(Chicago: University of Chicago Press, 1998); Betsy Lucal, "Seeing Ourselves Through Others' Eyes: An Examination of African American Perspectives on Whiteness" (unpublished paper presented at the Eastern Sociological Society in Philadelphia in 1998); Jane Davis, *The White Image in the Black Mind: A Study in African American Literature* (Westport, CT: Greenwood, 2000); Américo Paredes, *Uncle Remus con Chile* (Houston: Arte Publico Press, 1993); Du Bois, as reprinted in Julius Lester, ed., *The Seventh Son: The Thought and Writings of W. E. B. Du Bois*, 2 vols. (New York: Random House, 1971), 1:486.

38. Moraga, *The Last Generation*, 98–131; Gloria Anzaldúa, *Borderlands/La Frontera: The New Mestiza* (San Francisco: Spinsters/Aunt Lute, 1987), esp. 7–8, 102–3, and 134–35; Robert G. Lee, *Orientals: Asian Americans in Popular Culture* (Philadelphia: Temple University Press, 1999); Neil Foley, *The White Scourge: Mexicans, Blacks, and Poor Whites in Texas Cotton Culture* (Berkeley: University of California Press, 1997); john a. powell, "Whites Will Be Whites: The Failure to Interrogate Racial Privilege," *University of San Francisco Law Review* 34 (Spring 2000), 419–64; Toni Morrison, *Playing in the Dark: Whiteness and the Literary Imagination* (Cambridge, MA: Harvard University Press, 1990); Tómas Almaguer, *Racial Fault Lines: The Historical Origins of White Supremacy in California* (Berkeley: University of California Press, 1994), esp. 45–74.

39. Carl Abbott, "Tracing the Trends in U.S. Regional History" (American Historical Association) *Perspectives* 28 (February 1990), 8 (on Du Bois); on Silko, see Sharon Patricia Holland's important *Raising the Dead: Readings of Death and (Black) Subjectivity* (Durham and London: Duke University Press, 2000), 68 and 70–102, passim, and Leslie Marmon Silko, *Ceremony* (New York: Viking, 1977), 132–38.

40. Ralph Ellison, "The Little Man at Chehaw Station," in *Going to the Territory* (New York: Random House, 1987); Chester Himes, *If He Hollers Let Him Go* (New York: Doubleday, 1945), 42; Ethiop [William J. Wilson], "What Shall We Do with the White People?" *Anglo-African Magazine* 2 (February 1860), 41.

41. Morrison, *Playing in the Dark*, 47–50; Richard Dyer, "White," *Screen* 29 (1988), 141–63; Allan Bérubé, "How Gay Stays White" (paper delivered at "The Making and Unmaking of Whiteness" Conference, Berkeley, April 1997); Tracy D. Morgan, "Pages of Whiteness: Race, Physique Magazines and the Emergence of Public Gay Culture" in Brett Beemyn and Mickey Eliason, eds., *Queer Studies* (New York: New York University Press, 1997), passim; James Baldwin, "Here Be Dragons," in *The Price of the Ticket: Collected Nonfiction, 1948–1985* (New York: St. Martin's Press, 1985), esp. 682–83; John Howard, *Men Like That: A Southern Queer History* (Chicago and London: University of Chicago Press, 1999), 155 and 211; Siobhan Somerville, *Queering the Color Line: Race and the Invention of Homosexuality in American Culture* (Durham and London: Duke University Press, 2000), esp. 138–40; Mia Bay, *The White Image in the Black Mind* (Oxford and New York: Oxford University Press, 2000); Keith H. Basso, *Portraits of "The Whiteman": Linguistic Play and Cultural Symbols Among the Western Apache* (Cambridge, England, and New York: Cambridge University Press, 1978).

42. W. E. B. Du Bois, *Dusk of Dawn: An Essay Toward an Autobiography of a Race-Concept* (New York: Harcourt, Brace, 1940), 129; Du Bois, *Black Reconstruction in America, 1860–1880* (New York: Atheneum, 1992, originally 1935), 17–31 and 700–1; David R. Roediger, *The Wages of Whiteness: Race and the Making of the American Working Class* (New York and London: Verso, 1991); Eric Lott, *Love and Theft: Blackface Minstrelsy and the American Working Class* (New York and Oxford: Oxford University Press, 1993); Dana Frank, "White Working-Class Women and the Race Question," *International Labor and Working Class History* 54 (Fall 1998), 80–102; Lee, *Orientals*, 82; Bruce Nelson, *Divided We Stand: American Workers and the Struggle for Black Equality* (Princeton: Princeton University Press, 2001).

43. Piri Thomas, Down These Mean Streets (New York: New American Library, 1967), 33–47; James Baldwin, *The Price of the Ticket* and "On Being 'White' . . . and Other Lies," *Essence* (April 1984), 90–92; Noel Ignatiev, *How the Irish Became White* (New York and London: Routledge, 1995); Karen Brodkin, *How Jews Became White Folks and What That Says About Race in America* (New Brunswick, NJ: Rutgers University Press, 1998); Rogin, *Blackface, White Noise*; Matthew Jacobson, *Whiteness of a Different Color: European Immigrants and the Alchemy of Race* (Cambridge, MA: Harvard University Press, 1998); Robert Orsi, "The Religious Boundaries of an Inbetween People: Street *Feste* and the Problem of the Dark-Skinned 'Other' in Italian Harlem," *American Quarterly* 44 (September 1992), 313–47; Maurice Berger, *White Lies: Race and the Myths of Whiteness* (New York: Farrar, Straus & Giroux, 1999), esp. 5–8; Thandeka, *Learning to Be White: Money, Race and God in America* (New York: Continuum, 1999), 61–70; Camille O. Cosby, "America Taught My Son's Killer to Hate Blacks," *USA Today* (July 8, 1998), 15-A.

44. Lewis Gordon, *Bad Faith and Antiblack Racism* (Atlantic Highlands, NJ: Humanities Press, 1995); Cheryl Harris, "Finding Sojourner's Truth," *Cardozo Law Review* 18 (November 1998), 309–410; Ruth Frankenberg, *White Women, Race Matters: The Social Construction of Race* (Minneapolis: University of Minnesota Press, 1994); Vron Ware, *Beyond the Pale: White Women, Racism and History* (London: Verso, 1992); Louise Newman, *White Women's Rights: The Racial Origins of Feminism in the United States* (New York: Oxford University Press, 1999); Aida Hurtado, "The Trickster's Play: Whiteness in the Subordination and Liberation Process," in Rodolfo D. Torres, Louis F. Mirón, and Jonathan Xavier Inda, eds., *Race, Identity and Citizenship: A Reader* (Malden, MA: Blackwell, 1999), 229–36; Linda Martin Alcoff, "What Should White People Do?" *Hypatia* 13 (Summer 1998), 11–12.

45. Theodore W. Allen, *The Invention of the White Race*, 2 vols. (New York and London: Verso, 1994 and 1997); Saxton, *Rise and Fall of the White Republic*; Ian Haney Lopez, *White by Law: The Legal Construction of Race* (New York and London: New York University Press, 1996).

46. Paul Gilroy, *The Black Atlantic: Modernity and Double Consciousness* (Cambridge, MA: Harvard University Press, 1993), 174–75; bell hooks, *Black Looks: Race and Representation* (Boston: South End Press, 1992), 172; Ralph Ellison, "A Party Down at the Square," in John E. Callahan, ed., *Flying Home*

and Other Stories (New York: Random House, 1996), 3–11; Anzaldúa, *Borderlands/La Frontera*, 134–35; Roediger, ed., *Black on White*, 318–49;

47. Gordon, *Bad Faith and Antiblack Racism*; Trudier Harris, *Exorcising Blackness: Historical and Literary Lynching and Burning Rituals* (Bloomington: Indiana University Press, 1984); Robyn Wiegman, *American Anatomies: Theorizing Race and Gender* (Durham and London: Duke University Press, 1995); Grace Elizabeth Hale, *Making Whiteness: The Culture of Segregation in the South, 1890–1940* (New York: Pantheon, 1998); Nell Irvin Painter, "Soul Murder and Slavery: Toward a Fully Loaded Cost Accounting," in Linda K. Kerber, Alice Kessler Harris, and Kathryn Kish Sklar, eds., *U.S. History as Women's History: New Feminist Essays* (Chapel Hill and London: University of North Carolina Press, 1995), 125-46.

48. Cheryl Harris, "Whiteness as Property," 1710–91; Linda Lopez McAlister, "My Grandmother's Passing," and Linda M. Pierce, "Pinay White Woman," both in Chris J. Cuomo and Kim Q. Hall, eds., *Whiteness*, 15–27 and 45–52; George Lipsitz, *The Possessive Investment in Whiteness: How White People Profit from Identity Politics* (Philadelphia: Temple University Press, 1998), 1–23; Martha R. Mahoney, "Segregation, Whiteness, and Transformation," *University of Pennsylvania Law Review* 143 (1995); 1659–84.

49. Matt Wray and Annalee Newitz, *White Trash: Race and Class in America* (New York and London: Routledge, 1997). The most telling discussion of "poor whites" remains Ralph Ellison, "An Extravagance of Laughter," in *Going to the Territory*, 145–97. "Propertyless" whiteness is from Mike Hill's "Can Whiteness Speak?" in *White Trash*, 160. See also John Hartigan's provocative *Racial Situations: Class Predicaments of Whiteness in Detroit* (Princeton: Princeton University Press, 1999).

Chapter 2

1. Cheryl Harris, "Whiteness as Property," *Harvard Law Review* 106 (June 1993), 1710–1791; Toni Morrison, *Playing in the Dark: Whiteness and the Literary Imagination* (Cambridge, MA: Harvard University Press, 1990); Philip Deloria, *Playing Indian* (New Haven: Yale University Press, 1998); Cherrie Moraga, *The Last Generation* (Boston: South End Press, 1993); Thandeka, *Learning to Be White: Money, Race and God in America* (New York: Continuum, 1999); bell hooks, "Representations of Whiteness in the Black Imagination" in *Black Looks: Race and Representation* (Boston: South End Press, 1992), 165–79; W. E. B. Du Bois, "The Souls of White Folk," *Independent* 69 (August. 18, 1910), 339–42; Americo Paredes, *Uncle Remus con Chile* (Houston: Arte Publico Press, 1993); James Baldwin, *The Price of the Ticket* (New York: St. Martin's Press, 1985); Ida B. Wells-Barnett, *On Lynchings: Southern Horrors, A Red Record and Mob Rule in New Orleans* (New York: Arno Press, 1969). Thanks to Ana Chavier, Joel Helfrich, Robert Baum, and Mary Murphy-Gnatz for help with this project.

2. For the texts on which soundbites were based, see Giuliani's press releases and addresses on official websites of his administration, esp. his "Freedom of Expression Does Not Require Government Subsidization" as delivered

on WINS radio on September 26, 1999 (http://www.ci.nyc.ny.us/html/om
/html/99b/me 990926.html) and his WINS address, "The First Amendment
Does Not Require Public Subsidy," on October 3, 1999 (http://www.ci.nyc
.ny.us/html/om/html/99b/mc991003.html). For O'Connor, see "Taxpayers
Pay for 'Sick' Art," in *Artnewspaper.com* (October 27, 1999) at wysiwyg:
//116://artnewspaper.com/flash/Giulianiny.htm. Catholic League statements
throughout are taken from its website, (http://catholicleague.com/99press
_releases/pro399.htm). See also Peter Plagens, "Holy Elephant Dung!" *News-
week* (October 4, 1999), 71, and Cathleen McGuigan, "A Shock Grows in
Brooklyn," *Newsweek* (October 11, 1999), 68–70.

3. Southampton City Art Gallery and Serpentine Gallery, London, *Chris
Ofili* (London: Serpentine Gallery, 1998), Plate 15.

4. In the catalog cited in n. 3 above, see esp. Godfrey Worsdale, "Stereo
Type," 1–9, and Lisa G. Corrin, "Confounding the Stereotype," 15–16. For
Bowie, see www.thebee.com/bweb/iinfo118/htm. On "cruxification," see Benjamin Ivry, "'Modern Art Is a Load of Bullshit,'" *Salon* (online, February 10,
1999).

5. Lisa G. Corrin, "Confounding the Stereotype," 15–16, and Worsdale,
"Stereo Type," 4–6.

6. Peter Schjeldahl, "Those Nasty Brits," *New Yorker* 25 (October 11,
1999), 104; Redwing, "Tales of the New York Art Police," *Revolutionary
Worker*, October 10, 1999.

7. Worsdale, "Stereo Type," 8. See also Louisa Buck, "Chris Ofili," *Artfo-
rum* 36 (September 1997), 112; Kira Brunner, "Art, Politics, and Talk," *Dissent*
47 (Winter 2000), 7. Thanks to Professor Barbara Mooney of University of Illinois for information on Mary's attributes in Catholic art.

8. See Kodwo Eshun's essay "Plug Into Ofili" in the *Chris Ofili* catalog cited
in n. 3 above, esp. under "Lil' Kim" and "Porn," unpaginated.

9. On the exhibition and its marketing, see Katha Pollitt, "Catholic Bashing," *Nation* 269 (November 1, 1999), 10; Brunner, "Art, Politics and Talk,"
7–8; Arthur Danto, "'Sensation' in Brooklyn," *Nation* 269 (November 1, 1999),
25–26; "New York's Art Attack," *Time* 154 (October 4, 1999), 64: Plagens,
"Holy Elephant Dung!" 71; Schjeldahl, "Nasty Brits," 104–5.

10. David Barstow, "'Sensation' Exhibition Closes As It Opened, to
Applause and Condemnation," *New York Times*, January 10, 2000; "Brooklyn
Museum: Giuliani Isn't Its Biggest Problem" (editorial), *Minneapolis Star Tri-
bune*, November 3, 1999.

11. See n. 2 above.

12. Pollitt, "Catholic Bashing," 10.

13. Into the twentieth century, some Catholic immigrants dressed female
children in the Virgin's blue and white colors until their first Communion.
See Peter Murphy and Candice Ward, "'The Irish Thing': A Conversation on
the Australian and American Irish Diaspora," *South Atlantic Quarterly* 98
(Winter-Spring 1999), 130.

14. Peggy McIntosh, "White Privilege and Male Privilege: A Personal
Account of Coming to See Correspondences Through Work in Women's Studies" (Wellesley College Center for Research on Women, Working Paper No.

189, 1988) as reprinted in Richard Delgado and Jean Stefancic, eds., *Critical White Studies: Looking Behind the Mirror* (Philadelphia: Temple University Press, 1997), 291–99, esp. 293–94. In the same volume, see also Linda L. Ammons, "Mules, Madonnas, Babies, Bathwater: Racial Imagery and Stereotypes," 276–79. Barbara Reynolds, "Madonna and Child Stamp Leaves False Impression," *USA Today*, January 6, 1999; "Giuliani's Racist Holy War Against Brooklyn Museum," *Workers' Vanguard*, October 15, 1999 refers extensively to the *Amsterdam News* editorial. On Milwaukee, see Stephen Grant Meyer, *As Long As They Don't Move Next Door: Segregation and Racial Conflict in American Neighborhoods* (Lanham, MD: Rowman and Littlefield, 2000), 193.

15. Richard Dyer, *White* (London and New York: Routledge, 1997), 17 and 14–18.

16. Dyer, *White*, 66–67, 14–18, and 77. On milk and nursing in portrayals of Mary, see Marina Warner, *Alone of All Her Sex: The Myth and the Cult of the Virgin Mary* (New York: Knopf, 1976), 192; Saidiya Hartman, *Scenes of Subjection: Terror, Slavery, and Self-Making in Nineteenth Century America* (New York: Oxford University Press, 1997), 99–100; see also Donna Haraway, *Simians, Cyborgs, and Women: The Reinvention of Nature* (New York: Routledge, 1991), 146, on why the theorizing of gender "must simultaneously be a theory of racial difference in specific historical conditions of production and reproduction."

17. See the introduction to David Roediger, ed., *Black on White: Black Writers on What It Means to Be White* (New York: Schocken Book, 1998), 3–26; Kymberly N. Pinder, "Our Father, God; Our Brother, Christ; Or Are We 'Bastard Kin?': Images of Christ in African American Painting." *African American Review,* 31 (1997) 223–33; Mary Murphy-Gnatz, "Henry O. Tanner, Romare Bearden, and Chris Ofili: Art and Re-presentations of Blackness Syncretized with the White Ooze" (unpublished seminar paper, University of Minnesota, 1999); Judith Wilson, "Getting Down to Get Over: Romare Bearden's Use of Pornography and the Problem of the Black Female Body in Afro-U.S. Art," in Michele Wallace and Gina Dent, eds., *Black Popular Culture* (Seattle: Bay Press, 1983); Albert B. Cleage, Jr., *The Black Messiah* (New York: Sheed and Ward, 1968); Alain Locke, *The New Negro* (New York: Boni, 1925), frontispiece. On Samuel Cox, see Leslie Harris's forthcoming *In the Shadow of Slavery: African Americans, Class, Community and Political Activism in New York City.*

18. Jorge Amado, *Tent of Miracles*, trans. by Barbara Shelby (New York: Knopf, 1971); Arnold Rampersad and David Roessel, eds., *The Collected Poems of Langston Hughes* (New York: Knopf, 1994), 143.

19. For the official biography, see **http://hom.nyc.gov/portal/index.jsp ?pageID=nyc_mayor&catID=1194**; cf. "Rudy's White World," *Village Voice*, January 20–26, 1999.

20. Wayne Barrett with Adam Fifield, *Rudy!: An Investigative Biography of Rudolph Giuliani* (New York: Basic Books, 2000), 22–32. See below on the import of the casting by Lee.

21. James Barrett and David Roediger "Inbetween Peoples: Race, Nationality and the 'New Immigrant' Working Class," *Journal of American Ethnic*

History 16 (Spring 1997), 3–44; Rudolph Vecoli, "Are Italian Americans Just White Folks?" *Italian Americana* 13 (Summer 1995), 149–65; Robert Orsi, "The Religious Boundaries of an Inbetween People: Street *Feste* and the Problem of the Dark-Skinned Other in Italian Harlem, 1920–1990," *American Quarterly* 44 (September 1992), 313–47; Barrett with Fifield, *Rudy!*, 18–19.

22. Noel Ignatiev, *How the Irish Became White* (New York and London: Routledge, 1995); Karen Brodkin, *How Jews Became White Folks* (New Brunswick, NJ: Rutgers University Press, 1998); James Baldwin, "On Being 'White' . . . and Other Lies," *Essence* (April 1984), 90–92; Barrett and Roediger, "Inbetween Peoples," 3–44. Matthew Frye Jacobson, *Whiteness of a Different Color: European Immigrants and the Alchemy of Race* (Cambridge, MA, and London: Harvard University Press, 1998), esp. 56–62; David Richards, *Italian American: The Racializing of an Ethnic Identity* (New York: New York University Press, 1999).

23. Lucia Chiavola Birbaum, *Black Madonnas: Feminism, Religion and Politics in Italy* (Boston: Northeastern University Press, 1993); Salvatore Salerno, "The Black Madonna and Italian American Identity" (unpublished paper, Metropolitan State University, 1985); Richards, *Italian American*, 210–11: Warner, *Alone of All Her Sex*, 267 and 274–75; Leonard Covello, *The Social Background of the Italo-American Child: A Study of Southern Italian Family Mores and Their Effect on the School System in Italy and America* (Leiden: E. J. Brill, 1967), 121.

24. Leonard Moss and Stephen C. Cappannari, "In Quest of the Black Virgin: She Is Black Because She Is Black," in James J. Preston, ed., *Mother Worship: Theme and Variations* (Chapel Hill: University of North Carolina Press, 1982), 53-74; Moss and Cappannari, "The Black Madonna: An Example of Cultural Borrowing," *Scientific Monthly* 73 (1953), 319–24.

25. Salerno, "Black Madonna." At least one historian has suggested that Black Madonnas in Italy helped make Italian Americans more tolerant of African Americans in the United States. If so, the tolerance may have been quite specific as to time and place (turn-of-the-century Louisiana). See Richard Gambino's argument on tolerance and Madonnas as cited in Orsi, "Religious Boundaries," 342, n. 3. On Madonna and race, see hooks, "Madonna: Plantation Mistress or Soul Sister," in *Black Looks*, 157–64, and "Pepsi Cancels Madonna Ad," *New York Times*, April 5, 1989 and Elaine Louie, "Stylemakers," *New York Times,* April 9, 1989.

26. Orsi, "Religious Boundaries," 329 and passim; Covello, *Social Background*, 122 and 127.

27. Orsi, "Religious Boundaries," 331 and passim; John Coulsom, ed., *The Saints: A Concise Biographical Dictionary* (New York: Hawthorn Books, 1958), 114. Barrett with Fifield, *Rudy!*, 17–18; Anthony D'Angelo, "Italian Harlem's Saint Benedict the Moor," in Mary Jo Bona and Anthony Julian Tamburri, eds., *Through the Looking Class: Italian and Italian American Images in the Media* (Chicago: American Italian Historical Association, 1996), 236–39; on Marcantonio, see Gerald Meyer, *Vito Marcantonio: Radical Politician, 1902–1954* (Albany: State University of New York Press, 1989), esp. 76–77 and 149–62. Thanks to Sal Salerno for providing photos of San Benedetto and information on St. Ann's.

28. "New York's Art Attack," 64.

29. Wayne Barrett, "Rudy's Brooklyn Rampage: Papal Pandering," *Village Voice,* October 6-12, 1999.

30. Barrett, "Rudy's Brooklyn Rampage"; "Giuliani vs. Offensive Art," *Chicago Tribune,* February 27, 2001; Marc Humbert, "Aide: Giuliani Not Rethinking Abortion," at **http://www.cnn.com/ALLPOLITICS/** (August 18, 1999) from Associated Press wire; Richard Pérez-Peña, "Conservative Party Leader Says Republicans Can Do Better Than Giuliani," *New York Times,* February 8, 2000. For Giuliani's attack on the photograph of a Black female Jesus, see "Amidst Strong Debate, Mild Curiosity at the Exhibition," *New York Times,* February 17, 2000.

31. See, however, Barrett, "Rudy's Brooklyn Rampage." On Giuliani's marital problems, see Elisabeth Bumiller, "Giuliani and Wife of 16 Years Say They Will Seek Separation," *New York Times,* May 11, 2000, A-1.

32. On "Evans, Novak, Shields and Hunt," October 10, 1999; Catholic News Service (St. Paul), *Catholic Spirit,* October 14, 1999; Catholic League, "Catholics to Rally at Brooklyn Museum of Art," September 29, 1999.

33. Quoted in Barrett, "Rudy's Brooklyn Rampage."

34. Nabil Hanna, "Sensation and Endurance," sermon at St. George Orthodox Church in Indianapolis on October 10, 1999, at **http://www.stgindy.org**; "Giuliani's Racist Holy War Against Brooklyn Museum," *Workers' Vanguard,* October 15, 1999.

35. "Virgin Mary Painting Vandalized with Paint," Minneapolis *Star Tribune,* December 17, 1999.

36. Giuliani as quoted in Pollitt, "Catholic Bashing," 10. Dyer, *White,* 75–76, nicely sums up some of the psychoanalytic literature. See also Joel Kovel, *White Racism: A Psychohistory* (New York: Pantheon, 1970), 87–133; Sandor Ferenczi, "The Origins of Interest in Money," in *Contributions to Psychoanalysis* (Boston, R.C. Badger, 1916); Otto Fenichel, "The Drive to Amass Wealth," *Psychoanalytical Quarterly* 7 (1938); David Haight, "Is Money a Four-Letter Word?" *Psychoanalytic Review* 64 (1977), 621–29.

37. Giuliani on "Evans, Novak, Shields and Hunt," October 10, 1999; Worsdale, "Stereo Type," 7.

38. Michael Omi and Howard Winant, *Racial Formation in the United States* (New York and London: Routledge, 1994). See also Rochelle L. Stanfield, "The Wedge Issue," *National Journal,* April 1, 1995, 790–92.

39. The full name is Catholic League for Religious and Civil Rights; Giuliani, "The First Amendment Does Not Require Public Subsidy."

40. The most celebrated discussion of this phenomenon remains Thomas Bryne Edsall and Mary Edsall, *Chain Reaction: The Impact of Race, Rights and Taxes on American Politics* (New York: Norton, 1972). On Giuliani's own deftness at playing the race card, see Richard Goldstein, "The R-Word," *Village Voice,* April 6, 1999.

41. Doug Hartmann and Darren Wheelock, "Midnight Basketball and the 1994 Crime Bill Debates: The Cultural Politics of Race, Crime and Public Policy" (unpublished paper, American Sociological Association meetings, Washington, DC, August 2000).

42. See Martin Gilens, *Why Americans Hate Welfare: Race, Media, and the Politics of Antipoverty Policy* (Chicago: University of Chicago Press, 1999), 120; David Roediger, *Towards the Abolition of Whiteness: Essays on Race, Politics and Working Class History* (New York and London: Verso, 1994), 8; James Dao, "Master of Political Attack Ads Is Under Attack Himself," *New York Times,* September 15, 2000, A-22; Monte Poliawsky, "Racial Politics in the 1988 Presidential Election," *The Black Scholar* (January 1989), 32–35 and "Among the New Words," *American Speech* 68 (1993), 202–3.

43. Schjeldahl, "Those Nasty Brits," 104; Pollitt, "Catholic Bashing," 10.

44. Plagens, "Holy Elephant Dung!" 71 quotes Ofili; Hortense Spillers, "Interstices: A Small Drama of Words," in Carol Vance, ed., *Pleasure and Danger: Exploring Female Sexuality* (New York: Pandora, 1984), 73–100; Tricia Rose, "Rewriting the Pleasure/Danger Dialectic: Black Female Teenage Sexuality in the Popular Imagination," in Elizabeth Long, ed., *From Sociology to Cultural Studies: New Perspectives* (New York: Blackwell, 1997), 185-202; Rose, "'Two Inches or a Yard': Silencing Black Women's Sexual Expression," in Ella Shohat, ed., *Talking Visions: Multicultural Feminism in a Transnational Age* (Cambridge, MA: M.I.T. Press, 1999), 316–23. The religious historian Jaroslav Pelikan has argued that in more mainstream contexts, empowering images of Mary have hinged on women identifying "with her humility, yes; but also with her defiance and her victory." See Pelikan, *Mary Through the Centuries: Her Place in the History of Culture* (New Haven: Yale University Press, 1996), 219.

45. Rose, "Two Inches or a Yard," 323.

46. Roediger, *Abolition,* 14–15, reviews Clinton's use of attacks on the hiphop artist Sister Souljah to distance himself from Jesse Jackson and to win white votes. See also Manning Marable, "U.S. Commentary: At the End of the Rainbow," *Race and Class* 34 (October-December, 1992), 79, and Philip A. Klinkner, "Bill Clinton and the Politics of the New Liberalism," in Adolph Reed, Jr., ed., *Without Justice for All: The New Liberalism and Our Retreat from Racial Equality* (Boulder, CO: Westview, 1999), 16–18. For the original controversy, see *Washington Post,* May 13, 1992, B-1, and *New York Times,* June 15, 1992, A-22.

47. Pollitt, "Catholic Bashing," 10; Pérez-Peña, "Conservative Party Leader"; *New York Times,* May 20, 2000.

48. Pérez-Peña, "Conservative Party Leader."

49. Brunner, "Art, Politics and Talk," 7; "Artistic Freedom: See You in Court," *Economist* (U.S.), 353 (October 2, 1999), 94; Barstow, "Exhibition Closes."

50. Laolu Akande, "Ofili's Painting as New African Art?" *NigeriaWorld News* (online) at **http://nigeriaworld.com/news/daily/oct/111/html**. Related to the issues raised by Akande (and by Professor Niyi Osundare of the University of New Orleans in Akande's article) are reservations concerning Ofili's ease with hybridity that were expressed, in my view too flatly, in Niru Ratnam, "Chris Ofili and Limits of Hybridity," *New Left Review* 235 (May-June 1999), 153–59. Also noteworthy is Mary Schmidt Campbell's "Collisions at a Museum," *Nation,* 259 (November 22, 1999), 5–6.

51. The statement is at **http://www.blackradicalcongress.org**. and is dated April 12, 2001.

52. CNN television news (December 5, 1999).

Chapter 3

1. Anna Grimshaw and Keith Hart, "*American Civilization:* An Introduction," in C. L. R. James, *American Civilization* (Cambridge, MA: Blackwell, 1993), 10, and David Roediger's notes on a 1984 visit with James.

2. Michael North, "The Dialect in/of Modernism: Pound and Eliot's Racial Masquerade," *American Literary History* 4 (Spring 1992), 56–76.

3. Sterling Brown, *Southern Road* (Boston: Beacon Press, 1974, originally 1932), 70–72.

4. See Carolyn Karcher's remarkable *Shadow Over the Promised Land* (Baton Rouge: Louisiana State University Press, 1980), 256–57.

5. Eugene O'Neill, *The Hairy Ape, Anna Christie and The First Man* (New York: Boni and Liveright, 1923), 37–38, 30–31, 19, 33, and 39.

6. Ibid., 44, 84, and 42.

7. George Robertson, Melinda Mash, Lisa Tickner, Jon Bird, Barry Curtis and Tim Putnam, eds., *Travellers' Tales: Narratives of Home and Displacement* (New York: Routledge, 1994); Homi Bhabha, "The Other Questions: The Stereotype of Colonial Discourse," *Screen* 24 (1983), 16–36; Mary Louise Pratt, *Imperial Eyes: Travel Writing and Transculturation* (New York: Routledge, 1992); Catherine Lutz and Jane L. Collins, *Reading National Geographic* (Chicago: University of Chicago Press, 1993).

8. O'Neill, *The Hairy Ape*, 21; Donna Haraway, *Primate Visions: Gender, Race and Nature in the World of Modern Science* (New York: Routledge, 1989); Anne McClintock, "Soft-Soaping Empire: Commodity Racism and Imperial Advertising," in Robertson and others, eds., *Travellers' Tales*, 139, and Stephen Jay Gould, *The Mismeasure of Man* (New York: Norton, 1981), 113–45.

9. Phillips Verner Bradford and Harvey Blume, *Ota: The Pygmy in the Zoo* (New York: St. Martin's Press, 1992), 176 and 227–28; Robert Rydell, *All the World's a Fair: Visions of Empire at American International Exhibitions* (Chicago and London: University of Chicago Press, 1984); Corneilia Sears, "Man-like Apes and Ape-like Men: The Public Exhibition of African Peoples and Apes in Early Twentieth-Century America" (unpublished paper delivered to the Organization of American Historians Convention, Washington, DC, April 1995).

10. bell hooks, "Representations of Whiteness," in *Black Looks: Race and Representation* (London: Turnaround, 1992), 165–78, and Richard Dyer, "White," *Screen* 29 (1988), 44–65 anticipate some of the analysis of "white looks" offered here.

11. Eric Lott, *Love and Theft: Blackface Minstrelsy and the American Working Class* (New York and Oxford: Oxford University Press, 1993) and Alexander Saxton, "Blackface Minstrelsy and Jacksonian Ideology," *American Quarterly* 27 (1975), 3–28; Herbert Gutman, "As for the '02 Kosher-Food Rioters," in Maurianne Adams and John Bracey, eds., *Strangers and Neighbors:*

Relations Between Blacks and Jews in the United States (Amherst: University of Massachusetts Press, 1999), 709-11.

12. O'Neill, *The Hairy Ape,* 30-31; James Baldwin, "The Devil Finds Work," in *The Price of the Ticket, 1948–1985* (New York: St. Martin's Press, 1985).

13. See Shelley Fisher Fishkin, *Was Huck Black? Mark Twain and African American Voices* (New York and Oxford: Oxford University Press, 1993), esp. 96–99. For the text, see Charles Naider, ed., "A True Story," in *The Complete Stories of Mark Twain* (Garden City, NY: Hanover House, 1957), 94–98.

14. Pratt, *Imperial Eyes*, 7–9 discusses autoethnography.

15. Twain, "True Story," 94–95; James Fenimore Cooper, *Satanshoe* (Albany: State University of New York Press, 1990, originally 1845), 70 and 69–86; and Warren Hedges, "If Uncle Tom Is White, Should We Call Him 'Auntie'? Race and Sexuality in Postbellum U.S. Fiction," in Mike Hill, ed., *Whiteness: A Critical Reader* (New York: New York University Press, 1997), 231–41.

16. Twain, "True Story," 94–95.

17. Twain, "True Story," 95 and 98; Fishkin, *Was Huck Black?*, 7–9, 31–33, 36–38 and 99, (the quotation is from 8).

18. Karcher, *Promised Land*, 2 and 13; Twain, as quoted in Shelley Fisher Fishkin's excellent *Lighting Out for the Territory: Reflections on Mark Twain and American Culture* (New York and Oxford: Oxford University Press, 1998). Herman Melville, *Benito Cereno,* in *The Piazza Tales* (New York: Dix and Edwards, 1856).

19. Robin D. G. Kelley, "'We Are Not What We Seem': Rethinking Black Working-Class Opposition in the Jim Crow South," *Journal of American History* 80 (June 1993), 75; Leon Litwack, *Been in the Storm So Long: The Aftermath of Slavery* (New York: Knopf, 1979), 105–7, 136–38, 155–57; Elsa Barkley Brown, "Negotiating and Transforming the Public Sphere: African American Political Life and the Transformation from Slavery to Freedom," *Public Culture* 7 (1994), 107–46.

20. Coco Fusco, *English Is Broken Here* (New York: New Press, 1995) 37–63; Lutz and Collins, *Reading National Geographic;* Bluford Adams, *E Pluribus Barnum: The Great Showman and the Making of U.S. Popular Culture* (Minneapolis: University of Minnesota Press, 1997). Christine Sleeter, as quoted in Thomas K. Nakayama and Robert L. Kirzek, "Whiteness: A Strategic Rhetoric," *Quarterly Journal of Speech* 81 (1995), 298.

21. Giselda Pollock, "Territories of Desire: Reconsiderations of an African Childhood," in Robertson and others, eds., *Travellers' Tales,* 77; Pratt, *Imperial Eyes,* 221; Bhabha, "Other Question," 13. For a brilliant attempt by Isaac Julien to explore these matters, see Robert Stam, "Permutations of the Fanonian Gaze: Isaac Julian's 'Black Skin, White Mask,'" *Black Renaissance Noir,* 1 (Summer-Fall 1997), 187.

22. Nathan Huggins, *Harlem Renaissance* (New York: Oxford University Press, 1973), 264–74; Anne McClintock, *Imperial Leather: Race, Gender and Sexual Conquest* (New York and London: Routledge, 1995), 31–36 and 207–31; Cheryl Harris, "Whiteness as Property," *Harvard Law Review* 106

(June 1993), 1707–91; Maurice Manring, *Slave in a Box: The Strange Career of Aunt Jemima* (Charlottesville, VA: University of Virginia Press, 1998).

23. Michael Omi and Howard Winant, *Racial Formation in the United States* (New York: Routledge and Kegan Paul, 1994), 140–42.

24. See David Roediger, *Towards the Abolition of Whiteness* (London and New York: Verso, 1994), 8.

25. Rachel DuPlessis, "'Hoo, Hoo, Hoo': Some Episodes in the Construction of Modern Whiteness," *American Literature* 67 (December 1995), 671.

Chapter 4

1. Christopher Hitchens, *No One Left to Lie To: The Triangulations of William Jefferson Clinton* (New York and London: Verso, 1999); Adolph Reed, Jr., ed., *Without Justice for All: The New Liberalism and the Retreat from Racial Equality* (Boulder: Westview, 1999); Lydia Chávez, *The Color Bind: California's Battle to End Affirmative Action* (Berkeley: University of California Press, 1998), esp. 133–62.

2. Sachs, "Towards a Bill of Rights for a Democratic South Africa," *Journal of African Law* 35 (1991); 21 and 29, and ANC Constitutional Commission, *Discussion Document: Constitutional Principles and Structures for a Democratic South Africa* (Bellville: University of the Western Cape, 1991). Cheryl Harris's "Whiteness as Property," *Harvard Law Review* 106.8 (June 1993); 17, 89–90, alerted me to these sources.

3. A. Leon Higginbotham, "Racism in American and South African Courts: Similarities and Differences," *New York University Law Review* 65 (June 1990), 479–588; "Affirmative Action—Time for a Class Approach," *African Communist* (Third Quarter 1993), 4–6. See also the special section on affirmative action in South Africa in *Die Suid-Afrikaan* 44 (May-June 1993), particularly Vincent T. Maphai, "One Phrase, Two Distinct Concepts," 6–9, which reflects on the U.S. example, and Linda Loxton, "Empowering the People," 23–24.

4. Harris, "Whiteness as Property," 1713. Conversation with Wills, July 15, 1994.

5. Peter Brown, *Minority Party: Why the Democrats Face Defeat in 1992 and Beyond* (Washington, DC: Regnery Gateway, 1991); Philip A. Klinker, "Bill Clinton and the Politics of the New Liberalism," in Reed, Jr., ed., *Without Justice for All*, 15.

6. Wilson's most influential works are *The Declining Significance of Race* (Chicago: University of Chicago Press, 1980) and *The Truly Disadvantaged: The Inner City, The Underclass and Public Policy* (Chicago: University of Chicago Press, 1987). See also Thomas Bryne Edwall with Mary D. Edsall, *Chain Reaction: The Impact of Race, Rights, and Taxes on American Politics* (New York and London: Norton, 1992); Paul Starr, "Civil Reconstruction: What to Do Without Affirmative Action," *American Prospect* 9 (Spring 1992); Theda Skocpol; Skocpol, "The Choice," *American Prospect* 10 (Summer 1992); 86–90. Useful commentary on what Stephen Steinberg has called the "liberal retreat from race" includes Michael Omi and Howard Winant, *Racial Conditions: Politics, Theory, Comparisons* (Minneapolis: University of Minnesota Press, 1994); 30–51. Conservatives (neo- and otherwise) also continued

a relentless attack on affirmative action. Timur Kuran's remarkable "Seeds of Racial Explosion," *Society* 30 (September–October 1993); 55–67, aptly embodies the apocalyptic tone of the right-wing critique. For a good illustration of how blurred is the line between neoliberalism and conservatism on these matters, see Barry R. Gross, "The Intolerable Costs of Affirmative Action," *Reconstruction* 2 (1994); 58–63.

7. Edsall with Edsall, *Chain Reaction*, 256–57; William Julius Wilson, "The New Urban Poverty and the Problem of Race," and Terry Williams, "Moving Beyond the Academy," both in *Michigan Quarterly Review* 33 (Spring 1994), 253, 262, and 292–93.

8. David Oshinksy, review of *Chain Reaction*, in *New York Times Book Review* 96 (October 20, 1991), 1; Stanley B. Greenberg and the Analysis Group, *Report on Democratic Defection* (Washington, DC.: The Analysis Group, 1985), as cited in Edsall with Edsall, *Chain Reaction*, 182; Felicia Kornbluh, "Political Arithmetic and Racial Division in the Democratic Party," *Social Policy* 26 (Spring 1993), 49 and 51–63.

9. Thomas Bryne Edsall with Mary D. Edsall, "Race, "*Atlantic Monthly*, 267 (May 1991), 56.

10. Barry R. Gross, *Discrimination in Reverse: Is Turnabout Fair Play?* (New York: New York University Press, 1978), 31; Theda Skocpol, "The Choice," 89; James E. Jones, Jr., "The Rise and Fall of Affirmative Action," in Herbert Hill and Jones, Jr., *Race in America: The Struggle for Equality* (Madison: University of Wisconsin Press, 1993), 354 and *passim*; Edsall with Edsall, *Chain Reaction*, 186–87; Cornel West, *Race Matters* (Boston: Beacon Press, 1993), 64; Shelby Steele, *The Content of Our Character* (New York: St. Martin's Press, 1990); Jim Sleeper, *The Closest of Strangers: Liberalism and the Politics of Race in New York* (New York: Norton, 1990), 172–77; Wilson, *Truly Disadvantaged*, 115; Gertrude Ezorsky, *Racism and Justice: The Case for Affirmative Action* (Ithaca, NY: Cornell University Press, 1991), 63–65; Stephen Steinberg and Jerome Culp, in "Critiques of Stephen Carter's *Reflections of an Affirmative Action*," *Reconstruction*, 1 (1992), 116 and 124. On class and the benefits of affirmative action, see Adolph Reed, Jr., "Assault on Affirmative Action," *Progressive* 59 (June 1995), 20.

11. Edsall with Edsall, "Race," 56. On affirmative action, compare Edsall with Edsall, *Chain Reaction*, 122–29 and 186–91, with Thomas Bryne Edsall's, "Clinton, So Far," *New York Review of Books,* October 7, 1993, 6–7. Paul Sniderman and Thomas Piazza, in *The Scar of Race* (Cambridge, MA: Harvard University Press, 1993), argue that Nathan Glazer's fear that affirmative action would bring "an increasing divisiveness on the basis of race . . . a spreading resentment among the disfavored groups against the favored ones" has materialized, with neoracism being largely the result of affirmative action rather than a source of opposition to it. Cf. Glazer, *Affirmative Discrimination* (New York: Basic Books, 1975), 220.

12. Michael K. Brown, *Race, Money, and the American Welfare State* (Ithaca, NY: Cornell University Press, 1999), 5 and 372; Andrew Hacker, *Two Nations: Black and White, Separate, Hostile, Unequal* (New York: Scribner's, 1992), 84–92; Theda Skocpol, "The New Urban Poverty and U.S. Social Policy," *Michigan Quarterly Review* 33 (Spring 1994), 278–79, confuses the

debate on AFDC considerably by using *targeted* at times to refer to allegedly "race-based" programs and at other times to refer to "antipoverty" programs, both of which she regards as far more problematic than "universal social policies." See also Linda Gordon, "How 'Welfare' Became a Dirty Word," *Chronicle of Higher Education,* July 20, 1994, B-1; Jill Quadagno, *The Color of Welfare: How Racism Undermined the War on Poverty* (New York and Oxford: Oxford University Press, 1994), esp. 172–73. On the history of the decline of "race-specific" policies, see Gary Orfield, "Race and the Liberal Agenda: The Loss of the Integrationist Dream, 1965–1974," in Margaret Weir, Ann Shola Orloff, and Theda Skocpol, eds., *The Politics of Social Policy in the United States* (Princeton: Princeton University Press, 1988), 313–56.

13. George Lipsitz, *The Possessive Investment in Whiteness: How White People Profit from Identity Politics* (Philadelphia: Temple University Press, 1998), 1–23; Edsall, "Clinton, So Far," 6–7; Edsall with Edsall, *Chain Reaction,* 87, 198–214; esp. 203–04; Ruy Teixeira and Joel Rogers, *America's Forgotten Majority: Why the White Working Class Still Matters* (New York: Basic Books, 2000), 40–41; Martin Gilens, *Why Americans Hate Welfare: Race, Media, and the Politics of Antipoverty Policy* (Chicago: University of Chicago Press, 1999), esp. 173.

14. Massey, in Chris Shea, "A Prominent Scholar's Plan for Inner City Draws Fire," *Chronicle of Higher Education,* September 5, 1997, A-21.

15. Rustin's strategy and rationale are outlined in "From Protest to Politics: The Future of the Civil Rights Movement," *Commentary* 39 (February 1965), 25–31; see also Bayard Rustin, *Down the Line: The Collected Writings of Bayard Rustin* (Chicago: Quadrangle Press, 1971), and Margaret Weir, *Politics and Jobs: The Boundaries of Employment Policy in the United States* (Princeton: Princeton University Press, 1992), 95–96. On Hacker, see Roediger, "The Racial Crisis of American Liberalism," in *Towards the Abolition of Whiteness: Essays on Race, Politics and Working Class History* (New York and London: Verso, 1994), 122. Earl Black and Merle Black, *The Vital South: How Presidents Are Elected* (Cambridge, MA, and London: Harvard University Press, 1992), likewise ignore organized labor, labor issues, and indeed workers as a social category.

16. Stanley B. Greenberg, *Middle Class Dreams: The Politics and Power of the New American Majority* (New York: Times Books, 1995), 13, 22–54, 215–22, 263–64 and 284–85. Greenberg discussed the logic of the composition of the Macomb County focus groups in an interview on C-SPAN's "Booknotes" program in a discussion of *Middle Class Dreams* (1995).

17. Omi and Winant, *Racial Formation,* 147–57, offer acute criticism of Clinton's "handling" of race, but Edsall's praises on this score in "Clinton, So Far," 6–7, are equally revealing. Deirdre English, in "Clinton and the Left," *Nation* 258 (June 13, 1994), 818, and *Time,* 143 (June 20, 1994), 26 and 28–29. On California, see Chávez, *The Color Bind,* 83–85, 133–62, and 203–7. For recent figures on race and the death penalty in the United States, see Michael Ross, "A Matter of Life and Death," (London) *Socialist Review* (July–August, 1994); 17–19; Kenneth O'Reilly, *Nixon's Piano: Presidents and the Politics of Race from Washington to Clinton* (New York: Free Press, 1995), 407–23.

18. Edsall with Edsall, *Chain Reaction*, 227–32 and 183. See also Omi and Winant, *Racial Formation*, 150. Clearly, many such "middle-class" voters hold working-class jobs. Neoliberalism both validates suburbanized workers' identification as middle-class and closes possibilities for political action by whites mobilizing as workers.

19. Du Bois, *Black Reconstruction in America, 1860–1880* (New York: Atheneum, 1992, originally 1935), 55 and 727; Roediger, *The Wages of Whiteness: Race and the Making of the American Working Class* (New York and London: Verso, 1991), 65–92 and 144–45; Roediger, *Abolition of Whiteness*, 61–68; Edsall with Edsall, *Chain Reaction*, 343–48.

20. Greenberg, as quoted in Edsall with Edsall, *Chain Reaction*, 182; Halle, *America's Working Men: Work, Home and Politics Among Blue Collar Property Owners* (Chicago: University of Chicago Press, 1984), 202–03.

21. Fields, "Ideology and Race in American History," in J. Morgan Kousser and James M. McPherson, eds., *Region, Race, and Reconstruction* (New York: Oxford University Press, 1982), 159; Roediger, *Abolition of Whiteness*, 62–63.

22. Katherine Newman, *Falling From Grace: The Experience of Downward Mobility in the American Middle Class* (New York: Free Press, 1988), 193–96.

23. Omi and Winant, "Response to Stanley Aronowitz's 'The Situation of the Left in the United States,'" *Socialist Review* 93 (1994), 131.

24. Lott, *Love and Theft: Blackface Minstrelsy and the American Working Class* (New York and Oxford: Oxford University Press, 1993); Lott, "White Like Me: Racial Cross-Dressing and the Construction of American Whiteness," in Amy Kaplan and Donald E. Pease, eds., *Cultures of United States Imperialism* (Durham and London: Duke University Press, 1993), 474–95. Hall, "What Is This *Black* in Black Popular Culture?" *Social Justice* 20 (Spring-Summer 1993), 104–14.

25. Roediger, *Wages of Whiteness*, 76–77 and 115–31.

26. Stetson Kennedy, *Southern Exposure* (Garden City, NY: Doubleday, 1946), 67, citing a 1945 National Opinion Research Center poll; Horowitz, "White Southerners' Alienation and Civil Rights: The Response to Corporate Liberalism, 1956–1965," *Journal of Southern History* 54 (May 1988); 184. It is therefore especially distressing that such a committed scholar/activist as Mark Naison regards the spread of "affirmation action 'horror stories'" in white "folk culture" as a convincing argument against affirmative action. See Naison, "Jared Taylor's America: Black Man's Heaven, White Man's Hell," *Reconstruction* 2 (1994), 64–65. Interestingly, empirical research suggests that "policy exposure to affirmative action in the workplace leads to greater endorsement rather than [to] a 'backlash' against affirmative action." See Maura A. Belliveau, "The Paradoxical Influence of Policy Exposure on Affirmative Action Attitudes," *Journal of Social Issues* 52 (1996), 99–104.

27. See Stanley Lieberson, *A Piece of the Pie: Blacks and White Immigrants Since 1880* (Berkeley: University of California Press, 1980), 25 and 349.

28. Ambalavaner Sivanandan, *A Different Hunger: Writings on Black Resistance* (London: Pluto Press, 1982, originally 1974), 96. On the "destabilizing" character of affirmative action, see Harris, "Whiteness as Property," 1778–79. See also Kimberlé Crenshaw, "Race, Reform, and Retrenchment:

Transformation and Legitimation in Antidiscrimination Law," *Harvard Law Review* 101 (1988), 1361–62.

Chapter 5

1. See Rob Buchanan, "18 Holes with O. J. Simpson," *Golf,* December 1990, 100, 106, Lawrence Otis Graham, *Member of the Club* (New York: HarperCollins, 1995), p. 17; Joe Marshall, "Now You See Him, Now You Don't," *Sports Illustrated,* October 19, 1973, 30–43; Marc Cerasini, *O. J. Simpson: American Hero, American Tragedy* (New York: Windsor Publishing, 1994), 196, 226–27; Beth Ann Krier, "What Makes Simpson Run?" *Ebony,* December 1981, 109; Teresa Carpenter, "The Man Behind the Mask," *Esquire,* November 1994, 84–90; "Harsh Realities Haunt Simpson," Columbia (Missouri) *Daily Tribune,* June 25, 1994, 3–B; and especially *"Playboy* Interview: O. J. Simpson," *Playboy* 23 (December 1976); 92–94. Professor Josephine Lee (University of Minnesota) alerted me to the quotation in the epigraph.

2. Melanie Wells, "O. J. Agrees to Share Rights to His Initials" *USA Today,* February 22, 1996; Cerasini, *Simpson,*192; Michigan *Chronicle,* July 16, 1977, B-1; Louis J. Haugh, "O. J. Tops Year's Star Presenters," *Advertising Age,* June 20, 1977, 1; "The Juice Joins the Soda Wars," *Fortune,* September 30, 1985, 9-10; Jack Slater, "O. J. Simpson: The Problems of a Super Superstar," *Ebony,* November 1976, 164; Richard Hoffer, "Fatal Attraction," *Sports Illustrated,* June 27, 1994, 22, 31.

3. See, for example, Hugh Pearson, "Trial by T-Shirt," *Wall Street Journal,* August 12, 1994; "MAD's O. J. Pog Schtickers," *MAD Super Special* 105 (July 1995); 31–32; "Enough to Open a Library," *Newsweek,* March 25, 1996, 53; Clifford Linedecker, *O. J. from A to Z* (New York: St. Martin's Press, 1995), 37; "Cashing In on O. J., Reluctantly," *Harper's,* October 1994, 21; Adam Hochschild, "Closing Argument," *New York Times Book Review,* April 28, 1996, 14.

4. On these dynamics, and the connection of the verdict in the murder trial with unreason, see Ann DuCille, "The Blacker the Juice: O. J. Simpson and the Squeeze Play of Race," in DuCille's *Skin Trade* (Cambridge, MA and London: Harvard University Press, 1996), esp. 148 and 162–69; "The Pack in Search of O. J.'s Roots," *San Francisco Chronicle,* June 25, 1994, A–24; Greg Krikorian and Eric Lichtblau, "A Rising Star," *Los Angeles Times,* October 4, 1995, A–3; Richard C. Paddock and Jennifer Warren, "'I Was Somebody Who Didn't Care About Anything,'" *Los Angeles Times,* June 18, 1994, A–8; Evelyn C. White, "Fallen Hero Stirs Complicated Feelings," *San Francisco Chronicle,* October 4, 1995, A–6; Craig Marine and Leslie Goldberg, "The Hill O. J. Left Behind," *San Francisco Chronicle,* June 26, 1994, A–1, A–8; Simpson, I *Want to Tell You* (Boston: Little, Brown, 1995); 87–89; Michael Lind, "The End of the Rainbow," *Mother Jones,* September–October, 1997, 40.

5. Hoffer, "Fatal Attraction," p. 20. The 1996 HBO film of Arthur Ashe's *Hard Road to Glory: A History of the African-American Athlete Since 1946* (New York: Amistad Books, 1988) makes the point about Simpson's pioneering

in crossover advertising most acutely, perhaps because Ashe knew firsthand the long odds against such crossover. On advertising, see Roland Marchand, *Advertising and the American Dream* (Berkeley: University of California Press, 1985), 193; Jackson Lears, *Fables of Abundance* (New York: Basic Books, 1994), 123–24; Stephen Fox, *The Mirror Makers: A History of American Advertising and Its Creators* (New York: Morrow, 1984), 280–84; Harry Edwards, "The Black Professional Athlete," in John T. Talamini and Charles H. Page, eds., *Sport and Society: An Anthology* (Boston: Little, Brown, 1973), 260; Anne McClintock, *Imperial Leather: Race, Gender and Sexuality in the Colonial Conquest* (New York and London: Routledge, 1995), 31–35, 207–31.

6. Louis J. Haugh, "O. J. Tops Year's Star Presenters," *Advertising Age*, June 20, 1977, 1; Deford, "Ready If You Are," 16; Cerasini, *O. J. Simpson*, 84–85, 158–61, 192, 202–3; Edwin Shrake, "The Juice on a Juicy Road," *Sports Illustrated*, August 19, 1974, 36.

7. Carpenter, "The Man Behind the Mask," 87; James Brady, "Sunlit Afternoons and O. J.," *Advertising Age* (June 20, 1994), 34.

8. The best study of 1968 worldwide is George Katsiaficas, *The Imagination of the New Left: A Global Analysis of 1968* (Boston: South End Press, 1987); on the late 1960s in basketball and Chamberlain/Nixon, see Nelson George, *Elevating the Game; The History and Aesthetics of Black Men in Basketball* (New York: Fireside Books, 1992), 152–78.

9. Harry Edwards, *The Revolt of the Black Athlete* (New York: Free Press, 1970); Talamini and Page, eds., *Sport and Society,*259–61; Othello Harris, "Muhammad Ali and the Revolt of the Black Athlete," in *Muhammad Ali: The People's Champ*, Elliott J. Gorn, ed. (Urbana, IL, and Chicago: University of Illinois Press, 1995), 54–69.

10. Edwards, *Revolt of the Black Athlete*; Jack Scott, *The Athletic Revolution* (New York: Free Press, 1971), 86–88; Lee Ballinger, *In Your Face* (Chicago: Vanguard Books, 1981), 34–38; George, *Elevating the Game*, 147–48. See, however, Ashe's, *Hard Road to Glory*, 192, for Simpson's brief support of the antiracist boycott of the New York Athletic Club, and Earl Hutchinson, *Beyond O. J.: Race, Sex and Class Lessons for America* (Los Angeles: Middle Passage Press, 1996), 140, 149.

11. George, *Elevating the Game*, p. 142; Cromwell, quoted in Scott, *Athletic Revolution,* 81; "*Playboy* Interview: O. J. Simpson," 94; Dan Jenkins, "The Great One Confronts O. J.," *Sports Illustrated* November 20, 1967, 33, 38; Herman L. Masin, "All the Way with O. J.!" *Senior Scholastic*, October 18, 1968, 32; Carpenter, "The Man Behind the Mask," 87; A. S. Doc Young, "The Magnificent Six," Los Angeles *Sentinel,* January 17, 1980, A–7.

12. Louie Robinson, "Two Superstars Vie for Heisman Trophy," *Ebony*, December 1968, 173.

13. George, *Elevating the Game,*164; "*Playboy* Interview: O. J. Simpson," 78–B, 85–90, 98–99; Cerasini, *Simpson*, 56, 145, 177–78; Carpenter, "The Man Behind the Mask," 88–89; Frank Deford, "Ready If You Are, O. J.," *Sports Illustrated,* July 14, 1969, 19; Pete Axthelm, "The Juice Runs Wild," *Newsweek*, October 27, 1975, 10; Simpson with Axthelm, *O. J.: The Education of a Rich Rookie* (New York: Macmillan, 1970), 12–17; Jenkins, "Great

One Confronts O. J.," 34–38; Krier, "What Makes O. J. Run?" 110; Peter Wood, "What Makes Simpson Run?" *New York Times Magazine,* December 14, 1975, 6–38; Ballinger, *In Your Face,* 47–51; Dave Meggyesy, *Out of Their League* (New York: Ramparts Press, 1971), 172.

14. Michigan *Chronicle,* May 21, 1977; Jim Baker, *O. J. Simpson's Memorable Games* (New York: Putnam, 1978), 49.

15. Deford, "Ready If You Are," 16–19; Harry Edwards, *Sociology of Sport* (Homewood, IL: Dorsey, 1973), 279–80; Simpson with Axthelm, *Rich Rookie,* 9–17; Shrake, "First Taste of O. J.," 20–22; *"Playboy* Interview: O. J. Simpson," 78–85; Axthelm, "Juice Runs Wild," 72.

16. Robert Weems, "The Revolution Will Be Marketed," *Radical History Review* 59 (Spring 1994); 94–107; Fox, *Mirror Makers,* 281–84. On the "level playing field" image, see Mike Marquese, "Sport and Stereotype: From Role Model to Muhammad All," *Race and Class* 36 (April-June 1995); 4–5.

17. Cerasini, *Simpson,* 48–49; "Harsh Realities Haunt Simpson,"3-B; Robinson, "Two Superstars," 173; Simpson with Axthelm, *Rich Rookie,* 12; Edwin Shrake, "The First Taste of O. J. Is OK," *Sports Illustrated,* (August 25, 1969), 20; Darden, "The Bloody Glove," *Newsweek,* March 25, 1968, 57.

18. The most common misspelling, "Portrero," recurs in Pulitzer Prize–winning journalist Teresa Carpenter's recent attempt to tie the murders to Simpson's putatively underclass youth in her "The Man Behind the Mask," 84–100; Simpson's autobiographical work (with Axthelm) *Rich Rookie,* 10, comes no closer than "Patero." See also *"Playboy* Interview: O. J. Simpson," 97; "Countdown to Pasadena," *Time,* October 11, 1968, 43; Paul Zimmerman, "All Dressed Up," *Sports Illustrated,* November 26, 1979, 40; "Meet O. J. Simpson: Home Is Always Where the Heart Is," *Parents' Magazine,* February 1977, 42–43.

19. *"Playboy* Interview: O. J. Simpson," 97–99; Carpenter, "The Man Behind the Mask," 86; Warren and Paddock, "'I Was Somebody,'" A-8.

20. Robinson, "Two Superstars," 173; Brian Lowry, "Adams Turns Up the Juice with O. J. Simpson," *Advertising Age,* December 23, 1985, 6; Axthelm, "Juice Runs Wild," 70–71; "The Juice Joins the Soda Wars," *Fortune,* September 30, 1985, 9–10; Zimmerman, "All Dressed Up," 40; Paddocks and Warren, "'I Was Somebody,'" A-9.

21. Chuck Wingis, "O. J. Tells How Ads Led to His Tinseltown Success," *Advertising Age,* June 20, 1977, 82.

22. Edwards, "Black Professional Athlete," 263–64; Shrake, "First Taste of O. J.," 20.

23. *"Playboy* Interview: O. J. Simpson," 78-A, 78-B; Shrake, "First Taste of O. J.," 20; "Simpson Settles In," *Time,* October 8, 1973, 68; "O. J. to Go," *Newsweek* (January 13, 1969), 76; Jack Slater, "O. J. Simpson: The Problems of a Super Superstar," *Ebony,* November 1976, 164.

24. The Carson joke is in Robert F. Jones, "The $2.5 Million Dollar Man," *Sports Illustrated,* September 27, 1976, 20–21; see n. 23 above and, esp. for the quote, "Simpson Settles In," 68.

25. "Meet O. J. Simpson," 42, 43; Axthelm, "Juice Is Loose," 66; Joe Marshall, "What's Making O. J. Go?" *Sports Illustrated,* July 25, 1976, 20; Carpenter, "The Man Behind the Mask," 87. On debates over race, family, and

pathology in this period, see Lee Rainwater and William Yancey, eds., *The Moynihan Report and the Politics of Controversy* (Cambridge, MA: M.I.T. Press, 1967).

26. On Ali and style, see Jose Torres and Bert Sugar, *Sting Like a Bee* (New York: Abelard-Schuman, 1971); Jeffrey T. Sammons, "Rebel With a Cause," in Gorn, ed., *Ali,* 162–64; see also George, *Elevating the Game,* 132–68.

27. "Year of the Okey-Doke," *Time,* December 24, 1973, 57; Marshall, "Now You See Him," 37; Axthelm, "Juice Really Flows" 69–70; Bob Oates, "O. J.'s Way," Los Angeles *Times,* October 12, 1975, 3:1; "Simpson Settles In," 68; Robinson, "Two Supporters," 174; *"Playboy* Interview: O. J. Simpson" 102; Bob Oates, "There's a 'Coward' Loose in the NFL," Los Angeles *Times,* October 3, 1973. On *juke (jook),* see Clarence Major, *Dictionary of Afro-American Slang* (New York: International Publishers, 1970), 72; Robert L. Chapman, *New Dictionary of American Slang* (New York: Harper & Row, 1986), 239–40.

28. "Year of the Okey-Doke," 57; Herman L. Masin, "All the Way with O. J.," *Senior Scholastic,* October 18, 1968, 32. On Ali, Simpson, and style, see also Cuda Brown, "O. J. Who?" *Vibe Meanderings* 205 (1995): World Wide Web.

29. See n. 27 above and, on *okey-doke,* Major, *Dictionary of Afro-American Slang,* 87; Clarence Major, *Juba to Jive: A Dictionary of African-American Slang* (New York: Penguin, 1994), 329.

30. Dyson, "Be Like Mike? Michael Jordan and the Pedagogy of Desire," in *Reflecting Black: African-American Cultural Criticisms* (Minneapolis: University of Minnesota Press, 1993), 64–75, esp. 70.

31. Jenkins, "Great One Confronts O. J.," 38; Cerasini, *Simpson,* 61ff; Wingis, "Tinseltown Success," 30; Dan Jenkins, "The Juice Is Turned On Again," *Sports Illustrated,* October 13, 1975, 30; "O. J. Snags Real Juicy Contract with Tree Sweet," Los Angeles *Times,* July 14, 1976, section 3, 15; Chapman, *New Dictionary,* 303; Stuart Berg Flexner, *Listening to America* (New York: Simon and Schuster, 1982), 474. See also nn. 4 and 5 above.

32. Robinson, "Two Superstars," 173.

33. Gavin Power, "What the Marketing Experts See for O. J.," *San Francisco Chronicle,* June 16, 1994; *Time,* June 27, 1994, front cover.

34. Cited by Michael Oriard, "Order and Chaos, Work and Play," ch. 5 in *Reading Football, How the Popular Press Created an American Spectacle* (Chapel Hill: University of North Carolina Press, 1993), 185. See also Ballinger, *In Your Face,* 33–35.

35. From the beginning of his college career until the time of his trial, Simpson was constantly referred to by reporters as an affable, smiling Negro. For example, "The Great One Confronts O. J.," a 1967 *Sports Illustrated* story about a game between USC and UCLA, described O. J. as "a mild, warm, talkative transfer from City College of San Francisco," November 20, 1967, 37.

36. Shrake, "First Taste of O. J.," 20; Carpenter, "The Man Behind the Mask," 84, 88; Deford, "Ready If You Are," 16, 19; *Michigan Chronicle,* March 25, 1978, B–2; Zimmerman, "All Dressed Up," 38. See also Cerasini, *Simpson,* 196; Jenkins, "Great One Confronts O. J.," 38.

37. Perceptions of O. J.'s affability can be compared to the demonization of Kareem Abdul-Jabbar, who was deeply involved in Black protests. See also

Kareem Abdul-Jabbar, *Giant Steps* (New York: Bantam Books, 1983), 200: "My adversary relationship with the press started during my second week in the league."

38. Among the many accounts of Arledge's years as head of ABC sports are Ron Powers, *Supertube* (New York: Coward-McCann, 1984); Marc Gunther, *The House That Roone Built: The Inside Story of ABC News* (Boston: Little, Brown, 1994); Phil Patton, *Razzle Dazzle* (Garden City, NY: Dial Press, 1984); Terry O'Neil, *The Game Behind the Game: High Pressure, High Stakes in Television Sports* (New York: Harper & Row, 1989); Bert Randolph Sugar, *"The Thrill of Victory": The Inside Story of ABC Sports* (New York: Hawthorn, 1978); and Jim Spence, *Up Close and Personal: The Inside Story of Network Television Sports* (New York: Atheneum, 1988).

39. In *Supertube,* Ron Powers reproduces a memo in which Arledge maps out his philosophy of televised sports as spectacle designed to make specific gender appeals and talks about the role of slow motion in this effort; see 145–46. Patton elaborates on the history of slow motion in television, noting that NBC experimented with the technique before Arledge and CBS incorporated instant replay in the late 1950s. But Arledge perfected its use on live broadcasts, largely because he had access to video technology and especially to the mini-cam. See *Razzle Dazzle,* 63–75. Shortly after the first use of instant replay technology in a college football broadcast in 1963, the technique got its first mass exposure when it was used to replay Jack Ruby's shooting of Lee Harvey Oswald. See Erik Barnouw, *Tube of Plenty: The Evolution of American Television* (New York: Oxford University Press, 1975), 334, for an early example of the use of slow motion in sports. Also see Dan Streible, "A History of the Boxing Film, 1894–1915," *Film History* 3 (1989); 235–57.

40. Powers, *Supertube,* 160–70; Spence, "The Thrill of Victory . . . The Agony of Defeat: The Incredible Story of ABCs *Wide World of Sports,"* in *Up Close and Personal,* 66–79. The concept for *Wide World of Sports* was developed by Ed Sherick, Arledge's first boss at ABC Sports. Although Sherick developed the idea of covering offbeat sporting events, it was Arledge who figured out how to make the coverage "up close and personal."

41. Lisa Fluor, "God of the Stadium: National Socialist Aesthetics and the Body in Leni Riefenstahl's *Olympia*" (Ph.D. diss., Univ. of California at San Diego, 1992). Streible, "Boxing Film," 235–57 and n.39 above.

42. Ashe, *Hard Road to Glory,* 138–39, adds, "In the early 1970s, tickets for NFL games became more sought after than those for any other type of athletic contest. Corporations bought up sections of season tickets and sell-out crowds were the norm rather than the exception. There was a constant demand to make the game more exciting, and fans, especially those watching on television, wanted more scoring; rules were changed to accommodate them, and in nearly every instance black players benefited because, aside from the white quarterbacks, they were the most gifted performers on the field. On "supernatural," see Robinson, "Two Superstars," 171.

43. Gunther, in *House That Roone Built,* describes some of the panic that struck the ABC news division after Arledge's appointment as its head, noting that one journalist joked that Roone would soon be hiring the likes of Geraldo Rivera. Geraldo, in fact, was one of Arledge's first hires in the news division; see

32, 147. See also Howard Cosell, *I Never Played the Game* (New York: Avon, 1985), 154, 177; and note Axthelm's continuing praise of Simpson in *Newsweek* after the two collaborated on *Rich Rookie.*

44. Powers, *Supertube,* 146.

45. Ibid.,137–41; Spence, "Forever a Man's World? Why Women Sportscasters Are Still So Far from Winning Equal Air Time," in *Up Close and Personal,* 175–88.

46. O'Neill, *The Game Behind the Game,* 262–63.

47. Spence, *Up Close and Personal,* 147–48; Bill Russell, *Second Wind: The Memoirs of an Opinionated Man* (New York: Random House, 1979); Cosell, *I Never Played the Game,* 334.

48. Spence, *Up Close and Personal,* 149–50, Cosell, *I Never Played the Game,* 177–78.

49. Cosell, *I Never Played the Game,* 155, 158.

50. See, for example, Carpenter, "The Man Behind the Mask," 87–101; Hoffer, "Fatal Attraction"; and "Harsh Realities Haunt Simpson," 1-B, 3-B.

51. Interview with former *Newsday* writer Bob Drury, KFAN Radio in Minneapolis, May 8, 1996.

52. James McBride, *War, Battering and Other Sports* (Atlantic Highlands, NJ: Humanities Press, 1995).

53. Powers, *Supertube,* 138–41. See also Hoffer, "Fatal Attraction," 30–32.

54. Spence, *Up Close and Personal,* 6; Marlene Saunders, "Women in Management," in *Waiting for Prime Time* (Urbana, IL: University of Illinois Press, 1988), 158–90.

55. Kate Bertrand, "O. J. Simpson Juices Hertz's Image," *Business Marketing,* August 1992, 28.

56. Cerasini, *Simpson,* 180 82; Simpson with Axthelm, *Rich Rookie,* 16–17; "Chalk Up One More Score for 'The Juice,'" Michigan *Chronicle,* April 16, 1977, B-1; Krier, "What Makes O. J. Run?" 106, 110; Gertrude Gipson, "O. J. Signs Exclusive Contract with NBC-TV," Los Angeles *Sentinel,* May 5, 1977, Entertainment-1; Stu Black, "They Call Me Mister Juice," *Los Angeles Magazine,* April 1980, 174.

57. Buchanan, "18 Holes," 100; Lowry, "Adams Turns Up Juice," 6.

58. Deford, "Ready If You Are," 16; Bertrand, "Juices Hertz's Image," 28; Michigan *Chronicle,* July 16, 1977, B-1; Cerasini, *Simpson,* 204; Spangler, "Golf Legends," 26; Wood, "What Makes Simpson Run?" 38; "No Touchdowns," *Inc.,* October 1985, 18.

59. Lisa Disch and Mary Jo Kane, "When a Looker Is Really a Bitch: Lisa Olson, Sport and the Heterosexual Matrix," *Signs* 21 (Winter 1996); 284, 283–87.

60. Messner, as quoted in Disch and Kane, "Looker," 285.

61. Gates and West, "Affirmative Reaction," 181–83; "Harsh Realities Haunt Simpson," 3-B.

62. Messner, "Masculinities and Athletic Careers: Bonding and Status Differences," in Messner and Don Sabo, eds., *Sport, Men and the Gender Order* (Champaign, IL: Human Kinetics Books, 1990), 103; Zimmerman, "All Dressed Up," 39; Shrake, "Juice on Juicy Road," 37; Gates and West, "Affirmative Reaction," 181; Hoffer, "Fatal Attraction," 18, 20.

Chapter 7

1. Thanks go to Tiya Miles, Deirdre Murphy, and Gaye Johnson for assistance with this chapter and to Richard Davis, David Brion Davis, Stanley Engerman, Douglass North, Robert Gallman, David Montgomery, Amy Dru Stanley, Seymour Drescher, Robert Steinfeld, and Leon Fink for friendly criticisms.

2. Barry Goldberg, "'Wage Slaves' and White 'Niggers,'" *New Politics,* 2d ser., 3 (Summer 1991), 68.

3. David Brion Davis, *The Problem of Slavery in Western Culture* (Ithaca, NY: Cornell University Press, 1966), 90.

4. Goldberg, "'Wage Slaves,'" 68; Jonathan A. Glickstein, *Concepts of Free Labor in Antebellum America* (New Haven, CT: Yale University Press, 1991), 208 and 445.

5. I have been most influenced by the use of "simultaneity" in drafts of Tera Hunter's *To 'Joy My Freedom: Southern Black Women's Lives and Labors after the Civil War* (Cambridge, MA: Harvard University Press, 1997). See also Rose Brewer, "Theorizing Race, Class and Gender: The New Scholarship of Black Feminist Intellectuals and Black Women's Labor," in Abena Busia and Stanlie James, eds., *Theorizing Black Feminisms: The Visionary Pragmatism of Black Women* (London: Routledge, 1993), 16.

6. David Brion Davis, "Reflections on Abolitionism and Ideological Hegemony," in Thomas Bender, ed., *The Antislavery Debate: Capitalism and Abolitionism as a Problem in Historical Interpretation* (Berkeley: University of California Press, 1992), 162.

7. Blanche Glassman Hersh, "'Am I Not a Woman and a Sister?' Abolitionist Beginnings of Nineteenth-Century Feminism," in Lewis Perry and Michael Fellman, eds., *Antislavery Reconsidered: New Perspectives on the Abolitionists* (Baton Rouge, LA: Louisiana State University Press, 1979), 252. See also Hersh, *The Slavery of Sex: Feminist-Abolitionists in America* (Urbana, IL: University of Illinois Press, 1978). On the labor-abolitionist front, see Philip S. Foner, *History of the Labor Movement in the United States,* 10 vols. (New York: International Publishers, 1947–1999), vol. 1, 273; Marcus Cunliffe, *Chattel Slavery and Wage Slavery: The Anglo-American Context, 1830–1860* (Athens, GA: University of Georgia Press, 1979), 27; Goldberg, "'Wage Slaves,'" 67.

8. Ellen DuBois, *Feminism and Suffrage: The Emergence of an Independent Woman's Suffrage Movement in America* (Ithaca, NY: Cornell University Press, 1978); Amy Dru Stanley, "Conjugal Bonds and Wage Labor: Rights of Contract in the Age of Emancipation," *Journal of American History* 75 (December 1988); 471–500; Timothy Messer-Kruse, "The Yankee International: Marxism and the American Reform Tradition" (Ph.D. dissertation, University of Wisconsin–Madison, 1994).

9. Davis, "Abolitionism and Ideological Hegemony," in Bender, ed., *The Antislavery Debate,* 173.

10. William S. McFeely, *Frederick Douglass* (New York: Norton, 1991), 140–41; Frederick Douglass, *Narrative of the Life of Frederick Douglass, An American Slave* (New York: Anchor, 1989, originally 1845), 13.

11. "Address of the New York State Convention to Their Colored Fellow Citizens," *Colored American,* November 21, 1840; "An Appeal to the Colored

Citizens of Pennsylvania," reprinted in Philip S. Foner and George E. Walker, eds., *Proceedings of Black State Conventions, 1840–1865*, 2 vols. (Philadelphia: Temple University Press, 1979), vol. 1; 126–27. See also vol. 1, 234, for an 1850 Ohio convention's opposition to "iron manacles for the slave [and] unjust written manacles for the free." For Uriah Boston's December 1855 letter to Douglass, see C. Peter Ripley, ed., *The Black Abolitionist Papers*, 5 vols. (Chapel Hill: University of North Carolina Press, 1985–1992), vol. 4, 323–25.

12. Philip S. Foner and Ronald L. Lewis, eds., *Black Workers: A Documentary History from Colonial Times to the Present* (Philadelphia: Temple University Press, 1989), 112–14 and 122. See also "The Objects of the African Civilization Society" (1859) in Sterling Stuckey, ed., *The Ideological Origins of Black Nationalism* (Boston: Beacon, 1972), 182. For the contrary and unsupported view that "As for the Negro workers, there was little question in their minds or anyone else's that there was little to choose between their conditions and those of slaves," see Bernard Mandel's often valuable *Labor: Free and Slave* (New York: Associated Authors, 1955), 228.

13. C. L. R. James, "The Atlantic Slave Trade and Slavery: Some Interpretations of Their Significance in the Development of the United States and the Western World," in John R. Williams and Charles Harris, eds., *Amistad 1* (New York: Vintage, 1970), 142. See also John Ashworth, *Slavery, Capitalism and Politics in the Antebellum Republic* (Cambridge, England: Cambridge University Press, 1995): 4. For a recent analysis resembling James's in its conclusions and its Hegelianism, see Leonard Cassuto, "Frederick Douglass and the Work of Freedom: Hegel's Master-Slave Dialectic in the Fugitive Slave Narrative," *Prospects: An Annual of American Cultural Studies* 21 (1996), esp. 248–49.

14. Douglass, in his speech to the 1855 Negro convention in Troy, New York, as reprinted in Foner and Walker, eds., *Black State Conventions*, vol.1, 95. Douglass held to this sharp demarcation after slavery as well. See his "My Escape to Freedom," *Century Magazine* 23 (November 1881), 125–31. For a fuller account of Douglass and free labor, see David Roediger, "Why Douglass Knew: An Afterword" in Roediger and Martin Blatt, eds., *The Meaning of Slavery in the North* (New York and London: Garland, 1998), 177–85.

15. For the 1850 letter, see Foner and Walker, eds., *Black State Conventions*, vol. 1, 44–50; Harriet A. Jacobs, *Incidents in the Life of a Slave Girl* (New York: Oxford University Press, 1988, originally 1861), 290. See also Philip S. Foner and Ronald L. Lewis, eds., *The Black Worker: A Documentary History from Colonial Times to the Present*, 8 vols. (Philadelphia: Temple University Press, 1978–1984), vol. 1, 182–83; Foner and Walker, eds., *Black State Conventions*, vol. 2, 97 and 103. Douglass himself acknowledged his continuing liability to reenslavement by allowing friends to buy his freedom, while he was in Britain and contemplating return to the North in the United States in 1846. See Philip S. Foner, ed., *The Life and Writings of Frederick Douglass*, 5 vols. (New York: International Publishers, 1950–1975), vol. 1, 72–3.

16. The quotations as well as the account are from McFeely, *Douglass*, 104–8, except "mere dabbling with effects," which is from Davis, "Abolitionism and Ideological Hegemony," in Bender, ed., *The Antislavery Debate*, 173. See also Noel Ignatiev, *How the Irish Became White* (New York and London: Routledge, 1995), 9.

17. McFeely, *Douglass*, 141, on "metaphoric uses"; David Roediger, *The Wages of Whiteness: Race and the Making of the American Working Class* (New York and London: Verso, 1991), 65–77; Cunliffe, *Chattel Slavery and Wage Slavery*, 16–17.

18. The "Down with all slavery, both chattel and wages" phrasing is a formulation of the land reformer William West, a supporter of George Henry Evans. See Eric Foner, "Abolition and the Labor Movement in Antebellum America," in *Politics and Ideology in the Age of the Civil War* (New York: Oxford University Press, 1980), 70–72; Philip S. Foner and Herbert Shapiro, eds., *Northern Labor and Antislavery: A Documentary History* (Westport, CT: Greenwood, 1994), 19; Davis, "Abolitionism and Ideological Hegemony," in *Antislavery Debate*, 133; Noel Ignatiev, *How the Irish Became White* (New York: Routledge, 1995), 79–83.

19. *Liberator*, July 9, 1847.

20. Douglass, *My Bondage and My Freedom* (Chicago: Johnson Publications, 1970, originally 1855), 76; "Douglass to Friend Garrison," February 26, 1846, reprinted in Foner, ed., *Life and Writings* vol. 1; 138–42; Douglass, *Narrative*, 83–84. On abolitionism and Irish Americans, see Ignatiev, *Irish Became White*, 8-31; Gilbert Osofsky, "Abolitionists, Irish Immigrants and the Dilemmas of Romantic Nationalism," *American Historical Review* 80 (October 1975); 889–906.

21. John W. Blassingame et al., eds., *The Frederick Douglass Papers: Speeches, Debates and Interviews*, ser. 1, 5 vols. (New Haven, CT: Yale University Press, 1982), vol. 3, 139; Ignatiev, *Irish Became White*, 9; Foner, ed., *Life and Writings*, vol. 4, 266–67. See also, however, Blassingame et al, eds., *Douglass Paper*, vol. 5, 275–78 and 367–68.

22. Quotations from Blassingame et al., eds., *Douglass Papers*, vol. 2, 258–59; Jacobs, *Incidents*, 49. See also Ibid., vol. 2, 293 for an Irish/free Black comparison. Foner and Shapiro, eds., *Northern Labor and Antislavery*, 10–13 and 22–24.

23. Foner, ed., *Life and Writings*, vol. 1, 188; Blassingame et al, eds., *Douglass Papers*, vol. 2, 307.

24. Waldo Martin, *The Mind of Frederick Douglass* (Chapel Hill: University of North Carolina Press, 1984), 127; Herbert Aptheker, *Abolitionism: A Revolutionary Movement* (Boston: Twayne, 1989), 36 and 43; Phillips, "The Question of Labor," *Liberator*, July 9, 1847, as reprinted in Foner and Shapiro, eds., *Northern Labor and Antislavery*, 6–7. Garrison is quoted in Messer-Kruse, "The Yankee International," 64–65.

25. On abolitionist interest in "Saxon slavery" and other historical examples of white bondage, see Daniel J. McInerney, *The Fortunate Heirs of Freedom: Abolition and the Republican Thought* (Lincoln, NE: University of Nebraska Press, 1994), 40–42; and Mia Bay's impressive *The White Image in the Black Mind* (New York: Oxford University Press, 2000); Douglass, *My Bondage and My Freedom*, 162; Martin, *Mind of Frederick Douglass*, 128; William and Ellen Craft, *Running a Thousand Miles for Freedom* (New York: Arno, 1969, originally 1860), 4–7.

26. Eric Foner, "Workers and Slavery," in Paul Buhle and Alan Dawley, eds., *Working for Democracy: American Workers from the Revolution to the*

Present (Urbana, IL: University of Illinois Press, 1985), 23; Eric Lott, *Love and Theft: Blackface Minstrelsy and the American Working Class* (Oxford and New York: Oxford University Press, 1993), 200; Alan Dawley, *Class and Community: The Industrial Revolution in Lynn* (Cambridge, MA: Harvard University Press, 1976), 65. When Foner writes that the early labor movement's values were "obviously incompatible with the institution of slavery," the assumption is that defense of white privilege was not such a central value. On Britain, see especially Seymour Drescher, "Cart Whip and Billy Roller: Antislavery and Reform Symbolism in Industrializing Britain," *Journal of Social History* 15 (September 1981), 3–24.

27. *Voice of Industry*, May 7, 1847, and September 25, 1847; Foner and Shapiro, eds., *Northern Labor and Antislavery*, 213; Philip S. Foner, ed., *The Factory Girls* (Urbana, IL: University of Illinois Press, 1977), 279–81; for the Lynn quotes, Mary H. Blewett, *Men, Women, and Work: Class, Gender, and Protest in the New England Shoe Industry, 1780–1910* (Urbana, IL: University of Illinois Press, 1988), 132; and Foner, *Labor Movement*, vol. 1, 274. Clearly, some labor organizations took the form of their appeals from abolitionism. See Philip S. Foner, ed., *American Labor Songs of the Nineteenth Century* (Urbana, IL: University of Illinois Press, 1975), 68–69; Foner and Shapiro, eds., *Northern Labor and Antislavery*, xiv. For the British case, see Drescher, "Cart Whip and Billy Roller," 3–24. The emphasis in the United States on voting as differentiating white workers from slaves recurs interestingly. It unfolds in a context in which suffrage reformers had prevailed in early- and mid-nineteenth-century campaigns to extend voting rights to propertyless adult white males by arguing that dependence inhered in "natural" categories of gender, age, and race rather than in nonpossession of property. Such arguments clearly existed in considerable tension with ideas about wage slavery, which implied that the adult white males without property were dependent. See Robert Steinfeld, "Property and Suffrage in the Early American Republic," *Stanford Law Review* 41 (January 1989), 335–76.

28. Aptheker, *Abolitionism*, 35–49; Edward Magdol, *The Anti-Slavery Rank and File: A Social Profile of the Abolitionist Constituency* (Westport, CT: Greenwood, 1986); Bruce Levine, *The Spirit of 1848: German Immigrants, Labor and the Coming of the Civil War* (Urbana, IL: University of Illinois Press, 1992), esp. 149–51 and 187–88; John Jentz, "Artisans, Evangelicals and the City: A Social History of Abolition and the Labor Movement" (Ph.D. dissertation, City University of New York, 1977); Foner, "Abolitionism and the Labor Movement," 72. The support of *organized* labor's rank and file for abolition remains difficult to gauge. Anecdotal and statistical evidence, the latter mainly from analyses of petition signatures, shows a strong artisan base with some factory worker support. But it is possible that these signatures came as much or more from workers disinclined to unionism. See Roediger, *Wages of Whiteness*, 80–87. More broadly on abolition and the working class, see Betty Fladeland, *Abolitionists and the Working Class: Problems in the Era of Industrialization* (Baton Rouge, LA: Louisiana State University Press, 1984); and Robin Blackburn, *The Overthrow of Colonial Slavery, 1776–1848* (London: Verso, 1988).

29. Foner and Shapiro, eds., *Northern Labor and Antislavery*, 147 and 213; Foner, "Workers and Slavery," 22; Ignatiev, *How the Irish Became White*, 79.

30. Douglass, *Narrative*, 138–40 and 145; *Liberator*, December 1, 1837, and April 28, 1848; *National Era*, May 21, 1857; Philip S. Foner, *History of Black Americans from the Emergence of the Cotton Kingdom to the Eve of the Compromise of 1850* (Westport, CT: Greenwood, 1983), 477–78; Ripley, ed., *Black Abolitionist Papers*, vol. 1, 467.

31. Greeley found the chattel slaves' oppression less "proximate," Evans less pivotal. See *Working Man's Advocate*, July 6, 1844; Philip S. Foner, *American Socialism and Black Americans* (Westport, CT: Greenwood, 1977), 8–9; *Voice of Industry*, August 21, 1845; John R. Commons et al., eds., *Documentary History of Labor in the United States*, 10 vols. (Cleveland, OH: Russell and Russell, 1958, originally 1910), vol. 7, 211–13; (Lynn) *Awl*, Augist 23, 1845. Philip S. Foner and Herbert Shapiro graciously made available to me copies of the materials that went into their edited *Northern Labor and Antislavery*. See also Cunliffe, *Chattel Slavery and Wage Slavery*, 21; and Roediger, *Wages of Whiteness*, 77–80.

32. Mandel, *Labor: Free and Slave*, 229. On priority, see Foner and Shapiro, eds., *Northern Labor and Antislavery*, 9; Ignatiev, *How the Irish Became White*, 80–81; Norman Ware, *The Industrial Worker, 1840–1860* (Boston: Houghton Mifflin, 1924), 225.

33. See Roediger, *Wages of Whiteness*, 75–77; Foner, ed., *Factory Girls*, 278; Ignatiev, *How the Irish Became White*, 69; Cunliffe, *Chattel Slavery and Wage Slavery*, 1; Wilfred Carsel, "The Slaveholders' Indictment of Northern Wage Slavery," *Journal of Southern History* 6 (November 1940), 510–16.

34. Foner, ed., *Factory Girls*, 107; Roediger, *Wages of Whiteness*, 75–76.

35. Mandel, *Labor: Free and Slave*, 228, note 57; Roediger, *Wages of Whiteness*, 83–85. On the defense of the virtue of factory women against proslavery propagandists, see Harriet H. Robinson, *Loom and Spindle: Or Life among Mill Girls* (Boston: Crowell, 1898), 196–98; Ware, *Industrial Worker*, 93–94; Foner, ed., *Factory Girls*, 81 and 83. The last-named contains an atypically frank discussion of sexual harassment in the mills but also holds that slave women had masters to "protect" them. See also Benita Eisler, ed., *The Lowell Offering: Writings by New England Mill Women* (New York: Harper & Row, 1977), 188–89.

36. Roediger, *Wages of Whiteness*, 80–87; Frederick Douglass, *Life and Times of Frederick Douglass* (New York: Collier, 1973, originally 1892), 214; cf. Paul Gilroy, *The Black Atlantic: Modernity and Double Consciousness* (Cambridge, MA: Harvard University Press 1993), xiii and note 31 above.

37. Philip S. Foner, ed., *American Labor Songs*, 69. The song continued with a reference to the origins of union agitation for the 10-hour day lying in white workers desiring their own "abolition" societies after seeing the many "friends" of the "blackee." Eric Foner, "Workers and Slavery," in Buhle and Dawley, eds., *Working for Democracy*, 22; on the mathematical formulations, Roediger, *Wages of Whiteness*, 77; Foner and Shapiro, eds., *Northern Labor and Antislavery*, 15 and 23. On Douglass, see his *Narrative*, 148, and his *Life and Times*, 207–11; and *Bondage and Freedom*, 310. On the horses' comparison, see, for example, *Working Man's Advocate*, June 22, 1844; *Awl*, October 29, 1845.

38. See Karen Sanchez-Eppler, *Touching Liberty: Abolition, Feminism, and the Politics of the Body* (Berkeley: University of California Press, 1993); Gilroy, *Black Atlantic*, 117–20.

39. *Young America*, February 7, 1844; Foner and Shapiro, eds., *Northern Labor and Antislavery*, 23 and 186.

40. For a reading of the extent, logic, and limits of such identification in minstrelsy, see Lott, *Love and Theft*, passim.

41. Flexner, *Century of Struggle: The Woman's Rights Movement in the United States* (New York: Atheneum, 1973), 76; Martin, *Mind of Frederick Douglass*, 146–52; Foner, ed., *Douglass*, vol. 1, 320–21; Shirley J. Yee, *Black Women Abolitionists: A Study in Activism, 1828–1860* (Knoxville, TN: University of Tennessee Press, 1994), 140.

42. Blassingame et al. eds., *Douglass Papers*, vol. 2, 451; Foner, ed., *Douglass*, vol. 1, 321; Aptheker, *Abolitionism*, 87.

43. Hersh, "'Am I Not a Woman and a Sister?'" in Perry and Fellman, eds., *Antislavery Reconsidered*, 265; Flexner, *Century of Struggle*, 67.

44. Hersh, *Slavery of Sex*, 196 and 200; Sarah Grimké, *Letters on the Equality of the Sexes and Other Essays*, Elizabeth Ann Bartlett, ed. (New Haven: Yale University Press, 1988), 73; Antoinette Brown Bartlett and Susan B. Anthony, "Debates on Marriage and Divorce," in Mari Jo Buhle and Paul Buhle, eds., *The Concise History of Women's Suffrage: Selections from the Classic Work of Stanton, Anthony, Gage, and Harper* (Urbana: University of Illinois Press, 1978), 189; Ellen DuBois, ed., *The Elizabeth Cady Stanton-Susan B. Anthony Reader* (Boston: Northeastern University Press, 1992), 48.

45. The most brilliant study of such changes remains Jeanne Boydston, *Home and Work: Housework, Wages and the Ideology of Labor in the Early Republic* (New York: Oxford University Press, 1990); see also Rowland Berthoff, "Conventional Mentality: Free Blacks, Women and Business Corporations as Unequal Persons, 1820-1870," *Journal of American History* 76 (December 1989), 753–84.

46. DuBois, ed., *Stanton-Anthony Reader*, 47–50; Grimké, *Letters on Equality*, 48; Blassingame et al. eds., *Douglass Papers*, vol. 2, 451; Dana Greene, ed., *Lucretia Mott: Her Complete Sermons and Speeches* (New York: E. Mellen Press, 1980), 155, 213, and 232–33.

47. Kristin Hoganson, "Garrisonian Abolitionists and the Rhetoric of Gender, 1850–1860," *American Quarterly*, 45 (December 1993), 558–95. On exclusion, see Fee, *Black Women Abolitionists*, 140–41; on Truth, see Nell Irvin Painter, *Sojourner Truth: A Life, A Symbol* (New York: Norton, 1996), 227. For Grimké and Weld, see Katharine Du Pre Lumpkin, *The Emancipation of Angelina Grimké* (Chapel Hill: University of North Carolina Press, 1974), 120 and 121. See also Aileen S. Kraditor, *Means and Ends in American Abolitionism: Garrison and His Critics on Strategy and Tactics, 1834–1850* (New York: Pantheon, 1969), chap. 3.

48. Hersh, "'Am I Not a Woman and a Sister?'" 252; Jean Fagan Yellin, *Women and Sisters: The Antislavery Feminists in American Culture* (New Haven: Yale University Press, 1989); Ellen Carol DuBois, "Outgrowing the Compact of the Fathers: Equal Rights, Woman Suffrage and the United

States Constitution, 1820–1878," *Journal of American History* 74 (December 1989), 840.

49. In 1837 Angeline Grimké exposed the threat of women becoming "white slaves of the North" if prejudice barred them from speaking out against slavery. See Hersh, *Slavery of Sex*, 196. On Child, see Carolyn Karcher, *The First Woman of the Republic: A Cultural Biography of Lydia Maria Child* (Durham, NC: Duke University Press, 1994), 221–25; and David A. J. Richards, "Abolitionist Feminism, Moral Slavery and the Constitution," *Cardozo Law Review* 18 (November 1996), esp. 784–85.

50. Aptheker, *Abolitionism*, 82; Hersh, *Slavery of Sex*, 197; DuBois, ed., *Stanton-Anthony Reader*, 84–85; Nancy A. Hewitt, "On Their Own Terms: A Historiographical Essay," in Jean Fagan Yellin and John C. Van Horne, eds., *The Abolitionist Sisterhood: Women's Political Culture in Antebellum America* (Ithaca, NY: Cornell University Press, 1994), 23-30.

51. DuBois, ed., *Stanton-Anthony Reader*, 69.

52. Ibid., 83; Emily Collins, "Reminiscences" in Elizabeth Cady Stanton, Susan B. Anthony, and Matilda J. Gage, eds., *History of Woman Suffrage*, 2 vols. (Salem, NH: Ayer Company, 1985, originally 1882), vol. 1, 93; Alice Felt Tyler, *Freedom's Ferment* (Minneapolis: University of Minnesota Press, 1944), 439, quoting Swisshelm; Clement Eaton, "The Resistance of the South to Northern Radicalism," *New England Quarterly* 8 (1935), 218–19.

53. DuBois, ed., *Stanton-Anthony Reader*, 48; Buhle and Buhle, eds., *Concise History*, 73; Grimké, *Letters on Equality*, 72; Greene, ed., *Complete Sermons and Speeches*, 157; Hersh, *Slavery of Sex*, 197. [Emphases added].

54. C. B. McPherson, *The Political Theory of Possessive Individualism: Hobbes to Locke* (Oxford: Clarendon Press, 1962). On property, gender, and abolition, see Amy Dru Stanley, "Home Life and the Morality of the Market," in Melvyn Stokes and Stephen Conway, eds., *The Market Revolution in America: Social, Political, and Religious Expressions, 1800–1880* (Charlottesville: University of Virginia Press, 1996), 88–90.

55. S. E. P., "Appropriate Sphere of Woman,"*Liberator*, February 1, 1839, 20, as quoted in Matt Martin, "Nature, Gender and Political Action in the Women's Poetry: *Liberator*, 1837–1847" (MA paper, University of Minnesota, 1997); Sanchez-Eppler, *Touching Liberty*, 22; Hersh, *Slavery of Sex*, 197–98; Aptheker, *Abolitionism*, 79.

56. Douglass, *Narrative*, 148. Messer-Kruse's "Yankee International," passim, is indispensable on the postemancipation evolution of many abolitionists toward labor radicalism and on the antebellum roots of that evolution.

Chapter 8

1. Paul Gilroy, "Black British Cultural Studies and the Pitfalls of Identity," in Houston A. Baker, Jr., Manthia Diawara, and Ruth Lindeborg, eds., *Black British Cultural Studies: A Reader* (Chicago: University of Chicago Press, 1996), 224.

2. Alexander Saxton, *The Rise and Fall of the White Republic: Class Politics and Mass Culture in Nineteenth Century America* (New York and London: Verso, 1990); Theodore W. Allen, *The Invention of the White Race*; vol. 1;

Racial Oppression and Social Control (London and New York: Verso, 1994), and vol. 2, *The Origins of Racial Oppression in Anglo-America* (London and New York: Verso, 1997); Noel Ignatiev, *How the Irish Became White* (New York and London: Routledge, 1995); David R. Roediger, *The Wages of Whiteness: Race and the Making of the American Working Class* (London and New York: Verso, 1991). See also Michael Goldfield, *The Color of Politics: Race and the Mainsprings of American Politics* (New York: New Press, 1997), 74–112. Among the review essays, see especially, David Stowe, "Uncolored People: The Rise of Whiteness Studies," *Lingua Franca* 4 (September-October 1996), 68–77; George Lipsitz, "Swing Low Sweet Cadillac: White Supremacy, Antiblack Racism and the New Historicism," *American Literary History*, 7 (Winter 1995), 700–25 and Judith Levine, "The Heart of Whiteness," *Voice Literary Supplement* (Sept. 1994), 11–16.

3. Karen Brodkin, "How Did Jews Become White Folks?" in Roger Sanjek and Steven Gregory, eds., *Race* (New Brunswick, NJ: Rutgers University Press, 1996), 78–102; Eric Lott, *Love and Theft: Blackface Minstrelsy and the American Working Class* (Oxford and New York: Oxford University Press, 1993); Michael Rogin, *Blackface, White Noise: Jewish Immigrants in the Hollywood Melting Pot* (Berkeley, Los Angeles, and London: University of California Press, 1996); Susan Gubar, *Racechanges: White Skin, Black Face in American Culture* (New York: Oxford University Press, 1997); Richard Drinnon, *Facing West: The Metaphysics of Indian-Hating and Empire-Building* (New York: New American Library, 1980); Michael Paul Rogin, *Fathers and Children: Andrew Jackson and the Subjection of the American Indian* (New York: Knopf, 1975); Reginald Horsman, *Race and Manifest Destiny: The Origins of American Racial Anglo-Saxonism* (Cambridge, MA, and London: Harvard University Press, 1981); Richard Slotkin, *The Fatal Environment: The Myth of the Frontier in the Age of Industrialization, 1800–1890* (New York: Atheneum, 1985); Ronald Takaki, *Iron Cages: Race and Culture in Nineteenth-Century America* (New York and Oxford: Oxford University Press, 1990). See also Robert F. Berkhofer, Jr., *The White Man's Indian: Images of the American Indian from Columbus to the Present* (New York: Vintage, 1979); and Roy Harvey Pearce, *The Savages of America: A Study of the Indian and the Idea of Civilization* (Baltimore: Johns Hopkins University Press, 1953).

4. Matt Wray and Annalee Newitz, eds., *White Trash: Race and Class in America* (New York and London: Routledge, 1997). For a burlesque treatment of "whiteness studies" that rests on a caricature of the influence of cultural studies, see Margaret Talbot, "Getting Credit for Being White," *New York Times Magazine* (November 30, 1997), 116–19; Pat Jennings and Meredith Redlin, "Constituting White Identities: *disClosure* Interviews David Roediger," *disClosure* 7 (1998), 133–35 on history, cultural studies, and race; Cheryl Harris, "Whiteness as Property," *Harvard Law Review* 106 (June 1993), 1709–91; Saidiya Hartman, *Scenes of Subjection: Terror, Slavery, and Self-Making in Nineteenth-Century America* (New York and Oxford: Oxford University Press, 1997).

5. For a discussion of the older scholarly contention that the Declaration of Independence was Lockean at its core, with Jefferson more or less inexplicably

or magically substituting "pursuit of happiness" for Locke's emphasis on the right to property, see Garry Wills, *Inventing America: Jefferson's Declaration of Independence* (Garden City, NY: Doubleday, 1978), 229–55. Wills sharply and successfully challenges this view insofar as Jefferson's political philosophy is concerned. However, property and happiness were certainly paired in significant ways in and beyond Locke. See also Herbert L. Ganter, "Jefferson's 'Pursuit of Happiness' and Some Forgotten Men," *William and Mary Quarterly* 16 (July 1936), 422–34. See also Warren Montag, "The Universalization of Whiteness" in Mike Hill, ed., *Whiteness: A Critical Reader* (New York and London: New York University Press, 1997), esp. 287–89.

6. Edmund Morgan, *American Slavery, American Freedom: The Ordeal of Colonial Virginia* (New York: Norton, 1975); Orlando Patterson, *Freedom*, vol. 1, *Freedom in the Making of Western Culture* (New York: Basic Books, 1991); Herman Melville, *White-Jacket* (New York: Harper and Brothers, 1850); Samuel Otter, "Race in *Typee* and *White-Jacket*" in Robert S. Levine, ed., *The Cambridge Companion to Herman Melville* (Cambridge, England: Cambridge University Press, 1998), 23–33; Charles Mills, *The Racial Contract* (Ithaca, NY, and London: Cornell University Press, 1997), esp. 86–87 and 96 on John Locke, race, and property.

7. Mills, *The Racial Contract*, 41–53 and 27 (quote).

8. W. E. B. Du Bois, *Black Reconstruction in America, 1860–1880* (New York: Atheneum, 1969, originally 1935), 700–1 and 727; Stowe, "Uncolored People," 71.

9. Harris, "Whiteness as Property," 1721 and 1724.

10. Harris, "Whiteness as Property," 1734–36 and 1759–61, esp. 1760, note 226. The discussion of whiteness, property, and "reputation" in Harris opens onto critical connections among race, masculinity, and honor in the South. Cf. Ariela J. Gross, "'Like Master, Like Man': Constructing Whiteness in the Commercial Law of Slavery, 1800–1861," *Cardozo Law Review* 18 (November 1996), 265–66 and 298.

11. Harris, "Whiteness as Property," 1734.

12. Hartman, *Scenes of Subjection*, 23; cf. Eric Lott, "White Like Me: Racial Cross-Dressing and the Making of American Whiteness," in Amy Kaplan and Donald E. Pease, eds., *Cultures of United States Imperialism* (Durham, NC: Duke University Press, 1993), 482.

13. Ibid., 17–112 and esp. 32. Elsewhere (26) Hartman probes more deeply into property's links to minstrel happiness: "The fungibility of the commodity, specifically its abstractness and immateriality, enabled the black body or blackface mask to serve as the vehicle of white self-exploration, renunciation, and enjoyment."

14. Regarding African American thought on terror and whiteness, see David R. Roediger, ed., *Black on White: Black Writers on What It Means to Be White* (New York: Schocken, 1998), 14–17 and 317–49.

15. Hartman, *Scenes of Subjection*, 34–35. Cf. Robyn C. Wiegman, *American Anatomies: Theorizing Race and Gender* (Durham, NC; and London: Duke University Press, 1995), 193–201.

16. Lott, *Love and Theft*, passim; W. T. Lhamon, Jr., *Raising Cain: Blackface Performance from Jim Crow to Hip Hop* (Cambridge, MA, and London:

Harvard University Press, 1998); David Grimsted, "Review of Bluford Adam's *E Pluribus Barnum*," *American Historical Review* 103 (June 1998), 974–75. The overwrought comparison of blackface and abolitionism is found, incredibly enough, in the Spring–Summer 1998 catalog of Harvard University Press, advertising *Raising Cain*. See also William J. Mahar's *Behind the Burnt Cork: Early Blackface Minstrelsy and Antebellum American Popular Culture* (Urbana: University of Illinois Press, 1999).

17. Alexander Saxton, "Blackface Minstrelsy and Jacksonian Ideology," *American Quarterly* 27 (March 1975), 27; Roediger, *Wages of Whiteness*, 119; Hartman, *Scenes of Subjection*, 32; Kalpana Seshadri-Crooks, "The Comedy of Domination: Psychoanalysis and the Conceit of Whiteness," *Discourse* 19 (Winter 1997), 152–56. See also Saxton's insightful revisiting of these questions in his "Blackface Minstrelsy, Vernacular Comics, and the Politics of Slavery in the North," in David Roediger and Martin H. Blatt, eds., *The Meaning of Slavery in the North*, (New York and London: Garland, 1998), 157–75.

18. Paul M. Angle, ed., *Created Equal?: The Complete Lincoln-Douglas Debates of 1858* (Chicago: University of Chicago Press, 1958), 156. For emphases I have added in this version of this article, I am indebted to the apt published remarks of David Brion Davis. Davis suggests that at Freeport the shout "White, white" was repeated, whereas "White men, white men" was the isolated utterance of one person. The text reproduced in Angle is less than fully clear on this point, however. See Davis, "The Culmination of Racial Polarities and Prejudice," *Journal of the Early Republic* 19 (Winter 1999), 774–75.

19. Ignatiev, *How the Irish Became White*; Lott, *Love and Theft*; Hartman, *Scenes of Subjection*; Roediger, *Wages of Whiteness*; and Saxton, *White Republic*. See also Barry Goldberg, "Wage Slaves and White 'Niggers,'" *New Politics*, 2d series, 3 (Summer 1991), 64–83.

20. James Brewer Stewart, "The Emergence of Racial Modernity and the Rise of the White North, 1790–1840," *Journal of the Early Republic* 18 (Spring 1998), 181–217. Mary Cathryn Cain's forthcoming Emory University dissertation, tentatively titled "The Whiteness of White Women: Gender and the Use of Race Privilege in the Urban Northeast, 1820–1870" promises to make a substantial contribution to the history of middle-class whiteness. On the Irish and whiteness, see Catherine Eagan, "When Did the Irish Become White?" (Unpublished paper, American Studies Association, Washington, DC, 1997). On resistant Irish Americans, see Leslie M. Harris, "'Rulers of the Five Points': Irish and Black Workers in New York City," in her *In the Shadow of Slavery: African Americans, Class, Community and Political Activism in New York City, 1626–1863*, forthcoming; Graham Russell Hodges, *Slavery, Freedom, and Culture Among Early American Workers* (Annonk, NY, and London: M.E. Sharpe, 1998), 122–44; John Kuo Wei Tchen *New York before Chinatown: Orientalism and the Shaping of American Culture, 1776–1882*, (Baltimore: Johns Hopkins University Press, 1999); Michael Hogan, *The Irish Soldiers of Mexico* (Guadalajara: Fondo Editorial Universitario, 1997).

21. Bruce Levine, "'Against All Slavery, White or Black': German Americans and the Irrepressible Conflict," in David McBride, Leroy Hopkins, and C. Aisha Blackshire-Belay, eds., *Crosscurrents: African Americans, Africa and Germany in the Modern World* (Columbia, SC: Camden House, 1998), 53–64

and *The Spirit of 1848: German Immigrants, Labor Conflict, and the Coming of the Civil War* (Urbana: University of Illinois Press, 1992); see also Darlene Wilson, "'Black Dutch'—A Polite Euphemism?" *Appalachian Quarterly* 2 (December 1997), passim; Jon Gjerde, "'Here in America There Is Neither King Nor Tyrant': European Encounters with Race, Freedom and Their European Pasts," *Journal of the Early Republic* 19 (Winter 1999), 673–90; Maria Diedrich, *Love across Color Lines: Ottile Assing and Frederick Douglass* (New York: Hill and Wang, 1999); and new material in Matthew Jacobson's superb recent study, *Whiteness of a Different Color: European Immigrants and the Alchemy of Race* (Cambridge, MA: Harvard University Press, 1998), 46–48.

22. Richard Dyer's important overarching discussion of whiteness and Christianity in his *White* (London and New York: Routledge, 1997), esp. 14–18, makes specific studies for the United States still more urgent; see also Mason Stokes, "Someone's in the Garden with Eve: Race, Religion and the American Fall," *American Quarterly* 50 (December 1998), 719–25.

23. Dana Frank, "White Working Class Women and the Race Question," *International Labor and Working Class History* 54 (Fall 1998), 80–102; Angle, ed., *Created Equal?* 156; David Roediger, "Race, Labor and Gender in the Languages of Antebellum Social Protest," in Stanley L. Engerman, ed., *Terms of Labor: Slavery, Serfdom and Free Labor* (Stanford, CA: Stanford University Press, 1999), 168–87; Dana D. Nelson, *National Manhood: Capitalist Citizenship and the Imagined Fraternity of White Men* (Durham and London: Duke University Press, 1998), 395–415; Maggie Montesinos Sale, *The Slumbering Volcano: American Slave Revolts and the Production of Rebellious Masculinity* (Durham, NC: Duke University Press, 1997). On Lincoln, see George Fredrickson, "A Man But Not a Brother: Abraham Lincoln and Racial Equality," in *The Arrogance of Race: Historical Perspectives on Slavery, Racism and Social Inequality* (Middletown, CT: Wesleyan University Press, 1988), 54–72. Davis, "Culmination," 774–75 sharply raises this dimension of the Freeport debate.

24. Nancy Isenberg, *Sex and Citizenship in Antebellum America* (Chapel Hill and London: University of North Carolina Press, 1998), esp. 27–29, 33–36, and 122–27; Jeanne Boydston, *Home and Work: Housework, Wages and the Ideology of Labor in the Early Republic* (New York and Oxford: Oxford University Press, 1990). See also Amy Kaplan, "Manifest Domesticity," *American Literature* 70 (September 1998), 581–606. For promising new work that combines insights about gender and about whiteness, see Cain, "The Whiteness of White Women," forthcoming, and Lori Askeland, "Remodeling the Model Home in *Uncle Tom's Cabin* and *Beloved*," in Michael Moon and Cathy N. Davidson, eds., *Subjects and Citizens: Nation, Race and Gender from Oroonoko to Anita Hill* (Durham, NC: Duke University Press, 1995), 395–415. Particularly impressive for its insistence on whiteness as performance, and on the gendered nature of such performance, is Ariela J. Gross, "Litigating Whiteness: Trials of Racial Determination in the Nineteenth Century South," *Yale Law Journal*, 198 (October 1998), 109–88.

25. Martha Hodes, *White Women, Black Men: Illicit Sex in the Nineteenth Century South* (New Haven: Yale University Press, 1997); Nell Irvin Painter, "Soul Murder and Slavery: Towards a Fully Loaded Cost Accounting," in Linda Kerber, Alice Kessler-Harris, and Kathryn Kish Sklar, eds., *U.S. History*

as Women's History (Chapel Hill and London: University of North Carolina Press, 1995), 125–46; Victoria E. Bynum, *Unruly Women: The Politics of Social and Sexual Control in the Old South* (Chapel Hill: University of North Carolina Press, 1992), esp. 35–38; Elizabeth Fox-Genovese, *Within the Plantation Household: Black and White Women in the Old South* (Chapel Hill: University of North Carolina Press, 1988); Karen Sanchez-Eppler, *Touching Liberty: Abolition, Feminism and the Politics of the Body* (Berkeley and Los Angeles: University of California Press, 1993); Russ Castronovo, "Incidents in the Life of a White Woman: Economics of Race and Gender in the Antebellum Nation," *America Literary History* 10 (Summer 1998), 239–65; Gillian Brown, *Domestic Individualism: Imagining Self in Nineteenth Century America* (Berkeley: University of California Press, 1990), 3–38; Cheryl Harris, "Finding Sojourner's Truth: Race, Gender and the Institution of Slavery," *Cardozo Law Review* 18 (November 1998), 309–410.

26. Douglas as quoted in Robert W. Johannsen, *Stephen A. Douglas* (New York: Oxford University Press, 1973), 726. On the efforts, that were successful in Illinois in 1853, of midwestern states to exclude African American migrants, see Eugene Berwanger, *The Frontier against Slavery: Western Anti-Negro Prejudice and the Slavery Extension Controversy* (Urbana: University of Illinois Press, 1967), 44–59.

27. See, for example, Joe Trotter's review of *Wages of Whiteness* in *Journal of Social History* 25 (Spring 1992), 674–76. For rich studies of specific social histories of race, see Ignatiev, *How the Irish Became White*; Hodges, *Slavery, Freedom and Culture among Early American Workers*; John Kuo Wei Tchen, "Quimbo Appo's Fear of Fenians: Chinese-Irish-Anglo Relations in New York City," in Ronald Bayor and Timothy Meagher, eds., *The New York Irish* (Baltimore and London: Johns Hopkins University Press, 1996), 123–52. On free Blacks in the North, see James Brewer Stewart, "Modernizing 'Difference': The Political Meaning of Color in the Free States," *Journal of the Early Republic* 19 (Winter 1999), 691–712; Lois Horton, "From Class to Race in Early America: Northern Post-Emancipation Racial Reconstruction," *Journal of the Early Republic* 19 (Winter 1999), 629–50; Joanne Pope Melish, "The 'Condition' Debate and Racial Discourse in the Antebellum North," *Journal of the Early Republic* 19 (Winter 1999), 651–72. On the South, see Hodes, *White Women, Black Men*; Lacy K. Ford, Jr., "Making the White Man's Country White: Race, Slavery, and State-Building in the Jacksonian South," *Journal of the Early Republic* 19 (Winter 1999), 713–38.

28. For a vigorous endorsement of the superiority of local approaches, see Eric Arnesen's "Up from Exclusion: Black and White Workers, Race, and the State of Labor History," *Reviews in American History* 26 (1998), 162–67; Stuart Hall, "What Is This 'Black' in Black Popular Culture?' *Social Justice* 20 (Spring-Summer 1993), 111; John Kuo Wei Tchen, "Believing Is Seeing: Transforming Orientalism and the Occidental Gaze," in Margo Machida, eds., *Asia/America: Identities in Contemporary Asian American Art*, (New York: New Press, 1994), 12–25.

29. Joanne Pope Melish, *Disowning Slavery: Gradual Emancipation and 'Race' in New England, 1780–1860* (Ithaca, NY, and London: Cornell University Press, 1998), 5, 151–62 (Barbary slavery), 210 ("free white republic") and

passim. See also Paul Baepler, ed., *White Slaves, African Masters: An Anthology of American Captivity Narratives* (Chicago and London: University of Chicago Press, 1999).

30. Tchen, *New York before Chinatown*, passim.

31. Angle, ed., *Created Equal?* 201.

32. See the works cited in notes 2 and 22 above and George Lipsitz, *The Possessive Investment in Whiteness: How White People Profit from Identity Politics* (Philadelphia: Temple University Press, 1998).

33. Roediger, *Wages of Whiteness*, 21–23; Frank Dumont, *Burnt Cork; or, The Amateur Minstrel* (New York: DeWitt, 1881), 45; Martha Knack and Alice Littlefield, eds., *Native Americans and Wage Labor: Ethnohistorical Perspectives* (Norman, OK: University of Oklahoma Press, 1996); Jean M. O'Brien, "'Vanishing' Indians in Nineteenth-Century New England: Local Historians' Erasure of Still-Present Indian Peoples" (unpublished paper in possession of author, 1998); Lora Romero, "Vanishing Americans: Gender, Empire and the New Historicism," in Davidson and Moon, eds., *Subjects and Citizens*, 87–105. For the colonial studies, see Morgan, *American Slavery,* and Kathleen M. Brown, *Good Wives, Nasty Wenches and Anxious Patriarchs: Gender, Race and Power in Colonial Virginia* (Chapel Hill and London: University of North Carolina Press, 1998).

34. Philip Deloria, *Playing Indian* (New Haven and London: Yale University Press, 1998), 5; Susan Scheckel, *The Insistence of the Indian: Race and Nation in Nineteenth Century American Culture* (Princeton: Princeton University Press, 1998); Darlene Wilson and Patricia Beaver, "Embracing the Male Off-Shore Other: The Ubiquitous Native Grandmother in America's Cultural Memory," forthcoming in Barbara Smith, ed., *Links of Iron, Links of Gold: The Social Relations of Southern Women;* Cf. Neal Salisbury, "The Best Poor Man's Country as Middle Ground: Mainstreaming Indians in Early American Studies," *Reviews in American History* 26 (1998), 497–503.

35. On the Mexican War, see Paul W. Foos, "Mexican Wars: Soldiers and Society in an Age of Expansion, 1835–1855" (unpublished Ph.D. dissertation, Yale University, 1997), 6.

36. Tomás Almaguer, *Racial Fault Lines: The Historical Origins of White Supremacy in California* (Berkeley, Los Angeles, and London: University of California Press, 1994); Lisbeth Haas, *Conquests and Historical Identities in California, 1769–1936* (Berkeley: University of California Press, 1995); Ramón A. Gutiérrez, *When Jesus Came, the Corn Mothers Went Away: Marriage, Sexuality and Power in New Mexico, 1500–1846* (Stanford: Stanford University Press, 1991), 193–206 and 338–39. See also David Montejano, *Anglos and Mexicans in the Making of Texas, 1836–1986* (Austin: University of Texas Press, 1987) and Arnoldo De León, *They Called Them Greasers: Anglo American Attitudes Toward Mexicans in Texas* (Austin: University of Texas Press, 1983). On Marxism and raced categories, see Lisa Lowe, *Immigrant Acts: On Asian American Cultural Politics* (Durham, NC: Duke University Press, 1996), 24–28. Ronald Takaki, *Strangers from a Different Shore: A History of Asian Americans* (Boston: Little, Brown, 1989), 30–31. See also Patricia Nelson Limerick, *The Legacy of Conquest: The Unbroken Past of the American West* (New

York: Norton, 1987), esp. 179–292; Richard White, *"It's Your Misfortune and None of My Own": A History of the American West* (Norman: University of Oklahoma Press, 1991); Quintard Taylor, *In Search of the Racial Frontier: African Americans in the American West, 1528–1900* (New York: Norton, 1998), esp. 27–102.

37. Drinnon, *Facing West*; Rogin, *Fathers and Children*; Horsman, *Race and Manifest Destiny*; Slotkin, *The Fatal Environment*; Takaki, *Iron Cages*; Berkhofer, Jr., *The White Man's Indian,* and Pearce, *The Savages of America.*

38. James P. Ronda, "'We Have a Country': Race, Geography and the Invention of Indian Territory," *Journal of the Early Republic* 19 (Winter 1999), 739–56; Daniel K. Richter, "'Believing That Many of the Red People Suffer Much for the Want of Food': Hunting, Agrculture, and the Quaker Constructions of Indianness in the Early Republic," *Journal of the Early Republic* 19 (Winter 1999), 601–28; Nancy Shoemaker, "How Indians Got to Be Red," *American Historical Review* 102 (June 1997), 625–44; R. Keith Basso, *Portraits of "The Whiteman": Linguistic Play and Cultural Symbols Among the Western Apache* (Cambridge, England: Cambridge University Press, 1979); Herman Melville, *The Confidence-Man,* H. Bruce Franklin, ed. (Indianapolis: Bobbs-Merrill, 1967, originally 1857), 203.

39. Drinnon, *Facing West,* 198–99; Melville, *Confidence-Man,* 129–39; Eric Foner, *Free Soil, Free Labor, Free Men: The Ideology of the Republican Party before the Civil War* (New York: Oxford University Press, 1970).

40. Karl Marx, *Capital: A Critique of Political Economy,* vol. 1, trans. Ben Fowkes (London: Penguin, 1976, originally 1967), 914–26 and 915 (quote). On this point I am indebted to Peter Linebaugh, "Review of Robin Blackburn's *The Making of New World Slavery,*" *Historical Materialism* 1 (Autumn 1997), 185–96, esp. 190.

41. Slotkin, *Fatal Environment,* 235 (quote), 226–41, and 266–68. See also 117 for the link to Marx's point.

42. Takaki, *Iron Cages,* viii–x, 69–79, and 125–28.

43. Rogin, *Fathers and Children,* 19–279 and 8 (quote). George Rawick, *From Sundown to Sunup: The Making of the Black Community* (Westport, CT: Greenwood, 1972), 125–49, esp. 132–33.

44. Takaki, *Iron Cages,* 83, 90, and 139–42; Melville, *Confidence-Man,* 219.

45. Taylor, *In Search of the Racial Frontier*; Bruce M. White, "The Power of Whiteness, or the Life and Times of Joseph Roletter, Jr.," *Minnesota History* 56 (Winter 1998), 178–201; Sylvia Van Kirk, *"Many Tender Ties": Women in Fur-Trade Society, 1670–1870* (Norman: University of Oklahoma Press, 1983); Richard White, *The Middle Ground: Indian Empires and Republics in the Great Lakes Region, 1650–1815* (Cambridge, England, and New York: Cambridge University Press, 1991); June Namias, *White Captives: Gender and Ethnicity on the American Frontier* (Chapel Hill: University of North Carolina Press, 1993).

46. Drinnon, *Facing West,* 131–46 and 355 (quote).

47. Takaki, *Iron Cages,* 156–61 and 215–16; Helper, as quoted in Robert Lee, *Orientals: Asian Americans in Popular Culture* (Philadelphia: Temple University Press, 1999), 26.

48. Horsman, *Race and Manifest Destiny*, 208–71 (quoting Douglas at 251); and Saxton, *White Republic*. See also Jacobson, *Whiteness of a Different Color*.

49. Nelson, *National Manhood*, passim.

50. Nelson, *National Manhood*, 62.

51. Gesa Mackenthun, "Adding Empire to the Study of American Culture," *Journal of American Studies* 30 (1998), 263.

52. See, for example, Ann Laura Stoler, *Race and the Education of Desire: Foucault's "History of Sexuality" and the Colonial Order* (Durham, NC: Duke University Press, 1995); George Mosse, *Nationalism and Sexuality* (New York: Fertig, 1985); Homi Bhabha, "The Other Question: The Stereotype and Colonial Discourse," *Screen* 24 (November-December 1983), 18–36; Frantz Fanon, *The Wretched of the Earth* (New York: Grove Press, 1963); W. Jeffrey Bolster, *Black Jacks: African American Seamen in the Age of Sail* (Cambridge, MA, and London: Harvard University Press, 1997); Peter Linebaugh and Marcus Rediker, "The Many-Headed Hydra: Sailors, Slaves, and the Atlantic Working Class in the Eighteenth Century," *Journal of Historical Sociology* 3 (September 1990), 225–52. On Melville, see Leonard Cassuto, *The Inhuman Race: The Racial Grotesque in American Literature and Culture* (New York: Columbia University Press, 1997), 170-79 and 203–15; Carolyn Karcher, *Shadow over the Promised Land: Slavery, Race and Violence in Melville's America* (Baton Rouge and London: Louisiana State University Press, 1980); Sterling Stuckey, "The Death of Benito Cereno: A Reading of Herman Melville on Slavery," in *Going Through the Storm: The Influence of African American Art in History* (New York and Oxford: Oxford University Press, 1994), 158–69; Robert J. C. Young, *Colonial Desire: Hybridity in Theory, Culture and Race* (London and New York: Routledge, 1995), 118–41.

53. Allen, *Invention of the White Race*, vol. 1, 1.

Chapter 9

1. The epigraph is from John A. Fitch, *The Steel Workers* (New York: Russell Sage Foundation, 1910), 147. Joe Sauris, Interview with Joseph Loguidice, July 25, 1980, Italians in Chicago Project, copy of transcript, Box 6, Immigration History Research Center, University of Minnesota, St. Paul, MN. Such a sprawling essay would be impossible without help from students and colleagues, especially regarding sources. Thanks go to David Montgomery, Steven Rosswurm, Susan Porter Benson, Randy McBee, Neil Gotanda, Peter Rachleff, Noel Ignatiev, the late Peter Tamony, Louise Edwards, Susan Hirsch, Isaiah McCaffery, Rudolph Vecoli, Hyman Berman, Sal Salerno, Louise O'Brien, Liz Pleck, Mark Leff, Toby Higbie, Micaela di Leonardo, Dana Frank, and the Social History Group at the University of Illinois.

2. See, for example, Gerald Rosenblum, *Immigrant Workers: Their Impact on American Labor Radicalism* (New York: Basic Books, 1973); C. T. Husbands, "Editor's Introductory Essay," in Werner Sombart, *Why Is There No Socialism in the United States?* (White Plains, NY: International Arts and Sciences Press, 1976), xxix.

3. Robert Orsi, "The Religious Boundaries of an Inbetween People: Street *Feste* and the Problem of the Dark-Skinned 'Other' in Italian Harlem, 1920–1990," *American Quarterly* 44 (September 1992), 335. Michael Omi and Howard Winant, *Racial Formation in the United States from the 1960s to the 1980s* (New York and London: Routledge and Kegan Paul, 1986), 64–65; Gary Gerstle, "Working Class Racism: Broaden the Focus," *International Labor and Working Class History* 44 (1993), 38–39.

4. Sombart, *No Socialism*, 27–28; Stanford M. Lyman, "Race Relations as Social Process: Sociology's Resistance to a Civil Rights Orientation," in Herbert Hill and James E. Jones, Jr., *Race in America: The Struggle for Equality* (Madison: University of Wisconsin Press, 1993), 374–83; cf. Omi and Winant, *Racial Formation*, 15–17, for useful complications on this score; Thomas F. Gossett, *Race: The History of an Idea in America* (Dallas: Southern Methodist University Press, 1963); Barbara Solomon, *Ancestors and Immigrants* (Cambridge, MA: Harvard University Press, 1956); Gloria A. Marshall, "Racial Classification: Popular and Scientific," in Sandra Harding, ed., *The Racial Economy of Science* (Bloomington and Indianapolis: Indiana University Press, 1993), 123–24. On Park, race, and ethnicity, see also Omi and Winant, *Racial Formation*, 15–17; Stow Persons, *Ethnic Studies at Chicago, 1905–1945* (Urbana, IL: University of Illinois Press 1987), 602.

5. For historical invocations of "ethnicity" to explain situations experienced at the time as racial, in otherwise brilliant works, see Mary C. Waters, *Ethnic Options: Choosing Identities in America* (Berkeley: University of California Press, 1990), 79, and Werner Sollors, *Beyond Ethnicity: Consent and Descent in American Culture* (New York: Oxford University Press, 1986), 38-39. See also Michael Banton, *Racial Theories* (Cambridge, England: Cambridge University Press, 1988), and David Theo Goldberg, "The Semantics of Race," *Ethnic and Racial Studies* 15 (October 1992), esp. 554–55. The most devastating critique of the "cult of ethnicity" remains Alexander Saxton's review essay on Nathan Glazer's *Affirmative Discrimination* in *Amerasia Journal*, 4 (1977), 141–50. See also Gwendolyn Mink, *Old Labor and New Immigrants in American Political Development* (Ithaca, NY: Cornell University Press, 1986), esp. 46, note 1.

6. Peggy Pascoe, "Miscegenation Law, Court Cases, and Ideologies of 'Race' in Twentieth Century America," *Journal of American History* 83 (June 1996), 44–69; Peggy Pascoe, "Race, Gender, and Intercultural Relations: The Case of Interracial Marriage," *Frontiers: A Journal of Women's Studies* 12 (1991), 5–17, quotes; Paul Spickard, *Mixed Blood: Intermarriage and Ethnic Identification in Twentieth Century America* (Madison: University of Wisconsin Press, 1989), Appendix A, 374–75; See also Paul Siu, *The Chinese Laundryman: A Study of Social Isolation* (New York: New York University Press, 1987), 143 and 250–271.

7. We borrow "inbetween" from Orsi, "Religious Boundaries of an Inbetween People," passim and also from John Higham, *Strangers in the Land: Patterns of American Nativism, 1860–1925* (New York: Atheneum, 1974), 169. Herbert Gutman with Ira Berlin, "Class Composition and the Development of the American Working Class, 1840–1890," in Gutman, *Power and Culture:*

Essays on the American Working Class, Ira Berlin, ed. (New York: Pantheon, 1987), 380–94, initiates vital debate on immigration and the "remaking" of the U.S. working class over time. We occasionally use the phrase *new immigrants*, the same term that contemporaries sometimes employed to distinguish more recent—and "less desirable"—from earlier immigrant peoples, but we do so critically. To use the term indiscriminately tends not only to render Asian, Latin, and other non-European immigrants invisible but also to normalize a racialized language that we are trying to explicate.

8.   Lawrence Glickman, "Inventing the 'American Standard of Living': Gender, Race and Working-Class Identity, 1880–1925," *Labor History* 34 (Spring-Summer, 1993): 221–35; David Montgomery, *Beyond Equality: Labor and the Radical Republicans, 1862–1872* (Urbana: University of Illinois Press, 1981), 254. Richard Williams, *Hierarchical Structures and Social Value: The Creation of Black and Irish Identities in the United States* (Cambridge, England, and New York: Cambridge University Press, 1990); Edward P. Thompson, *Customs in Common: Studies in Traditional Popular Culture* (London: Merlin, 1991), 320.

9.   On the history of *guinea*, see Roediger, "*Guineas, Wiggers* and the Dramas of Racialized Culture," *American Literary History* 7 (Winter 1995): 654–68. On post-1890 usages, see William Harlen Gilbert, Jr., "Memorandum Concerning the Characteristics of the Larger Mixed-Blood Islands of the United States," *Social Forces* 24 (March 1946), 442; *Oxford English Dictionary*, 2d ed. (Oxford, 1989), vol. 6; 937–38; Frederic G. Cassidy and Joan Houston Hall, eds., *Dictionary of American Regional English* (Cambridge, MA, and London: Harvard University Press, 1991), vol. 2, 838; Harold Wentworth and Stuart Berg Flexner, *Dictionary of American Slang* (New York: Crowell, 1975), 234, and Peter J. Tamony, research notes on *guinea*, Tamony Collection, Western Historical Manuscripts Collection, University of Missouri, Columbia.

10.   Tamony's notes on *hunky* (or *hunkie*) speculate on links to *honkie* (or *honky*) and refer to the former as an "old labor term." By no means did *Hun* refer unambiguously to Germans before World War I. See, for example, Henry White, "Immigration Restriction as a Necessity," *American Federationist* 4 (June 1897), 67; Paul Krause, *The Battle for Homestead, 1880–1892: Politics, Culture and Steel* (Pittsburgh: University of Pittsburgh Press, 1992), 216–17; Stan Kemp, *Boss Tom: The Annals of an American Anthracite Mining Village* (Akron, OH: Saalfield Publishing Company, 1904), 258; Thames Williamson, *Hunky* (New York: Coward-McCann, 1929), slipcover; Thomas Bell, *Out of This Furnace* (Pittsburgh: University of Pittsburgh Press, 1976; originally 1941), 124–25; David Brody, *Steelworkers in America: The Nonunion Era* (New York: Harvard University Press, 1969), 120–121; Josef Barton, *Peasants and Strangers: Italians, Rumanians, and Slovaks in an American City, 1890–1950* (Cambridge, MA: Harvard University Press,1975), 20; Theodore Radzialowski, "The Competition for Jobs and Racial Stereotypes: Poles and Blacks in Chicago," *Polish American Studies* 22 (Autumn 1976), note 7; Upton Sinclair, *Singing Jailbirds* (Pasadena: the author, 1924). Remarks regarding the use of *mill hunky* in the 1970s are based on Barrett's anecdotal observations in and around Pittsburgh at the time. See also the *Mill Hunk Herald*, published in Pittsburgh throughout the late 1970s.

11. Dollard, *Caste and Class in a Southern Town* (Garden City, NY: Doubleday, 1949), 93; Barry Goldberg, "Historical Reflections on Transnationalism, Race, and the American Immigrant Saga" (unpublished paper delivered at the Rethinking Migration, Race, Ethnicity, and Nationalism in Historical Perspective Conferences, New York Academy of the Sciences, May 1990).

12. Albert S. Broussard, "George Albert Flippin and Race Relations in a Western Rural Community," *The Midwest Review* 12 (1990), 15, note 42; J. Alexander Karlin, "The Italo-American Incident of 1891 and the Road to Reunion," *Journal of Southern History* 8 (1942); Gunther Peck, "Padrones and Protest: 'Old' Radicals and 'New' Immigrants in Bingham, Utah, 1905–1912," *Western Historical Quarterly* (May 1993), 177; Dan Georgakas, *Greek America at Work* (New York: n.p., 1992), 12 and 16–17; A. Yvette Huginnie, *Strikitos: Race, Class, and Work in the Arizona Copper Industry*, forthcoming; Ruth Shonle Cavan and Katherine Howland Ranck, *The Family and the Depression: A Study of One Hundred Chicago Families* (Chicago: University of Chicago Press, 1938), 38–39; Isaiah McCaffery, "An Esteemed Minority? Greek Americans and Interethnic Relations in the Plains Region" (unpublished paper, University of Kansas, 1993); see also Donna Misner Collins, *Ethnic Identification: The Greek Americans of Houston, Texas* (New York: AMS Press, 1991), 201–11. For the African American slang, see Clarence Major, ed., *From Juba to Jive: A Dictionary of African-American Slang* (New York: Penguin, 1994), 213.

13. Donna Gabaccia, "The 'Yellow Peril' and the 'Chinese of Europe': Italian and Chinese Laborers in an International Labor Market" (unpublished paper, University of North Carolina at Charlotte, c. 1993).

14. Matthew Frye Jacobson, *Whiteness of a Different Color: European Immigrants and the Alchemy of Race* (Cambridge, MA, and London: Harvard University Press, 1998), 4 and 65; George E. Cunningham, "The Italian: A Hindrance to White Solidarity in Louisiana, 1890–1898," *Journal of Negro History* 50 (January 1965): 34, includes the quotes.

15. Higham, *Strangers in the Land*, 66; Gary R. Mormino and George E. Pozzetta, *The Immigrant World of Ybor City: Italians and Their Latin Neighbors in Tampa, 1885–1985* (Urbana, IL: University of Illinois Press, 1987), 241; Micaela diLeonardo, *The Varieties of Ethnic Experience* (Ithaca, NY: Cornell University Press, 1984), 24, note 16; Georgakas, *Greek Americans at Work*, 16. See also Karen Brodkin's superb *How Jews Became White Folks and What That Says About Race in America* (New Brunswick, NJ: Rutgers University Press, 1998).

16. Quoted in Brody, *Steelworkers*, 120; W. Lloyd Warner and J. O. Low, *The Social System of the Modern Factory, The Strike* (New Haven: Yale University Press, 1947), 140; Gershon Legman, *The Horn Book* (New Hyde Park, NY: University Books, 1964), 486–87; *Anecdota Americana: Five Hundred Stories for the Amusement of the Five Hundred Nations That Comprise America* (New York: W. Faro, 1933), 98; Nathan Hurvitz, "Blacks and Jews in American Folklore," *Western Folklore* 33 (October 1974), 304–7; Emory S. Bogardus, "Comparing Racial Distance in Ethiopia, South Africa, and the United States," *Sociology and Social Research* 52 (January 1968), 149–56; F. James Davis, *Who Is Black? One Nation's Definition* (University Park, PA: Pennsylvania State University Press, 1991), 161.

17. Thomas G. Dyer, *Theodore Roosevelt and the Idea of Race* (Baton Rouge: Louisiana State University Press, 1980), 131 and 143–44; On "stock," see M. G. Smith's "Ethnicity and Ethnic Groups in America: The View from Harvard," *Ethnic and Racial Studies* 5 (January 1982), 17–18.

18. On race and naturalizaton law, see Ian F. Haney Lopez, *White by Law: The Legal Construction of Race* (New York and London: New York University Press, 1996), esp. 37–154; A. William Hoglund, *Finnish Immigrants in America, 1908–1920* (Madison: University of Wisconsin Press, 1960), 112–14; Peter Kivisto, *Immigrant Socialists in the United States: The Case of Finns and the Left* (Rutherford, NJ: Fairleigh Dickinson University Press, 1984), 127–28. The whiteness of Armenians was also sometimes at issue, even if they lived on "the west side of the Bosphorus." See *In re Halladjian* 174 F. 834 (C.C.D. Mass., 1909) and *U.S. v. Cartozian*, 6 Fed. 2d 919 (1925).

19. *U.S. v. Thind*, 261 U.S. 204 (1923); Joan M. Jensen, *Passage from India: Asian Indian Immigrants in North America* (New Haven: Yale University Press, 1988), 246–69. On the nonwhite status of Asians, see also *In re Ah Yup*, 1 Fed. Cas. 223 (C.C.D. Cal., 1878); *Ozawa v. U.S.* 260 U.S. 178 (1922). Williams, *Hierarchical Structures*, passim; David Montejano, *Anglos and Mexicans in the Making of Texas, 1836–1986* (Austin: University of Texas Press, 1987); Sharon M. Lee, "Racial Classifications in the U.S. Census, 1890–1990," *Ethnic and Racial Studies* 16 (January 1993), 79: Tomas Almaguer, *Racial Faultlines: The Historical Origins of White Supremacy in California* (Berkeley: University of California Press, 1994), 55-57; George Sanchez, *Becoming Mexican American: Ethnicity, Culture and Identity in Chicano Los Angeles, 1900–1945* (Oxford and New York: Oxford University Press, 1993), 29–30.

20. Oscar Handlin, *Race and Nationality in American Life* (Boston: Little, Brown, 1957), 205; Cunningham, "Hindrance to White Solidarity," 33–35, and especially Jean Scarpaci, "A Tale of Selective Accommodation: Sicilians and Native Whites in Louisiana," *Journal of Ethnic Studies* 3 (1977), 44–45, who notes the use of *dago clause* to describe the provision. For the Irish, see David R. Roediger, *The Wages of Whiteness: Race and the Making of the American Working Class* (New York and London: Verso, 1991), 140–43, and Steven P. Erie, *Rainbow's End: Irish-Americans and the Dilemmas of Urban Machine Politics, 1840–1985* (Berkeley: University of California Press, 1988), 25–66 and 96, Table 10.

21. Reginald Horsman, *Race and Manifest Destiny: The Origins of American Racial Anglo-Saxonism* (Cambridge, MA: Harvard University Press, 1981), 250–53. Dyer, *Idea of Race*, 131; Mink, *Old Labor and New Immigrants*, 224–27.

22. Dyer, *Idea of Race*, 29–30 and 10–44, passim. Stephan Thernstrom, ed., *Harvard Encyclopedia of American Ethnic Groups* (Cambridge, MA: Harvard University Press, 1980), 379; quotations, Dyer, *Idea of Race*, 55, 66, 132.

23. Dyer, *Idea of Race*, 132; and, for Roosevelt's revealing exchanges with Madison Grant, 17.

24. Higham, *Strangers in the Land*, 238–62.

25. Quoted in Mink, *Old Labor and New Immigrants*, 71–112, 109–10; Grant quoted in Higham, *Strangers in the Land*, 156–57.

26. Jane Addams, *Twenty Years at Hull House* (New York: Macmillan, 1910); Mink, *Old Labor and New Immigrants*, 223 and 226 for the quotes.

27. James Weinstein, *The Corporate Ideal in the Liberal State, 1900–1918* (Boston: Beacon, 1968).

28. Stephen Meyer III, *The Five-Dollar Day: Labor Management and Social Control in the Ford Motor Company, 1908–1921* (Albany: State University of New York Press, 1981), 176–85; Higham, *Strangers in the Land*, 138, 261–62, 316–17.

29. Cf. Dyer, *Idea of Race*, 42–44, 63, 130–31; Higham, *Strangers in the Land*, 317; John F. McClymer, "The Americanization Movement and the Education of the Foreign-Born Adult, 1914–1925," in Bernard J. Weiss, ed., *American Education and the European Immigrant, 1840–1940* (Urbana, IL: University of Illinois Press 1982), 96–116; Herbert Gutman, *Work, Culture and Society in Industrializing America: Essays in Working-Class and Social History* (New York: Knopf, 1976), 7–8, 22–25. On the curricula in factory-based Americanization programs, see Gerd Korman, "Americanization at the Factory Gate," *Labor and Industrial Relations Review* 18 (1965), 396–419.

30. Higham, *Strangers in the Land*, 263.

31. Quotes from ibid., 273 and 321. See also 300–330, passim. On the triumph of terror and exclusion and the consequent turn by leading liberal intellectuals to a defeatism regarding "race and ethnicity," see Gary Gerstle, "The Protean Character of American Liberalism," *American Historical Review* 99 (October 1994), 1055–67.

32. Richard Slotkin, *Gunfighter Nation: The Myth of the Frontier in Twentieth-Century America* (New York: Atheneum, 1992); Michael Rogin, "'The Sword Became a Flashing Vision': D. W. Griffith's *The Birth of a Nation*," in *Ronald Reagan: The Movie and Other Essays in Political Demonology* (Berkeley: University of California Press, 1987), 190–235. "Incontestably mulatto" comes from Albert Murray, *The Omni-Americans: Some Alternatives to the Folklore of White Supremacy* (New York: Vintage, 1983), 22; Zena Pearlstone, *Seeds of Prejudice: Racial and Ethnic Stereotypes in American Popular Lithography, 1830–1918*, forthcoming. See especially Michael Rogin, "Blackface, White Noise: The Jewish Jazz Singer Finds His Voice," *Critical Inquiry* 18 (Spring 1992), 417–53; Rogin, "Making America Home: Racial Masquerade and Ethnic Assimilation in the Transition to Talking Pictures," *Journal of American History* 79 (December 1992), 1050–77.

33. Gads Hill Center, "May Report" (1915) and "Minstrel Concert" flyer. Thanks to Steven Rosswurm for identifying this source. See also Elisabeth Lasch-Quinn, *Black Neighbors: Race and the Limits of Reform in the American Settlement House Movement, 1890-1945* (Chapel Hill: University of North Carolina Press, 1993), esp. 14–30, quote 22; Krause, *Battle for Homestead*, 218.

34. Kathleen Neils Conzen, David A. Gerber, Ewa Morawska, George E. Pozzetta, and Rudolph J. Vecoli, "The Inventory of Ethnicity: A Perspective from the U.S.A.," *Journal of American Ethnic History* 12 (Fall 1992), 27.

35. Stanley Lieberson, *A Piece of the Pie: Black and White Immigrants Since 1880* (Berkeley: University of California Press, 1980), 301–59; John Bodnar,

Roger Simon, and Michael P. Weber, *Lives of Their Own: Blacks, Italians, and Poles, 1900–1960* (Urbana, IL: University of Illinois Press, 1982), 141–49; Suzanne Model, "The Effects of Ethnicity in the Workplace on Blacks, Italians, and Jews in 1910 New York," *Journal of Urban History* 16 (November 1989), 33–39.

36. Ibid. See also Sterling D. Spero and Abram L. Harris, *The Black Worker* (New York: Atheneum, 1969; originally 1931), 149–81, 221, and David Ward, *Poverty, Ethnicity and the American City: 1840–1925* (Cambridge, England: Cambridge University Press, 1989), 211.

37. Harold M. Baron, *The Demand for Black Labor* (Somerville, MA: New England Free Press, n.d.), 21–23; Spero and Harris, *Black Worker*, 174–77; Edward Greer, "Racism and U.S. Steel," *Radical America*, 10 (September-October 1976), 45-68; Paul F. McGouldrick and Michael Tannen, "Did American Manufacturers Discriminate against Immigrants before 1914?" *Journal of Economic History* 37 (September 1977), 723–46; Allan Kent Powell, *The Next Time We Strike: Labor in Utah's Coal Fields, 1900–1933* (Logan: Utah State University Press, 1985), 92; John R. Commons, "Introduction to Volumes III and IV," Commons and others, *History of Labour in the United States*, 4 vols. (New York: Kelley, 1966; originally 1935), vol. 3: xxv. Bodnar, Simon, and Weber, *Lives of Their Own*, 5; quote, Montgomery, *The Fall of the House of Labor: The Workplace, the State and American Labor Activism, 1865–1925* (Cambridge, England: Cambridge University Press, 1987), 243. For the cartoon, see Ernest Riebe, *Mr. Block* (Chicago: Charles Kerr Company, 1984; originally 1913), unpaginated. See also David Gordon, Richard Edwards, and Michael Reich, *Segmented Work, Divided Workers: The Historical Transformation of Labor in the United States* (Cambridge, England: Cambridge University Press, 1982), 141–43.

38. Ross, as quoted in Lieberson, *A Piece of the Pie*, 25; Brody, *Steelworkers*, 120. Peter Speek, "Report on Psychological Aspect of the Problem of Floating Laborers," United States Commission on Industrial Relations Papers (June 25, 1915); 31. Thanks to Tobias Higbie for the citation. Huginnie, *Strikitos*, forthcoming; Georgakas, *Greek Americans at Work*, 17; John Bukowczyk, "The Transformation of Working-Class Ethnicity: Corporate Control, Americanization, and the Polish Immigrant Middle Class in Bayonne, New Jersey, 1915–1925," in Robert Asher and Charles Stephenson, eds., *Labor Divided: Race and Ethnicity in United States Labor Struggles, 1835–1960* (Albany: State University of New York Press, 1990), 291; Higham, *Strangers in the Land*, 173. See also Saxton, *Indispensable Enemy*, 281; Richard W. Steele, "No Racials: Discrimination against Ethnics in American Defense Industry, 1940–1942," *Labor History* 32 (Winter 1991), 66–90.

39. Jean Scarpaci, "Immigrants in the New South: Italians in Louisiana's Sugar Parishes, 1880–1910," *Labor History* 16 (Spring 1975); 175–77; Lieberson, *Piece of the Pie*, 346–50. The judgment changed briefly in African Americans' favor in the early 1920s. See Peter Gottlieb, *Making Their Own Way: Southern Blacks' Migration to Pittsburgh, 1916–30* (Urbana: University of Illinois Press, 1987), 126, 162; Baron, *Demand for Black Labor*, 22; quotes from Lieberson, *Piece of the Pie*, 348; Thaddeus Radzialowski, "The Competition

for Jobs and Racial Stereotypes: Poles and Blacks in Chicago," *Polish American Studies* 33 (Autumn 1976), 16.

40. Lieberson, *Piece of the Pie*, 299–327; John Bodnar, Roger Simon, and Michael Weber, "Blacks and Poles in Pittsburgh, 1900–1930," *Journal of American History* 66 (1979), 554.

41. Bodnar, Simon, and Weber, *Lives of Their Own*, 141, Table 16.

42. Steve Nelson, James R. Barrett, and Rob Ruck, *Steve Nelson, American Radical* (Pittsburgh: University of Pittsburgh Press, 1981), 16.

43. Model, "Effects of Ethnicity," 41–42. Cf. Bodnar, Simon, and Weber, *Lives of Their Own*, 141.

44. Bell, *Out of This Furnace*, 124; Attaway, *Blood on the Forge* (New York: Monthly Review Press, 1987, originally 1941), 122–23.

45. Roger Horowitz, "'Without a Union, We're All Lost': Ethnicity, Race and Unionism among Kansas City Packinghouse Workers, 1930–1941" (unpublished paper given at the "Reworking American Labor History" conference, State Historical Society of Wisconsin, April 1992), 4. On marriage between Catholics but across "ethnic" lines, see Spickard, *Mixed Blood*, 8, 450, note 70.

46. Mark Wyman, *Round Trip to America: The Immigrants Return to Europe, 1880-1930* (Ithaca, NY: Cornell University Press, 1993), 10–12; see also Michael J. Piore, *Birds of Passage: Migrant Labor and Industrial Societies* (New York: Cambridge University Press, 1978), passim.

47. See Arnold Shankman, "This Menacing Influx: Afro-Americans on Italian Immigration to the South," *Mississippi Quarterly* 31 (Winter 1977–78), 82 and 79–87 passim; Scarpaci, "Immigrants in the New South," 175; Robert Asher, "Union Nativism and Immigrant Response," *Labor History* 23 (Summer 1982), 328; Gabaccia, "'Chinese of Europe',"16–18; Scarpaci, "Sicilians and Native Whites," 14.

48. Ibid., and, for the quotation, Harold David Brackman, "The Ebb and Flow of Race Relations: A History of Black-Jewish Relations through 1900" (unpublished Ph.D. dissertation, University of California, Los Angeles, 1977), 450. See James W. Loewen, *The Mississippi Chinese: Between Black and White* (Cambridge, MA: Harvard University Press, 1971), 58–72; Youn-Jin Kim, "From Immigrants to Ethnics: The Life Worlds of Korean Immigrants in Chicago" (unpublished Ph.D. dissertation, University of Illinois at Urbana-Champaign, 1991).

49. Adam Walaszek, "'For in America Poles Work Like Cattle': Polish Peasant Immigrants and Work in America, 1880–1921," in Marianne Debouzy, ed., *In the Shadow of the Statue of Liberty: Immigrants, Workers and Citizens in the American Republic, 1880–1920* (Urbana: University of Illinois Press, 1992), 86–88, 90–91; Bodnar, Simon, and Weber, *Lives of Their Own*, 5, 60.

50. David Roediger, *Towards the Abolition of Whiteness: Essays on Race, Politics, and Working Class History* (London and New York: Verso, 1994), 163; Tamony Papers, on *hunkie*, excerpting *American Tramp and Underworld Slang*; Scarpaci, "Immigrants in the New South," 174; Andrew Neather, "Popular Republicanism, Americanism and the Roots of Anti-Communism,

1890–1925" (unpublished Ph.D. dissertation, Duke University, 1993), 242; Model, "Effects of Ethnicity," 33; Bodnar, Simon and Weber, *Lives of Their Own*, 60, and note 49 above.

51. Ibid.; Neather, "Roots of Anti-Communism," 138–223; James Barrett, "Americanization from the Bottom Up: Immigration and the Remaking of the Working Class in the United States, 1880–1930," *Journal of American History* 79 (December 1992), 1009.

52. Barrett, "From the Bottom Up," 1002; Higham, *Strangers in the Land*, 305, 321–22.

53. Neather, "Roots of Anti-Communism," 235–40; Mink, *Old Labor and New Immigrants*, 71–112; Messer-Kruse, "Chinese Exclusion and the Eight-Hour Day: Ira Steward's Political Economy of Cheap Labor" (unpublished paper, University of Wisconsin, Madison, 1994), 13 and passim. The classic expression of both the biological and the cultural racism, and much else, is Samuel Gompers and Herman Guttstadt, "Meat vs. Rice: American Manhood against Asiatic Coolieism: Which Shall Service?" (San Francisco, 1902). On the distinction between opposition to coolies and to the Chinese "race," see Andrew Gyory, *Closing the Gate: Race, Politics, and the Chinese Exclusion Act* (Chapel Hill: University of North Carolina Press, 1998).

54. Ibid.; Glickman, "American Standard," 221–35.

55. Krause, *Battle for Homestead*, 216.

56. Collomp, "Unions, Civics, and National Identity: Organized Labor's Reaction to Immigration, 1881–1897," in Debouzy, ed., *Shadow of the Statue of Liberty*, 240, 242, 246.

57. Neather, "Roots of Anti-Communism," 242; White, "Immigration Restriction as a Necessity," 67–69; A. A. Graham, "The Un-Americanization of America," *American Federationist* 17 (April 1910): 302, 303, 304.

58. Asher, "Union Nativism," 328; Neather, "Roots of Anti-Communism," 242, 267; Gompers as in Arthur Mann, "Gompers and the Irony of Racism," *Antioch Review* 13 (1953), 212; in Mink, *Old Labor and New Immigrants*, 97; and in David Brody, *In Labor's Cause: Main Themes on the History of the American Worker* (New York and Oxford: Oxford University Press, 1993), 117. Cf. Prescott F. Hall, "Immigration and the Education Test," *North American Review* 165 (1897), 395.

59. McGovern, quoted in David Montgomery, *House of Labor*, 25; Asher, "Union Nativism," 338–42. *Internal protectionism* is Mink's term, from *Old Labor and New Immigrants*, 203; Lieberson, *Piece of the Pie*, 341–44. Cf. the explicit Anglo-Saxonism of *Railroad Trainmen's Journal*, discussed in Neather, "Roots of Anti-Communism," 267–68.

60. Lieberson, *Piece of the Pie*, 342–43; Gabaccia, "Chinese of Europe," 17–19; Mink, *Old Labor and New Immigrants*, 108. See also A. T. Lane, *Solidarity or Survival: American Labor and European Immigrants, 1830–1924* (New York: Greenwood, 1987). A. A. Graham, "The Un-Americanizing of America," runs in *American Federationist* 17 (April 1910) alongside "Where Yanks Meet Orientals" and "The International Fraternity of Labor"; see 302–4 and passim. J. A. Edgerton's "Brotherhood of Man," *American Federationist* 12 (April 1905), 213, runs one issue before A. H. Pio's "Exclude Japanese

Labor." On "race suicide," see Lizzie M. Holmes's review of *The American Idea* in *American Federationist* 14 (December 1907), 998.

61. Asher, "Union Nativism," passim; Mink, *Old Labor and New Immigrants*, 198–203.

62. Asher, "Union Nativism," 345, for the quote. See also Philip S. Foner, *History of the Labor Movement in the United States*, 10 vols. (New York: International Publishers, 1947–82), vol. 3; 256–81.

63. Barrett, "From the Bottom Up," 1010 and passim; cf. Brody, *In Labor's Cause*, 128.

64. Asher, "Union Nativism," 330; Covington Hall, "Labor Struggles in the Deep South" (unpublished manuscript, Labadie Collection, University of Michigan, 1951), 122, 138, 147–48, 183; *Voice of the People* (March 5, 1914); Roediger, *Towards the Abolition of Whiteness*, 149, 150, and 175, note 75. See also Peck, "Padrones and Protest," 172.

65. Speek, "Floating Laborers," 31, 34, 36; plasterer quoted in Asher, "Nativism," 330.

66. *New Majority* (November 22, 1919), 11. See John Howard Keiser, "John Fitzpatrick and Progresssive Unionism, 1915–1925" (unpublished Ph.D. dissertation, Northwestern University, 1965), 38–41; William D. Haywood, *Bill Haywood's Book* (New York: International Publishers, 1929), 241–42; James R. Barrett, *Work and Community in the Jungle: Chicago's Packinghouse Workers, 1894-1922* (Urbana: University of Illinois Press, 1987), 138–142.

67. Du Bois, as quoted in Thomas Holt, "The Political Uses of Alienation: W. E. B. Du Bois on Politics, Race and Culture," *American Quarterly* 42 (June 1990), 313; Peck, "Padrones and Protest," 173.

68. Dominic A. Pacyga, *Polish Immigrants and Industrial Chicago: Workers on the South Side, 1880–1930* (Columbus: Ohio State University Press, 1991), 172; Barrett, *Work and Community in the Jungle*, 172–74. If newly organized Poles read John Roach's "Packingtown Conditions," *American Federationist* 13 (August 1906), 534, they would have seen strikebreaking described as an activity in which "the illiterate southern negro has held high carnival" and would have wrongly learned that the stockyards strike was broken simply by Black strikebreakers, "ignorant and vicious, whose predominating trait was animalism."

69. Gompers, "Talks on Labor," *American Federationist* 12 (September 1905), 636–37.

70. Quoted in Robert L. Allen with Pamela P. Allen, *Reluctant Reformers: Racism and Social Reform Movements in the United States* (Garden City, NY: Doubleday, 1975), 213; Mark Pittenger, *American Socialists and Evolutionary Thought, 1870–1920* (Madison: University of Wisconsin Press, 1993); Higham, *Strangers in the Land*, 172; London's animus was characteristically directed against both 'racial' and 'semi-racial' groups, against 'Dagoes and Japs.' See his *The Valley of the Moon* (New York: Macmillan, 1913), 21–22.

71. Roediger, *Towards the Abolition of Whiteness*, 158–69; Powell, *Next Time We Strike*, 236, note 11; Barry Goldberg, "'Wage Slaves' and 'White Niggers,'" *New Politics*, 2d Series, 3 (Summer 1991), 64–83.

72. Warren C. Whatley, "African-American Strikebreaking from the Civil War to the New Deal," *Social Science History* 17 (1993), 525–58; Allen with Allen, *Reluctant Reformers*, 183; Roach, "Packingtown Conditions," 534; Radzialowski, "Competition for Jobs," 8, note 7, and passim; Leslie Fishel, "The North and the Negro, 1865–1900: A Study in Race Discrimination" (unpublished Ph.D. dissertation, Harvard University, 1953), 454–71; Ray Ginger, "Were Negroes Strikebreakers?" *Negro History Bulletin* (January 1952), 73–74; on the *niggerscab* image, see Roediger, *Towards the Abolition of Whiteness*, 150–53.

73. Higham, *Strangers in the Land*, 172, 321–22; Mink, *Old Labor and New Immigrants*, 234; James R. Barrett, "Defeat and Decline: Long Term Factors and Historical Conjunctures in the Decline of a Local Labor Movement, Chicago, 1900–1922," unpublished manuscript in Barrett's possession; Quinn, "Americanism and Immigration," *American Federationist* 31 (April 1924), 295; Gompers linked support for the 1924 restrictions to "maintenance of racial purity and strength." See Brody, *In Labor's Cause*, 117.

74. Scarpaci, "Immigrants in the New South," 177; Radzialowski, "Competition for Jobs," 17.

75. The first quote is from David Montgomery to Jim Barrett, May 30, 1995. On old-world prejudices, see Orsi, "Inbetween People," 315; Mormino, *Immigrants on the Hill: Italian-Americans in St. Louis,* (Urbana: University of Illinois Press, 1986), 74–75. For popular anti-semitism in Poland in the era of massive Polish and eastern European Jewish immigration to the United States, see Celia S. Heller, *On the Edge of Destruction: Jews in Poland between the Two World Wars* (New York: Columbia University Press, 1977), 38–76.

76. Ronald L. Lewis, *Black Coal Miners in America: Race, Class, and Community Conflict, 1780–1900* (Lexington: University Press of Kentucky, 1987), 110; Allen with Allen, *Reluctant Reformers*, 180. For a recent expression of the common-oppression argument, see Paul Berman, "The Other and the Almost the Same," introducing Paul Berman, ed., *Blacks and Jews: Alliances and Arguments* (New York: Delacorte Press, 1994), 11–30.

77. Peck, "Padrones and Protest," 172–73; "The Greatness of the Greek Spirit," (Chicago) *Saloniki* (January 15, 1919); Georgakas, *Greek Americans at Work*, 17; Kivisto, *Immigrant Socialists*, 127–28; Thomas Lee Philpott, *The Slum and the Ghetto: Neighborhood Deterioration and Middle Class Reform, Chicago, 1930* (New York: Oxford University Press, 1978), 195.

78. Brackman, "Ebb and Flow of Conflict," 461–64; Marilyn Halter, *Between Race and Ethnicity: Cape Verdean American History, 1860–1965* (Urbana: University of Illinois Press, 1993), 146–49; Mormino and Pozzetta, *Ybor City*, 241.

79. Radzialowski, "Competition for Jobs," 14, note 20.

80. Rogin, "Making America Home," 1053; Robert W. Snyder, *The Voice of the City: Vaudeville and Popular Culture in New York* (New York and Oxford: Oxford University Press, 1989), 120; Lewis Erenberg, *Steppin' Out: New York Nightlife and the Transformation of American Culture, 1890–1930* (Chicago: University of Chicago Press, 1981), 195; Rogin, "Blackface, White Noise," 420, 437–48; Brackman, "Ebb and Flow of Conflict," 486.

81. Collins, *Ethnic Identification*, 210–11; Georgakas, *Greek Americans at Work*, 9–12. Hodding Carter, *Southern Legacy* (Baton Rouge: Louisiana State University Press, 1950), 106; John B. Kennedy, "The Knights of Columbus History Movement," *Current History* 15 (December 1921), 441–43; Herbert Aptheker, "Introduction" to W. E. B. Du Bois, *The Gift of Black Folk* (Millwood, NY: Kraus-Thomson Organization, 1975; originally 1924), 7–8; Rudolph J. Vecoli, "Free Country: The American Republic Viewed by the Italian Left, 1880–1920," in Debouzy, ed., *Shadow of the Statue of Liberty*, 38, 33, 34, for the quotes from the Italian American press; and (Chicago) *Daily Jewish Courier* (August 1912).

82. See Noel Ignatiev, *How the Irish Became White* (New York: Routledge, 1996).

83. Barrett, *Work and Community in the Jungle*, 219–223; On the highpoint for Polish American and Lithuanian American nationalism in the World War I era, see Victor Greene, *For God and Country: The Rise of Polish and Lithuanian Ethnic Consciousness in America, 1860–1910* (Madison: University of Wisconsin Press, 1975), chapters 7–9.

84. Radzialowski, "Competition for Jobs," 16; *Glos Polek* (July 31, 1919); cf. *Daily Jewish Courier* (April 22, 1914). and *Narod Polski* (August 6, 1919).

85. Luigi Villari, "Relazione dell dott. Luigi Villari gugli Italiani nel Distretto Consolare di New Orleans," *Bolletino Dell Emigrazione* (Italian Ministry of Foreign Affairs, Royal Commission on Emigration, 1907), 2439, 2499, 2532. Thanks to Louise Edwards for the source and the translations.

86. Barrett, "From the Bottom Up," esp. 1012–1013; John McClymer, "Gender and the "'American Way of Life'": Women in the Americanization Movement," *Journal of American Ethnic History* 11 (Spring 1991), 5–6.

87. Niles Carpenter with Daniel Katz, "The Cultural Adjustment of the Polish Group in the City of Buffalo: An Experiment in the Technique of Social Investigation," *Social Forces* 6 (September 1927), 80–82. For further evidence of such "indifference," see Scarpaci, "Immigrants in the New South," 175, and Edward R. Kantowicz, *Polish American Politics in Chicago, 1880–1940* (Chicago: University of Chicago Press, 1975), 149.

Chapter 11

1. Saxton's "Discrimination on the Railroads" is in his possession in typescript and will appear in a new collection of his historical essays. On the hearings, the delays, and the history of discrimination in railroad labor, see Herbert Hill, *Black Labor and the American Legal System* (Madison: University of Wisconsin Press, 1985), 334–72. For "Nordic closed shop," see Charles Houston, "Foul Employment Practice on the Rails," *Crisis* 56 (October 1949), 270. Eric Arnesen alerted me to Houston's article. This chapter is best read in counterpoint with Alice Kessler Harris's pioneering "Treating the Male Worker as Other: Redefining the Parameters of Labor History," *Labor History* 34 (Spring-Summer 1993), 190–204.

2. Reed, "Accommodation Between Negro and White Employees in a West Coast Aircraft Industry, 1942–1944," *Social Forces* 26 (1947), 76–77 and

76–84 passim. I take "whiteness as property" from Cheryl Harris's remarkable "Whiteness as Property," *Harvard Law Review* 106 (June 1993), 1701–91.

3. Herbert Northrup, *Organized Labor and the Negro* (New York and London: Harper & Brothers, 1944), 16. Toni Morrison, *Playing in the Dark: Whiteness and the Literary Imagination* (Cambridge, MA: Harvard University Press, 1992), 47.

4. John R. Commons and others, *History of Labour in the United States*, 4 vols. (New York: A.M. Kelley, 1966, originally 1918–35), vol. 2; 252–53; Herbert Hill, "Anti-Oriental Agitation and the Rise of Working-Class Racism," *Society* 10 (January-February 1973), 48–51; Dana Frank, *Purchasing Power: Consumer Organizing, Gender and the Seattle Labor Movement, 1919–1929* (Cambridge, England: Cambridge University Press, 1994), 228–32.

5. See Philip S. Foner and Ronald L. Lewis, eds., *Black Workers: A Documentary History from Colonial Times to the Present* (Philadelphia: Temple University Press, 1989), 567–70; Philip S. Foner, *Organized Labor and the Black Worker, 1619–1973* (New York: Praeger, 1976), 328–46; The quotation on seniority rights is from an AFL-CIO position regarding congressional antidiscrimination legislation in 1964, as quoted in Herbert Hill, "Black Workers, Organized Labor, and Title VII of the 1964 Civil Rights Act: Legislative History and Litigation Record," in Hill and James E. Jones, eds., *Race in America: The Struggle for Equality* (Madison: University of Wisconsin Press, 1993), 272. On labor's propagation of the idea and language of "reverse discrimination," see Foner, "Black Workers and the Labor Movement: Recent Transformations," in Lajos Biro and Marc J. Cohen, eds., *The United States in Crisis: Marxist Analyses* (Minneapolis: Marxist Educational Press, 1979), 55–56; Foner, *Organized Labor and the Black Worker*, 259, 289, 308.

6. Hill, "Black Workers, Organized Labor, and Title VII," 272; Foner and Lewis, eds., *Black Workers*, 621; Harris, "Whiteness as Property," passim.

7. Howard Fullerton, Jr., "The 2005 Labor Force: Growing, But Slowly," *Monthly Labor Review* 118 (November 1995), 29–44, calculations from Table 1, on 30; Roberta Spalter-Roth, Heidi Hartman, and Nancy Collins, "What Do Unions Do for Women?" in Sheldon Friedman, ed., *Restoring the Promise of American Labor Law* (Ithaca, NY: ILR Press 1995), 195. Union membership statistics are from U.S. Bureau of Labor Statistics news release (February 9, 1996), accessible at **ftp://ftp.bls.gov/pub/news.release/History/union2.020996nous**.

8. Alan Draper, *Conflict of Interests: Organized Labor and the Civil Rights Movement in the South, 1954–1968* (Ithaca, NY: ILR Press, 1994), 4–5.

9. David Moberg, "Gritty Strikers Chip Away at Pittston Intransigence," *In These Times* (November 15–21, 1989), 22; "Malcolm X: Labor's Ally?" (Service Employees International) *Union*, 7 (Winter 1993), 26–27; C. J. Hawking, "Staley Union Builds Community Support," *Labor Notes*, April 1994, 3; the chants and music in Decatur are from the 1994 Labor Day demonstrations there, attended by the author; Peter Rachleff, *Hard-Pressed in the Heartland: The Hormel Strike and the Future of the Labor Movement* (Boston: South End Press, 1993), 65, 85; interview with Rachleff (St. Paul, July 26, 1996).

10. For recent attempts to historicize labor's current position, see Lichtenstein, "Revitalizing America's Labor Movement," *Chronicle of Higher Education*, May 31, 1996, B-1, B-2; Elizabeth Faue, "Anti-Heroes of the Working

Class," forthcoming in *International Review of Social History*, explicitly refers to a membership "less white" and "more female" than ever in discussing possibilities for change; Iain Boal and Michael Watts, "Working Class Heroes," *Transition* 68 (Winter 1995), passim, and Mike Davis, *Magical Urbanism: Latinos Reinvent the U.S. City* (London and New York: Verso, 2000), 143–49.

11. Hill, "Black-Jewish Relations in the Labor Context," *Race Traitor* 5 (Winter 1996), 81–92.

12. Glenn Burkins, "In Switch, Employers Accuse Labor Unions of Playing Race Card," *Wall Street Journal*, May 28, 1996. See also Paul Johnston, *Success While Others Fail: Social Movement Unionism and the Public Workplace* (Ithaca, NY: ILR Press, 1994), esp. 213–14; Robert Perkinson, "A New Voice at Old Blue," Z, (July-August), 1996, 19–21.

13. Barry Herbert Goldberg, "Beyond Free Labor: Labor, Socialism, and the Idea of Wage Slavery, 1890–1920" (unpublished Ph.D. dissertation, Columbia University, 1979), 281–82 (for Haywood) and passim; Barry Herbert Goldberg, "'Wage Slaves' and White 'Niggers,'" *New Politics*, 2d series, 11 (Summer 1991), 64–83; Lawrence B. Glickman, "Wage Slavery and American Labor, 1865–1910" (paper presented at the Organization of American Historians convention, Atlanta, April 16, 1994).

14. Burkins, "In Switch, Employers Accuse Labor Unions of Playing Race Card"; Lawrence Levine, "Slave Songs and Slave Consciousness," in Allen Weinstein, David Sarasohn, and Frank Otto Gatell, eds., *American Negro Slavery* (New York: Oxford University Press, 1976), 143–72. Sterling Stuckey, *Slave Culture: Nationalist Theory and the Foundations of Black America* (Oxford and New York: Oxford University Press, 1987); Elsa Barkley Brown, "Negotiating and Transforming the Public Sphere: African American Political Life in the Transition from Slavery to Freedom," *Public Culture* 7 (Fall 1994), 107–46.

15. Mary Blewett, *Men, Women and Work: Class, Gender and Protest in the New England Shoe Industry, 1780–1860* (Urbana: University of Illinois Press, 1988); Christine Stansell, *City of Women: Sex and Class in New York, 1789–1860* (New York: Knopf, 1986); Alice Kessler-Harris, *A Woman's Wage: Historical Meaning and Social Consequences* (Lexington: University of Kentucky Press, 1990); Nan Enstad, *Ladies of Labor, Girls of Adventure: Working Women, Popular Culture, and Labor Politics at the Turn of the Twentieth Century* (New York: Columbia University Press, 1999); Thomas Dublin, *Transforming Women's Work: New England Lives in the Industrial Revolution* (Ithaca, NY: Cornell University Press, 1994); Susan Porter Benson, *Counter Cultures: Saleswomen, Managers and Customers in American Department Stores, 1890–1910* (Urbana: University of Illinois Press, 1986).

16. Robin D. G. Kelley, "'We Are Not What We Seem': Rethinking Black Working Class Opposition in the Jim Crow South," *Journal of American History* 80 (June 1993), 75–112; Earl Lewis, *In Their Own Interests: Race, Class, and Power in Twentieth Century Norfolk, Virginia* (Berkeley: University of California Press, 1991); Joe William Trotter, *Coal, Class and Color: Blacks in Southern West Virginia, 1915–1932* (Urbana: University of Illinois Press, 1990); Zaragosoa Vargas, *Proletarians of the North: A History of Mexican Industrial Workers in Detroit and the Midwest, 1917–1933* (Berkeley: University of California Press, 1993). See also James Grossman, *Land of Hope:*

Chicago, Black Southerners, and the Great Migration (Chicago: University of Chicago Press, 1989); Chris Friday, *Organizing Asian-American Workers: The Pacific Coast Salmon Industry, 1870–1942* (Philadelphia: Temple University Press, 1994).

17. Alice Littlefield and Martha C. Knack, eds., *Native Americans and Wage Labor: Ethnohistorical Perspectives* (Norman: University of Oklahoma Press, 1996); Peter Linebaugh and Marcus Rediker, *The Many-Headed Hydra: Sailors, Slaves, Commoners, and the Hidden History of the Revolutionary Atlantic* (Boston: Beacon, 2000); Peter Linebaugh, "All the Atlantic Mountains Shook," *Labour/Le Travail* 10 (Autumn 1982), 87-121.

18. Neil Foley, *The White Scourge: Mexicans, Blacks, and Poor Whites in the Cotton Culture of Central Texas* (Berkeley: University of California Press, 1997); Ronald Takaki, *Paui Hana: Plantation Life and Labor in Hawaii, 1835–1920* (Honolulu: University of Hawaii Press, 1983); Tomas Almaguer, *Racial Fault Lines: The Historical Origins of White Supremacy in California* (Berkeley: University of California Press, 1994); Bruce Nelson, *Divided We Stand: American Labor and the Struggle for Black Equality* (Princeton, NJ: Princeton University Press, 2001).

19. Vicki Ruiz, *Cannery Women, Cannery Lives: Mexican Women, Unionization and the California Food Processing Industry, 1930–1950* (Albuquerque: University of New Mexico Press, 1987); Evelyn Nakano Glenn, "The Dialectics of Wage Work: Japanese-American Women and Domestic Service, 1905–1940," in Ellen Dubois and Vicki Ruiz, eds., *Unequal Sisters: A Multicultural Reader in U.S. Women's History* (New York: Routledge, 1990); Kelley, "'We Are Not What We Seem,'" 75–112; Tera Hunter's *To 'Joy My Freedom: Southern Black Women's Lives and Labors after the Civil War* (Cambridge, MA: Harvard University Press, 1997) sets new standards in this area; equally impressive is Barkley Brown, "Negotiating and Transforming the Public Sphere," 107–46.

20. Roediger, "Precapitalism in One Confederacy: A Note on Genovese, Politics and the Slave South," in *Towards the Abolition of Whiteness: Essays on Race, Politics, and Working Class History* (London and New York: Verso, 1994); Martin Glaberman, "Slaves and Proletarians: The Debate Continues" and Noel Ignatiev, "Reply to Martin Glaberman," *Labour/Le Travail* 36 (Fall 1995), 207–16.

21. Kevin Boyle, "The Kiss: Racial and Gender Conflict in a 1950s Automobile Factory," *Journal of American History* 84 (September 1997) 496–523; Dolores Janiewski, *Sisterhood Denied: Race, Gender, and Class in a New South Community* (Philadelphia: Temple University Press, 1985); Eileen Boris, "'You Wouldn't Want One Dancing with Your Wife': Racialized Bodies on the Job in World War II," *American Quarterly* 50 (March 1998), 77–108.

22. Jacqueline Dowd Hall and others, *Like a Family: The Making of the Southern Cotton Mill World* (Chapel Hill: University of North Carolina Press, 1987); Frank, *Purchasing Power*; Lewis, *In Their Own Interests*; Barkley Brown, "Negotiating and Transforming the Public Sphere," 107–46; Lisa Norling, *Captain Ahab Had a Wife: New England Women and the Whale Fishery, 1720–1870* (Chapel Hill: University of North Carolina Press, 2000); Elizabeth Faue, *Community of Suffering and Struggle: Women, Men and the Labor*

Movement in Minneapolis, 1915–1945 (Chapel Hill: University of North Carolina Press, 1991).

23. Ava Baron, *Work Engendered: Towards a New History of Men, Women, and Work* (Ithaca, NY: Cornell University Press, 1991); Patricia Cooper, *Once a Cigarmaker: Men, Women and Work Culture in American Cigar Factories* (Urbana: University of Illinois Press, 1987); Joshua Freeman, "Hardhats: Construction Workers, Manliness and the 1970 Pro-War Demonstrations," *Journal of Social History* 26 (Summer 1993), 725–44; Paul Taillon, "By Every Right and Tradition: Racism and Fraternalism in the Railway Brotherhoods, 1880–1910" (unpublished paper delivered to the American Studies Association convention, Baltimore, November 1991); Robert G. Lee, *Orientals: Asian Americans in Popular Culture* (Philadelphia: Temple University Press, 1999), esp. 51–82; George Chauncey, *Gay New York: Gender, Urban Culture, and the Making of the Gay Male World, 1890–1940* (New York: Basic Books, 1994).

24. Paul Gilroy, *The Black Atlantic: Modernity and Double Consciousness* (Cambridge, MA: Harvard University Press, 1993), 85; Eric Lott, *Love and Theft: Blackface Minstrelsy and the American Working Class* (New York and Oxford: Oxford University Press, 1993).

25. Noel Ignatiev, *How the Irish Became White* (New York and London: Routledge, 1995); Karen Brodkin Sacks, "How Did Jews Become White Folks?" in Roger Sanjek and Steven Gregory, eds., *Race* (New Brunswick, NJ: Rutgers University Press, 1995); Rudolph Vecoli, "Are Italian Americans Just White Folks?" *Italian Americana* (Summer 1995), 149–65; James Barrett and David Roediger, "Inbetween Peoples: Race, Nationality and the 'New Immigrant' Working Class," *Journal of American Ethnic History* 16 (Spring 1997), 3–44.

26. Herbert Hill, "Race, Ethnicity and Organized Labor: The Opposition to Affirmative Action," *New Politics*, 2nd series, 1 (Winter 1987), 31–82; Herbert Hill, "Myth-Making as Labor History: Herbert Gutman and the United Mine Workers of America," *International Journal of Politics, Culture and Society* 2 (Winter 1988), 12–99; Stephen Brier, "In Defense of Gutman: The Union's Case," *International Journal of Politics, Culture and Society* #2, (Spring, 1989), 394 (quoting Salvatore) and passim.

27. Lichtenstein, "Revitalizing America's Labor Movement," B-2 on "white male job trusts."

28. Du Bois as quoted in Ben Keppel, *The Work of Democracy: Ralph Bunche, Kenneth B. Clark, Lorraine Hansberry, and the Cultural Politics of Race* (Cambridge, MA, and London: Harvard University Press, 1995), 50, from a letter to George Streator; Francille Rusan Wilson, "Black Workers' Ambivalence Toward Unions," *International Journal of Politics, Culture and Society* 2 (Spring 1989), 378–81.

29. On Cayton, see Herbert Hill, "The Problem of Race in Labor History," *Reviews in American History* 24 (June 1996), 199, and St. Clair Drake and Horace Cayton, *Black Metropolis: A Study of Negro Life in a Northern City* (New York: Harcourt, 1945), 314, 341.

30. Eric Arnesen, "'Like Banquo's Ghost, It Will Not Down': The Race Question and the American Railroad Brotherhoods, 1880–1920," *American Historical Review* 99 (December 1994), 1601–33.

31. See note 9 above and Daniel Walden, ed., *W. E. B. Du Bois, The Crisis Writings* (Greenwich, CT: Fawcett, 1972), 380, 388, 389; Du Bois, "Behold the Land," *New Masses,* (January 1947), 362–64.

32. Bert Cochran, "American Labor in Midpassage," in Cochran, ed., *American Labor in Midpassage* (New York: Monthly Review Press, 1959), 57.

33. Cf. Hill, "Myth-Making as Labor History," 195; Brier, "In Defense of Gutman: The Union's Case," 393.

34. Though overgeneralized into a sweeping critique of Marxism, Steven Shulman, "Racism and the Making of the American Working Class," *International Journal of Politics, Culture and Society* 2 (Spring 1989), 362, is acute on these matters. See also W. E. B. Du Bois, *Black Reconstruction in America* (New York: Atheneum, 1992, originally 1935), 700–701.

35. George Rawick, *From Sundown to Sunup: The Making of the Black Community* (Westport, CT: Greenwood, 1972), 156. I take the tone of Hill, "Problem of Race," and of remarks on race in the recent *Labor History* symposium on Robert Zieger's *The CIO* to be possible harbingers of fuller and more productive debate. See Bruce Nelson, Ruth Milkman, Dorothy Sue Cobble, Nelson Lichtenstein, Earl Lewis, and Robert Zieger, "Robert Zieger's *History of the CIO*: A Symposium," *Labor History* 37 (Spring 1996), 157–88.

36. Michael Goldfield, "Race and the CIO: The Possibilities for Racial Egalitarianism during the 1930s and 1940s," *International Labor and Working Class History* 44 (1993), 1–32, is a well-done recent example. Considerable emphasis is placed on whether the union leadership or the white rank and file deserves the blame for lack of antiracist progress in unions. See, for example, Martin Glaberman, "Review of Nelson Lichtenstein's *The Most Dangerous Man in Detroit: Walter Reuther and the Fate of American Labor,*" *Impact* (May 1996), back cover.

37. Eric Arnesen, *Waterfront Workers of New Orleans: Race, Class and Politics, 1863–1923* (New York: Oxford University Press, 1991); Trotter, *Coal, Class and Color;* Michael Honey, *Southern Labor and Black Civil Rights: Organizing Memphis Workers* (Urbana: University of Illinois Press, 1994); Daniel Letwin, *The Challenge of Interracial Unionism: Alabama Coal Miners, 1878–1921* (Chapel Hill: University of North Carolina Press, 1997); Rick Halpern, *Down on the Killing Floor: Black and White Workers in Chicago's Packinghouses, 1904–54* (Urbana: University of Illinois Press, 1997); David Wellman, *The Union Makes Us Strong: Radical Unionism on the San Francisco Waterfront* (Cambridge, England, and New York: Cambridge University Press, 1995); Roger Horowitz, *Negro and White, Unite and Fight! A Social History of Industrial Unionism in Meatpacking* (Urbana: University of Illinois Press, 1997).

38. Gwendolyn Mink, *Old Labor and New Immigrants in American Political Development: Union, Party and State, 1875–1920* (Ithaca, NY, and London: Cornell University Press, 1986); Alexander Saxton, *The Indispensable Enemy: Labor and the Anti-Chinese Movement in California* (Berkeley: University of Illinois Press, 1971), 201–84.

39. Bruce A. Olson and Jack L. Howard, "Armed Elites Confront Labor: The Texas Militia and the Houston Strikes of 1880 and 1898," *Labor's Heritage* 8 (Summer 1995), 52–63; Alex Lichtenstein, *Twice the Work of Free Labor:*

The Political Economy of Convict Labor in the New South (London and New York: Verso, 1996).

40. David Roediger, "Gaining a Hearing for Black-White Unity," in *Towards the Abolition of Whiteness*, 127–80.

41. On the Commons School and race, see David Roediger, *Towards the Abolition of Whiteness*, 22–23.

42. Michael Kazin, "Do What We Can: The Limits and Achievements of American Labor Politics," *New Labor Forum* 5 (Fall/Winter 1999), 21–31; Richard Schneirov, "Labor and the New Liberalism in the Wake of the Pullman Strike," in Schneirov, Shelton Stromquist, and Nick Salvatore, eds., *The Pullman Strike and the Crisis of the 1890s* (Urbana, and Chicago: University of Illinois Press, 1999), 204–5.

43. Kazin, "Do What We Can," 23.

44. Daniel Letwin, Review of Robert H. Zieger, ed., *Southern Labor in Transition, 1940–1995, International Labor and Working-Class History* 57 (Spring 2000), 154.

45. Kazin, "Triumph of the Will? A Reply to Nikhil Singh," *New Labor Forum* 6 (Spring/Summer 2000), 41.

46. Nelson, *Divided We Stand*; Kazin, "Do What We Can," 30; Nikhil Singh, "Irritants or Apologists: A Reply to Michael Kazin," *New Labor Forum* 5 (Fall/Winter 1999), 35; Fernando E. Gapasin, "Race, Gender and Other 'Problems' of Unity for the American Working Class," *Race, Gender and Class* 4 (1996), 42–43.

47. Michael Goldfield, "The Color of Politics in the United States," in Dominick La Capra, ed., *The Bounds of Race: Perspectives on Hegemony and Resistance* (Ithaca, NY: Cornell University Press, 1991), 124.

48. Foner, *Organized Labor and the Black Worker*, 20, 23, and 17–46 passim; William H. Harris, *The Harder We Run: Black Workers Since the Civil War* (New York and Oxford: Oxford University Press, 1982), 25–26; Commons and others, *History of Labour in the United States*, vol. 2, 113 and 134–37; Sumner E. Matison, "The Labor Movement and the Negro During Reconstruction," *Journal of Negro History* 33 (October 1948); John R. Commons and others, *A Documentary History of American Industrial Society*, 10 vols. (Cleveland: Russell and Russell, 1958, originally 1910), vol. 9, 135 and 485–88.

49. Foner, *Organized Labor and the Black Worker*, 23, 25–26; Myers's speech was in the (Chicago) *Workingman's Advocate* (September 1, 1869).

50. Rayford W. Logan, *The Betrayal of the Negro from Rutherford B. Hayes to Woodrow Wilson* (New York: Collier Books, 1965), 149; Philip S. Foner and Ronald Lewis, eds., *The Black Worker: A Documentary History from Colonial Times to the Present*, 8 vols. (Philadelphia: Temple University Press, 1978–1984), vol. 1, 407 and vol. 3, 66; Spero and Harris, *The Black Worker*, 18; David R. Roediger, "Racism, Reconstruction and the Labor Press: The Rise and Fall of the Saint Louis *Daily Press*, 1864–1866," *Science and Society* 42 (Summer 1978), 156–77; Commons and others, *History of Labour*, vol. 2, 135; Foner, *Organized Labor and the Black Worker*, 27, 21–22; Harris, *Harder We Run*, 25–26; Eric Foner, *Reconstruction: America's Unfinished Revolution, 1863–1877* (New York: Harper & Row, 1988), 479–81.

51. For superb accounts of this issue and of the moral stakes involved for organized labor, see Saxton, *The Indispensable Enemy*, and Timothy Messer-Kruse, "Chinese Exclusion and the Eight-Hour Day: Ira Steward's Political Economy of 'Cheap Labor'" (unpublished paper, 1994). Professor Messer-Kruse is at the University of Toledo.

52. James C. Sylvis, ed., *The Life, Speeches, Labors and Essays of William H. Sylvis* (Philadelphia: Claxton, Remsen, and Haffelfinger, 1872), 339–46; Foner and Lewis, eds., *Black Workers*, 160.

53. Foner, *Organized Labor and the Black Worker*, 23–24, 48; Foner and Lewis, eds., *Black Workers*, 9–10.

54. Spero and Harris, *The Black Worker*, 27, 29–34; Eric Foner, *Reconstruction*, 480; Foner, *Organized Labor and the Black Worker*, 23; Foner and Lewis, eds., *Black Workers*, 12–13, 453–54.

55. Cf. Foner, *Organized Labor and the Black Worker*, 16–46, and Du Bois, *Black Reconstrction*, 3–31, 352–70. For the votes, see *Black Reconstruction*, 727, and Harris, *Harder We Run*, 7.

56. Du Bois, *Black Reconstruction*, 370, 577, 596; Northrup, *Organized Labor and the Negro*, 7–8.

57. Du Bois, *Black Reconstruction*, 354–55; Foner and Lewis, eds., *The Black Worker*, vol. 1, 407. See also Foner, *Organized Labor and the Black Worker*, 27; Foner and Lewis, eds., *The Black Worker*, vol. 1; 408; Paul Krause, *The Battle for Homestead, 1888–1892: Politics, Culture and Steel* (Pittsburgh and London: University of Pittsburgh Press, 1992), 113–14; *Boston Daily Evening Voice*, May 21, 1866. Alexander Saxton, *The Rise and Fall of the White Republic: Class Politics and Mass Culture in Nineteenth-Century America* (New York and London: Verso, 1990), 301–304, offers useful commentary on failed efforts to extend "producerism" to Black workers.

58. David Saposs, "Interview with Elmer Carter," Saposs Collection, State Historical Society of Wisconsin (Madison) series 4, box 21, folder 5; Du Bois, *Black Reconstruction*, 354–55.

59. Foner and Lewis, eds., *The Black Worker*, vol. 1; 379.

60. Ibid, vol. 1; 385. Labor historiography at times reproduces this logic. Thus Sumner Rosen could write in 1968 that the "Textile Workers Union, although squarely within the CIO tradition of racial equality, [has] found itself forced to accept Southern practices of segregation in hiring and assignment. . . ." See Rosen, "The CIO Era, 1935-55," in Julius Jacobson, ed., *The Negro and the Labor Movement* (Garden City, NY: Doubleday, 1968), 202.

61. On "stomach equality," see David R. Roediger, "Gaining a Hearing," 139–48; Sylvis, ed., *Life of Sylvis*, 339–46; Foner, *Organized Labor and the Black Worker*, 26.

62. Roediger, "Gaining a Hearing," 140–44; Shubel Morgan, "The Negro and the Union: A Dialogue," in Cochran, ed., *American Labor in Midpassage*, 144–49; Cochran, "American Labor in Midpassage," 57.

63. Roediger, "Gaining a Hearing," 154; Hill, "Black Workers, Organized Labor and Title VII," 275–81; Norrell, "Caste in Steel," passim.

64. Spero and Harris, *Black Worker*, 67. On "intermingling" and Myers, see Foner, *Organized Labor and the Black Worker*, 35.

65. Spero and Harris, *Black Worker*, 58, 66–68; Boyle, "The Kiss," passim; Claude McKay, *The Negroes in America*, ed. Alan McLeod and trans. Robert J. Winter (Port Washington, NY, and London: Kennikat Press, 1979), 38; Foner and Lewis, eds., *The Black Worker*, vol. 1, 372; on the costs of the lack of "bridges" between Black and white workers, see Peter Rachleff's fine *Black Labor in Richmond, 1865–1890* (Urbana, and Chicago: University of Illinois Press, 1989), 137–38.

66. Quoted in Grace Palladino, "Forging a National Union: Electrical Workers Confront Issues of Craft, Race and Gender, 1890–1902," *Labor's Heritage* 3 (October 1990), 13–14.

67. Eric Foner, *Reconstruction*, 480; (Chicago) *Workingman's Advocate*, March 27, 1869; Foner and Lewis, *The Black Worker*, vol. 2; 144–48; Du Bois, *Black Reconstruction*, 283 (on Johnson). On the NLU and the charge of reverse racism against a prominent CNLU leader, see Spero and Harris, *Black Worker*, 29.

68. See Eric Foner, *Nothing But Freedom: Emancipation and Its Legacy* (Baton Rouge and London: Louisiana State University Press, 1983), 85–100; on state power, violence, and Black labor in Reconstruction, see Julie Saville, *The Work of Reconstruction: From Slave to Wage Labor in South Carolina, 1860–1870* (Cambridge, England: Cambridge University Press, 1994), 177–89.

69. Du Bois, *Black Reconstruction*, 357–70, esp. 55–83, 381–486 and quotation from 596; cf. Spero and Harris, *Black Worker*, 28.

70. Du Bois, *Black Reconstruction*, 357–70, esp. 368; Messer-Kruse, "Chinese Exclusion," 22, 28; Foner, *Organized Labor and the Black Worker*, 34–37; Hill, "Problem of Race," 193–95; the cooperative that Myers headed, which formed as a result of a hate strike by whites, employed white workers. See Foner and Lewis, eds., *Black Workers*, 155–56.

71. Roediger, *Wages of Whiteness*, 173–76.

72. Foner, *Organized Labor and the Black Worker*, 20 (Cameron); Marx in Saul K. Padover, ed., *Marx on America and the Civil War* (New York: McGraw-Hill, 1972), 244. The CNLU branded exclusion "an insult to God, injury to us and disgrace to humanity." See Preston Valien, "The 'Mentalities' of Negro and White Workers," *Social Forces* 29 (May 1949), 436.

73. Foner, *Organized Labor and the Black Worker*, 43; David R. Roediger, "Albert Parsons," in Roediger and Franklin Rosemont, eds., *Haymarket Scrapbook* (Chicago: Charles Kerr Company, 1986), 27. In the same volume, see Roediger, "Strange Legacies: The Black International and Black America," 93–96.

74. See for example, Palladino, "Forging a National Union," 14; Roediger, "Racism, Reconstruction and the Labor Press," 70. See also Foner and Lewis, eds., *Black Worker*, vol. 3, 131, and Ray Marshall, "The Negro in Southern Unions," in Jacobson, ed., *The Negro and the American Labor Movement*, 138–39.

75. On the dynamism and militancy of postbellum Blacks in the South, including many tramping strikes and some armed ones, see Foner, *Nothing But Freedom*, 83–106; Saville, *Work of Reconstruction*, 177; Foner and Lewis, eds., *The Black Worker*, vol. 1, 344–64; vol. 2, 144, 162–64, 183, 277–78; vol. 3,

65, 75, 275; Lerone Bennett, Jr., *The Shaping of Black America* (Chicago: Johnson Publications, 1975), 247; Eric Foner, "Black Labor Conventions During Reconstruction," in Ronald C. Kent, Sara Markham, David R. Roediger, and Herbert Shapiro, eds., *Culture, Gender, Race and U.S. Labor History* (Westport, CT: Greenwood, 1993), 91–104; Foner, *Organized Labor and the Black Worker*, 47–63; Rachleff, *Black Labor in Richmond*, esp. 28–29.

76. Isaac Hourwich, *Immigration and Labor: The Economic Aspect of European Immigration to the United States* (New York and London: Putnam's, 1912), 327. Warren C. Whatley, "African-American Strikebreaking from the Civil War to the New Deal," *Social Science History* 17 (Winter 1993), 530–32; Foner and Lewis, eds. *Black Workers*, 15, 18, 19–20; Eric Foner, *Nothing But Freedom*, 106; Foner and Lewis, eds., *The Black Worker*, vol. 1, 357–58; vol. 2, 141–47; vol. 3, 53, 66–67, 91–93, 141, 272; Jonathan W. McLeod, *Workers and Workplaces in Reconstruction-Era Atlanta: A Case Study* (Los Angeles: UCLA Center for Afro-American Studies, 1989); Olson and Howard, "Armed Elites Confront Labor," 52–56. Jerrell H. Shofner, "Militant Negro Laborers in Reconstruction Florida," *Journal of Southern History* 39 (1973), 397–408; *Minutes of the General Council of the First International, 1870–1871* (Moscow: Foreign Languages Publishing House, n.d.), 228; George Tindall, *South Carolina Negroes, 1877–1900* (Columbia: University of South Carolina Press, 1952), 138; Paul Ortiz, "'Like Water Covering the Sea': The African American Freedom Struggle in Florida, 1877–1920" (Ph.D. dissertation, Duke University, 2000), 41–43. The two counterexamples of African American strikebreaking in "white" strikes not listed in Whatley are noted in McLeod (98) and in Foner and Lewis, eds., *The Black Worker*, vol. 3, 52.

77. Hill, "Problem of Race," 197 and 206, note 23; David Montgomery, *Beyond Equality: Labor and the Radical Republicans, 1862–1872* (New York: Knopf, 1967); David Roediger and Philip S. Foner, *Our Own Time: A History of American Labor and the Working Day* (London and New York: Verso, 1989), xi. See for example, Amy Dru Stanley, "Conjugal Bonds and Wage Labor: Rights of Contract in the Age of Emancipation," *Journal of American History* 75 (September 1988), 471–500, for delineation of the profound issues raised by the study of gender and labor.

Chapter 12

1. "Bay Area Typographical Union Local 21 (Communications Workers of America) to Governor Tom Ridge" (February 8, 1995). Copy in possession of the author. Thanks go to Marcus Rediker for helping to provide this and other documentation. On Abu-Jamal's case, see Amnesty International, "A Life in the Balance: The Case of Mumia Abu-Jamal" (New York: Amnesty International, 2000).

2. Larry Adams, "The Labor Movement and Mumia," (New York City) *Working People's News* (February-March 1999), 1: on the report, see "Sam Donaldson, Hanging Judge," *FAIR* (February 1999) and archived at **http://www.fair.org/extra/9902/hanging-judge.html**.

3. Adams, "Labor Movement and Mumia," 1; "ILWU Shuts Down 30 West Coast Ports for Mumia Abu-Jamal!" (New York City), *Fighting Words*,

Supplement Number One (May 13, 1999), 1–2; Mumia Abu-Jamal, "A Philly Union Fights for Its Life," (New York City) *Workers Vanguard* (undated clipping, 1998); San Francisco Labor Council AFL-CIO, "Resolution [on Mumia Abu-Jamal]" (January 11, 1999).

4. See note 3 above and "Canadian Labor Supports Mumia," *Labor Notes* 251 (February 2000) 2; Randy Christensen, "Labor Speaks Up for Mumia," *Against the Current* 87 (July-August 2000), 3; Jeff Mackler, "Support Grows for Mumia and April 24," *Socialist Action* (April 1999), 4; "Motion for the Alameda County Central Labor: In Solidarity with Political Prisoner Mumia Abu-Jamal" (January 4, 1999); Oakland Education Association, "Minutes, Executive Board Meeting," (November 17, 1998); "Hotel and Restaurant Employees Union Local 2 to The Mobilization to Free Mumia Abu-Jamal" (November 9, 1998); "United Brotherhood of Carpenters and Joiners of America Local 1713 to Mobilization to Free Mumia Abu-Jamal" (January 19, 1999); "Brian McWilliams to Governor Ridge" (February 10, 1995), for International Longshoremen's and Warehousemen's Union (ILWU); ILWU Longshore Clerk and Bosses Caucus, "Resolution: Mumia Abu-Jamal" (September 30, 1995); "Inlandboatmen's Union of the Pacific to Governor Casey" (June 25, 1990); Barbara Jean Hope and Rosita Johnson, "Thousands March for Mumia, against Death Penalty," *People's Weekly World* (May 1, 1999), 9; Workers to Free Mumia, "Labor Supports Millions for Mumia" in "Why Justice for Mumia Abu-Jamal Is a Labor Issue" (brochure); "Madison Federation of Labor, AFL-CIO Mumia Resolution" (March 15, 1999); "Call for Labor Conference for Mumia (May 12, 2000); "Justice for Mumia Abu-Jamal," *Labor Standard* 1 (November-December 1999), back cover; "Mumia Backers Renew Plea to Justice to Review Cop-Killer's Trial," *Philadelphia Daily News* (December 12, 2000) and the website of the Labor for Mumia group at http//www.aspenlinx. com/labor/labor4Mumia/laborconference.htm.

5. Hope and Johnson, "Thousands March," 9; "ILWU Shuts Down 30 West Coast Ports," 1–2.

6. Michael Moore, "Is the Left Nuts? (Or Is It Me?)," *Nation* 265 (November 17, 1997), 18. Mark Cooper, "What's Mumia Got to Do with It?" at www.motherjones.com/magazine/classics.html (February 9, 2000); see also Katha Pollitt, "The Death Penalty in Theory and Practice," *Nation*, 270 (March 6, 2000), 10, for an apt response to Cooper. "Good Leftist" is from the *Mother Jones* introduction to Cooper's piece.

7. Adolph Reed, Jr., *Class Notes: Posing as Politics and Other Thoughts on the American Scene* (New York: New Press, 2000), 69. Christopher Hitchens astoundingly uses one of the very few column inches that the *New York Times Book Review* (*NYTBR*) rations to leftists to endorse and considerably extend Reed's more careful views on Abu-Jamal's possible guilt. See Hitchens, "Erasing the Color Line," *NYTBR*, May 7, 2000, 20.

8. Adams, "Labor Movement and Mumia," 1; Heyman in "ILWU Shuts Down 30 West Coast Ports," 2. See also Jack Heyman, "Why Labor Is Marching for Mumia Abu-Jamal," *San Francisco Chronicle* (April 23, 1999).

9. George Lipsitz, "We Know What Time It Is: Race, Class and Youth Culture in the Nineties," in Andrew Ross and Tricia Rose, eds., *Microphone Fiends: Youth Music and Youth Culture* (New York and London: Routledge, 1994),

17; Stanley Aronowitz, *From the Ashes of the Old* (New York: Houghton Mifflin, 1998), xiii; Steven Fraser and Joshua B. Freeman, "Introduction," Fraser and Freeman, eds, *Audacious Democracy: Labor, Intellectuals, and the Social Reconstruction of America* (New York: Houghton Mifflin, 1997), 5.

10. Sweeney, "America Needs a Raise," in Fraser and Freeman, eds., *Audacious Democracy*, 13–21.

11. Paul Buhle, *Taking Care of Business: Samuel Gompers, George Meany, Lane Kirkland and the Tragedy of American Labor* (New York: Monthly Review Press, 1999), 244–48: Steven Fraser, "Is Democracy Good for Unions?" *Dissent* 45 (Summer 1998). See also Kim Moody, "Is Bureaucracy 'Best' for Unions?" *New Politics* 7, new series (Winter 1999), 126–32.

12. Eric Foner, "Intellectuals and Labor: A Brief History," 55; and Fraser and Freeman, "Introduction," in Fraser and Freeman, eds., *Audacious Democracy*. In the same volume, see Betty Friedan, "History's Geiger Counter," 22–31.

13. Howard Fullerton, Jr., "The 2005 Labor Force: Growing, But Slowly," *Monthly Labor Review* 118 (1995), 29–44; union membership estimates are from the U.S. Bureau of Labor Statistics news release (February 9, 1996) at **ftp://ftp.bls.gov./pub/news.release/History/union2.020996.news.**

14. See Michael Goldfield, "Race and Labor Organization in the United States," *Monthly Review* 49 (July-August 1997), 80–97; Ruy Teixeira and Joel Rogers, *America's Forgotten Majority: Why the White Working Class Still Matters* (New York: Basic Books, 2000), xii–xiv and 38–43; Roberta Spalter-Roth, Heidi Hartman, and Nancy Collins, "What Do Unions Do for Women?" in Sheldon Friedman, ed., *Restoring the Promise of American Labor Law* (Ithaca: ILR Press, 1995), 195 and passim. On the history of white workers moving in egalitarian directions when they do not dominate a workplace demographically, and on attacks on diverse unions, see Chapter 11 in this book.

15. William V. Flores, "*Mujeres en Huelga:* Cultural Citizenship and Gender Empowerment in a Cannery Strike," in Flores and Rina Benmayor, eds., *Latino Cultural Citizenship: Claiming Identity, Space and Rights* (Boston: Beacon Press, 1997), 210–54 and in the same volume, Flores, "Citizens v. Citizenry: Undocumented Immigrants and Latino Cultural Citizenship," 261; David Bacon, "Labor's About-Face," *Nation* 270 (March 20, 2000), 6–7; George Lipsitz, "Immigrant Labor and Identity Politics," in *The Possessive Investment in Whiteness: How White People Profit from Identity Politics* (Philadelphia: Temple University Press, 1998), 52; Peter Kwong, *Forbidden Workers: Illegal Chinese Immigration and American Labor* (New York: New Press, 1997), 207–11.

16. Bacon, "Labor's About Face," 6–7; Teófilo Reyes, "In Dramatic Turnaround, AFL-CIO Endorses Amnesty for Undocumented Workers," *Labor Notes* 253 (April 2000), 1, 14; David Montgomery, "Planning Our Futures," in Fraser and Freeman, eds., *Audacious Democracy*, 71; Andy Merrifield, "The Urbanization of Labor: Living-Wage Activism in the American City," *Social Text* 62 (2000), 31–42. Kwong, *Forbidden Workers*, 209, provides the quoted summary of "timeworn" AFL-CIO dogma on immigration. See also 207–12 passim; Reyes, "Dramatic Turnaround," 14, quotes Velasquez. For suspicions regarding AFL-CIO delays, see Teofilo Reyes, "As Multiple Coalitions Press for

a General Amnesty for Immigrants, Frictions Raise Concerns," *Labor Notes*, 260 (November 2000), 3.

17. Bill Fletcher, Jr., and Richard Hurd, "Is Organizing Enough? Race, Gender and Union Culture," *New Labor Forum* 6 (Spring-Summer 2000) 60, 61, 64, 59–69 passim; Alicia Schmidt Camacho, "On the Borders of Solidarity: Race and Gender Contradictions in the 'New Voice' Platform of the AFL-CIO," *Social Justice* 26 (1999), 79–90. See also Fletcher, Jr., "Putting Away the Hatchets" *Ahora Now* 6 (1998), 7–9, for a view emphasizing "opportunities posed by changes in the AFL-CIO "in light of the centrality of the Black working class" (9). See also Daniel HoSang, "Is the AFL-CIO Changing Colors?" *ColorLines* 3 (Summer 2000), 23 and in the same issue, HoSang's "All the Issues in Workers' Lives: Labor Confronts Race in Stamford," 21–23.

18. Schmidt Camacho, "Borders of Solidarity," 90; Fletcher, Jr., and Hurd, "Is Organizing Enough?" 59, 65, 62.

Chapter 13

1. Susan Gubar, *Racechanges: White Skin, Black Face in American Culture* (Oxford and New York: Oxford University Press, 1997). On crossover, see Nelson George, *The Death of Rhythm and Blues* (New York: Pantheon, 1988), 81–82, 147–56, 194; Brian Ward, *Just My Soul Responding: Rhythm and Blues, Black Consciousness and Race Relations* (Berkeley: University of California Press, 1998), 127–42; the working file on *crossover* in the Peter J. Tamony Collection, Western Historical Manuscripts Collection, University of Missouri, at Columbia, and Laura Helper's forthcoming *Whole Lot of Shakin' Going On: An Ethnography of Race Relations and Crossover Audiences for Rhythm and Blues and Rock 'n' Roll in 1950s Memphis.*

2. Gubar, *Racechanges*, 244, 249.

3. W. H. Lhamon, *Raising Cain: Blackface Performance from Jim Crow to Hiphop* (Cambridge, MA: Harvard University Press, 1998).

4. Howard Winant, "Behind Blue Eyes: Whiteness and Contemporary U.S. Racial Politics," in Michelle Fine, Lois Weis, Linda C. Powell, and L. Mun Wong, eds., *Off White: Readings on Race, Power, and Society* (New York and London: Routledge, 1998), 48, 50.

5. See, for example, David R. Roediger, *Towards the Abolition of Whiteness: Essays on Race, Politics, and Working Class History* (London and New York: Verso, 1994), 15.

6. Michael T. Bertrand, *Race, Rock, and Elvis* (Urbana and Chicago: University of Illinois Press, 2000), 114–15, 160.

7. King, as quoted in Ward, *Just My Soul Responding*, 232. See also 173 and Bertrand, *Race, Rock, and Elvis*, 41–58.

8. See George Lipsitz's introduction to Johnny Otis, *Upside Your Head! Rhythm and Blues on Central Avenue* (Hanover, NH, and London: University Press of New England, 1993) xxiv–xxxiv; Lipsitz, "Land of a Thousand Dances: Youth, Minorities, and the Rise of Rock and Roll," in Lary May, ed., *Recasting America: Culture and Politics in the Age of Cold War* (Chicago and London: University of Chicago Press, 1989), 267–82.

9. Michael Lind, "The End of the Rainbow," *Mother Jones* (September-October 1997), 39–43 and 75, esp. 43; on the issue's political agenda, see Jeffrey Klein's editor's introduction, "The Race Curse," 3–4.

10. On Elvis's memory, see Erika Doss, *Elvis Culture: Fans, Faith, and Image* (Lawrence: University of Kansas Press, 1999); Presley took his law enforcement activities equally seriously. See Peter Guralnick, *Careless Love: The Unmaking of Elvis Presley* (Boston: Little, Brown & Company, 1999), 415–29; Alanna Nash with Billy Smith, Marty Lacker, and Lamar Fike, *Elvis Aaron Presley: Revelations from the Memphis Mafia* (New York: HarperCollins, 1995), 496–502. For a published version of the joke, see Kevin O'Kelley, Review of Diane Roberts's *The Myth of Aunt Jemima*, *Southern Exposure* 24 (Spring 1996), 62; on fans' reactions to the marriage, see Doss, *Elvis Culture*, 164–67.

11. Nash, *Presley*, 256–57. On the controversy over Elvis's alleged slur regarding African Americans, records, and shining shoes, see G. B. Rudman, "A Hero to Most? Elvis, Myth and the Politics of Race," *Cultural Studies* 8 (October 1994), 462–72. On the "Mexican woman" controversy, see Peter Whitmer, *The Inner Elvis: A Psychological Biography of Elvis Aaron Presley* (New York: Hypernion, 1996), 228, 288; Nash, *Presley*, 272; and Eric Zolov, *Refried Elvis: The Rise of the Mexican Counterculture* (Berkeley: University of California Press, 1999), 40–47.

12. For both Goldman and Dundy, see Dorothy Nelkin and M. Susan Lindee, "Elvis' DNA: The Gene as a Cultural Icon," *The Humanist* 55 (May/June 1995), 10.

13. Bertrand, *Race, Rock, and Elvis*, 105 and 256, note 54.

14. Bob Michaels, "Oprah's Amazing Link to Elvis," *Globe* (September 20, 1994), 30–32.

15. Peter Guralnick, *Last Train to Memphis: The Rise of Elvis Presley* (Boston: Little, Brown, 1994), 2, 25, 75, and 11–158 passim; George, *Death of Rhythm and Blues*, 62–63; Nash, *Presley*, 20; Louis Cantor, *Wheelin' on Beale* (New York: Pharos Books, 1992), 164–66, 189–96.

16. Ward, *Just My Soul Responding*, 134–42. On "reverse crossover," see Dave Marsh, *Elvis* (New York: Times Books , 1982), 38; Guralnick, *Last Train*, 243, 299. See also Greil Marcus, *Mystery Train: Images of America in Rock 'n' Roll Music* (New York: Dutton, 1990), 152–55.

17. George, *Death of Rhythm and Blues*, 63; James Brown as quoted in George and Jill Pearlman, *Elvis for Beginners* (London and Sydney, 1986), unpaginated. See also Pete Daniel, *Lost Revolutions: The South in the 1950s* (Chapel Hill: University of North Carolina Press, 2000), 167.

18. George, *Death of Rhythm and Blues*, 63. On racist opposition to rock and to Elvis particularly, see Linda Martin and Kerry Segrave, *Anti-Rock: The Opposition to Rock 'n' Roll* (Hamden, CT: Archon Books, 1988), 41–43 and 63; Bertrand, *Race, Rock, and Elvis*, 160–65; Ward, *Just My Soul Responding*, 95–109.

19. On the decline of minstrelsy, see Michael Rogin, "'Democracy and Burnt Cork': The End of Blackface, the Beginning of Civil Rights," *Representations* 46 (Spring 1994), 3–34; Peter Stanfield, "' An Octoroon in the Kindling'" American Vernacular and Blackface Minstrelsy in 1930s Hollywood," *Journal*

of American Studies 31 (1997), 407–38. See also Jon Dolan, "Lights! Camera! Elvis!" (Minneapolis) *City Pages* (December 3, 1997), 42; I modify "postminstrel" from W. T. Lhamon, Jr., *Deliberate Speed: The Origins of a Cultural Style in the American 1950s* (Washington, DC and London: Smithsonian Institution Press, 1990), 90. For a thoughtful attempt to historicize Griffin's project in relation to minstrelsy, see Eric Lott, "White Like Me: Racial Cross-Dressing and the Construction of American Whiteness," in Amy Kaplan and Donald E. Pease, eds., *Cultures of United States Imperialism* (Durham and London: Duke University Press, 1993), 474–95.

20. M. Alison Kibler, "Black and White Choruses: White Women's Contrasting Use of Racial Masquerades in Vaudeville" (unpublished paper, 1996); David R. Roediger, *The Wages of Whiteness: Race and the Making of the American Working Class* (London and New York: Verso, 1991), 117; Harold Brackman, "The Ebb and Flow of Race Relations: A History of Black-Jewish Relations" (unpublished Ph.D. dissertation, University of California, Los Angeles, 1977), 486; Bart Bull, *Does This Road Go to Little Rock? Blackface Minstrelsy Then and Now, Now and Then* (n.p., n.d.) 18; on moving on from blackface, see Stanfield, "Octoroon in the Kindling," 435; Michael Rogin, *Blackface, White Noise: Jewish Immigrants and the Hollywood Melting Pot* (Berkeley: University of California Press, 1996), 52, 112; Jeffrey Melnick, *A Right to Sing the Blues: African Americans, Jews, and American Popular Song* (Cambridge, MA, and London: Harvard University Press, 1999), 112-13.

21. Pauline Bartel, *Reel Elvis* (Dallas: Taylor Publishers, 1994), 27–29, 37–41, 130–34 with the quotation from 132; Nash, *Presley*, 2, 187–89, 282.

22. Bartel, *Reel Elvis*, esp. 63–75, 96–100, 106–10. On Kwoh, see Henry Yu, *Thinking Orientals: Migration, Contact and Exoticism in Modern America* (New York: Oxford University Press, 2001), 171–72. On Elvis and Valentino, see David R. Shumway, "Watching Elvis: The Male Rock Star as Object of the Gaze," in Joel Foreman, ed., *The Other Fifties: Interrogating Midcentury American Icons* (Urbana and Chicago: University of Illinois Press, 1997), 129–31.Whitmer, *The Inner Elvis*, 341; Nash, *Presley*, 77, and displays at the Sincerely Elvis Museum, near Graceland. Whitmer, *The Inner Elvis*, 356, discusses the proposed role in a John Brown film.

23. Guralnick, *Careless Love*, 547, 530–32, 546, 548–552.

24. Guralnick, *Careless Love*, 197–200, 222, 243; Nash, *Presley*, 549, 589–90; Amit Rai, "An American Raj in Filmistan: Images of Elvis in Indian Films," *Screen* 35 (Spring 1994), 51–77; Zolov, *Refried Elvis*; Doss, *Elvis Culture*, 177–78; Martin and Segrave, *Anti-Rock*, 81.

25. Greil Marcus, *Dead Elvis: A Chronicle of a Cultural Obsession* (London and New York: Doubleday, 1992), 3.

26. Martin and Segrave, *Anti-Rock*, 62.

27. Guralnick, *Careless Love*, 27–28; Whitmer, *The Inner Elvis*, 301.

28. Nash, *Presley*, 49, 95–97, 125. Guralnick, *Last Train*, 11–29, 395–402; Helper, *Whole Lot of Shakin' Going On*, forthcoming.

29. Guralnick, *Careless Love*; 223, 228, 239 ("memorable" and "seldom"), 318, 333–34, 584, 596. For Elvis's increasing discomfort in clubs, for reasons that went beyond his celebrity, see Nash, *Presley*, 379.

30. Doss, *Elvis Culture*, 163–211, esp. 183 and 208–10; Bertrand, *Race, Rock, and Elvis*, 48, 224; Ward, *Just My Soul Responding*, 298 (on Hamilton and Wilson). See also, however, Eric Lott, "All the King's Men: Elvis Impersonators and White Working-Class Masculinity," in Harry Stecopoulos and Michael Uebel, eds., *Race and the Subject of Masculinities* (Durham and London: Duke University Press, 1997), esp. 203–9 for impersonators who do not recall an "all-white Elvis," at least not in any simple way.

31. On Presley and Sinatra, see Guralnick, *Last Train*, 437; Nash, *Presley*, 434; Bertrand, *Race, Rock, and Elvis*, 139 (for the quotes from Sinatra); Guralnick, *Careless Love*, 3, 6, 61–63 and 74. Rose Clayton and Dick Heard, eds., *Elvis Up Close: In the Words of Those Who Knew Him Best* (Atlanta: Turner Publications, 1994), 170 (Axton) and 177–78; Patricia J. Pierce, *The Ultimate Elvis: Elvis Presley Day by Day* (New York: Simon and Schuster, 1994), 134; Patrick Higgins, *Before Elvis There Was Nothing* (New York: Carroll and Graf, 1994), 68 ("rancid"). On Sinatra, race, and victimization, see Tom Kuntz and Phil Kuntz, eds., *The Sinatra Files: The Secret Dossier* (New York: Three Rivers Press, 2000), esp. 42–52.

32. Tad Friend, "The White Trashing of America," *New York* 27 (August 22, 1994), 30 quoting Murray.

33. Robin D. Givhan, "Wiggers See Style as a Way into Another Culture," (Detroit) *Free Press* (June 21, 1993), 1-D; Molly O'Neill, "Hip-Hop at the Mall," *New York Times Magazine* (January 9, 1994), 43. Charles Aaron, "Black Like Them" at http://www.utne.com/ (1999).

34. James Ledbetter, "Imitation of Life," *VIBE*, Special Preview Issue (September 1992), 114; Greg Tate, "The Sound and the Fury," *VIBE*, Special Preview Issue (September 1992), 15.

35. Neil Bernstein, "Goin' Gangsta, Choosin' Cholita," as reprinted in *UTNE Reader* (March-April 1995), 87–90 from *West*, a Sunday Supplement to the (San Jose) *Mercury News*. Bernstein uses *cholita* as a stand-in for "Mexican gangsta' girl" (86).

36. Ralph Ellison, "The Little Man at Chehaw Station," in *Going to the Territory* (New York: Random House, 1987), 21; A. Sivanandan, *Communities of Resistance: Writings on Black Struggles for Socialism* (London: Verso, 1990), 66.

37. Telephone interview with Terry Moore in Detroit (October 25, 1992); Denise Sanders, "Black Is In," (Madison) *Isthmus* (October 29, 1993), 1, 20; letter to author from Tom Sabatini in Warren, Ohio (November 7. 1993); Richard Roeper, "Fashion Statement Gets an Ugly Reply," (Chicago) *Sun Times* (November 29, 1993), 11; "Wiggers Attacked," MTV News (November 24, 1993); Kathy Dobie, "Heartland of Darkness," *VIBE* 2 (August 1994), 63–67, 124, 126; E. Jean Carroll, "The Return of the White Negro," *Esquire* (June 1994), 100–107; Pistol Pete, "Media Watch," *Source* (December 1993), 17.

38. On these usages, see Roediger, *Wages of Whiteness*, 68, 145; and "*Guineas, Wiggers* and the Dramas of Racialized Culture," *American Literary History* 7 (Winter 1995), 654–58; Steve Pond, "The Hard Reign of a Country Music King," *Rolling Stone* (December 10, 1992), 122; Serch quoted in David Samuels, "The Rap on Rap," *The New Republic* (November 11, 1991), 24–29. On the 1868 incident, see Michael Newton and Judy Ann Newton, *Racial and Religious Violence in America: A Chronology* (New York: Garland, 1991), 200.

39. Telephone interview with Gary Miles in Los Angeles (November 15, 1992); Alice Echols, "'We Gotta Get Out of This Place': Notes Toward a Remapping of the Sixties," *Socialist Review* 22 (1992), 9–34. For "Whatinas," see Becky Thompson and White Women Challenging Racism, "Home/Work: Antiracism Activism and the Meaning of Whiteness," in Fine, Weis, Powell, and Wong, eds., *Off White*, 358.

40. Telephone interview with Steve Meyer in Milwaukee (November 29, 1992); Abra Quinn, "Field Notes from Milwaukee on *Wigger*" (December, 1992); Clarence Major, *From Juba to Jive: A Dictionary of African-American Slang* (New York: Penguin, 1994), 122.

41. Miles interview and interview with Sundiata Cha-Jua in Columbia, Missouri (January 25, 1993); Clarence Major, *Dictionary of Afro-American Slang* (New York: International Publishers, 1970), 122; "Notes on *Wigged*," Peter J. Tamony Collection, Western Historical Manuscripts Collection, Ellis Library, University of Missouri at Columbia. The link to jazz usages meaning "crazy" is proposed in Robert Chapman, ed., *American Slang* (New York: HarperPerennial, 1998), 546–47.

42. Aaron, "Black Like Them"; Interview with Brendan Roediger in Columbia, Missouri (March 16, 1993); Interview with name withheld in Cambridge, MA (February 20, 1993); Nadia Shihata, to *VIBE* 2 (November 1994), 26; Conversation with Noel Ignatiev in Lowell, MA (June 4, 1993).

43. Ledbetter, "Imitation of Life," 112–14; William Upski Wimsatt, "We Use Words Like 'Mackadocious,'" *Source* (May 1993), 64–66; Tate, "Sound and Fury," 15. See Also Wimsatt, "*Wigger:* Confessions of a White Wannabe," (Chicago) *Reader* (July 8, 1994), 1; Aaron, "Black Like Them," on the demographics of rap purchasers.

44. Donald Tricarico, "Guido: Fashioning an Italian-American Youth Style," *Journal of Ethnic Studies* 19 (1991), 56–57; Venise Wagner, "Crossover: The Rest of America Is Still Deeply Divided by Race. So How Come So Many White Suburban Youths Want to Be Black?" (San Francisco) *Examiner* (November 10, 1996); Leslie Fiedler, *Waiting for the End* (New York: Stein and Day, 1964), 134; Joplin, in Ledbetter, "Imitation of Life," 114.

45. Robin D. G. Kelley, "Straight from Underground," *Nation* (June 8, 1992), 793–96; Brent Staples, "Dying to Be Black," *New York Times* (December 9, 1996). Barbara Ransby and Tracye Matthews, "Black Popular Culture and the Transcendence of Patriarchal Illusions," *Race and Class* 35 (1993), 57–68; Leerom Medovoi, "Mapping the Rebel Image," *Cultural Critique* 20 (1991–1992), 153–88; *VIBE* Special Preview Issue (September 1992), center spread. On nudity in *National Geographic*, see Catherine A. Lutz and Jane L. Collins, *Reading National Geographic* (Chicago: University of Chicago Press, 1993), esp. 172–78; June Jordan, "Owed to Eminem," *VIBE* (January 2001); Davey D as quoted in Wagner, "Crossover." For "hardest-core element," see Norman Kelley, "Rhythm Nation: The Political Economy of Black Music," *Black Renaissance Noire* 2 (Summer 1999), 16, 8–22. Compare, in the same issue, Davarian Baldwin, "Black Empires, White Desires: The Spatial Politics of Identity in the Age of Hip-Hop," esp. 146–50.

46. Norman Mailer, "The White Negro," in *Advertisements for Myself* (New York: Putnam, 1959), 341, 349; on *Soul Man*, see Margaret M. Russell,

"Race and the Dominant Gaze: Narrative of Law and Inequality in Popular Film," in Richard Delgado, ed., *Critical Race Theory: The Cutting Edge* (Philadelphia: Temple University Press, 1995), 59–63; Roediger, *Wages of Whiteness*, 119; Amiri Baraka in William J. Harris, ed., *The Le Roi Jones/Amiri Baraka Reader* (New York: Thunder's Mouth Press, 1995), xiii.

47. On "white culture," see Roediger, *Towards the Abolition of Whiteness* (London and New York: Verso, 1994), 1–17; on hybridity in Black culture, see Lester Bowie's remarks in Dave Marsh, "Grave Dancers Union," *Rock and Rap Confidential* (September 1993), 7; Stuart Hall, "What Is This 'Black' in Black Popular Culture?" *Social Justice* 20 (1993), 104–14.

48. Wagner, "Crossover," unpaginated. I thank Professor Rachel Buff (history) for sending me the unsigned Bowling Green State University paper. See also Mumia Abu-Jamal's acute "A Rap Thing" in his *All Things Censored*, Noelle Hanrahan, ed. (New York: Seven Stories Press, 2000), 124–25.

49. Matthew Durington, "Racial (Co)option: Visualizing Whiteness in Suburban Space" (unpublished paper, American Anthropological Association, Temple University, 1998) and available at **http://astro.temple.edu/ruby/aaa/matt.html**. See also Rhonda B. Sewall, "Black Like Me," (St. Louis) *Post-Dispatch* (November 23, 1999); Farai Chideya, *The Color of Our Future* (New York: Morrow, 1999), 86–112. On Hoch, see Charles Aaron, "What the White Boy Means When He Says Yo," *Spin* 14 (November, 1998), 124–26 and passim.

50. Rogers, as quoted in Wagner, "Crossover," unpaginated.

51. Rose Farley, "Wiggers," *Twin Cities Reader* (March 6–12, 1996), 8–14.

52. For Wimsatt's quote, which first appeared in *In Context* in 1993, see **http://www.context.org./CLIB/permiss.htm**.

53. Charles Baron, "Even Homeboys Get the Blues," *Spin* 15 (June 1999), 86, in an insert titled "Signifying Whiteys." Emphasis original. On Eminem's positioning, see Anthony Bozza, "Eminem Blows Up," *Rolling Stone* 811 (April 29, 1999), 43–47, 72. See also the issue's front cover.

54. Zaid Ansari on *Tony Brown's Journal* (Public Broadcasting Company, March 1993).

55. David Dalby, " The African Element in American English," in Thomas Kochman, ed., *Rappin' and Stylin' Out: Communication in Urban Black America* (Urbana: University of Illinois Press, 1972), 180–81; Major, *Juba to Jive*, 234.

56. Dalby, "African Element," 180–82.

57. Franklin Rosemont, "Bugs Bunny," in Rosemont and others, eds., *Surrealism and Its Popular Accomplices* (San Francisco: City Lights Books, 1980), 55; Joe Adamson, *Bugs Bunny: Fifty Years and Only One Grey Hare* (New York: Holt, 1991), 50. Sterling Stuckey's brilliant *Going Through the Storm: The Influence of African American Art in History* (New York: Oxford University Press, 1994), 165–67, places Senegal, home of Wolof speakers, at the center of the creation and elaboration of Brer Rabbit tales. On Harris and Brer Rabbit, see Alice Walker, "Uncle Remus: No Friend of Mine," *Southern Exposure* 8 (1981), 29–31.

58. For a recent and challenging use of the Fiedler quotation, see Kelley, "Rhythm Nation," 16, 8–21. On youth hiphop and marketing, see M. Eliza-

beth Blair, "Commercialization of the Rap Music Youth Subculture," *Journal of Popular Culture* 27 (Winter 1993), 21–33, and "Bazooka Joe RAPS," Number 23 (gum wrapper in possession of the author, c. 1998).

59. Kellogg's Raisin Bran box, back cover (c. 1995); Timberland advertisement from *New York Times Magazine* (April 25, 1993), 51; Anne McClintock, *Imperial Leather: Race, Gender and Sexuality in the Colonial Conquest* (New York and London: Routledge, 1995), 31–35, 207–31.

60. Tamar Lewin, "Growing Up, Growing Apart," *New York Times* (June 25, 2000).

61. On Trammell, see Ward, *Just My Soul Responding*, 227.

62. Greg Tate, "The GOP Throws a Mammy-Jammy: Black Stars Bowl Over Bush at Blues Summit," in *Flyboy in the Buttermilk: Essays on Contemporary America* (New York: Simon and Schuster, 1992), 104, 99–107.

63. "Memories and an Apology by a Gravely Ill Atwater," *New York Times* (January 13, 1991); Monte Poliawsky, "Racial Politics in the 1988 Presidential Election," *Black Scholar* (January 1989), 32–35.

64. Mingus in "Playboy Summit Meeting, 1964," in Robert Walser, ed., *Keeping Time: Readings in Jazz History* (New York and London: Oxford University Press, 1998) as quoted in Nichole Rustin's important forthcoming study of Mingus; Cf. Benjamin Gendron, "Moldy Figs and Modernists," *Discourse: Theoretical Studies in Media and Culture* 15 (Spring 1993), 147–48; Aaron, "What the White Boy Means," 128–32; Martha Bayles, "Hollow Rock," *Wilson Quarterly* (Summer 1993), 26; Samuels, "Rap on Rap," 29.

65. Tate, "Mammy-Jammy," 106.

66. Michaelene Zawistowski, "Beach Music," *World Traveler* (January 1997), 79–80.

67. Peter Leki, "Why Be White?" *Chicago Reader* (June 28, 1996), 16–17. For a fascinating account of connections among class, hopelessness, and defensive assertions of white masculinity, see Michelle Fine, Lois Weis, Judi Addelston, and Julia Maruza, "(In)Secure Times: Constructing White Working Class Masculinities in the Late 20th Century," *Gender & Society* 11 (February 1997), 52–68.

68. Roediger, *Wages of Whiteness*, 120–21; Rogin, *Blackface, White Noise*, 109–13; Gayle Wald, "'A Most Disagreeable Mirror': Reflections on White Identity in *Black Like Me*," in Elaine Ginsburg, ed., *Passing and the Fictions of Identity* (Durham, NC: Duke University Press, 1996), 162; Wald's point is deepened in Deborah E. McDowell, "Pecs and Reps: Muscling In on Race and the Subject of Masculinities," in Stecopoulos and Uebel, eds., *Race and the Subject of Masculinities*, 366. Marybeth Hamilton, *When I'm Bad, I'm Better: Mae West, Sex, and American Entertainment* (New York: HarperCollins, 1995); Gayle Wald, "One of the Boys: Whiteness, Gender, and Popular Music Studies," in Mike Hill, ed., *Whiteness: A Critical Reader* (New York and London: New York University Press, 1997), 151–67. For Toll, see Heather Leitner, "Can a Sex Symbol Be a Soloist? Gender Constructions and Jazzwomen" (senior thesis, American Studies Program, Scott Hall, University of Minnesota, 1998).

69. Wini Breines, *Young, White, and Miserable: Growing Up Female in the Fifties* (Boston: Beacon Press, 1992), 151–59 with the quotation on soul (from

Gerri Hirshey) at 154; Bayles, "Hollow Rock," 18 ("sugary"). See also Breines, "Postwar White Girls' Dark Others," in Foreman, ed., *The Other Fifties*, 53–77. On gender and dance, see Randy McBee, *Dance Hall Days: Intimacy and Leisure Among Working-Class Immigrants in the United States* (New York and London: New York University Press, 2000).

70. See especially David Gates, "White Male Paranoia," *Newsweek* (March 29, 1993), 48–53; Steven Roberts, "Affirmative Action on the Edge," *U.S. News & World Report* 118 (February 13, 1995), 32–37; Richard Goldstein, "Save the Males," *Village Voice* (March 7, 1995), 25–29; Lydia Chávez, *The Color Bind: California's Battle to End Affirmative Action* (Berkeley: University of California Press, 1998).

71. Gregory Stephens, "Interracial Dialogue in Rap Music: Call-and-Response in a Multicultural Style," *New Formations* 16 (Spring 1992), esp. 74–76; Deborah Wong, "The Asian American Body in Performance," in Ronald Radano and Philip V. Bohlman, eds., *Music and the Racial Imagination* (Chicago and London: University of Chicago Press, 2000), 57–94; in the same volume, see also Rafael Pérez-Torres, "*Mestizaje* in the Mix: Chicano Identity, Cultural Politics, and Postmodern Music," 206–30.

72. Rachel Barrett Martin, "Feathers in Their Hair: Race and Tribal Trespass at the Psychedelic Frontier" (unpublished paper, 1998). Martin's almost completed University of Minnesota dissertation develops this material at length. For "Weskimos," see "Meet the Hermaneuts," *Lingua Franca* 9 (October 1999), 19; Yvonne Tasker, "Fists of Fury: Discourses of Race and Masculinity in the Martial Arts Cinema," in Stecopoulos and Uebel, eds., *Race and the Subject of Masculinities*, 315–36.

73. Bernstein, "Goin' Gangsta, Choosin' Cholita," 87–90; Tasker, "Fists of Fury," 315–36; Rachel Buff, *Immigration and the Political Economy of Home*, forthcoming from University of California Press, 2001.

74. Sunaina Maira, "Identity Dub: The Paradoxes of Indian American Youth Subculture," *Cultural Anthropology* 14 (February 1999), 40–41, 29–60; Rogin, *Blackface, White Noise*.

75. Maira, "Identity Dub," 41, quoting Sanjay Sharma. See also Vijay Prashant, *The Karma of Brown Folk* (Minneapolis: University of Minnesota Press, 2000) and Monisha Das Gupta, "'A Footnote to Whites'?: Race, Rights, the Census, and the Vexing Case of South Asians in the U.S." (Unpublished paper, 2001). Professor Gupta is in the Department of Sociology at Syracuse University.

76. Maira, "Identity Dub," 41. See also Tony Tiongson, "Asian American Criminality and Popular Culture" (Association for Asian American Studies Annual Conference, Toronto, March, 2001) for important commentary on Filipino American rap as both "relying on" and "distinct from" African American forms.

77. I thank Professor Michael Willard for this information, communicated via email on June 9, 1998.

78. Wong, "Asian American Body," 88–89.

79. Hung C. Trai, "'Splitting Things in Half Is So White!'": Conceptions of Family Life and Friendship and the Formation of Ethnic Identity among Second Generation Vietnamese Americans," *Amerasia Journal* 25 (1999), 53–88.

80. Cherrie Moraga, *The Last Generation: Prose and Poetry* (Boston: South End Press, 1993), 128.

81. Janine Y. Kim, "Are Asians Black? The Asian-American Civil Rights Agenda and the Contemporary Significance of the Black/White Paradigm," *Yale Law Journal* 108 (June 1999), 2385–412; Clare Jean Kim, "The Racial Triangulation of Asian Americans," *Politics & Society* 27 (March 1999), 105–38. Especially useful in opening up these complexities is Gary Okihiro's "Is Yellow Black or White?" in his *Margins and Mainstreams: Asians in American History and Culture* (Seattle: University of Washington Press, 1994), 31–63. Evelyn Hu-Dehart led an excellent discussion on the racial futures of Asian American identity and whiteness at the University of California, Riverside, "Then What Is White?" conference in February 1998.

82. Wong, "Asian American Body," 71; Randall Robinson, *The Debt: What America Owes to Blacks* (New York: Dutton, 2000).

83. James Baldwin, "On Being 'White' . . . and Other Lies," *Essence* (April 1984), 90–92; Gary Gerstle, *American Crucible*, forthcoming from Princeton University Press; Matthew Frye Jacobson, *Whiteness of a Different Color: European Immigrants and the Alchemy of Race* (Cambridge, MA: Harvard University Press, 1998).

Credits

Chapter 3: Adapted from "White Looks: Hairy Apes, True Stories and Limbaugh's Laughs," by David R. Roediger, in *Minnesota Review* 47 (1997). Reprinted with permission of the publisher.

Chapter 4: Adapted from "White Workers, New Democrats, and Affirmative Action," by David Roediger, in Wahneema Lubiano, ed., *The House That Race Built*. (New York: Vintage, 1998). © 1997 David R. Roediger.

Chapter 5: Adapted from "'Hertz, Don't It?' Becoming Colorless and Staying White in the Crossover of O. J. Simpson," by Leola Johnson and David R. Roediger, in Toni Morrison and Claudia Brodsky Lacour, eds., *Birth of a Nation 'hood: Gaze, Script, and Spectacle in the O. J. Simpson Case.* © Leola Johnson and David R. Roediger. Reprinted with permission of Leola Johnson.

Chapter 6: Adapted in part from "John Brown and Black Revolt," by David Roediger, in *Race Traitor* 11 (Spring 2000). © David R. Roediger.

Chapter 7: Adapted from "Race, Labor, and Gender in the Language of Antebellum Social Protest," by David R. Roediger, in Stanley B. Engerman, ed., *Terms of Labor: Slavery, Serfdom, and Free Labor*, with the permission of the publishers, Stanford University Press. © 1999 by the Board of Trustees of the Leland Stanford Junior University.

Chapter 8: Adapted from "The Pursuit of Whiteness: Property, Terror, and Expansion," by David R. Roediger, in *Journal of the Early Republic* 19 (Winter 1999). © Society for Historians of the Early Republic. Reprinted with permission of the Society.

Chapter 9: Adapted from "Inbetween Peoples: Race, Nationality, and the 'New Immigrant' Working Class," by James R. Barrett and David R. Roediger,

Index